Instructor's Manual

to accompany

Social Psychology

Seventh Edition

David G. Myers
Hope College

Prepared by
K. Paul Nesselroade
Simpson College

McGraw Hill

Boston   Burr Ridge, IL   Dubuque, IA   Madison, WI   New York   San Francisco   St. Louis
Bangkok   Bogotá   Caracas   Kuala Lumpur   Lisbon   London   Madrid   Mexico City
Milan   Montreal   New Delhi   Santiago   Seoul   Singapore   Sydney   Taipei   Toronto

McGraw-Hill Higher Education
A Division of The McGraw-Hill Companies

Instructor's Manual to accompany
SOCIAL PSYCHOLOGY, SEVENTH EDITION
DAVID G. MYERS

Published by McGraw-Hill Higher Education, an imprint of The McGraw-Hill Companies, Inc., 1221 Avenue of the Americas, New York, NY 10020. Copyright © The McGraw-Hill Companies, Inc., 2002, 1999, 1996, 1993, 1990. All rights reserved.

The contents, or parts thereof, may be reproduced in print form solely for classroom use with SOCIAL PSYCHOLOGY, provided such reproductions bear copyright notice, but may not be reproduced in any other form or for any other purpose without the prior written consent of The McGraw-Hill Companies, Inc., including, but not limited to, in any network or other electronic storage or transmission, or broadcast for distance learning.

This book is printed on acid-free paper.

2 3 4 5 6 7 8 9 0 QPD/QPD 0 3 2 1

ISBN 0-07-241389-1

www.mhhe.com

CONTENTS

INTRODUCTION	vi
CHAPTER 1: INTRODUCING SOCIAL PSYCHOLOGY	1
Lecture and discussion ideas	2
Demonstration and project ideas	10
Demonstration and project materials	16
Films/Videos	33
CHAPTER 2: THE SELF IN A SOCIAL WORLD	34
Lecture and discussion ideas	36
Demonstration and project ideas	45
Demonstration and project materials	52
Films/Videos	72
CHAPTER 3: SOCIAL BELIEFS AND JUDGMENTS	73
Lecture and discussion ideas	75
Demonstration and project ideas	84
Demonstration and project materials	96
Films/Videos	110
CHAPTER 4: BEHAVIOR AND ATTITUDES	111
Lecture and discussion ideas	112
Demonstration and project ideas	121
Demonstration and project materials	126
Films/Videos	130
CHAPTER 5: GENES, CULTURE, AND GENDER	131
Lecture and discussion ideas	132
Demonstration and project ideas	139
Demonstration and project materials	144
Films/Videos	147
CHAPTER 6: CONFORMITY	149
Lecture and discussion ideas	150
Demonstration and project ideas	158
Demonstration and project materials	164
Films/Videos	170
CHAPTER 7: PERSUASION	171
Lecture and discussion ideas	172
Demonstration and project ideas	178
Demonstration and project materials	182
Films/Videos	187

CHAPTER 8: GROUP INFLUENCE	188
Lecture and discussion ideas	190
Demonstration and project ideas	198
Demonstration and project materials	203
Films/Videos	210
CHAPTER 9: PREJUDICE: DISLIKING OTHERS	211
Lecture and discussion ideas	212
Demonstration and project ideas	218
Demonstration and project materials	225
Films/Videos	236
CHAPTER 10: AGGRESSION: HURTING OTHERS	237
Lecture and discussion ideas	238
Demonstration and project ideas	246
Demonstration and project materials	249
Films/Videos	255
CHAPTER 11: ATTRACTION AND INTIMACY: LIKING AND LOVING OTHERS	256
Lecture and discussion ideas	257
Demonstration and project ideas	265
Demonstration and project materials	270
Films/Videos	279
CHAPTER 12: ALTRUISM: HELPING OTHERS	280
Lecture and discussion ideas	282
Demonstration and project ideas	289
Demonstration and project materials	293
Films/Videos	303
CHAPTER 13: CONFLICT AND PEACEMAKING	304
Lecture and discussion ideas	305
Demonstration and project ideas	313
Demonstration and project materials	320
Films/Videos	327
MODULE A: SOCIAL PSYCHOLOGY IN THE CLINIC	328
Lecture and discussion ideas	329
Demonstration and project ideas	337
Demonstration and project materials	343
Films/Videos	353
MODULE B: SOCIAL PSYCHOLOGY IN COURT	354
Lecture and discussion ideas	355
Demonstration and project ideas	365

Demonstration and project materials	367
Films/Videos	374
MODULE C: SOCIAL PSYCHOLOGY AND THE SUSTAINABLE FUTURE	375
Lecture and discussion ideas	376
Demonstration and project ideas	377
Demonstration and project materials	379
Films/Videos	383
FILM PRODUCER/DISTRIBUTOR LIST	384
REFERENCES	387

INTRODUCTION: HOW TO USE THIS MANUAL

In this manual we provide suggestions for teaching each chapter of David G. Myers' Social Psychology, Seventh Edition. Our aim is not only to identify supplementary sources, but also to digest this information into ready-to-use form. By so doing we hope to help you create a stimulating course in social psychology and to save you time.

If your students have purchased Myers' Social Psychology you have permission to photoduplicate any page of this manual for class use in conjunction with the text. The resources for each chapter are organized into five sections:

Chapter Outline. The chapter overview appears on a separate page, in case you wish to reproduce it for students.

Lecture and Discussion Ideas. These are practical ideas for how to supplement the chapter, and how to stimulate students' thinking about the chapter. Other possible resources are identified—usually books or magazine articles in which research is digested into a form suitable for lay audiences.

Demonstration and Project Ideas. Sometimes we instructors get so preoccupied with teaching the content of our discipline that we forget to teach the student. We give students more information than they can incorporate into true understanding. One remedy is to activate the learner. Doing so puts into practice social psychological insights concerning how attitudes and cognitive insights are nurtured by action and experience. For each chapter, several classroom exercises and student projects are suggested.

The classroom exercises allow students to experience phenomena described in the chapter (e.g., the "I-knew-it-all-along-phenomenon" discussed in Chapter 1), and so should be conducted BEFORE students read the chapter. This means that you should scan the chapter ideas a week ahead of when your students are due to read the chapter.

It might be wise to reassure students with some demonstration ground rules at the beginning of the semester: 1) Students will never be asked to identify themselves; privacy and anonymity will always be protected. 2) Only demonstrations judged to be nonstressful have been included. 3) Although the demonstrations are intended to be educational and interesting, anyone at any time may decline to participate. 4) Students can expect the instructor to clarify confusing instructions, but should allow the instructors not to disclose the purpose of the demonstration until after the data are gathered. Occasionally, there may be a little temporary deception, but usually not. When there is, it is for a constructive purpose—to allow students to experience phenomena or to allow the class to test some conclusion drawn by the text.

Projects are to be performed out of class by students, either individually or in groups. The projects are intended to promote student interest and understanding of the subject matter and to provide them with a feeling for the process of psychological research. Results of these projects can be reported orally and discussed in class, or students may be assigned written reports. (Many of the classroom exercises, particularly the self-assessment measures, can also be used as projects.)

Demonstration and Project Materials. Materials for demonstrations and projects are on a separate page, all ready for you simply to duplicate and carry to class. No need to locate, adapt, or type them!

Suggestion: On a master copy of each demonstration, tally the results across sections. Doing so will a) allow you to determine which demonstrations work for you most powerfully and reliably, and b) to have a larger data base to report to students (especially after obtaining unusual results from a small class!).

Films/Videos. Each suggested program is briefly described and identified by a producer/distributor code. See the end of the manual for identification of these sources. Better yet, Bowker's Complete Video Directory 1997, prepared by Judy Salk, provides ordering information for virtually all the videos in this manual. Video 1 includes entertainment and performance titles. Volumes 2 and 3 list educational and special-interest videos. Together, the three volumes list more than 110,000 programs and include a variety of indexes for ease of use.

CHAPTER 1
INTRODUCING SOCIAL PSYCHOLOGY

Social Psychology and Related Disciplines
Social Psychology and Sociology
    Social Psychology and Personality Psychology
    Social Psychology and Biology
    Levels of Explanation
Social Psychology and Human Values
    Obvious Ways in Which Values Enter Psychology
    Not-So-Obvious Ways in Which Values Enter Psychology
    The Subjective Aspects of Science
    Psychological Concepts Contain Hidden Values
    There is No Bridge from "Is" to "Ought"
I Knew It All Along: Is Social Psychology Simply Common Sense?
How We Do Social Psychology
    Forming and Testing Hypotheses
    Correlational Research: Detecting Natural Associations
    Correlation Versus Causation
    Survey Research
    Experimental Research: Searching for Cause and Effect
    Control: Manipulating Variables
    Random Assignment: The Great Equalizer
    The Ethics of Experimentation
    Generalizing from Laboratory to Life
Personal Postscript: Why I Wrote This Book

LECTURE AND DISCUSSION IDEAS

1. Social Psychology Web Sites

Both teachers and students of social psychology will find many useful resources on the Internet. Among the sites to share with students are the following:

Social Psychology Network (www.socialpsychology.org), maintained by Scott Plous of Wesleyan University, is a comprehensive source of information for exploring virtually every major topic in the textbook. Students preparing writing assignments will find links to other sites organized by topic such as conformity, cultural influences, prejudice, and aggression. Students can also participate in online social psychology studies from around the world, visit social psychology research groups and journals, browse through a list of social psychology textbooks, and visit the homepages of individual social psychologists (Demonstration 1-12 provides a ready-to-use handout for students to explore this site).

Allen McConnell's Compendium of Social Psychology Web Resources (http://www.msu.edu/user/amcconne/social.html) is presently divided into links to general social psychology resources, such as the Society for Personality and Social Psychology and the Journal for Experimental Social Psychology, and links to specific social psychology programs and researchers.

Psychology Web Archive: Jumping Off Place for Social Psychologists (http://swix.ch/clan/ks/CPSP1.htm), maintained by Karsten Schwarz, provides worldwide links and is organized into sections that include articles and references, libraries and journals, gopher resources, and available software.

Richard Sherman's Weblinks to Social Psychology in Cyberspace (http://Miavx1.MUOhio.edu/~psy2cwis/webinfo.html) includes a special section devoted specifically to teaching resources as well as separate categories of research resources and links to general information resources.

Eliot R. Smith of Purdue University maintains an archive of social-cognition papers and information (www.psych.purdue.edu/~esmith/scarch.html). The cite offers a search engine to navigate through the entries as well as links to a couple dozen other resources on the web.

Instructors may also be interested in joining a discussion group (LISTSERV@UGA.CC.UGA.EDU) that provides a forum for considering current theory and research in social psychology as well as the teaching of social psychology. To join the list, send an e-mail to the above address with the body of message as follows: subscribe socpsy-L your first name then last name.

2. Introducing Social Psychology with McGraw-Hill Videotapes

Both the McGraw-Hill Videotape in Social Psychology and the McGraw-Hill Videotape of Candid Camera Classics in Social Psychology are excellent sources of material for introducing social psychology. The former provides brief motion clips from research studies and everyday life that serve to introduce the discipline's content and methods. For example, there is coverage of Milgram's obedience study, Zimbardo's prison simulation, and Bandura's Bobo doll experiment. There are clips from the Interpersonal Perception Task as well as CBS coverage of the rescue of Jessica McClure, resistance at Tiananmen Square, and the Waco tragedy. For a lighter introduction and one that is sure to break the tension of the first class day, you might use some clips from the Candid Camera disc/tape. "Face the Rear," "Don't Eat Light," and "Delaware Closed Today" are among the most hilarious.

3. Introducing Social Psychology's Content

Chapter 1 begins with three specific questions that illustrate social psychology's focus on how people think about, influence, and relate to one another. In introducing the discipline you may want to supplement these with additional examples from the research literature and current events.

To highlight social psychology's concern with social thinking you might cite Rosenthal's studies of self-fulfilling prophecy, particularly the effects of teachers' expectations (Chapter 3), or Rosenhan's controversial demonstration of the biasing power of diagnostic labels (Module A). Or note some common misconceptions such as those identified by Gilovich in How We Know What Isn't So: for example, the mistaken notion that infertile couples who adopt a child are more likely to conceive than couples who don't; admission committees' false assumption that they can make better decisions if they see candidates in brief, personal interviews; and basketball fans' misconception of the "hot hand." Why do people hold firmly to these beliefs in the absence of supporting evidence? Social psychology is concerned with understanding the errors that contaminate our thought processes.

For social influence you might complement the text's treatment of groupthink in the Bay of Pigs fiasco by noting flaws in the group decision-making process that led to the Challenger explosion (Chapter 8). Or recall the Jonestown massacre (Chapter 7), noting how it raises questions about the dynamics of human persuasion. The felony conviction of former East German border guards for shooting those who were fleeing toward freedom in West Berlin raises anew the question of obedience to authority and our capacity to resist (Chapter 6).

For social relations, citing examples of the bystander phenomenon, such as the now classic Kitty Genovese case (Chapter 12), stimulates students' interest in the study of altruism. Contrast Kitty's case with that of 18-month-old Jessica McClure who, in 1988, fell 22 feet into an abandoned mine shaft. The people of Midland, Texas, worked nonstop for almost three days to free her. What accounts for this difference? When do people help?

4. Introducing the Idea of "Ah-Ha!" Moments

The book tries to further highlight the relevancy of social psychology by including a series of "Taking Social Psychology Into Life" vignettes. The goal of increasing the student's awareness of the near ubiquitous applicability of social psychological principles can also be supported by periodically asking students to report instances in their daily lives that reminded them of principles and concepts learned in their social psychology class—so called "Ah-Ha!" moments. Students enjoy the opportunity to share with the class their personal stories and it is a good opening exercise that can be used repeatedly throughout the semester. This idea is included here because of its general applicability, but it is best used after at least a few class periods (and lectures) have occurred.

5. Introducing Research Methodology: A Decision-Making Perspective

Gordon Wood (1984) suggests that students' understanding and appreciation of research methodology may be enhanced by our adopting a decision-making perspective. That is, the necessity for systematic procedures to avoid bias—a research methodology—will become clear if students are shown that they do have biases that influence their judgments and decisions. Wood identifies three categories of biases: general biases, those involved in assessing covariation, and those that contaminate our judgments of causation. All are readily demonstrated in Chapters 2 and 3 of the Myers' text, and accompanying demonstrations are provided in this manual. Some could be used in your coverage of methodology.

A. General biases.

1. Self-serving bias. Our tendency to see ourselves favorably is discussed in Chapter 2 and is evident in the better-than-average bias. (See Demonstration 2-6 in this manual.)
2. The I-knew-it-all-along phenomenon. (See Demonstrations 1-1, 1-2, and 1-3 in this chapter.)
3. Intuitions about randomness. Two basic features of research methodology are random sampling and random assignment. Our intuitions about randomness, however, are biased.

   Wood suggests asking students to simulate a random number generator. Tell them to imagine that there are 10 balls of equal size in an urn. Each has one of 10 digits from 1 to 10 printed on it. The balls are mixed and one is drawn by a blindfolded person. The number on the ball is recorded, the ball is returned, and a second is drawn. Tell students to write down the numbers that might be selected if this process is repeated 30 times. Given this assignment, students will show a bias against repeating a digit. While probability tells us that on the average there will be three repeats, many students will not have any.

   Asked to generate a sequence of 100 coin flips, people show a similar bias. The proportion of heads to tails stays very close to even throughout the entire series. Wood writes, "In order to have students appreciate this point, have them compare their sequence of 100 simulated coin flips with a sequence generated by using a table of random numbers. I generated the following sequence using a table of random numbers: H H H T H H H H H H H H T H T H H T T T H H T H H T H H T H H H T T T T H H H H H H T T H H H T H H T H H H T H H H T H T H T H T T H H H H H H T T T H T T H H H H H T T H H T T T T T T T T."

   To demonstrate misperceptions of randomness (as well your ESP ability) you might try a variation on this exercise recommended by Donald McBurney and Greg Lockhead. Tell your class that while you are out of the room they are to generate a random series of the letters A, B, and C about 50 letters long.

   When you come back begin guessing the string they created. After your first guess have the class give immediate feedback on the correct answer. From that trial on, always guess one of the responses that was not correct on the previous trial, e.g., if the correct letter on the last trial was "A," then say "B" or "C." You will have about 50 percent success compared to an expected value of 33 percent.

B. Biases in assessing covariation.
   1. Illusory correlation. We sometimes see relationships where none exist. This bias is discussed in Chapters 2 and Module A of the text. (See Demonstration MA-5 in this manual.)
   2. Data-based versus theory-based covariation. While our theories may lead us to see relationships where none exist, we also fail to detect true relationships when simply presented the data. (See Demonstration MA-4 in this manual.)

C. Biases in inferring causation.
   1. The fundamental attribution error. The tendency for observers to underestimate the impact of the situation and overestimate the impact of inner disposition upon another's behavior is discussed in Chapter 3. (See Demonstration 3-2 in this manual.)
   2. Illusion of control. People often believe they are in control when they are not. This bias is discussed in Chapter 3 of the text. Wood suggests a simple coin-flipping demonstration to illustrate how quickly we may be inclined to an illusion of control. Ask all students to stand up and flip a coin in an effort to get heads. They remain standing and continue to flip until they get tails. Approximately half the people standing should sit down after every flip.

Beginning, say, with a total of 256 people, the number standing will go to 128 to 64 to 32 to 16 to 8 to 4 to 2 to 1. Do students find themselves making skill attributions to the individual who remains standing?

6. Testing Facilitated Communication

Chapter 6 of this manual describes the use of facilitated communication with autistic children. Presumably such children could communicate using a keyboard if someone simply steadied their arms. Simple experiments in which the child responded after the facilitator and the child saw the same or different pictures demonstrated that the facilitator rather than child authored the communications. You can use this case early in the course both to introduce social influence as one of social psychology's chief topics and also to highlight the value of the experiment in helping us to evaluate everyday claims.

The PBS production Prisoners of Silence (Call 800-344-3337 to order) provides an excellent review of facilitated communication including the use of controlled experiments to test its validity. You may choose to show all of it (56 minutes) or only the eight-minute segment showing the experiments that begin 25 minutes into the film. After showing it, ask students to analyze the experimental design including both independent and dependent variables.

7. Give Your Own "Behind the Scenes" Story

Chapter 1 stresses that social psychologists view human nature from a particular perspective, and that their personal values influence their work in subtle ways. You might therefore begin by telling the story of your own involvement in social psychology. How did your interest begin? How was it developed? What are your special interests? What are your own presuppositions and commitments, and how do they influence your teaching and research? Revealing such information will introduce you to your students, and will embody the main point of the text section on "Social Psychology and Human Values."

8. Encouraging Class Participation

Randolph Smith suggests a technique for encouraging classroom participation and, at the same time, has the added benefit of allowing you to monitor class attendance efficiently. At your first class session, explain to students that each day, as they enter the class, they will receive a small slip of paper on which they are to sign their name. They may also write down any question(s) they did not wish to raise in class. On the way out, they should leave the paper on your desk. You can then devote the first part of the next lesson to a discussion of the issues raised. Not only does this give you time to prepare your response to students' questions and concerns, it also gives you a chance to review the highlights of the previous day's presentation. Equally important, you will have a good idea of how well students comprehend your lecture. Smith reports that this technique increases both the quantity and quality of questions and raises the general level of classroom discussion.

9. Complementary Levels of Explanation

The text notes that the different disciplines, which study human functioning, provide different levels of explanation that are complementary rather than contradictory. This notion can be further developed in class with a simple illustration suggested by Stephen Evans. Have students imagine a poem that has been handwritten with pen and ink. It is possible to describe the poem in purely physical terms as a set of ink marks on paper. This description could be made even more basic by providing a chemical analysis of the ink and paper. Such a description could be very useful if someone wished to know whether the poem is likely to fade and become illegible over time. A third level of explanation would be to view the poem as a collection of letters of the English alphabet. Still a fourth would be to view the poem as a collection of English words. Finally, someone might describe the poem as a literary creation. In analyzing these different perspectives, should we ask, "Which one is true?" Certainly not. While they state very different things, they are complementary perspectives. Each account is accurate and potentially useful. They are simply different ways of looking at the same event.

William Doise (1986) suggests that even within social psychology there are complementary levels of explanation: 1) The <u>intrapersonal</u> level deals with individuals' traits and their ways of perceiving and thinking about their social world. 2) The <u>interpersonal</u> level deals with how individuals influence and relate to one another. 3) The <u>intergroup</u> level deals with how our group identifications influence our behavior. 4) The <u>societal</u> level deals with the impact of shared cultural norms and ideas. Applying this analysis to prejudice, we see how prejudice is influenced by how we individually organize information about our social worlds, how we absorb the ideas of our peers, how our division into social groups fuels dislike for "outgroups," and how the assumptions and ideology of our culture feed our stereotypes. (Note that Doise's definition of social psychology is more inclusive than that of the text, which emphasizes Doise's first two levels of explanation as the unique province of social psychology.)

10. The Hindsight Bias

We tend to exaggerate our ability to have foreseen how something would turn out, <u>after</u> learning the outcome. For example, before the 1985 Super Bowl, Brigham (1986) asked students to predict its outcome. An overwhelming majority (81 percent) predicted the Miami Dolphins would win and 40 percent said by more than 10 points. A week after the San Francisco 49er's decisive victory, Brigham asked another group to remember their pre-game predictions. No one remembered thinking Miami would win by at least 10 points. More recently Demakis (1997) reported hindsight bias in connection with pre- and postverdict predictions of the outcome of the O.J. Simpson criminal trial. Students who made postverdict ratings were more likely to say they expected a not guilty verdict and less likely to have expected a hung jury than those who made pre-verdict predictions. You may want to replicate the hindsight bias by having some of your students predict the outcome of some sporting event or election (local or national) and having other students remember their predictions after the outcome is known (this is most easily done if you have more than one psychology class). As the text notes, we did this with the Clarence Thomas case, and like Brigham and Demakis, found dramatic evidence for the hindsight bias. (Also see Demonstrations 1-1, 1-2, and 1-3.)

Fischhoff and Beyth (1975) demonstrated how the hindsight bias strengthens over time. Prior to President Nixon's trips to China and Russia in 1972, they asked students to estimate the probability of a number of events, e.g., that the United States would establish a permanent diplomatic mission in Peking, that President Nixon would meet Mao Tse-Tung at least once, that Nixon would see Soviet demonstrators, etc. After the trip, students were asked in hindsight to remember their original estimates. When the interval between the two tests was just two weeks, 67 percent thought their original estimates were closer to the truth than they actually were. When a four-to-eight-month interval had elapsed, 84 percent showed the hindsight bias.

Russo and Schoemaker (1989) suggest that we see more reasons for an event when it <u>has already happened</u> than when we simply ask why it <u>might occur</u>. They asked managers and MBA students who had been given a brief description of a new employee why he <u>might</u> quit six months from now. They generated a mean of 3.5 reasons per person. However, when told that the new employee had already quit, the hindsight group generated 25 percent more reasons on average (4.4 reasons). Moreover, the reasons were more specific and more closely tied to the description of the employee. The investigators further suggest that by merely pretending that an event has occurred leads us to see more reasons for its occurrence and ultimately assigning it a higher probability of becoming reality. For example, they indicate that people who imagine that a woman has been elected president of the United States in 2000 come up with more reasons why this occurred than those who are simply asked why a woman might be elected in 2000. Moreover, when finally asked to estimate the probability of the hypothetical event becoming reality. the former give a higher estimate than the latter. Russo and Schoemaker conclude that although hindsight usually obstructs learning, sometimes "prospective hindsight" can be turned to advantage in contemplating the future. If you doubt whether people have sufficient insight into the myriad of causes that could produce success or failure for an important project, it may be useful to have them engage in some "mental time travel."

11. Survey Research

Given the glut of popular books reporting survey results of Americans' attitudes and behaviors (e.g. Harris's Inside America, Patterson and Kim's The Day America Told the Truth, Poretz and Sinrod's The First Really Important Survey of American Habits as well as their Do You Do It with the Lights On?), you may want to highlight the potentially biasing influences cited in the text.

For example, Poretz and Sinrod's survey asked respondents about their eating, sleeping, and dressing habits, as well as for information about their special abilities and eccentricities. They found 68 percent roll toilet paper over the spool, 79 percent squeeze toothpaste from the top, 7 percent look behind the shower curtain when using someone else's bathroom, and 80 percent eat corn on the cob in circles rather than from side to side. How did the authors reach these conclusions? They sent surveys to 25,000 people and a total of 7,000 returned them. It is unlikely we have a representative sample of all Americans.

Pratkanis and his colleagues (1989) provide a delightful example of how response options can influence results. Some students were asked to select A or B: A. Nutri-burger: a tofu burger that is rated very good on nutrition but only average on taste, or B. Tasti-burger: a hamburger that is rated very good on taste but only average on nutrition. Others were asked to select from three alternatives: A, B, or C. Bummer-burger: a hamburger that is rated only good on taste and only average on nutrition. As predicted, virtually no one selected the inferior C over A or B. But the addition of C significantly increased the choice of the Tasti-burger over the Nutri-burger. Why? Very likely the "C" option made the very good tasting Tasti-burger appear to be even better tasting and the average tasting Nutri-burger to be even poorer tasting.

Demonstration 1-10 illustrates anchoring effects. Russo and Schoemaker (1989) show how even random and thus clearly irrelevant anchors can influence responses in a survey. In one hilarious demonstration they even had respondents provide their own anchor. They asked: "What are the last three digits of your home phone number?" If the last three digits for a particular person were XYZ, they then said, "I'm going to add 400 to your answer. Do you think Attila the Hun was defeated in Europe before or after A.D. (XYZ + 400)?" After respondents answered (and without telling them whether they were right), they inquired, "In what year would you guess Attila the Hun was actually defeated?" Few knew (A.D. 451). However, the telephone-number anchor dramatically affected their answers. For example, if the range of the initial anchor (last three digits plus 400) was 400 to 599, the average estimate of Attila's defeat was 629. When the anchor range was 1200 to 1399, the average estimate was 988.

12. Challenge Students with Case Examples of Correlational vs. Experimental Research

Chapter 1 emphasizes the distinction between correlational and experimental research, and the problems with drawing cause-effect conclusions from the former. Emphasize the importance of making this distinction when evaluating conclusions drawn by researchers and journalists. Stimulate students' facility at making this distinction by challenging them with case examples, such as:

A. Researchers have consistently found that heavy cigarette smoking is associated with lung cancer. The more one smokes, the more likely one is to get cancer and to die early. If this smoking-cancer relationship is indeed reliable, may we conclude that smoking increases one's chances of lung cancer? (Answer: The correlation does not prove cause and effect. In The Causes and Effects of Smoking, Sage, 1981, Hans Eysenck argues that the correlation may occur simply because some people have a genetic personality disposition, such as a reactive temperament, that a) inclines them to heavy smoking, and b) makes them more vulnerable to lung cancer.) How could one study whether smoking actually does increase one's vulnerability to cancer? (Answer: By training animals to inhale smoke with or without nicotine; by experimentally studying the health benefits of an antismoking treatment program; by statistically extracting the influence of plausible "third factors," such as personality; etc.)

B. If researchers were to discover that joggers live longer, what would this tell us about the effects of jogging on longevity? (Answer: Nothing, necessarily. The text suggests three types of explanation are possible for any correlation.)

C. Hippocrates' Good News Survey (Tierney, 1987) found that people who often ate Frosted Flakes as children had half the cancer rate of those who never ate the cereal. Conversely, those who frequently ate oatmeal as children were four times as likely to develop cancer than those who did not. Does this mean that eating Frosted Flakes prevents cancer while eating oatmeal causes it? Ask your students to explain these correlations. The answer? Cancer tends to be an illness of later life. Those who ate Frosted Flakes are younger. In fact, the cereal was not around when older respondents were children; they were much more likely to have eaten oatmeal.

D. Keith Stanovich (1995) correctly notes that the nature of the relationship between two variables influences the likelihood of our interpreting a correlation in causal terms. Several years ago a research team in Taiwan found the best predictor of the adoption of birth-control methods was the number of electric appliances in the home. Stanovich asks, "Does this finding suggest that the teenage pregnancy problem should be dealt with by passing out free toasters in the schools?" Obviously not. With this example, students will quickly recognize that a correlation does not necessarily imply causation. It may exist because of a mediating variable. What would it be in this case? Education is one likely candidate. Education is related to contraceptive use as well as to socioeconomic status. Since families at higher socioeconomic levels tend to have more electric appliances in their homes, the linkage is complete.

13. Exploring the Use of Deception in Social Psychological Research

Chapter 1 notes that achieving experimental realism often requires the use of deception. Although deception is used in experiments for other disciplines, social psychology's use is much more frequent than most other experimental disciplines. As a result, students are most likely to understand the importance of thinking through the "deception issue" while taking a social psychology class. The 7th Edition of "Taking sides: Clashing views on controversial psychological issues" (Slife & Rubinstein, 1992) contains two articles (Part 1, Issue 1) arguing the pro and con for the question "Can deception in research be justified?" Although the title suggests a more general discussion on deception, both of the authors (Stanley Milgram and Thomas Murray) use social psychological examples. The book also contains several "challenge questions" after the readings to facilitate critical thinking about this debate. Some additional questions are: "What do you think of Milgram's argument against using the word deception?" Do you agree with Murray's assertion that the experimenter is simply unable to remove all psychological trauma during the debriefing time?

14. Popular Sources for Additional Classroom Material

Aron, A., & Aron, E. (1990). <u>The heart of social psychology</u>, 2nd ed. Lexington, MA: D.C. Heath. A brief and popular account of some of social psychology's major findings. Based on interviews with researchers active in the field. Complements the textbook's treatment.

Brannigan, C.G., & Merrens, M.R. (Eds.). (1995). <u>The social psychologists: Research adventures</u>. New York: McGraw-Hill. A collection of first-person accounts of research by leading social psychologists including Susan Fiske, Mark Snyder, Robert Cialdini, and Leonard Berkowitz. Topics cover all of the major research areas in social psychology.

Coats, E.J., & Feldman, R. S. (Eds.). (1998). <u>Classic and contemporary readings in social psychology</u>, 2nd ed. Upper Saddle River, NJ: Prentice Hall. Provides a unique set of 30 paired selections, a classic and a contemporary, from articles and books covering all the major topics in social psychology.

Dane, F. C. (1988). <u>The common and uncommon sense of social behavior</u>. Pacific Grove, CA: Brooks/Cole. A very brief overview of social psychology. A blend of research findings and everyday examples.

Davis, M.H. (Ed.). (2000). <u>Annual editions: Social psychology 01/02</u>. Guilford, CT: Dushkin/McGraw-Hill. Updated annually, this volume provides convenient access to a wide range of current articles on social psychology appearing in magazines, newspapers, and journals.

Ellyson, S.J., & Halberstadt, A.G. (Eds.) (1995). <u>Explorations in social psychology: Readings and research.</u> New York: McGraw-Hill. A collection of 30 classic and contemporary articles from all areas of social psychological research organized under social thought, influence, and relations. Each reading is accompanied by a short introduction. Highly readable!

Fein, S., & Spencer, S. (Eds.). (1996). <u>Readings in social psychology: The art and science of research</u>, 3rd ed. Boston: Houghton Mifflin. A collection of 16 short readings on various topics dealing with social perception, social interaction, social influence, and applying social psychology. Each entry includes a brief introduction by the editor and a set of critical thinking questions at the end.

Gilbert, D. T., Fiske, S.T., & Lindzey, G. (Eds.) (1997). <u>Handbook of social psychology</u>, 4th ed. Cary, NC: Oxford University Press. An authoritative overview of the methods and findings of social psychology. Two volumes and nearly 2,000 pages contributed by leading researchers.

Hendricks, B., Marvel, M.K., & Barrington, B. L. (1990). The dimensions of psychological research. <u>Teaching of Psychology, 17</u>, 76-82. Presents a methodological cube that classifies studies along three dimensions: research design (descriptive, correlational, or experimental), data-collection method (self-report or observational), and research setting (laboratory or field). Examples are drawn from the aggression literature.

Higgins, E. T., & Kruglanski, A.W. (Eds.) (1996). <u>Social psychology: Handbook of basic principles</u>. New York: Guilford. Provides an overview of the central principles that guide social psychological investigation. Each chapter describes alternative conceptualizations of a particular principle and reviews relevant research.

Kohn, A. (1990). <u>You know what they say</u>. New York: HarperCollins. Analyzes the truth of familiar proverbs, many of them relating to social behavior. Some are true, others are not. Demonstrates the value of careful, systematic research.

Jordan, C.H., & Zanna, M. P. (1999). How to read a journal article in social psychology. In R. F. Baumeister (Ed.), <u>The self in social psychology</u> (p.461–470). Philadelphia, PA: Psychology Press. A wonderfully informative introduction for students who are new to reading journal articles. It breaks the article down into its main parts and helps the student understand the logic behind article construction. This is a great resource to use early in the semester if you are planning on asking students to do a research project.

Lesko, W. A. (Ed.). (2000). Readings in social psychology; General, Classic and Contemporary selections, 4th ed. Boston: Allyn and Bacon. A collection of 42 articles covering all of the major sub-disciplines in social psychology. Each entry includes a brief introduction by the editor and a set of critical thinking questions at the end.

Pacanowsky, M. (1978). Salt passage research: The state of the art. Change, 10(8), 41-43. A very funny application of popular social psychological theories and methods to predicting reactions for the request, "Please pass the salt."

Pettijohn, T.F. (Ed.). (1998). Sources: Notable selections in social psychology, 2nd ed. Guilford, CT: Dushkin/McGraw-Hill Publishing. A collection of 42 classic articles, book excerpts, and research studies that have shaped the discipline of social psychology. The selections are organized around the major areas of study within social psychology.

Sapsford, R, Still, A., Wetherell, M., Miell, D., & Stevens, R. (Eds.). (1998). Theory and Social Psychology. London: Sage. A collection of 11 short essays on topics pertaining to nature and origins, making sense of diversity, and applying social psychology. Excellent supplemental material for creating lectures. The reading, however, may be somewhat difficult for average undergraduate students.

Stanovich, K.E. (1995). How to think straight about psychology, 4th ed. New York: HarperCollins. Teaches students to examine critically the claims that are made about human behavior in the popular media.

Tesser, A. (Ed.). (1995). Advanced social psychology. Boston: McGraw-Hill. This text has 12 chapters covering many of the topics in Myers' text by noted authors such as Cialdini, Fiske, and Batson. Excellent resource for instructors who want to take their students beyond the text but need to get back up-to-speed with what is going on in social psychology.

Zimbardo, P. (June 1985). Laugh where we must, be candid where we can. Psychology Today, p. 43–47. A conversation with Allen Funt, creator of Candid Camera. Funt describes the potential educational value of the show and also responds to concerns about his use of deception and the potential for harm to his subjects. Good background for the use of McGraw-Hill's Candid Camera Classics for Social Psychology.

DEMONSTRATION AND PROJECT IDEAS

1. **Social Psychology Essays**

If you want student involvement to move beyond text-reading and note-taking, Ann Weber (1984) suggests the assignment of brief, one-page essays. Each should provide (1) a short description of a personal experience or an observation, which illustrates or exemplifies one of the social psychological phenomena covered in class lecture or the text; (2) a brief explanation of the theory or research dealing with the phenomenon or process discussed in 1, complete with references; and (3) an application of the research or theory in 2 to the observation described in 1, together with an evaluation of the "fit" of the theory to the life experience. If each essay is evaluated on a 4-or-5-point scale, the grading proves simple and fast. A package of 5 to 10 essays can tell much about a student's level of interest and comprehension.

2. **A Social Psychology Portfolio**

Rider's (1992) suggestion for having students create a portfolio of news clippings that illustrate psychological concepts is particularly applicable to social psychology courses. To encourage students to apply what they have learned to everyday life, have them, in the course of the term, collect newspaper and magazine clippings and write an explanation of each using course material. They can use articles, editorials, advertisements, advice columns, photographs, and cartoons. You might suggest that students find at least one item for each chapter in the text. Rider found that for her introductory students the median number of portfolio entries was 20 with students' accompanying explanations ranging from two sentences to two paragraphs.

3. Reenacting Social Psychological Experiments

Wann (1993) reports success in helping students comprehend social psychological research and methodology by having small groups each select a different experiment and develop a dramatic script to describe the research. Each group of four to six individuals was responsible for obtaining a copy of the relevant article (e.g., Milgram's study of obedience), using the article to write a script, and developing the props necessary to perform the play. Students play the roles of experimenters, confederates, and subjects with each play approximately 10 minutes long. Students are instructed to pay attention to detail in an effort to reenact the study as accurately as possible. Poetic license is allowed where authors were not explicit.

4. The I-Knew-It-All-Along Phenomenon

This hindsight bias enables a powerful, memorable demonstration that what's "obvious common sense" often becomes so *after* the facts are known. BEFORE students read Chapter 1, duplicate copies of Demonstration 1-1 or of Demonstration 1-2. Cut the sheets in half and alternate the two versions, so that after the questions are distributed and completed, each person can compare with an adjacent person to confirm the contradictory versions. The procedure is simple: after everyone has answered the questions, explain the phenomenon and then demonstrate it by asking, "How many of you found the finding 'surprising'?" Few hands will rise. "How many of you found it, 'not surprising'?" Many hands will rise. "Now let me tell you a secret. Half of you were given a finding opposite to the other half."

The hindsight bias may also be illustrated with Demonstration 1-3, which is adapted from Fischhoff (1977). Give half the class the first version of this questionnaire; this tells them the answers to factual questions and asks them, in essence, whether they knew-it-all-along. Give the other half of the class the second version, which does not inform them that the answer they are rating is, in fact, the correct answer. Then have all students average their probability estimates, and do a quick tally to see whether the answers seem more obvious to those who have been told them.

R. E. Goranson's experiment cited by Gordon Wood (1984) provides the basis for another quick yet dramatic illustration. Write the following anagrams with their solutions in parentheses on the chalkboard: WREAT (WATER), ETRYN (ENTRY), OCHSA (CHAOS), GRABE (BARGE). Ask students to write down an estimate of how long it would have taken them to correctly solve each anagram if they had not been given the solution. Then ask students to raise their hands if their estimates were lower than the actual solution times. Those reported by Goranson were 158, 182, 224, and 173 seconds, respectively. Knowing the outcome, the answer seems so obvious and students will grossly underestimate solution times.

As Gordon Wood (1984) suggests, throughout the course it is probably wise to have students predict the results of a study before presenting the findings. Very likely they will become less vulnerable to the hindsight bias.

5. Social Psychology and Common Sense

Although the chapter does not maintain that most social psychological findings are counterintuitive, it can be demonstrated that some are. Our students miss most of the questions in Demonstration 1-4. Do yours? These questions can also serve to introduce the range of topics studied by social psychologists.

Here is the answer key; evidence supporting each answer will be encountered in the text chapters indicated.

1.F(Chapter 2)	10.F(Chapter 6)	19.F(Chapter 11)
2.F(Chapter 2)	11.F(Chapter 7)	20.F(Chapter 11)
3.F(Chapter 3)	12.F(Chapter 7)	21.T(Chapter 11)
4.F(Chapter 3)	13.F(Chapter 8)	22.T(Chapter 12)
5.F(Chapter 4)	14.F(Chapter 8)	23.T(Chapter 13)
6.T(Chapter 4)	15.F(Chapter 9)	24.F(Module A)
7.F(Chapter 4)	16.T(Chapter 9)	25.T(Module A)
8.T(Chapter 5)	17.F(Chapter 10)	26.F(Module B)
9.T(Chapter 5)	18.T(Chapter 11)	27.F(Module C)

6. Social Psychology and Classic Wisdom

Demonstration 1-5 contrasts the wisdom of various sages on topics pertinent to social psychology. Stress to students that the point is not that the sages were not sage, but that no matter what answers research might reveal on these issues, there will already be people who anticipated the findings. Completing this demonstration should sensitize students to this point. It will also introduce them to the 15 chapter topics. Finally, it should prevent their misinterpreting the marginal quotes appearing throughout the text as indicating that the research was unnecessary.

7. The Framing of Survey Questions and Life Decisions

Tversky and Kahneman (1981) demonstrated how trivial changes in the formulations of questions can dramatically affect people's choices. The two versions of Demonstration 1-6 allow you to replicate their findings. Make copies, cut the sheets in half, and randomly distribute to your class, making sure each student receives only one form of the question. The authors found that those given the choices in the top half favored Program A by about 3 to 1. Those given the same choices but expressed as in the bottom half preferred Program B by 3 to 1. Demonstration 1-7 provides another pair of questions, again each question to be distributed to half the class. When the odds were given in terms of mortality, more than 40 percent chose radiation. But when the odds were given in terms of survival, the number choosing radiation was cut in half. Demonstration 1-8 presents yet another pair. Despite the fact that both cases involve the loss of $40, most people will buy a ticket after losing cash but not after losing the ticket.

The range of alternatives on a survey question can also distort responses. When people have no well-formed opinion they may gravitate toward a seemingly moderate answer. But what is moderate may depend on the "end anchors" provided in the question. Demonstration 1-9 provides two forms of the same question for distribution to separate groups. Tally responses by a show of hands for each group, using the following format. Inevitably the group that received the question with the "small fine" option will advise lighter sentences.

Group with "small fine"	Group with "life imprison"	Sentence recommended
_____	_____	Six months <u>or less</u>
_____	_____	Two years
_____	_____	Five years <u>or more</u>

You may accompany this exercise with results from some national surveys. For example, in a recent survey of more than 1,200 American adults, New York's American Museum of Natural History and Louis Harris found that 77 percent were interested in plants and trees but only 39 percent expressed interest in botany. Similarly, 48 percent were interested in fossils but only 39 percent were interested in paleontology. Of the total sample, only 42 percent were interested in rocks and minerals, but 53 percent were interested in geology. Sometimes respondents simply lie. In 1996, exit polls in New Hampshire showed Democrat Dick Sivett leading Republican Senator Bob Smith 52 to 47 percent. The actual vote was the other way around. Some speculate that this was voters' reaction to the fact that mainline media coverage of public life is to the left of where many citizens' sympathies lie. Respondents may tell pollsters what they think they want to hear.

H. Ross Perot's 1992 mail-in survey results may have been contaminated by both wording and a biased sample. His questionnaire was published in <u>TV Guide,</u> and the magazine's readers were asked to reply. A total of 97 percent answered "yes" to the question, "Do you believe that for every dollar of tax increase there should be $2 in spending cuts with the savings earmarked for deficit reduction?" Using the same wording with a random sample, Yankelovich found 67 percent agreed. And the more neutrally worded "Would you favor or oppose a proposal to cut spending by $2 for every dollar in new taxes, with the savings earmarked for deficit reduction, even if that meant cuts in domestic programs like Medicare and education?" elicited approval from only 33 percent. Perot's question "Should laws be passed to eliminate all possibilities of special interests giving huge sums of money to candidates?" elicited a whopping 99 percent from <u>TV Guide</u> readers but only 80 percent from Yankelovich's random sample. The latter's more neutral "Should laws be passed to prohibit interest groups from contributing to campaigns or do groups have a right to contribute to the candidate they support" elicited 40 percent wanting to prohibit and 55 percent believing groups had the right to contribute.

Polls taken at the same time produce different results depending on how the question is phrased. <u>Time</u> magazine (April 5, 1993) reported that approval ratings for "Hillary Clinton" were 56.8 percent while those for "Hillary Rodham Clinton" were only 49.4 percent. Similarly, 8 in 10 Americans believe that "Women with young children should be able to work outside the home." But 7 in 10 also believe that "Women should stay home if they have young preschool children." Twenty-nine percent favored a constitutional amendment "prohibiting abortions" but 50 percent favored a constitutional amendment "protecting the life of the unborn." Sixty-one percent believed we are spending too little on "assistance to the poor" but only 22 percent believed we are spending too little on "welfare."

8. Demonstrating the Anchoring Bias

Demonstration 1-10 illustrates anchoring effects. Make copies, cut the sheets in half, and randomly distribute to your class making sure each student receives only one form of the question. Compared to those provided an anchor of 500 miles, those given a 3,000-mile anchor will give a higher estimate. You can collect the responses and tabulate the mean estimates for each group or, more simply, by a show of hands ask each group provided a different anchor whether their own estimate was greater than 1,500 miles. A majority of those given 3,000 miles will raise their hands but a minority of those given 500 miles will do so. (The actual length of the Mississippi is 2,348 miles).

Replication of Amos Tversky and Daniel Kahneman's (1973) experiment will help students appreciate the significance of the "anchoring bias." Have them give friends the following problem: "Estimate quickly the product of $1 \times 2 \times 3 \times 4 \times 5 \times 6 \times 7 \times 8$." They should instruct an equal number of respondents: "Estimate quickly the product of $8 \times 7 \times 6 \times 5 \times 4 \times 3 \times 2 \times 1$." In each case, they should ask for an answer after only a few seconds. Tversky and Kahneman found the median estimates to be 512 and 2,250, respectively. The first group's estimates were anchored to "$1 \times 2 \times 3 \ldots$"; the second group's responses were anchored to "$8 \times 7 \times 6. \ldots$"

9. Conducting a National Survey—In Class

One way to prove that a true random sample of 1,500 people can estimate the responses of 200 million people is mathematically. A more vivid and memorable way to make the point is to demonstrate it with an in-class simulation of a national survey. It's easy:

1. Obtain a wide-mouth gallon glass jug (perhaps from your campus food service).
2. Purchase a large supply of small white beans and of identically sized colored beans. (Alternatively, stain half of the white beans in a solution of water and food coloring.)
3. Place a large <u>known</u> quantity (more than 5,000) of each color in the jug. This will be the population, which, numbering more than 10,000, will be essentially infinite. If the beans are indeed of identical size (e.g., both colors have been soaked and dried identically, one with coloring added), then you need only measure a known proportion of each (e.g., 53 percent white, 47 percent green).
4. Now simulate the survey by having each student act as survey taker as he or she takes a <u>small</u> number from the jug (a small handful tends to have more than the student imagines). You might say: "We're surveying voter preferences for the next presidential election. The white beans represent Gore supporters and the green beans Bush supporters. Our first survey taker is sampling neighborhoods in western Washington," etc. If there are 30 people in the class, have each person drop 50 beans from a closed hand, counting the two colors.
5. The counting completed, it's time to tabulate the results. Tallying 15 groups of 100 will demonstrate a 95 percent confidence interval of about +/- 10 percent about the true population mean. Clustering those into three groups of 500 should demonstrate that the margin of error is reduced to about +/- 5 percent. Chances are 95 percent that the population estimate based on the total sample of 1,500 will be within +/- 3 percent.
6. Emphasize that the sampling principles demonstrated are identical to those involved in large national surveys (assuming true random sampling), and that it makes little difference whether the population is 10,000+ or 200 million.

10. Demonstrating Non-representative Sampling in Class

Chapter 1 suggests surveys are only helpful if the sampling procedure used is representative of the population from which it comes. This importance of representative samples can be demonstrated in class by having students answer the series of personal preference questions asked in Demonstration 1-11. While they are filling them out, suggest that this data may be used by the school's radio station and/or the student activities committee as an indication of the student body's interests in popular culture events on campus. Before gathering up the forms, suggest that you really don't need a very big sample and that maybe you'll only need a sub-set of the classes' responses. Then attempt to gather up the forms from only those in the back rows or maybe only a small pack of students sitting off to one side. (You might try to defend this action by suggesting the analysis is long and difficult.) At this point, the students will begin to object and the value of sample representativeness can be made. You may also wish to ask students how fair it would be if the radio station or student activities committee only sampled their class. You may also choose this opportunity to introduce the concept of "response bias" and the problems that arise when people who are asked to complete surveys fail to do so.

11. Assessing Human Values

Chapter 1 contends that one's values are important; they affect one's thinking. Milton Rokeach's (1973) research on values documents this point, and also illustrates both <u>correlational</u> and <u>experimental</u> methodology. Demonstration 1-12 is Form E of Rokeach's survey of "terminal values." Form G of the Value Survey, the alternate form most widely used, presents each value printed on a removable gummed label and is commercially produced by Consulting Psychologists Press, P.O. Box 10096, Palo Alto, CA 94303. Rokeach reports that value rankings <u>correlate</u> with various social attitudes and behaviors. For example, higher rankings of equality are associated with more favorable attitudes and actions toward the poor and minority groups. More recently he (Rokeach, 1989) reported that from 1968–1981, the ranking of equality decreased more than any other value. He also reports that <u>experimentally</u> identifying inconsistencies—"you put freedom high and equality low, which means you care more about your own freedom than others"—promotes both value change (equality ranked higher) and behavior change (greater willingness to contribute to NAACP solicitation, to sign up for race relations course, etc). In a recent field experiment Ball-Rokeach, Rokeach, and Grube (1984) have shown how a single 30-minute exposure to TV can significantly alter basic beliefs, attitudes, and behaviors of large numbers of people for at least several months. Here are rankings from a national sample of Americans (Ball-Rokeach, Rokeach, & Grube, 1984):

8	A COMFORTABLE LIFE	11	INNER HARMONY
17	AN EXCITING LIFE	14	MATURE LOVE
7	A SENSE OF ACCOMPLISHMENT	13	NAT'L SECURITY
2	A WORLD AT PEACE	16	PLEASURE
15	A WORLD OF BEAUTY	10	SALVATION
12	EQUALITY	4	SELF-RESPECT
1	FAMILY SECURITY	18	SOCIAL RECOGNITION
3	FREEDOM	9	TRUE FRIENDSHIP
5	HAPPINESS	6	WISDOM

12. Exploring Social Psychology on the Web

If you intend to use the Internet in your course, you may want to get students started early. Students may complete Demonstration 1-13 as an out-of-class project. It will introduce them to Social Psychology Network (www.socialpsychology.org), a comprehensive source of information for exploring virtually every major topic in the textbook. It is maintained by Scott Plous of Wesleyan University.

13. The Social Connection Video Series

One of the entries in the video instructional supplement (The Social Connection Video Series), entitled "Role Playing: The Power of the Situation," addresses some questions raised in Chapter 1 regarding the ethics of social research. See the Faculty Guide accompanying the video series for a program summary, pause points, and a classroom activity.

Demonstration 1-1
Bolt & Myers
©McGraw-Hill, 1999

Research suggests that the more romantically in love two people are, the more attractive they find all others of the opposite sex.

In a sentence or two, why do you suppose this is?

Does this finding strike you as surprising or not surprising?
___ surprising
___ not surprising

Demonstration 1-1
Bolt & Myers
©McGraw-Hill, 1999

Research suggests that the more romantically in love two people are, the less attractive they find all others of the opposite sex.

In a sentence or two, why do you suppose this is?

Does this finding strike you as surprising or not surprising?
___ surprising
___ not surprising

Demonstration 1-2

Research suggests that people with high self-esteem are more susceptible to flattery than those with low self-esteem.

In a sentence or two, why do you suppose this is?

Does this finding strike you as surprising or not surprising?
_____ surprising
_____ not surprising

Demonstration 1-2

Research suggests that people with low self-esteem are more susceptible to flattery than those with high self-esteem.

In a sentence or two, why do you suppose this is?

Does this finding strike you as surprising or not surprising?
_____ surprising
_____ not surprising

Demonstration 1-3

(with permission of B. Fischhoff)

Below are a number of factual questions, each of which has two possible answers. We are interested in studying the perceived difficulty of these items. <u>The correct answer has a blank beside it.</u> Pretend you hadn't been told the right answer. What probability would you have assigned to the answer with the blank beside it?

Here is a sample question:

Absinthe is

        a.   a precious stone

__%__   b.   a liqueur

Your task on this would be to pretend we hadn't told you that absinthe is a liqueur and to indicate the probability (from 0 to 100 percent) you would have believed that absinthe is indeed a liqueur. If you would have been pretty sure that absinthe is a liqueur, you might mark, say, 85 percent. If you would have felt equally sure that absinthe is <u>not</u> a liqueur, you might put 15 percent. If you felt it 50-50 (you would have had no idea), you might put 50 percent. In summary, your task is simply to estimate what odds you would have given to the answer with the blank if we hadn't told you the right answer.

1.   About how many known active volcanoes exist in the world?

__%__   a.   445

        b.   45

2.   Which magazine had the highest circulation in 1970?

        a.   <u>Time</u>

__%__   b.   <u>Playboy</u>

3.   Aesop, the fabulist, lived in

__%__   a.   The sixth century B.C.

        b.   The sixth century A.D.

4.   Potatoes are native to

__%__   a.   Peru

        b.   Ireland

5.   The first air raid in history took place in

__%__   a.   1849

        b.   1937

6.   Aladdin's nationality was

        a.   Persian

__%__   b.   Chinese

7.   Aardvarks eat mostly

        a.   Ants

__%__   b.   Termites

8.   3/4ths of the world's cacao (used in chocolate) comes from

__%__   a.   Africa

        b.   South America

Demonstration 1-3

(with permission of B. Fischhoff)

Below are a number of factual questions, each of which has two possible answers. We are interested in studying the perceived difficulty of these items. In each case, one answer has a blank beside it, which may or may not be the correct answer. In the blank, assign a probability that it is in fact the right answer.

Here is a sample question:

Absinthe is

a.   a precious stone

__%__   b.   a liqueur

Your task on this would be to indicate what probability (from 1 to 100 percent) you believe that absinthe is indeed a liqueur. If you are pretty sure that absinthe is a liqueur, you might mark, say, 85 percent. If you felt equally sure that absinthe is not a liqueur, you might put 15 percent. If you felt it 50-50 (you have no idea), you might put 50 percent. In summary, your task is simply to estimate what odds you would have given to the answer with the blank.

1.   About how many known active volcanoes exist in the world?
   __%__   a.   445
            b.   45

2.   Which magazine had the highest circulation in 1970?
            a.   <u>Time</u>
   __%__   b.   <u>Playboy</u>

3.   Aesop, the fabulist, lived in
   __%__   a.   The sixth century B.C.
            b.   The sixth century A.D.

4.   Potatoes are native to
   __%__   a.   Peru
            b.   Ireland

5.   The first air raid in history took place in
   __%__   a.   1849
            b.   1937

6.   Aladdin's nationality was
            a.   Persian
   __%__   b.   Chinese

7.   Aardvarks eat mostly
            a.   Ants
   __%__   b.   Termites

8.   3/4ths of the world's cacao (used in chocolate) comes from
   __%__   a.   Africa
            b.   South America

Demonstration 1-4
Bolt & Myers
©McGraw-Hill, 1999

True or False?

T F 1. Most of us have quite accurate insight into the factors that influence our moods.

T F 2. Most people rate themselves as worse-than-average in rating themselves on socially desirable characteristics.

T F 3. Memory is like a storage chest in the brain, into which we deposit material and from which we can withdraw it later if needed. Occasionally, something gets lost from the "chest" and then we say we have forgotten.

T F 4. People's behavior is best predicted in terms of their personalities or inner dispositions.

T F 5. To alter the way people act, one needs first to change their hearts and minds.

T F 6. People who are made self-conscious by looking into a mirror act more in line with their attitudes.

T F 7. The greater the reward promised for an activity, the more one will come to enjoy the activity.

T F 8. In overall vocabulary, happiness, and intelligence, males and females are not noticeably different.

T F 9. In countries everywhere, girls spend more time helping with housework and child care, while boys spend more time in unsupervised play.

T F 10. Most people would disobey an authority who orders them to hurt a stranger.

T F 11. Persuaders will always be more effective if they acknowledge opposing arguments.

T F 12. In a formal debate, it is always to your advantage to be the last speaker.

T F 13. People pull harder in a tug-of-war when part of a team than when pulling by themselves.

T F 14. The greater the cohesiveness or "we feeling" in a group, the more likely the group will make a good decision.

T F 15. When white and black students are shown faces of a few white and black individuals and then asked to pick these individuals out of a photographic lineup, both white and black students more accurately recognize the white faces than the black.

T F 16. In a recent national survey, only a minority of Americans indicated that they would be willing to see a homosexual doctor.

T F 17. To be mentally healthy, people need an opportunity to act out, and thus to vent, their aggression.

T F 18. The more often we see something—even if we don't like it at first—the more we grow to like it.

T F 19. As suggested by the dumb-blonde idea, physically attractive men and women tend to be looked on by others as colder, dumber, and less moral than the plainer people.

T F 20. Opposites attract.

T F 21. One of the best predictors of whether any two people are friends is their sheer proximity, or geographical nearness, to one another.

T F 22. When we feel guilty, we are more likely to help those around us.

T F 23. If you want to buy a new car at the best price, it is best to adopt a tough bargaining stance by opening with a very low offer rather than with a sincere, "good faith" offer.

T F 24. Depressed persons tend to be unrealistic in their perceptions of themselves.

T F 25. People who favor the death penalty are also more prone to vote a defendant guilty.

T F 26. Eyewitnesses' <u>certainty</u> about their own accuracy in viewing a crime is highly related to their actual <u>accuracy</u>.

T F 27. Research clearly shows a strong positive relationship between material wealth and life satisfaction.

Demonstration 1-5
Bolt & Myers
©McGraw-Hill, 1999

The Wisdom of the Past: Who Is Right?

The following 15 questions will be discussed in the textbook's 15 chapters. (Chapter 1 will speak to question 1, Chapter 2 to question 2, and so forth.) Indicate your own hunches, prior to reading the text.

1. What is the relationship between science and common sense? Shall we agree with
    ___a. Thomas H. Huxley that "science is nothing but trained and organized common sense?"

    Or with

    ___b. E. B. Titchener, that "common sense is the very opposite of science?"

2. Do people more commonly have deflated or inflated self-images? Shall we agree more with
    ___a. Carl Rogers that "the central core of difficulty in people . . . is that in the great majority of cases they despise themselves, and regard themselves as worthless and unlovable?"

    Or shall we agree more with

    ___b. Henry Ward Beecher that "conceit is the most incurable disease that is known to the human soul?"

3. Concerning the rationality of our social thinking, who is closer to the truth?
    ___a. Shakespeare's Hamlet: "What a piece of work is man! How noble in reason! How infinite in faculty! . . . in apprehension how like a god!" Or
    ___b. Madeline L'Engle's Mr. Murry: "The naked intellect is an extraordinarily inaccurate instrument?"

4. Consider the relationship between our actions and our convictions. Is it more true that
    ___a. "The ancestor of every action is a thought" (Ralph Waldo Emerson)? Or that
    ___b. "Thought is the child of action" (Benjamin Disraeli)?

5. Which sex exerts more social power? Is it more often true
   ___a. as Alfred Lord Tennyson declared: "Man to command, and woman to obey?" Or
   ___b. as Thomas Moore believed: "Disguise our bondage as we will, Tis woman, woman rules us still?"
6. Are most evil acts willfully performed by evil individuals, or by ordinary people who have been corrupted by an evil influence? Whose experience is the more typical, that of
   ___a. Euripides: "I know indeed what evil I intend to do?" Or that of
   ___b. St. Paul: "The evil which I would not, that I do?"
7. Are people more persuaded by reason or emotion? Was
   ___a. Shakespeare's Lysander correct that "The will of man is by his reason sway'd?"
   Or was
   ___b. Lord Chesterfield's advice wiser: "Address yourself generally to the senses, to the heart, and to the weaknesses of mankind, but rarely to their reason?"
8. Who makes better decisions—individuals ("too many cooks spoil the broth") or groups ("two heads are better than one")? Is it more true that
   ___a. "The mass never comes up to the standard of its best member, but on the contrary degrades itself to a level with the lowest" (Henry David Thoreau)? Or that
   ___b. "About things on which the public thinks long, it commonly attains to think right" (Samuel Johnson)?
9. How do people evaluate innocent victims of oppression? Was
   ___a. Juvenal, the Roman satirist, correct that people "hate those who have been condemned?"
   Or is it more often true that
   ___b. "The martyr cannot be dishonored" (Ralph Waldo Emerson)?
10. Is aggression instinctive? Was
    ___a. George Santayana correct that "To fight is a radical instinct. . . . To knock a thing down is a deep delight to the blood?" Or was
    ___b. Bronislaw Malinowski closer to the truth: "Is war a biological necessity? As regards the earliest cultures the answer is emphatically negative. . . . Nor is head-hunting, body snatching, or killing for food instinctive or natural?"
11. How does repeated contact with another usually affect our liking for the person? Does
    ___a. "Familiarity breed contempt" while "Absence makes the heart grow fonder?"
    Or is it more true that
    ___b. "Love depends on frequent meetings" (Leo Tolstoy)?
12. What motivates helpfulness? Is it more true that
    ___a. "Men do not value a good deed unless it brings a reward" (Ovid)? Or that
    ___b. "True goodness springs from man's own heart. All men are good" (Confucius)?

13. Is another's being of equal status more likely to trigger friendship, or rivalry and conflict? Who is more right?
    ___a. Samuel Johnson: "Friendship is seldom lasting but between equals?" Or
    ___b. Francis Bacon: "There is little friendship in the world, and least of all between equals?"
14. What shapes our beliefs? Was
    ___a. Julius Caesar correct that "Men freely believe that which they desire?" Or
    ___b. Sophocles that "The truth is always the strongest argument?"
15. Are juries more influenced by the evidence or by their personal biases and sympathies? Can a jury be impartial? Which assumption is more accurate, that of
    ___a. The Sixth Amendment to the U.S. Constitution: "The accused shall enjoy the right to a speedy and public trial, by an impartial jury?" Or that of
    ___b. Clarence Darrow: "Jurymen seldom convict a person they like, or acquit one they dislike. . . . Facts regarding the crime are relatively unimportant?"

Demonstration 1-6

Imagine that the United States is preparing for the outbreak of an unusual Asian disease, which is expected to kill 600 people. Two alternative programs to combat the disease have been proposed. Assume that the exact scientific estimate of the consequences of the programs are as follows:

If Program A is adopted, 200 people will be saved.
If Program B is adopted, there is 1/3 probability that 600 people will be saved, and 2/3 probability that no people will be saved.
Which of the two programs would you favor?

(From Tversky, A., Kahneman, D. The framing of decisions and the psychology of choice. Science, 1981, 211, 453–458. Copyright 1981 by the American Association for the Advancement of Science.)

Demonstration 1-6

Imagine that the United States is preparing for the outbreak of an unusual Asian disease, which is expected to kill 600 people. Two alternative programs to combat the disease have been proposed. Assume that the exact scientific estimate of the consequences of the programs are as follows:

If Program A is adopted, 400 people will die.
If Program B is adopted, there is 1/3 probability that 600 people will be saved, and 2/3 probability that 600 people will die.
Which of the two programs would you favor?

(From Tversky, A., Kahneman, D. The framing of decisions and the psychology of choice. Science, 1981, 211, 453-458. Copyright 1981 by the American Association for the Advancement of Science.)

Demonstration 1-7

(with permission of A. Tversky)

Imagine you have operable lung cancer and must choose between two treatments—surgery and radiation therapy. Of 100 people having surgery, 10 die during the operation, 32 (including those original 10) are dead after one year, and 66 after five years. Of 100 people having radiation therapy, none die during treatment, 22 are dead after one year and 78 after five years. Which treatment would you prefer?

___ Surgery

___ Radiation therapy

Demonstration 1-7

(with permission of A. Tversky)

Imagine you have operable lung cancer and must choose between two treatments—surgery and radiation therapy. Of 100 people having surgery, 90 survive the operation, 68 are alive after one year, and 34 after five years. Of 100 people having radiation therapy, all survive the treatment, 78 are alive after one year, and 22 after five years. What treatment would you prefer?

___ Surgery

___ Radiation therapy

Demonstration 1-8

(with permission of A. Tversky)

You've decided to see a Broadway play for which the ticket price is $40. As you enter the theater to buy your ticket, you discover you've lost $40 from your pocket. Would you still buy the ticket? (Assume you have enough cash left to do so.)

_____ Yes
_____ No

Demonstration 1-8

(with permission of A. Tversky)

You've decided to see a Broadway play and have bought a $40 ticket. As you enter the theater, you realize you've lost your ticket. You can't remember the seat number, so you can't prove to the management that you bought a ticket. Would you spend $40 for a new ticket?

_____ Yes
_____ No

Demonstration 1-9

Bolt & Myers

©McGraw-Hill, 1999

George is a 19-year-old male who has been arrested for assault and battery with intent to commit murder. George is pleading guilty to the charge. It is his first offense. On the basis of this limited information what sentence would you recommend?

A small fine
A brief probationary period
One-month jail sentence
Six-month sentence
Two-year sentence
Five-year sentence

Demonstration 1-9

Bolt & Myers

©McGraw-Hill, 1999

George is a 19-year-old male who has been arrested for assault and battery with intent to commit murder. George is pleading guilty to the charge. It is his first offense. On the basis of this limited information what sentence would you recommend?

Six-month sentence
Two-year sentence
Five-year sentence
Ten-year sentence
Twenty-five-year sentence
Life imprisonment

Demonstration 1-10

Is the Mississippi River longer or shorter than 500 miles? _____
How long is it? _____ Miles

Demonstration 1-10

Is the Mississippi River longer or shorter than 3000 miles? _____
How long is it? _____ miles

Demonstration 1-11

Student Preferences Survey

Please identify your favorite style of music. _____

Please identify three of your favorite current music groups. _____

_____

_____

Please circle the time of day when you are most likely to listen to the radio.
    Early morning   Middle of the day   Afternoon   Evening

Please circle the time in the semester when you are most likely to attend a musical concert.
    First few weeks   Middle of the semester   Near the end   Anytime

Demonstration 1-12

Rokeach Value Survey

Below is a list of 18 values arranged in alphabetical order. We are interested in finding out the relative importance of these values for you.

Study the list carefully. Then place a 1 next to the value, which is most important for you, place a 2 next to the value, which is second most important for you, etc. The value, which is least important, relative to the others, should be ranked 18.

When you have completed ranking all of the values, go back and check over your list. Please take all the time you need to think about this, so that the end result is a true representation of your values.

A COMFORTABLE LIFE (a prosperous life)
AN EXCITING LIFE (a stimulating, active life)
A SENSE OF ACCOMPLISHMENT (lasting contribution)
A WORLD AT PEACE (free of war and conflict)
A WORLD OF BEAUTY (beauty of nature and the arts)
EQUALITY (brotherhood, equal opportunity for all)
FAMILY SECURITY (taking care of loved ones)
FREEDOM (independence, free choice)
HAPPINESS (contentedness)
INNER HARMONY (freedom from inner conflicts)
MATURE LOVE (sexual and spiritual intimacy)
NATIONAL SECURITY (protection from attack)
PLEASURE (an enjoyable, leisurely life)
SALVATION (saved, eternal life)
SELF-RESPECT (self-esteem)
SOCIAL RECOGNITION (respect, admiration)
TRUE FRIENDSHIP (close companionship)
WISDOM (a mature understanding of life)

©1967 by Milton Rokeach. Reproduced with the permission of the publisher, Halgren Tests, NW 1145 Clifford, Pullman, WA 99163.

Demonstration 1-13

Bolt & Myers

©McGraw-Hill, 1999

Visit the Social Psychology Network at http://www.socialpsychology.org to answer the following questions:

1. Identify three specific topics in social psychology and give the address of a web site providing information on each:

   _____

   _____

   _____

2. Identify three journals that publish research in social psychology:

   _____

   _____

   _____

3. Identify one important research group studying social psychology in the United States and one outside the United States. Briefly describe the primary interests of each:

   _____

   _____

   _____

4. What are the primary research interests of David G. Myers, author of your text?

   _____

   _____

FILMS/VIDEOS

McGraw-Hill Videodisc/Videotape in Social Psychology (MGH, 30-60 min., 1994). The disc and tape contain 10 motion clips ranging from 2 to 5 minutes covering classic research studies as well as news events of particular interest to social psychologists. Accompanied by a viewer's guide.

Candid Camera Classics in Social Psychology (MCG, 58 min., 1994). A total of 15 clips selected and edited by Philip Zimbardo and Allen Funt from the original Candid Camera series to illustrate basic social psychological concepts.

Social Psychology (Insight, 30 min., 1990). Introduces social psychology's attempt to understand the social forces that influence our attitudes and actions. Covers many of social psychology's primary concerns including attribution theory, stereotyping and prejudice, and the power of social roles.

Constructing Social Reality (ANN, 26 min., 1990) From the Discovering Psychology series, this video examines how our perceptions and interpretations shape all our social relationships and behaviors. Covers Rosenthal's self-fulfilling prophecy, Cialdini's persuasion principles, and Aronson's jigsaw classroom.

The Power of the Situation (ANN, 26 min., 1990) From the Discovering Psychology series, this program shows how the social context shapes our behavior for good and for ill. Portrays Lewin's work on leadership, Milgram's obedience studies, and Zimbardo's prison simulation.

Inferential Statistics: Hypothesis Testing—Rats, Robots, and Roller Skates (WIL, 28 min., 1976). Basic principles of hypotheses testing, control groups, random assignment, statistical inference are highlighted through four humorous sketches.

Methodology: The Psychologist and the Experiment (CRM, 31 min., 1975). Introduces research methods, emphasizes experimental design. Schachter's fear and affiliation experiment and Riesen's experiment on the development of visual motor coordination are given extensive treatment.

Two Research Styles (Insight, 28 min., 1991). Examines the observational method using Dr. Jenny Hewison's research on how patients decide when to go the doctor and the experimental method using Dr. Chris Alford's studies of the effects of alcohol on daily activities.

Understanding Research (ANN, 30 min., 1990). From the "Discovering Psychology" series. Introduces the scientific method and the ways data are collected and analyzed. Includes examples from social psychology and emphasizes the development of critical thinking.

CHAPTER 2
THE SELF IN A SOCIAL WORLD

Self-Concept: Who Am I?
    At the Center of Our Worlds: Our Sense of Self
    Self-Reference
    Possible Selves
    What is Self-Esteem?
    Development of the Social Self
    The Roles We Play
    Social Identity
    Social Comparisons
    Success and Failure Experiences
    Other People's Judgments
    Self and Culture
    Self-Knowledge
    Explaining Our Behavior
    Predicting Our Behavior
    Prediction Our Feelings
    The Wisdom and Delusions of Self Analysis
Perceived Self-Control
    Self-Efficacy
    Locus of Control
    Learned Helplessness Versus Self-Determination
Self-Serving Bias
    Explaining Positive and Negative Events
    Can We All Be Better Than Average?
    Unrealistic Optimism
    False Consensus and Uniqueness
    Other Self-Serving Tendencies
    Self-Esteem Motivation
    The Dark Side of Self-Esteem
    Reflections on Self-Efficacy and Self-Serving Bias
    The Self-serving Bias as Adaptive
    The Self-serving Bias as Maladaptive
Self-Presentation
    False Modesty

Self-Handicapping
Impression Management
Personal Postscript: Twin Truths-The Perils of Pride, the Power of Positive Thinking

LECTURE AND DISCUSSION IDEAS

1. The Nature of "The Self"

Chapter 2 asks the question "Who am I?" Students can be made aware of some of the previous thinking on this topic, as well as trying their hand at describing themselves, by reading an except from Jonathan Brown's (1998) book "The Self" (see this chapter's "Popular Sources for Additional Classroom Material") found in the 01/02 edition of the "Annual Editions—Social Psychology" edited by Davis (see Chapter 1 references). Here Brown uses William James' (1890) analytical work on the "self" and brings it to life for undergraduate students. It includes a discussion on the material self, social self, spiritual self, and collective self. As hinted above, there are two exercises students can complete within the text of the article.

In addition to discussing the student's responses you may want to ask some of the following questions: Did you agree with James' taxonomy of the empirical self? More components? Less components? Different components? Do you agree with James' hierarchy of the components of self? Does Table 4 do an adequate job of describing the possible ways people of ethnic minority status create an identity once introduced to a majority group? As a result of doing the exercises, what did you learn about yourself that you did not previously know? What, to you, was the most surprising finding, statement, or concept in the article?

2. The Limits of Self-Insight

Chapter 2 argues that our self-understandings are subject to error. You may wish to emphasize this point, since it is fundamental to why social psychologists do experiments and not just rely upon people's introspective self-reports.

To reinforce the point, you may introduce the results of Janet Swim and Lauri Hyers' (1997) dramatic experiment briefly reported in Chapter 6 of the text. In fact, you might ask your students to play the role of the subject and predict how they themselves would respond to Swim and Hyers' hypothetical situation. In the study, students are asked to imagine themselves discussing with three others whom to select for survival on a desert island. In the course of the conversation, one in the group, a man, makes three sexist comments, including "I think we need more women on the island to keep the men satisfied." How would they react to such remarks? A mere 5 percent predicted they would ignore each of the comments or wait to see how others would react. However, when Swim and Hyers engaged other students in discussions where such comments were actually made by a male confederate, 56 percent (not 5 percent) said nothing. Clearly it is difficult to predict behavior, even our own.

Such findings do <u>not</u> indicate that we never have genuine self-insight, only that when influences are subtle, self-insight is vulnerable to error. This is why we need a science of behavior. And it is also why people's explanations of their own thoughts and actions are suggestive, yet not as trustworthy as commonly believed.

3. The Mirror Has Two Faces: Other People's Judgments

According to Charles H. Cooley's <u>looking-glass self</u>, we see our reflection in how we appear to others. As the text notes, George Herbert Mead argued that what matters for our self-concept is not what others actually think but what we <u>perceive</u> them as thinking.

You might introduce the importance of other people's judgments, specifically of our physical appearance, with a three-minute clip from the feature film <u>The Mirror Has Two Faces</u>. Eighty-six minutes into the film the central character Rose Morgan (played by Barbra Streisand) leaves her husband, returns home late at night, and has a poignant exchange with her elderly mother. Having experienced a blow to her self-esteem and now struggling with her self-concept she asks, "When I was a baby, did you think I was pretty?" When her mother avoids the question, she reflects on how as a child she experienced the pain of her mother's negative evaluations. Finally, she asks her mother, who at one time had been beautiful, "What was it like to have others admire you?" Now there is an immediate, straightforward response, "It was wonderful." After watching this clip you might have students reflect on the following questions in small groups:

Who have provided the most memorable reflected appraisals in your life—parents, teachers, or peers? Which of these was most positive? How have the appraisals of others served to threaten or boost your sense of self-esteem? Do you have any personal traits, abilities, or physical characteristics that have been socially distinctive? Did you like or dislike being distinctive?

4. The Dark Side of Self-Esteem

In reviewing the literature on the relationship of self-esteem to aggression, Roy Baumeister, Laura Smart, and Joseph Boden (1996) conclude that "The societal pursuit of high self-esteem for everyone may literally end up doing considerable harm." They note that the conventional wisdom regards low self-esteem as an important cause of violence. If this were indeed the case, "it would be therapeutically prudent to make every effort to convince rapists, murderers, wife-beaters, professional hit men, tyrants, torturers, and others that they are superior beings." However, there is clear evidence that this is something they already believe. "If any modifications to self-appraisals were to be attempted," suggest Baumeister and his colleagues, "then perhaps it would be better to try instilling modesty and humility."

A careful review of the relevant research revealed that high not low self-esteem underlies violent behavior, particularly "favorable self-appraisals that may be inflated or ill-founded and that are confronted with an external evaluation that disputes them." Teenagers who do not feel that they have received the respect they deserve are more likely to strike out than are those who genuinely believe themselves unworthy. Studies of murder, rape, domestic abuse, and even terrorism show that violence occurs when a person with a high, often inflated, opinion of himself or herself is challenged by someone considered inferior. For example, one study of sexual offenders found that rapists sometimes choose a particular victim in order "to disabuse her of her sense of superiority. That is, the woman gave the man the impression that she thought she was better than he was and so he raped her as a way of proving her wrong."

5. Individualism Versus Collectivism

Triandis, Brislin, and Hui (1988) present differences between collectivism and individualism in the form of advice to individualists moving into a collective culture and collectivists moving into an individualist culture.

They suggest that individualists interacting with collectivists heed the following:

A. Attend to the other's group memberships and authorities for they define appropriate attitudes and behaviors.

B. Recognize that the person is more comfortable in vertical than in horizontal relationships. Persuade by getting the other's superiors to show approval and by demonstrating how a new behavior will benefit the other's ingroups.

C. Criticize sparingly. Emphasize harmony and cooperation. Recognize that the person will be uncomfortable in competitive situations.

D. Expect extraordinary and unjustified modesty, particularly if the person is from east Asia. If you give presentations, begin more modestly than you would in your own country.

E. Cultivate long-term relationships. Be patient. Spend time chatting with people. The person values doing business with old friends. If resources are to be distributed among peers, expect the other to use equity in the early phases of a relationship, and equality or need in later stages.

F. Expect that initially, at least, social behavior will be formal. It will be polite, correct, but not especially friendly. Gift giving is important. One must be generous and not expect immediate repayment. However, if you are helpful, the other person is likely to repay much more than you expect.

G. Remember that your social position based on age, sex, and family name is more important than what you have accomplished. Informing the person of your status will ease the acquaintanceship process.

H. Expect the person to spend a great deal of time with you, even accompanying you to such places as the doctor's office. Only in this way can a long-term relationship be established. In fact, a collectivist may find it unimaginable and painful to be without company.

Recommendations to collectivists interacting with individualists include the following:

A. Attend more to the other person's personal beliefs and principles than to his or her ingroups.

B. Expect the other to be more involved in horizontal and less involved in vertical relationships. What superiors approve of is less important than what peers think.

C. Expect relationships to be superficial, short-termed, but good-natured. Do not confuse friendliness with intimacy.

D. Do not be threatened if the other acts competitively. In fact, learn to expect competition more than cooperation. Recognize that the other person defines status more in terms of accomplishment than in terms of sex, age, or family name.

E. Expect that you can do business soon after you meet. The other person is likely to be impatient with ceremony. Time is money and getting down to business is important.

F. Pay attention to contracts, signatures, and to the written word. Informal agreements mean much less than in your own culture.

G. Recognize that the principle of equity is likely to be followed even when you would favor distributing rewards equally or on the basis of need.

H. Do not expect to be accompanied or assisted all the time. By letting you go alone they are expressing confidence in you.

6. Self-Discrepancy Theory

You can readily extend the text's discussion of self-esteem by introducing E. Tory Higgins's (1989) self-discrepancy theory. His theory distinguishes between <u>domains of the self</u> and <u>standpoints on the self</u>. The three types of self-domains are (1) the actual self, the traits that someone (yourself or another) believes you possess; (2) the ideal self, the traits that someone (yourself or another) would like you to possess; and (3) the ought self, the traits that someone (yourself or another) believes you should possess. Two standpoints on the self include (1) your own personal standpoint; and (2) the standpoint of some significant other (e.g., mother, father, spouse, and close friend). Combining the domains on the self with the different standpoints creates six basic types of self-state representations including actual/own, actual/other, ideal/own, ideal/other, ought/own, and ought/other. The first two self-state representations, particularly the actual/own, constitute a person's self-concept. The four remaining self-state representations are self-directive standards, or what Higgins labels <u>self-guides</u>. The degree of discrepancy between one's self-concept and self-guides determines one's self-esteem. The theory further assumes that people are strongly motivated to reach a condition in which their self-concept matches their personally relevant self-guides. Self-discrepancy is unique in that it predicts specific emotional consequences for failure to achieve specific self-guides. For example, discrepancy of the self-concept with the ought/own guide leads to guilt, with the ought/other guide produces shame, with the ideal/own guide leads to disappointment, and with the ideal/other guide leads to dejection and lack of pride. Finally, the discomfort created by self-discrepancy varies not only with its amount but also its accessibility, that is, the degree to which people are aware of it.

An effective strategy for introducing self-discrepancy theory is to have students, as Higgins does in his research, generate a list of up to 10 attributes for each of the different self-states, e.g., "list up to 10 attributes of the type of person you think you actually are," then "list up to 10 attributes of the type of person your mother thinks you should or ought to be," etc. After students have generated these lists, have them compare and contrast the different lists, reflecting on the feelings they generate.

7. Schindler's List: Perceived Self-Control

A five-minute clip from the feature film Schindler's List provides a powerful introduction to the literature on personal control. At 98 minutes 16 seconds into the film, Schindler, while at the commandant's house party, walks down the steps into the basement where he meets Helen, a Jewish maid and prisoner. She discloses her innermost thoughts and feelings, particularly her despair over there no longer being a connection between her actions and outcomes. After vividly describing the arbitrary beating she received at the hands of brutal commandant, she reports how he recently shot and killed a passerby without reason. "There are no set rules to live by," she complains. Although Schindler attempts to comfort her, it is clear that Helen has lost all sense of personal control.

8. Locus of Control

This construct always fascinates students and can generate a lively classroom discussion. You might begin by having students complete the locus of control scale in the "Demonstrations" section of this chapter, then carefully define the important differences between internals and externals, and conclude by raising a number of discussion questions.

Internals believe the rewards and punishments they receive in life are produced by their own actions and thus they have a sense of personal control. Internals take credit for their success, but also accept responsibility for failure. They have great incentive to engage in operant behavior if the subjective value of reinforcement is high. They perceive themselves as more active, powerful, independent, and effective than do externals. Even when faced with obstacles, internals are likely to take an active, controlling approach to life. They have a "can do" mentality. In contrast, externals believe the reward and punishments they receive in life occur quite independently of whatever they do and thus they have a sense of helplessness. Because they believe their successes and failures in life are due to luck, chance, fate, social forces, or powerful others, externals neither take credit for their success nor accept blame for failure. They feel that operant behavior is somewhat futile even if the subjective value of reinforcement is high. They perceive themselves as relatively powerless, dependent, and ineffective. Even when life is good to them, externals approach tasks in a passive, helpless, fatalistic manner.

To stimulate classroom discussion, pose some of the following questions: What relationship would you anticipate between locus of control orientation and gender, age, race, religious affiliation, conformity to peer pressure, academic achievement, and participation in lotteries? How would this dimension influence the extent to which people are superstitious, believe in horoscopes, quack remedies, and magical rituals? Who is most likely to demonstrate ego strength by choosing a delayed but valuable reward over an immediate momentary pleasure? Do you feel more or less external in some areas of life (e.g., politics) than others (e.g., academic)? What childhood experiences or characteristics of your family may have contributed to your own locus of control expectancies?

9. Self-Serving Bias: Who's Going to Heaven?

Reporting the results of a recent U.S. News & World Report poll (March 31, 1997, p. 18) provides an effective, humorous introduction to the literature on self-serving bias. The poll asked 1,000 Americans whether they thought various celebrities were likely to go to heaven. For example, 66 percent thought that Oprah Winfrey is "very likely" or "somewhat likely" to go to heaven. Princess Diana (before her death five months later) scored 60 percent, Michael Jordan received a 65 percent positive rating, Bill Clinton got the nod from 52 percent, Dennis Rodman scored only 28 percent, and O.J. Simpson received a mere 19 percent. Mother Teresa's 79 percent was only the second highest. The top vote-getter? More than 87 percent of Americans surveyed believed themselves likely to go to heaven.

The text notes that self-inflation is found most strikingly in Western countries. In this context, Newsweek (February 26, 1996, p. 21) quotes Japanese bar association official Koji Yanase explaining why there are half as many lawyers in his country as in the Greater Washington area alone: "If an American is hit on the head by a ball at the ballpark, he sues. If a Japanese person is hit on the head he says, 'It's my honor. It's my fault. I shouldn't have been standing there.'"

10. Dimensions of Causality

The text's distinction between internal and external causes can be readily extended to include other dimensions of causality such as those suggested by Weiner's attributional model of achievement. In addition to difference in locus (internal versus external), causes may vary in their stability and controllability. For example, the internal causes for achievement outcomes may include aptitude (stable but uncontrollable), mood (unstable and uncontrollable), typical effort (stable and controllable), temporary effort exerted for a specific task (unstable but controllable). External causes may include task difficulty (stable but uncontrollable), luck (unstable and uncontrollable), some forms of teacher bias (stable and controllable) and having received unusual help from another person (unstable but controllable).

In reviewing Weiner's model, Fiske and Taylor (1991) note that the stability dimension indicates whether or not the cause will change and is strongly associated with subsequent expectations of success or failure. The locus dimension concerns whether the cause is internal or external, and is related to changes in self-esteem, including feelings of pride and shame. Judgments regarding controllability are also used as a basis for judging oneself as well as others and may be important in decisions on offering another person help.

You may want to introduce Russell's (1982) Causal Dimension Scale in class. It attempts to assess judgments on the three causal dimensions by people's responses to a series of nine questions. After analyzing the cause of an event, the respondent is asked to indicate the degree to which the cause "reflects an aspect of yourself or of the situation" (internal versus external), "is something for which someone or no one is responsible" (controllable versus uncontrollable), and "is permanent or temporary" (stable versus unstable). The scale has been used to assess judgments regarding a variety of outcomes, not only those relating to achievement.

11. Excuses

The text reports on drivers' descriptions of their accidents. Here are a few more to give in class that are sure to elicit a chuckle: "The pedestrian had no idea which direction to go so I ran over him," "A truck backed through my windshield and into my wife's face," "The guy was all over the road. I had to swerve a number of times before I hit him," "I had been driving my car for 40 years when I fell asleep at the wheel and had an accident," "To avoid hitting the bumper of the car in front, I hit the pedestrian," "The telephone pole was approaching fast. I was attempting to swerve out of its path when it hit my front end."

C. R. Snyder, Raymond L. Higgins, and Rita J. Stucky's (1983) <u>Excuses: Masquerades in Search of Grace</u> is an excellent resource for extending the text's discussion of the self-serving bias. According to the authors, excuses come in three forms: "I didn't do it," "It's not so bad," and "Yes, but. . . ."

The most rudimentary form of excuse-making is to refuse ownership of a bad performance. Children frequently use simple denial "Who, me?" If we are not responsible, someone else must be, and it helps if we can give some clue as to who the real culprit is.

When we cannot sever our own ties to the poor performance, we may admit, "I did it," but really, "it's not <u>so</u> bad." "I only hit him once," "I'm only 45 minutes late," or "It was only a small piece of cake."

The major category of excuses usually grants "Yes, I did it" and "It was bad" but . . . "I couldn't help it" or "I didn't mean to." Often these admit to ignorance or incompetence but not the maliciousness.

Snyder and his colleagues suggest that excuses serve to preserve our self-image and to reduce the stress associated with failure. They are also a social lubricant that enables us to continue interactions with friends, co-workers, and bosses when we foul up. By providing an excuse we also acknowledge the validity of the standards we have violated. Finally, excuses help us to take chances. A world of total accountability would be overwhelming. With our excuses we can take risks and try again.

12. Self-Serving Biases Outside of the Self?

Students may be surprised to find that some research suggests self-serving biases extend outside of judgments about their own abilities, talents, habits, and skills—even beyond the boundaries of their own skin. For example, Beggan (1992) ran three studies, which found evidence that participants valued even a trivial object (like a cold drink insulator) more if they owned it then if they did not own it. One of Beggan's proposed explanations for this effect, later supported by further research using other trivial and nontrivial objects (Nesselroade, Beggan & Allison, 1999) suggests people can indirectly generate a self-serving bias by enhancing external agents, which are merely associated with the self—sometimes referred to as "self-extensions" (e.g., owned objects).

Discussions of this research should dovetail nicely with theoretical discussions about William James's work (1890) on the nature of the self. Also, the instructor may want to introduce the counterintuitive idea that nonsocial objects may, in certain circumstances, take on social characteristics. Here's a theoretical zinger: Can viewing an owned object be understood in terms of social perception as well as nonsocial perception? Maybe, if the evaluation of that object has implications for the self—See Fiske and Taylor (1991) p. 18 & 19 for a list of criteria distinguishing social perception from nonsocial perception.

13. The Barnum Effect

In discussing "Other Self-Serving Tendencies." the text notes that if a test or some other source of information, for example, a horoscope, flatters us, then we believe it, and we evaluate positively both the test and any evidence suggesting that the test is valid. In class, you might introduce students to the <u>Barnum effect</u>—named in honor of circus entrepreneur P.T. Barnum who said, "There's a sucker born every minute." It refers to our tendency to accept as valid favorable descriptions of our personality that are generally true of everyone. Interestingly, if forewarned that that description is true of most people, people usually say it fits so-so. However, if told it is designed specifically for them on the basis of psychological tests or astrological sign, they will say the description is very accurate. In fact, research suggests that given a choice between a phony description and an actual test-based description of themselves, people usually judge the fake description as equally or more accurate. Human susceptibility to the Barnum effect explains why so many of us fall victim to the methods of astrologers, palm readers, and fortune tellers. Peter Glick and his colleagues (1989) found that even skeptics of astrology, who are given an astrologer's positive description of themselves, conclude that "maybe there's something to this astrology business after all."

You can demonstrate the Barnum effect by having students complete some bogus personality instrument and then, the next class period, giving them each a computerized personality description, supposedly drawn from observations of other people who answered similarly. (Alternatively, you could have them provide some simple items of individuating information, such as their birthdate, hair color, sex, and height.)

The following program, written in Basic, will produce a set of Barnum descriptions, which come from Forer (1949), for your class. After distributing the "confidential" report to each person, invite each person to evaluate its accuracy: Excellent? Good? Fair? Poor? Most will agree that the fit is excellent or good. You can then reveal the hoax—and use the opportunity to make the serious point about the Barnum effect and its use (whether intentionally or not) by astrologers, palm readers, and clinicians.

Forer's BASIC Program

```
01   REM PERSONALITY DESCRIPTION PROGRAM (WRITTEN FOR A TRS-80)
02   MAX=200:REM MAX # OF PRINTOUTS AT ONE TIME
03   CLS:PRINT:REM CLEAR THE SCREEN
04   PRINT"I will create PERSONALIZED PERSONALITY DESCRIPTIONS for your"
05   PRINT"class. However, first you will have to tell me their names."
06   PRINT
07   PRINT"How many people do you want me to handle this time";
08   INPUT NUM
09   IF NUM<=0 THEN 48
10   IF NUM<=MAX GO TO 12
11   PRINT:PRINT"I'm sorry. I can only handle";MAX:;"people at once.":GOTO 7
12   DIM NAME$(NUM)
13   PRINT:PRINT"OK. Now type their names one at a time."
14   FOR I=1 TO NUM
15   PRINT"Person #";I;:INPUT NAME$(I)
16   IF NAME$(I)="" THEN PRINT"Try again,":GOTO 15
17   NEXT I
18   PRINT"Prepare printer, then press <ENTER>":INPUT D$
19   FORI=1 TO NUM
20   LPRINTCHR$(12):REM FORM FEED FOR NEW PAGE (IF PRINTER ALLOWS)
21   PRINT"#";I;"of";NUM
22   REM LINE 21 ALLOWS YOU TO SEE HOW FAR YOU ARE. IT IS NOT PRINTED.
23   LPRINT:LPRINT:LPRINT:REM 'LPRINT' SENDS THE LINE TO THE LINE PRINTER
24   LPRINT"PERSONALIZED PERSONALITY DESCRIPTION for ";NAME$(I)
25   LPRINT:LPRINT:LPRINT
26   LPRINT"You have a strong need for other people to like you and for"
27   LPRINT"them to admire you. You have a tendency to be critical of"
28   LPRINT"yourself. You have a great deal of unused energy which you"
29   LPRINT"have not turned to your advantage. While you have some"
30   LPRINT"personality weaknesses, you are generally able to compensate"
31   LPRINT"for them. Your sexual adjustment has presented some problems"
32   LPRINT"for you."
33   LPRINT
```

```
34  LPRINT"Disciplined and controlled on the outside, you tend to be"
35  LPRINT"worrisome and insecure inside. At times you have serious"
36  LPRINT"doubts as to whether you have made the right decisions or done"
37  LPRINT"the right thing. You prefer a certain amount of change and"
38  LPRINT"variety and become dissatisfied when hemmed in by restrictions"
39  LPRINT"and limitations."
40  LPRINT
41  LPRINT"You pride yourself on being an independent thinker and do not"
42  LPRINT"accept other opinions without satisfactory proof. You have"
43  LPRINT"found it unwise to be too frank in revealing yourself to"
44  LPRINT"others. At times you are extraverted, affable, and sociable,."
45  LPRINT"while at other times you are introverted, wary, and reserved."
46  LPRINT"Some of your aspirations tend to be pretty unrealistic."
47  NEXT I
48  PRINT:PRINT"That's all. Come again."
```

Personalized Personality Description for _ _ _ _ _ _ _ _ _ _ _ _ _ _ _ _ _

You have a strong need for other people to like you and for them to admire you. You have a tendency to be critical of yourself. You have a great deal of unused energy, which you have not turned to your advantage. While you have some personality weaknesses, you are generally able to compensate for them. Your sexual adjustment has presented some problems for you.

Disciplined and controlled on the outside, you tend to be worrisome and insecure on the inside. At times you have serious doubts as to whether you have made the right decision or done the right thing. You prefer a certain amount of change and variety and become dissatisfied when hemmed in by restrictions and limitations.

You pride yourself on being an independent thinker and do not accept other opinions without satisfactory proof. You have found it unwise to be too frank in revealing yourself to others. At times you are extraverted, affable, and sociable, while at other times you are introverted, wary, and reserved. Some of your aspirations tend to be pretty unrealistic.

14. Self-Presentational Strategies

The text's discussion of impression management can be readily extended using Edward E. Jones' (1990) taxonomy of self-presentational strategies. Jones argues that the motive underlying impression management is the desire to maintain or augment social power. The major strategies include ingratiation, intimidation, self-promotion, exemplification, and supplication.

Through ingratiation, people try to elicit the <u>affection</u> of others by conforming to others' opinions, by doing favors, or by praising others' achievements.

Through intimidation, people try to elicit <u>fear</u> in others by projecting both the capacity and inclination to deliver negative outcomes. Typically this strategy is used in relationships that are nonvoluntary rather than in freely formed relationships among peers.

Through self-promotion, people try to elicit the <u>respect</u> of others by highlighting their prior successes and excusing previous failures.

Through exemplification, people try to elicit <u>guilt</u> in others by creating the impression of moral superiority. They may do this by deliberately seeking out ways to make their own self-sacrifice and self-denial public.

Through supplication, people try to elicit the nurturance of others through self-deprecation and entreaties for help. This is the last resort and typically used by low-power persons who have little else going for them.

15. Self-Monitoring

The self-monitoring tendency is introduced toward the end of this chapter and is discussed at greater length later in the text. Chapter 4 of this manual contains a discussion of this important personality variable as well as Mark Snyder and Steve Gangestad's (1986) Self-Monitoring Scale with directions for scoring. You may choose to use that material for lecture and demonstration now.

16. Popular Sources for Additional Classroom Material

Bandura, A. (1997). Self-efficacy: The exercise of control. New York: W. H. Freeman. Discusses the nature and development of self-efficacy and examines its application to health, clinical, athletic, and organizational functioning.

Baumeister, R. F. (Ed.). (1999). The self in social psychology. Philadelphia, PA: Psychology Press. A collection of 23 readings covering a variety of topics. Some of the articles may be difficult for undergraduates, although each area contains a set of discussion questions. Excellent resource for generating topics in class, which take the students into deeper theoretical arenas.

Baumeister, R.F., Heatherton, T.F., & Tice, D.M. (1994). Losing control: How and why people fail at self-regulation. San Diego: Academic Press. Excellent survey of theory and research on self-control. Separate chapters are devoted to specific behavioral control problems such as alcohol abuse, overeating, and smoking.

Brown, J. (1998). The Self. New York: McGraw-Hill. Excellent overview of social psychological research on the self. Includes discussions of the nature and development of the self as well as separate chapters on self-regulation, self-presentation, and self-esteem.

Fiske, S., & Taylor, S. (1991). Social cognition, 2nd ed. New York: McGraw-Hill. Provides an excellent overview of the elements and processes of social cognition. Includes discussion of attribution theory, and of our perceptions of self and others.

Goleman, D. (1985). Vital lies, simple truths: The psychology of self-deception and shared illusions. New York: Simon and Schuster. Goleman examines how and why we fool ourselves. Excellent source for lecture examples and illustrations.

Jones, E. (1990). Interpersonal perception. New York: Freeman. A leading researcher explores how we perceive and explain people's behavior, including our own.

Leary, M. R. (1996). Self-presentation: Impression management and interpersonal behavior. Boulder, CO: Westview Press. A state of the art analysis of the motives and tactics underlying our self-presentations, and of the effects they have on others—and ourselves.

Myers, D. G. (1980). The inflated self. New York: Seabury Press. The author of the text explores the human capacity for illusion and self-deception. This book documents the extent of human pride, both personal and collective, and explores some of its applications.

Seligman, M. (1991). Learned optimism. New York: Knopf. Describes research on learned helplessness and optimism, showing why optimism is important and how to gain it.

Snyder, C. R., Higgins, R. L., & Stucky, R. J. (1983). Excuses: Masquerades in search of grace. New York: John Wiley & Sons. This book provides an excellent extension of the text's treatment of self-serving bias. Examines the subtlety, complexity, effectiveness, and pervasiveness of excuses.

Swann, W. B., Jr. (1996). Self-traps: The elusive quest for higher self-esteem. New York: W. H. Freeman. Provides an overview of the self-esteem literature. Explores how people's self-conceptions guide their lives. Excellent in moving from the research laboratory to everyday experience.

Taylor, S. E. (1989). Positive illusions. New York: Basic Books. Excellent review of the self-serving bias. Unrealistically positive views of the self seem to promote the ability to care about others, the ability to be happy or contented, and the ability to engage in productive and creative work.

Tesser, A., Felson, R. B., & Suls, J. M. (Eds.). (2000). Psychological perspectives on self and identity. Washington D.C.: American Psychological Association. Consists of eight chapters on the structure and dynamics of the self, self motives, and the self in interpersonal processes. Excellent collection of articles reflecting the expanding growth of knowledge on the self.

DEMONSTRATION AND PROJECT IDEAS

1. We Often Do Not Know Why We Do What We Do

In this and later chapters the text provides repeated examples of people's failure to appreciate what has influenced them. For example, participants in research on bystander intervention routinely denied being influenced by the presence or absence of other bystanders—a powerfully important factor.

You can attempt to demonstrate a similar phenomenon by partially replicating a study by Richard Nisbett and Timothy Wilson (1977). In the guise of a consumer survey, they invited passers-by in a shopping mall to examine four identical nylon pantyhose and to say which was the best quality. There was a pronounced position effect, with the right-most pantyhose heavily favored over the left-most. Asked about the reasons for their choice, no one ever mentioned the position of the item. When probed directly about the possibility of a position effect, "virtually all subjects denied it, usually with a worried glance at the interviewer suggesting that they felt either that they had misunderstood the question or were dealing with a madman."

Replicating this study requires a) purchasing four pair of pantyhose (or more, if you have a large class), b) inviting people individually to come forward to make the comparisons (perhaps as people file in for class), and then c) asking them each to write a sentence explaining their choice. Finally ask for a show of hands for the left-most and right-most item and (assuming the expected result) solicit people's written explanations. How many recognized the position effect?

This demonstration idea is not yet time-tested. You can turn this to your advantage, and prevent embarrassment in the event of unexpected results, by telling the class beforehand that you are informally replicating an intriguing finding to see whether it is reliable or not. Either way, you've gained some information.

2. Who Am I? ✓

Before your students have read Chapter 2, you might have them complete the "Who am I?" exercise suggested in the text. Ask them to take out a clean sheet of paper and write 20 different statements in response to the simple question, "Who am I?" They should begin each statement with "I am. . . ." Have them write in the order that they occur and instruct them to go fairly fast.

Use the exercise as the basis for a small-group or class discussion on the nature of the self-concept. Taken together, the answers define one's self-concept. The specific beliefs by which we define ourselves are our self-schemas. Ask volunteers to share specific items from their lists. What are some of the common categories included on students' lists? Physical characteristics? Individual traits? Social roles?

You can also use the exercise to introduce the text's discussion of cultural influences on the self. Have your students count the number of their answers that are linked to social identity (e.g., "I am a son" or "I am a Roman Catholic"). They might also assess how high on their lists these answers occur. People in industrialized western cultures are more likely to demonstrate an independent self, defining their identity in terms of their personal attributes rather than their social groups. In contrast, many in nonwestern cultures are likely to have an interdependent self in which identity is defined more in relation to others.

3. Rosenberg Self-Esteem Scale

The text defines self-esteem as a person's overall self-evaluation or sense of self worth. Handout 2-1, the Rosenberg Self-Esteem Scale (SES), has been the most frequently used instrument in the literature for assessing global self-esteem. In scoring it, students should first reverse the numbers placed in front of items 3, 5, 8, 9, and 10, and then add the numbers in front of all 10 items to obtain a total score. Scores can range from 10 to 40 with higher scores reflecting a greater sense of self worth.

The SES is designed to assess the degree to which people are generally satisfied with their lives and consider themselves worthy people. Other researchers have attempted to measure self-judgments relative to specific areas of daily functioning with self-esteem being a summation of subscale scores. As the text indicates, research suggests that those with global self-esteem are more likely to accept their appearance, abilities, and so forth. That is, feeling good about oneself in a general way casts a rosy glow over one's specific self-schemas and possible selves.

An excellent resource for self-esteem measures is John P. Robinson et al.'s <u>Measures of Personality and Social Psychological Attitudes</u>, a 1991 publication of Academic Press. This volume devotes an entire chapter to measures of self-esteem and includes the actual scales. More generally, if you like to include self-assessment measures in your teaching, you will want to add the Robinson volume to your personal library. It includes measures of locus of control, authoritarianism, interpersonal trust, sex roles, values, social anxiety, loneliness, depression, and subjective well-being.

4. Independent and Interdependent Selves

Demonstration 2-2 provides Theodore M. Singelis's (1994) revised measures of independent and interdependent self-construals. Students should add up the numbers they have placed before items 1, 2, 5, 7, 9, 10, 13, 15, 18, 20, 22, 24, 26, and 28 to assess the strength of their independent self. Similarly, they should add up the numbers they have placed before items 3, 4, 6, 8, 11, 12, 14, 16, 17, 19, 21, 23, 25, and 27 to assess the strength of their interdependent self. In each case, total scores can range from 14 to 98 with higher numbers reflecting higher scores. Singelis's research has indicated that these two aspects of self are separate factors and thus do not constitute a continuum.

Singelis (1995) explains that an independent self-construal includes an emphasis on (1) internal abilities, thoughts, and feelings; (2) being unique and expressing the self; (3) realizing internal attributes and promoting one's own goals; and (4) being direct in communication. Similarly, he explains that an interdependent self-construal is a "flexible, variable self" that emphasizes (1) external, public features such as status, roles, and relationships; (2) belonging and fitting-in; (3) occupying one's proper place and engaging in appropriate action; and (4) being indirect in communication and "reading others' minds."

In a number of recent studies, Singelis has shown that self-construals provide an important link between culture and behavior. Collectivism encourages the development of the interdependent self, while individualism promotes the independent self. Among the fascinating links Singelis has uncovered between these two selves and behavior is one between self-construal and embarrassability. As predicted, he found embarrassabilty to be negatively associated with an independent self-construal and positively related to an interdependent self-construal. In addition, Asian-Americans were more susceptible to embarrassment than Euro-Americans. Other studies have linked self-construal to attributions to the situation and conversational constraints.

5. Locus of Control Scale

Demonstration 2-3 is a locus of control scale designed originally for children by Stephen Nowicki, Jr., and B. Strickland (1973) and revised for adult use by Nowicki and Marshall Duke. Scoring is as follows:

1. Yes   11. Yes   21. Yes   31. Yes

2. No	12. Yes	22. No	32. No
3. Yes	13. No	23. Yes	33. Yes
4. No	14. Yes	24. Yes	34. No
5. Yes	15. No	25. No	35. Yes
6. No	16. Yes	26. No	36. Yes
7. Yes	17. Yes	27. Yes	37. Yes
8. Yes	18. Yes	28. No	38. No
9. No	19. Yes	29. Yes	39. Yes
10. Yes	20. No	30. No	40. No

About one-third of the people taking the test score from 0 to 8 and demonstrate an internal locus of control. They believe they control their own destiny and see themselves as responsible for the reinforcements they receive in life. Most respondents score between 9 and 16 and answer some of the questions in each direction. Locus of control may be situation specific. For example, some may see themselves as externally controlled in their work but internally controlled in their social lives. Approximately 15 percent score 17 or higher. High scorers may see life more as a game of chance than as one where their skills make a difference.

6. Self-Efficacy

In his delightful book, Body Magic, John Fisher (1979) proposes a way to demonstrate learned helplessness. Distribute Demonstration 2-3 (with the words BAT and LEMON) to the left half of the room, and the other form of Demonstration 2-4 to the right half. Acknowledge that you are testing two different sets of items with the two halves of the room. Tell them all that their first task is to solve the first anagram—to construct a new word using all the letters of the first word, and to look up and raise their hands when they have reached a solution. (Hands should rise only on the side given BAT [TAB], since the item on the other list is impossible.) Go on to the second item, with the same instructions. Again, only those given LEMON (MELON) display hands. Finally, have them do the third word, which is the same for all, CINERAMA (AMERICAN). Observe: On the third word, do hands rise more slowly for those who have experienced repeated failure? Likely yes. You can relate this demonstration to people's real life failure experiences in school and work, leading some to feelings of self-efficacy and others to feelings of helplessness and incompetence.

7. Introducing the Self-Serving Bias and Explaining Good Events and Bad

The self-serving bias can be demonstrated easily and powerfully. In discussing self-serving bias, someone may argue a point, which the text acknowledges—that some individuals, and some groups of individuals, may be less likely to exhibit the bias. For example, if women have been socialized into self-disparaging modesty, and men into self-aggrandizing bravado, then perhaps men will exhibit self-serving bias more strongly than women. You and your students can research this question by comparing the responses of men and women on some of the following demonstrations.

Dana Dunn (1989) suggests that, after informing students that the psychology of self will be the next topic, distribute a sheet of paper to each member of your class and ask them to first write down what they believe are their personal strengths and then to list their weaknesses. Tell them not to put their names on the sheet. Collect the responses and simply tabulate the number of strengths and weaknesses, recording the mean for each category. Dunn reports that typically students report almost twice as many positive as negative attributes. Report your results at the next class period and introduce the self-serving bias. Ask students to speculate why we tend to see ourselves favorably. Is it a matter of self-presentation, information-processing, self-justification, or some combination of these?

Demonstration 2-5 provides the materials for a replication of the Susan Green and Alan Gross (1979) study in which students read paragraphs describing something that happened either to them or to someone else. Note that in the four versions of the story, something desirable or undesirable happens to "David" or to oneself. Green and Gross reported both self-enhancing and self-protective biases. Students claimed significantly more credit (than that given David) when Roger called early, but significantly less when he called late. You will need to randomly mix and distribute the four versions (so that each student responds to one of the versions). Then you may either collect them to compute the average response to answer "B" in each of the four versions, or you may ask for a show of hands ("How many of you who had the version in which Roger called <u>you sooner</u> than expected (pause) put a number in line <u>B</u> (pause) that was 30 or greater?" etc.)

This demonstration provides the opportunity to explain a 2 x 2 design and the predicted interaction effect (dispositional attributions being greater for self only for the desirable outcome). Alternatively (e.g., if you have fewer than 50 or so students), you could simplify the demonstration by using only the two desirable outcome versions.

8. Explaining Success and Failure

You can offer your students a success or failure treatment—by handing back the first exam. After doing so, distribute Demonstration 2-6, inviting students to explain the score they received. This requires your collecting the questionnaires and intercorrelating the variables. The prediction: internal attributions (to ability or study) should be positively correlated with score on the exam; those who succeed will accept more responsibility for their performance. It would probably be diplomatic to add, as the text does, that professors exhibit the same tendencies in explaining their scholarly successes and failures.

9. Can We All Be Better Than Average?

This is the question raised by Demonstrations 2-7 and 2-8. To avoid invading privacy, both should be tabulated outside of class, <u>not</u> by a show of hands. Alternatively, collect students' responses, shuffle, redistribute, and have each student score another student's responses, calculating the mean. Ask, "How many have a mean greater than 5.00?" On Demonstration 2-7 the overwhelming majority of the class will rate themselves higher.

Demonstration 2-8 reproduces items from the College Board survey described in the text. When presenting the results, ask students to guess which items will show the most positive self-evaluations. The answer is those characteristics that are both subjective and socially desirable (ability to get along with others, leadership ability, etc.). The alternate form of Demonstration 2-8 allows you to examine the effect of the skewed response scale used in the College Board survey. By distributing each version to half the class you could assess the biasing effect of the skewed scale.

As a final demonstration of self-serving bias you might replicate James Friedrich's (1996) classroom exercise on what he calls the "ultimate self-serving bias," namely the tendency to see oneself as less self-serving than others. After his students were informed of the research on the self-serving bias, he had them respond to one of two versions of the following question: "How often do you think (you; the average person) makes this kind of mistake when judging or evaluating (yourself: him- or herself)? The self and average person's versions were randomized before distribution and students were asked to provide an answer by circling the appropriate number on a scale ranging from 1 (almost never) to 9 (nearly all the time). Students who responded to the questions about their own tendency to fall victim to this bias gave significantly lower ratings than did those who rated the same tendency for the average person.

10. Unrealistic Optimism

Neil Weinstein's (1982) research on "Unrealistic Optimism About Susceptibility to Health Problems" lends itself to classroom replication. Have students respond to Demonstration 2-9. Weinstein observed some tendency for people to be especially optimistic about <u>controllable</u> health problems. Health problems that are beyond one's control are less related to one's self-image, which may explain why people exhibit less self-serving bias concerning these. Explain this to the class and then invite students to identify which three health problems are most under one's personal control (answer: the even items). Instruct them to average their responses to the odd items, and to average their responses to the even items. Then ask: "How many of you were on average more optimistic about the even numbered items?" Virtually all hands should rise. (On the even numbered items Weinstein found that Rutgers students averaged -1.46; on the odd numbers they averaged -0.16).

C. R. Snyder (1997) demonstrated the tenacity of the illusion of invulnerability by forewarning students that a demonstration of unique invulnerability would occur later in the class. In an exercise you can replicate with your own class, Snyder informed students that the actuarially predicted age of death for U.S. citizens (men and women together) is 75 years. Then he asked them to write down anonymously on a blank slip of paper their estimated ages of death and their gender. After the estimates were handed in, a student read aloud each anticipated age of death, which Snyder plotted in a vertical array on a transparency. Another class member calculated the means. Results? Students overestimated their life expectancy by 9 years.

Demonstration 2-10, designed by John Brink, provides a marvelous example of unrealistic optimism as it relates to students' academic work. It is best used early in the course, preferably before the first test is given. Questions 2, 3, and 5 are the critical ones; you can modify the rest to best fit your particular situation. Collect student responses anonymously, tabulate the results for the entire class, and report the findings at your next session. Invariably students are wildly optimistic about their future success both in terms of predicting overall GPA for the upcoming semester and their performance in the course. It's a rare student who does not think his or her GPA will be significantly higher and who does not expect at least a "B" in your course.

These demonstrations could provide the springboard for an interesting discussion about optimism. Are people really being unrealistically optimistic about their own futures, or are they instead unduly pessimistic about others? What are the <u>benefits</u> of optimistic thinking? (In response to this question, one has a whole positive thinking cultural tradition to draw from.) What are the <u>perils</u> of optimism? (The Pollyanna optimism of the American military helped leave the United States unprepared for the Japanese attack on Pearl Harbor. Those who shun negative thinking about future energy supplies and the possibility of nuclear war are not likely to be much concerned with conservation or nuclear disarmament. Those who are unrealistically optimistic about their future health are <u>least</u> interested in taking steps to reduce their health risks. Students who are overconfident tend to underprepare.)

11. The False Consensus Bias

Kite (1991) describes a brief classroom exercise for demonstrating the false consensus bias. Ask your students to identify an opinion, for example, "I like David Letterman," or "George W. Bush is a good president," and identify their degree of agreement with the statement on a scale ranging from (1) strongly agree to (5) strongly disagree. Also ask students to estimate the percentage of people in the class that they believe share their opinion. By a show of hands, ask how many selected each response and record the number on the board. After computing the percentage of students choosing each option, have students indicate again by a show of hands whether they overestimated the number of people in agreement with them. Kite reports that in three social psychology classes at least 60 percent of the students overestimated the commonality of their opinions.

Kite also suggests some topics for classroom discussion. First, the bias seems to hold across various reference groups (e.g., friends versus college students in general) and issues (e.g., preferred type of bread or preferred presidential candidate). However, the strongest false consensus effects occur with factual information or political expectations (e.g., future use of nuclear weapons or outcome of presidential elections). Second, false consensus may reflect the operation of the availability heuristic, our tendency to overestimate the probability of events easily brought to mind. Third, ask students what might be the possible social costs and benefits of a false consensus bias for both individuals and society. Finally, ask whether having others agree with us makes our opinions "correct."

12. Self-Ratings and Perceived Importance of a Trait

The more favorably we perceive ourselves on some dimension, the more important we perceive the dimension to be, and as the text indicates, the more we use it as a basis for judging others. This self-serving tendency is readily illustrated in class with a demonstration designed by John Brink. Distribute a copy of Demonstration 2-11 to each member of your class. Although you may want to collect the responses and calculate the correlations for the entire class, it's really not necessary. The effect is so powerful students will see it by simply examining their own responses.

13. The Pollyanna Principle

Margaret Matlin and David Stang's <u>The Pollyanna Principle</u> (1980) reviews more than one thousand studies indicating that in perception, language, memory, and thought, the pleasant predominates over the unpleasant. William Dember and Larry Penwell (1980) report that this "Pollyanna Principle" is easily demonstrated. First, ask students simply to write down the names of 10 vegetables. Then ask them to "write down 10 pairs of antonyms, pairs such as 'good-bad' and 'unattractive-attractive.'" Then have them a) rank order the vegetables from 1, the most preferred, to 10, the least preferred, and b) average the ranks given to the first five vegetables names, and to the second five. A show of hands should reveal that most students rank the five vegetables that came to mind first as the more pleasant. Finally, have them a) circle the more positive word in each of the antonym pairs and b) count the number of times the circled word was named first. About 75 percent of the time it will be, so virtually all hands will be raised if you ask, "how many of you put the positive word first more than half the time?" Finally, you might point out that these rather trivial positive thinking tendencies are symptomatic of what Matlin and Stang contend is a deep human tendency to look on the bright side, playing the glad game, seeing, hearing, and speaking no evil.

14. Overrecalling One's Own Behavior

The text suggests that one possible source of self-serving bias is cognitive rather than motivational. We more easily recall what we've done than what others have done, or than what we have not done. For example, Michael Ross and Fiore Sicoly (1979) had student experimenters interrupt couples talking in cafeterias and lounges and ask each person to estimate how much he or she had spoken during the conversation. On the average, each estimated having spoken 59 percent of the time. We have successfully replicated this effect as a class project, though with less dramatic results. You can, too, by having class members each administer Demonstration 2-12 to two or three couples. Do the summed estimates average more than 100 percent?

15. Self-Handicapping Scale

Edward Jones and Steven Berglas (1979) have described self-handicapping as a set of behavioral strategies enacted before a performance that permits the individual to externalize failure and internalize success. The Self-Handicapping Scale, Demonstration 2-13, was designed by Jones and Frederick Rhodewalt to assess the respondent's tendency to use such self-handicapping behaviors as lack of effort, illness, or procrastination in conjunction with evaluative performances. For items 3, 5, 6, 10, 13, 20, 22, and 23, score as follows: AVM=0, APM=1, AL=2, DL=3, DPM=4, DVM=5. All remaining items are reversed scored: AVM=5, APM=4, AL=3, DL=2, DPM=1, DVM=0. The reported mean for a total of 685 college undergraduates was 67.5. Rhodewalt, Saltzman, and Wittmer (1984) report two field studies investigating individual differences among competitive athletes. Their findings indicated that high self-handicapping intercollegiate swimmers and golfers withheld practice effort relative to low self-handicappers prior to competitions that posed a threat to self-esteem.

16. Aspects of Identity Questionnaire

An excellent complement and extension of the research discussed in Chapter 2 of the text is to have students explore Jonathan M. Cheek's comprehensive web site atwww.wellesley.edu/Psychology/ Cheek/jcheek.html. Handout 2-14 asks students to do that. According to Cheek, identity orientations refer to the "relative importance that individuals place on various identity attributes or characteristics when constructing their self definitions." His Aspects of Identify Questionnaire is at the site along with a scoring key. The questionnaire distinguishes between personality identity, social identity, and communal or collective identity. The site includes abstracts of research utilizing the questionnaire.

17. The Social Connection Video Series

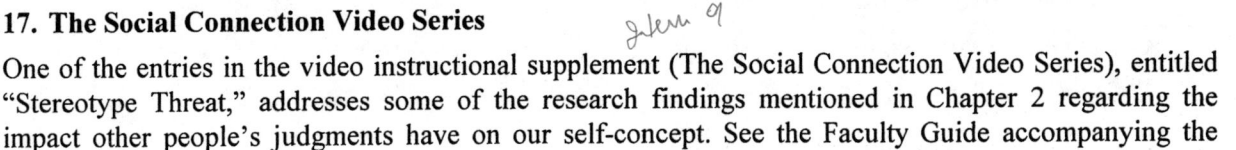

One of the entries in the video instructional supplement (The Social Connection Video Series), entitled "Stereotype Threat," addresses some of the research findings mentioned in Chapter 2 regarding the impact other people's judgments have on our self-concept. See the Faculty Guide accompanying the video series for a program summary, pause points, and a classroom activity.

Demonstration 2-1

Listed below are a number of statements. Indicate your agreement or disagreement with each statement using the following scale:

    1 = strongly agree
    2 = agree
    3 = disagree
    4 = strongly disagree

___ 1. I feel that I am a person of worth, at least on an equal basis with others.
___ 2. I feel that I have a number of good qualities.
___ 3. All in all, I am inclined to feel that I am a failure.
___ 4. I am able to do things as well as most other people.
___ 5. I feel I do not have much to be proud of.
___ 6. I take a positive attitude toward myself.
___ 7. On the whole, I am satisfied with myself.
___ 8. I wish I could have more respect for myself.
___ 9. I certainly feel useless at times.
___ 10. At times, I think I am no good at all.

Source: M. Rosenberg (1989). Society and the Adolescent Self-Image (Rev. ed.). Hanover, NH: University Press of New England, p. 325–327.

Demonstration 2-2

(with permission of T. Singelis)

This is a questionnaire that measures a variety of feelings and behaviors in various situations. Listed below are a number of statements. Read each one as if it refers to you. Indicate your agreement or disagreement with the statement using the following scale:

1 = strongly disagree
2 = disagree
3 = disagree somewhat
4 = don't agree or disagree
5 = agree somewhat
6 = agree
7 = strongly agree

___ 1. I enjoy being unique and different from others in many respects.
___ 2. I feel comfortable using someone's first name soon after I meet them, even when they are much older than I am.
___ 3. Even when I strongly disagree with group members, I avoid an argument.
___ 4. I have respect for the authority figures with whom I interact.
___ 5. I do my own thing, regardless of what others think.
___ 6. I respect people who are modest about themselves.
___ 7. I feel it is important for me to act as an independent person.
___ 8. I will sacrifice my self-interest for the benefit of the group I am in.
___ 9. I'd rather say "No" directly, than risk being misunderstood.
___ 10. Having a lively imagination is important to me.
___ 11. I should take into consideration my parents' advice when making education/career plans.
___ 12. I feel my fate is intertwined with the fate of those around me.
___ 13. I prefer to be direct and forthright when dealing with people I've just met.
___ 14. I feel good when I cooperate with others.
___ 15. I am comfortable with being singled out for praise or rewards.
___ 16. If my brother or sister fails, I feel responsible.
___ 17. I often have the feeling that my relationships with others are more important than my own accomplishments.
___ 18. Speaking up during a class is not a problem for me.
___ 19. I would offer my seat in a bus to my professor.
___ 20. I act the same way no matter who I am with.
___ 21. My happiness depends on the happiness of those around me.
___ 22. I value being in good health above everything.
___ 23. I will stay in a group if they need me, even when I'm not happy with the group.

Demonstration 2-2 (cont.)

___ 24. Being able to take care of myself is a primary concern for me.
___ 25. It is important to me to respect decisions made by the group.
___ 26. My personal identity independent of others is very important to me.
___ 27. It is important for me to maintain harmony within my group.
___ 28. I act the same way at home that I do at school.

Singelis, T. M. (1994). The measurement of independent and interdependent self-construals. Personality and Social Psychology Bulletin, 20, 585. Copyright by Sage Publications, Inc. Reprinted by permission.

Demonstration 2-3

(with permission of S. Nowicki)

We are trying to find out what men and women think about certain things. We want you to answer the following questions the way you feel. There are no right or wrong answers. Don't take too much time answering any one question, but do try to answer them all.

One of your concerns during the test may be, "What should I do if I can answer both yes and no to a question?" It's not unusual for this to happen. If it does, think about whether your answer is just a little more one way than the other. For example, if you'd assign a weighting of 51 percent to "yes" and assign 49 percent to "no," mark the answer "yes." Try to pick one or the other responses for all questions and not leave any blank.

Yes No

___ ___ 1. Do you believe that most problems will solve themselves if you just don't fool with them?
___ ___ 2. Do you believe that you can stop yourself from catching a cold?
___ ___ 3. Are some people just born lucky?
___ ___ 4. Most of the time do you feel that getting good grades means a great deal to you?
___ ___ 5. Are you often blamed for things that just aren't your fault?
___ ___ 6. Do you believe that if somebody studies hard enough he or she can pass any subject?
___ ___ 7. Do you feel that most of the time it doesn't pay to try hard because things never turn out right anyway?
___ ___ 8. Do you feel that if things start out well in the morning it's going to be a good day no matter what you do?
___ ___ 9. Do you feel that most of the time parents listen to what their children have to say?
___ ___ 10. Do you believe that wishing can make good things happen?
___ ___ 11. When you get punished does it usually seem it's for no good reason at all?
___ ___ 12. Most of the time do you find it hard to change a friend's opinion?
___ ___ 13. Do you think that cheering more than luck helps a team to win?
___ ___ 14. Did you feel that it was nearly impossible to change your parents' minds about anything?
___ ___ 15. Do you believe that parents should allow children to make most of their own decisions?
___ ___ 16. Do you feel that when you do something wrong there's very little you can do to make it right?
___ ___ 17. Do you believe that most people are just born good at sports?
___ ___ 18. Are most of the other people your age stronger than you are?
___ ___ 19. Do you feel that one of the best ways to handle most problems is just not to think about them?
___ ___ 20. Do you feel that you have a lot of choice in deciding who your friends are?
___ ___ 21. If you find a four-leaf clover, do you believe that it might bring you good luck?
___ ___ 22. Did you often feel that whether or not you did your homework had much to do with what kind of grades you got?
___ ___ 23. Do you feel that when a person your age is angry at you, there's little you can do to stop him

___ or her?
___ 24. Have you ever had a good-luck charm?
___ 25. Do you believe that whether or not people like you depends on how you act?
___ 26. Did your parents usually help you if you asked them to?
___ 27. Have you felt that when people were angry with you it was usually for no reason at all?
___ 28. Most of the time, do you feel that you can change what might happen tomorrow by what you do today?
___ 29. Do you believe that when bad things are going to happen they just are going to happen no matter what you try to do to stop them?
___ 30. Do you think that people can get their own way if they just keep trying?
___ 31. Most of the time do you find it useless to try to get your own way at home?
___ 32. Do you feel that when good things happen they happen because of hard work?
___ 33. Do you feel that when somebody your age wants to be your enemy there's little you can do to change matters?
___ 34. Do you feel that it's easy to get friends to do what you want them to do?
___ 35. Do you usually feel that you have little to say about what you get to eat at home?
___ 36. Do you feel that when someone doesn't like you there's little you can do about it?
___ 37. Did you usually feel that it was almost useless to try in school because most other children were just plain smarter than you were?
___ 38. Are you the kind of person who believes that planning ahead makes things turn out better?
___ 39. Most of the time, do you feel that you have little to say about what your family decides to do?
___ 40. Do you think it's better to be smart than to be lucky?

Demonstration 2-4

1. BAT
2. LEMON
3. CINERAMA

Demonstration 2-4

1. WHIRL
2. SLAPSTICK
3. CINERAMA

Demonstration 2-5

(with permission of S. Green)

Assume that David attended a party last week. At this party David met and had a 15-minute conversation with Roger whom David found to be a very interesting person. Roger has just moved to this area and doesn't yet have a telephone. Near the end of the conversation Roger obtained David's phone number but said it would not be possible to call him during that week. However, Roger called David only two days later and arranged to have lunch with him. Why did Roger phone David sooner than he said he would?

How much did each of the following factors probably account for Roger phoning sooner than he said he would? Express your hunch by distributing 100 percentage points among these three possible explanations:

__A. Something about Roger probably caused him to phone David sooner than he said he would.

__B. Something about David probably caused Roger to phone David sooner than he said he would.

__C. Something about the particular situation or circumstances (not related to the personal characteristics of David or Roger) probably caused Roger to call David sooner than he said he would.

100%

Demonstration 2-5

(with permission of S. Green)

Assume that you attended a party last week. At this party you met and had a 15-minute conversation with Roger whom you found to be a very interesting person. Roger has just moved to this area and doesn't yet have a telephone. Near the end of the conversation Roger obtained your phone number but said it would not be possible to call you during that week. However, Roger called you only two days later and arranged to have lunch with you. Why did Roger phone you sooner than he said he would?

How much did each of the following factors probably account for Roger phoning sooner than he said he would? Express your hunch by distributing 100 percentage points among these three possible explanations:

__A. Something about Roger probably caused him to phone you sooner than he said he would.

__B. Something about you probably caused Roger to phone you sooner than he said he would.

__C. Something about the particular situation or circumstances (not related to the personal characteristics of you or Roger) probably caused Roger to call you sooner than he said he would.

100%

Demonstration 2-5

(with permission of S. Green)

Assume that David attended a party last week. At this party David met and had a 15-minute conversation with Roger whom David found to be a very interesting person. Roger has just moved to this area and doesn't yet have a telephone. Near the end of the conversation Roger obtained David's phone number and promised to call before the end of the week so that he could meet him for lunch. However, the week is over and David has not yet heard from Roger. Why didn't Roger phone David when he said he would?

How much did each of the following factors probably account for Roger not phoning when he said he would? Express your hunch by distributing 100 percentage points among these three possible explanations:

__A. Something about Roger probably caused him not to phone David when he said he would.

__B. Something about David probably caused Roger not to phone David when he said he would.

__C. Something about the particular situation or circumstances (not related to the personal characteristics of David or Roger) probably caused Roger not to call David when he said he would.

100%

Demonstration 2-5

(with permission of S. Green)

Assume that you attended a party last week. At this party you met and had a 15-minute conversation with Roger whom you found to be a very interesting person. Roger has just moved to this area and doesn't yet have a telephone. Near the end of the conversation Roger obtained your phone number and promised to call before the end of the week so that he could meet you for lunch. However, the week is over and you have not yet heard from Roger. Why didn't Roger phone you when he said he would?

How much did each of the following factors probably account for Roger not phoning when he said he would? Express your hunch by distributing 100 percentage points among these three possible explanations:

__A. Something about Roger probably caused him not to phone you when he said he would.

__B. Something about you probably caused Roger not to phone you when he said he would.

__C. Something about the particular situation or circumstances (not related to the personal characteristics of you or Roger) probably caused Roger not to call you when he said he would.

100%

Demonstration 2-6
Bolt and Myers
©McGraw-Hill, 1999

To what extent do you think your score on this test was due to:

1. This particular test—how easy or difficult it was:

    Not at all   0 1 2 3 4 5 6 7 8 9   To a great extent

2. My academic ability or lack of ability:

    Not at all   0 1 2 3 4 5 6 7 8 9   To a great extent

3. Study—how much or little I studied:

    Not at all   0 1 2 3 4 5 6 7 8 9   To a great extent

4. Luck—good or bad:

    Not at all   0 1 2 3 4 5 6 7 8 9   To a great extent

5. What score did you receive on the test? _____

6. How satisfied are you with this score?

    Not at all
    satisfied   0 1 2 3 4 5 6 7 8 9   Very satisfied

7. Was this test:

    A poor measure of   An excellent measure
    what I knew   0 1 2 3 4 5 6 7 8 9   of what I knew

8. Are you   ___female   ___male?

Demonstration 2-7

Compared to other college students of the same class level and sex as yourself, how would you rate yourself on the following characteristics? Use the following scale in making your response.

    1 = considerably well below average
    2 = well below average
    3 = below average
    4 = slightly below average
    5 = average
    6 = slightly above average
    7 = above average
    8 = well above average
    9 = considerably well above average

_____ 1. leadership ability
_____ 2. athletic ability
_____ 3. ability to get along with others
_____ 4. tolerance
_____ 5. energy level
_____ 6. helpfulness
_____ 7. responsibility
_____ 8. creativeness
_____ 9. patience
_____ 10. trustworthiness
_____ 11. sincerity
_____ 12. thoughtfulness
_____ 13. cooperativeness
_____ 14. reasonableness
_____ 15. intelligence

Demonstration 2-8

These questions are, for the most part, drawn from "The Student Descriptive Questionnaire," put out by the College Board. The questions concern how you feel you compare with other people your own age in certain areas of ability. On the answer sheet, mark the letter

hi 1   if you feel you are in the <u>highest 1 percent</u> in that area of ability

hi 10 if you feel you are in the <u>highest 10 percent</u> in that area of ability

aa   if you feel you are <u>above average</u> in that area of ability

a   if you feel you are <u>average</u> in that area of ability

ba   if you feel you are <u>below average</u> in that area of ability

hi 1	hi 10	aa	a	ba	
( )	( )	( )	( )	( )	Acting ability
( )	( )	( )	( )	( )	Artistic ability
( )	( )	( )	( )	( )	Athletic ability
( )	( )	( )	( )	( )	Getting along with others
( )	( )	( )	( )	( )	Leadership ability
( )	( )	( )	( )	( )	Mathematical ability
( )	( )	( )	( )	( )	Mechanical ability
( )	( )	( )	( )	( )	Musical ability
( )	( )	( )	( )	( )	Organizing work
( )	( )	( )	( )	( )	Sales ability
( )	( )	( )	( )	( )	Scientific ability
( )	( )	( )	( )	( )	Spoken expression
( )	( )	( )	( )	( )	Written expression

(From <u>College Descriptive Questionnaire</u>. College Entrance Examination Board, N.Y. Used by permission of Educational Testing Service, the copyright owner.)

Demonstration 2-8

These questions are, for the most part, drawn from "The Student Descriptive Questionnaire," put out by the College Board. The questions concern how you feel you compared with other people your own age in certain areas of ability. On the answer sheet, mark the letter

- hi 1   if you feel you are in the <u>highest 1 percent</u> in that area of ability
- hi 10 if you feel you are in the <u>highest 10 percent</u> in the area of ability
- aa   if you feel you are <u>above average</u> in that area of ability
- a   if you feel you are <u>average</u> in that area of ability
- ba   if you feel you are <u>below average</u> in that area of ability
- lo 10 if you feel you are in the <u>lowest 10 percent</u> in that area of ability
- lo 1   if you feel you are in the <u>lowest 1 percent</u> in that area of ability

hi 1	hi 10	aa	a	ba	lo 10	lo 1	
( )	( )	( )	( )	( )	( )	( )	Acting ability
( )	( )	( )	( )	( )	( )	( )	Artistic ability
( )	( )	( )	( )	( )	( )	( )	Athletic ability
( )	( )	( )	( )	( )	( )	( )	Getting along with others
( )	( )	( )	( )	( )	( )	( )	Leadership ability
( )	( )	( )	( )	( )	( )	( )	Mathematical ability
( )	( )	( )	( )	( )	( )	( )	Mechanical ability
( )	( )	( )	( )	( )	( )	( )	Musical ability
( )	( )	( )	( )	( )	( )	( )	Organizing work
( )	( )	( )	( )	( )	( )	( )	Sales ability
( )	( )	( )	( )	( )	( )	( )	Scientific ability
( )	( )	( )	( )	( )	( )	( )	Spoken expression
( )	( )	( )	( )	( )	( )	( )	Written expression

(From <u>College Descriptive Questionnaire</u>. College Entrance Examination Board, N.Y. Used by permission of Educational Testing Service, the copyright owner.)

Demonstration 2-9

(with permission of N. Weinstein)

Compared to other students of your sex at your college, what do you think are the chances that the following health problems will trouble you at some point in the future? Respond by choosing a number from the following scale:

Compared to other students of my sex, the chances of my experiencing this problem are:

    -3 = much below average
    -2 = below average
    -1 = slightly below average
     0 = average
    +1 = slightly above average
    +2 = above average
    +3 = much above average

__1. Arthritis
__2. Suicide
__3. Pneumonia
__4. Being 40 or more pounds overweight
__5. Laryngitis
__6. Alcoholism
__7. Being killed in an auto accident
__8. Lung cancer

Demonstration 2-10

Academic Survey: Social Psychology

1. Please indicate your current enrollment status. (Check one).

    _____ Freshman

    _____ Sophomore

    _____ Junior

    _____ Senior

    _____ Other

2. What was your overall Grade Point Average (G.P.A.) for the college courses you completed last semester? (Use numbers, for example 2.87)

3. Try to predict what your Grade Point Average for the upcoming semester will be. (Use numbers)

4. Why did you enroll in Social Psychology?

    _____ To satisfy a requirement related to my college major

    _____ The catalogue description sounded interesting

    _____ My academic advisor recommended it

    _____ A family member or friend recommended it

5. Last year over 150 students took Social Psychology from your professor. The average grade these students received in this course was a B-. What do you think your final grade in this course will be?

    _____ A

    _____ A-

    _____ B+

    _____ B

    _____ B-

    _____ C+

    _____ C

    _____ C-

    _____ D+

    _____ D

    _____ D-

    _____ F

Demonstration 2-11

(with permission of J. Brink)

Please try to respond to the following questions as honestly as you can. Circle the number that best corresponds to your feelings. Your answers will remain completely confidential.

1. How athletic are you?
   Not at all   1 2 3 4 5 6 7   Very much

2. How much do you care about whether or not you are athletic?
   Not at all   1 2 3 4 5 6 7   Very much

3. How intelligent are you?
   Not at all   1 2 3 4 5 6 7   Very much

4. How much do you care about whether or not you are intelligent?
   Not at all   1 2 3 4 5 6 7   Very much

5. How physically attractive are you?
   Not at all   1 2 3 4 5 6 7   Very much

6. How much do you care about whether or not you are physically attractive?
   Not at all   1 2 3 4 5 6 7   Very much

7. How creative are you?
   Not at all   1 2 3 4 5 6 7   Very much

8. How much do you care about whether or not you are creative?
   Not at all   1 2 3 4 5 6 7   Very much

9. How mechanically skilled are you?
   Not at all   1 2 3 4 5 6 7   Very much

10. How much do you care about whether or not you are mechanically skilled?
    Not at all   1 2 3 4 5 6 7   Very much

Demonstration 2-12

For about how many minutes have the two of you been talking together?
_____ minutes

About what percent of the talking has been contributed by you?
_____%

Demonstration 2-12

For about how many minutes have the two of you been talking together?
_____ minutes

About what percent of the talking has been contributed by you?
_____%

Demonstration 2-13

(with permission of E. Jones and F. Rhodewalt)

Please indicate the degree to which you agree with each of the following statements as a description of the kind of person you think you are most of the time. Code for responses: AVM = agree very much, APM = agree pretty much, AL = agree a little, DL = disagree a little, DPM = disagree pretty much, and DVM = disagree very much. Place the appropriate abbreviation in the space before each item.

____ 1. When I do something wrong, my first impulse is to blame circumstances.

____ 2. I tend to put things off until the last moment.

____ 3. I tend to overprepare when I have an exam or any kind of "performance."

____ 4. I suppose I feel "under the weather" more often than most people.

____ 5. I always try to do my best, no matter what.

____ 6. Before I sign up for a course or engage in any important activity, I make sure I have the proper preparation or background.

____ 7. I tend to get very anxious before an exam or "performance."

____ 8. I am easily distracted by noises or my own creative thoughts when I try to read.

____ 9. I try not to get too intensely involved in competitive activities so it won't hurt too much if I lose or do poorly.

____ 10. I would rather be respected for doing my best than admired for my potential.

____ 11. I would do a lot better if I tried harder.

____ 12. I prefer small pleasures in the present to larger pleasures in the dim future.

____ 13. I generally hate to be in any condition but "at my best."

____ 14. Someday I might "get it all together."

____ 15. I sometimes enjoy being mildly ill for a day or two because it takes off the pressure.

____ 16. I would do much better if I did not let my emotions get in the way.

____ 17. When I do poorly at one kind of thing, I often console myself by remembering I am good at other things.

____ 18. I admit that I am tempted to rationalize when I don't live up to other's expectations.

____ 19. I often think I have more than my share of bad luck in sports, card games, and other measures of talent.

____ 20. I would rather not take any drug that interfered with my ability to think clearly and do the right thing.

____ 21. I overindulge in food and drink more often than I should.

____ 22. When something important is coming up, like an exam or a job interview, I try to get as much sleep as possible the night before.

____ 23. I never let emotional problems in one part of my life interfere with other things in my life.

____ 24. Usually, when I get anxious about doing well, I end up doing better.

____ 25. Sometimes I get so depressed that even easy tasks become difficult.

Demonstration 2-14

To answer the following questions visit Dr. Jonathan M. Cheek's Web site at www.wellesley.edu/Psychology/Cheek/jcheek.html.

1. Briefly explain what is meant by "identity orientation."

   _____
   _____
   _____
   _____
   _____

2. What three types of identity are assessed by the Aspects of Identity Questionnaire (AIQ-IIIx)?

   _____   _____   _____

3. Complete the AIQ-IIIx and indicate your mean score for each aspect of identify.

   _____   _____   _____

4. How are different identities related to other personality dimensions, attitudes, or behaviors? Cite at least three important research findings.

   _____
   _____
   _____
   _____
   _____
   _____
   _____
   _____
   _____

FILMS/VIDEOS

Looking Out for Number One (FIL, 52 min., 1987). Discusses conflict between individualism and social responsibility. Examines signs of self-indulgence, concern with success and material comforts. Can be used to extend text's discussion of the self-serving bias.

Predicting Our World (UFC, 28 min., 1975). Discussion of learned helplessness, the need for control, "just world" theory, and risk-taking.

The Self (ANN, 26 min., 1989). From the Discovering Psychology series, this video examines the role of the self-concept in behavior. It examines how different psychologists have viewed the self, includes treatment of Bandura's concept of self-efficacy, and discusses the ways in which people try to protect their self-esteem.

Self-Esteem and Social Development (Insight, 18 min. each, 1991). This two-part program examines how self-esteem develops in children. It discusses and demonstrates six specific principles that promote social-skills development in infants, toddlers, and preschoolers.

Self-Esteem and How We Learn (Insight, 30 min., 1992). This video explores the relationship of self-esteem to personal satisfaction and academic success. It suggests that a positive self-image decreases the likelihood of drug abuse, teenage pregnancy, and involvement in crime.

The Truth About Lies (PBS, 60 min., 1989). Narrated by Bill Moyers, this program examines how deception has influenced some of the major events of our recent past. Of particular interest to this chapter is the treatment of self-deception and of how it shapes our personal lives and the public mind.

CHAPTER 3
SOCIAL BELIEFS AND JUDGMENTS

Explaining Others
    Attributing Causality: To the Person or the Situation?
    Inferring Traits
    Commonsense Attributions
    Information Integration
    The Fundamental Attribution Error
    The Fundamental Attribution Error in Everyday Life
    Why Do We Make the Attribution Error?
    Perspective and Situational Awareness
    Cultural Differences
    How Fundamental Is the Fundamental Attribution Error?
    Why We Study Attribution Errors
Constructing Interpretations and Memories
    Perceiving and Interpreting Events
    Belief Perseverance
    Constructing Memories
    Reconstructing Past Attitudes
    Reconstructing Past Behavior
    Reconstructing Our Experiences
Judging Others
    Thinking Without Awareness
    The Powers of the Unconscious
    The Limits of Intuition
    Judgmental Overconfidence
    Remedies for Overconfidence
    Heuristics
    Representativeness Heuristic
    The Availability Heuristic
    Counterfactual Thinking
    Illusory Thinking
    Illusory Correlation
    Illusion of Control
    Mood and Judgment
Self-Fulfilling Beliefs

    Teacher Expectations and Student Performance
    Getting from Others What We Expect
Conclusions
Personal Postscript: Reflecting on Intuition's Powers and Limits

LECTURE AND DISCUSSION IDEAS

1. Introducing Social Perception: The Interpersonal Perception Task

This 40-minute video prepared by Dane Archer and Mark Costanzo provides an excellent introduction to social perception and attribution theory. (Available from the University of California Extension Center for Media and Independent Learning Center, 2000 Center Street, Fourth Floor, Berkeley, CA 94704, 510-642-0460.) The video presents 30 brief scenes, each 30 to 60 seconds in length that depict common types of social interaction. Each scene is paired with a question that has two or three possible answers and gives viewers the opportunity to "decide" something important about the people they have just seen. Archer and Costanzo have published a guide for instructors that suggests a variety of ways of using the IPT. It also contains an answer sheet that can be duplicated for in-class use. (The IPT-15, released in 1993, is a 20-minute program containing 15 of the original 30 scenes, and is also available through the University of California Extension Media Center. In addition, the McGraw-Hill Social Psychology Videotape/Videodisc contains three scenes from the ITP, running just under three minutes.)

2. Attributional Complexity

The text notes that Fletcher and his colleagues (1986) found that psychology students explain behavior less simplistically than equally able natural science students. This finding emerged from their research on attributional complexity, a construct you may want to discuss in class.

In developing a measure of individual differences, the researchers postulated that the following seven attributional constructs can be viewed as ranging along a simple-complex dimension:

A. Level of interest or motivation. Attributionally complex people possess higher levels of intrinsic motivation to explain human behavior ("I really enjoy analyzing the reasons or causes for people's behavior").

B. Preference for complex rather than simple explanations. All other things being equal, explanations that contain more causes are considered more complex ("Once I have figured out a single cause for a person's behavior, I don't usually go any further" [reversed scored]).

C. Presence of metacognition concerning explanations. The attributionally complex tend to think about the underlying processes involved in causal attribution ("I am very interested in understanding how my own thinking works when I make judgments about people or attach causes to their behavior").

D. Awareness of the extent to which people's behavior is a function of interaction with others. Attributionally complex people are more aware of the power of the social situation both in terms of the influence other people have on their own behavior and in terms of the impact their own behavior has on others ("I think a lot about the influence I have on other people's behavior").

E. Tendency to infer abstract or causally complex internal attributions. Some dispositions seem to be summary terms for specific behaviors (e.g., punctuality). Others refer to more abstract cognitive mental structures (e.g., beliefs, attitudes, abilities). Moreover, internal causes can be linked in complex chains (e.g., shyness causes anxiety, which causes insomnia). Abstract or causally complex internal explanations are associated with increased attributional complexity ("To understand a person's behavior, I have found it is important to know how that person's attitudes, beliefs, and character traits fit together").

F. Tendency to infer external causes operating at a spatial distance. External causes can be viewed as radiating out spatially, however contemporaneously, from the person. The more physically removed the cause, moving, say, from the immediate environment to societal causes, the more complex it is judged to be ("I think a lot about the influence that society has on other people").

G. Tendency to infer external causes operating at a temporal distance. Some external causes exert their influence from the distant past, perhaps through a chain of intermediary causes. The perception of more distant causes are considered more complex ("I have often found that the basic cause for a person's behavior is located far back in time").

3. A Demonstration of Harold Kelley's Attribution Model

Michael J. White of Ball State University has created a 20-minute videotape that provides an overview and application of Kelley's attribution model. The tape first describes the basic components of the theory and then illustrates them using a naturalistic social situation. Purchase price is $50, plus postage and handling. Copies may be obtained by contacting the Office of Research, Ball State University, Muncie, IN 47304, 317-285-1600.

4. Actor versus Observer Perspectives of the "Who" Concert

John Brink (personal communication) cites an excellent example of the actor-perceiver difference in perception. In 1979, rock fans were waiting to get into Riverfront Coliseum for a "Who" concert. When the coliseum doors were finally opened, a stampede ensued and several people were trampled to death. Among the letters to Time magazine, which had earlier reported on the tragedy, were those of an outside observer and an actor participant. To whom does each attribute the cause?

First, the observer's comments:

> The violently destructive message that The Who and other rock groups deliver leaves me little surprised that they attract a mob that will trample human beings to death to gain better seats. Of greater concern is a respected news magazine's adulation of this sick phenomenon.

Next, the actor's comments:

> While standing in the crowd at Riverfront Coliseum, I distinctly remember feeling that I was being punished for being a rock fan. My sister and I joked about this, unaware of the horror happening around us. Later, those jokes came back to us grimly as we watched the news. How many lives before the punitive and inhuman policy of festival seating at rock concerts is outlawed?

5. Public and Private Self-Consciousness

The text notes that some people are typically quite self-conscious. Those who report themselves as privately self-conscious view themselves more as observers typically do; that is, they attribute their behavior more to internal factors and less to the situation.

In class you can extend the research on private self-consciousness and also introduce the related construct of public self-consciousness. Whereas private self-consciousness refers to a focus on personal aspects of the self, including bodily sensations, beliefs, moods, and feelings, public self-consciousness involves a more outward concern, particularly an awareness of how one is seen by others. Typical questionnaire items that reflect private self-consciousness are: "I reflect about myself a lot," and "I'm always trying to figure myself out." Items reflecting public self-consciousness include: "I'm concerned about what other people think of me," and "One of the last things I do before I leave my house is look in the mirror."

In a simple exercise to test for public self-consciousness, have students draw a capital E on their forehead using their dominant hand. Ask "What direction does the 'E' face?" If it is oriented so that someone looking at the student would have seen it in the correct position, it is likely that the student is high in public self-consciousness. According to Hass (1984), people who are low in public self-consciousness are more likely to draw an E from an internal perspective.

Individual differences in both forms of self-consciousness have been linked to relevant behaviors. Research suggests that people high in private self-consciousness are more likely to base their behaviors on internal standards and beliefs and less likely to comply with social pressure. They are more consistent in expressing their attitudes and are more aware of their emotional reactions to events. Those high in public self-consciousness are more concerned with fashion and physical appearance. They are more sensitive to what others think of them, conform to social pressure to avoid negative evaluations, and are more likely to engage in self-handicapping.

6. Reasons and Causes

In pondering the sections on fundamental attribution error, some students may wonder: why do actors tend to attribute their behavior to the situation if they also prefer a sense of self-efficacy? Isn't viewing one's behavior as caused by the situation contradictory to feelings of personal efficacy and internal control?

The answer is that when people explain their own behavior they typically are giving <u>reasons,</u> not causes. They are not viewing themselves as mere billiard balls, buffeted by situational causes. Rather, they are explaining their actions by giving reasons (in terms of the situation) that <u>justify</u> how they chose to behave. Reasons are justifications as perceived by the actor. Causes are objective factors (features of the environment, the actor, and so on) as discerned by external observers. For further commentary, see Locke and Pennington (1982).

7. Marvels of the Human Mind

Chapter 3 includes a discussion of the powers and limits of human intuition. Are we wise or foolish? You may want to precede (or end) the discussion of human error by noting some of Morton Hunt's (1982) marvels of the human mind. First is the sheer intricacy of the neural pathways by which the human brain transmits and processes information. According to one estimate, the circuitry in the human brain has 60 times the informational capacity of the entire U.S. telephone system! A second marvel is the mind's information-storage capacity. Donald Norman, Director of the Program in Cognitive Science at the University of California at San Diego, believes that each of us holds something like 50,000 facts about every topic on which we are reasonably knowledgeable—our own bodies, our personal idiosyncrasies, the arrangement of our homes and environs, the words and grammar of our native language. Mathematician John Griffith calculates that in the course of a lifetime the average person can accumulate 500 times as much information as is contained in the <u>Encyclopedia Britannica</u>.

We take for granted, suggests Hunt, the enormously complex mental acts we routinely perform every day. To illustrate, he poses several questions, which you can also present to your class.

1. What's a seven-letter word ending in "y" that means a "group of interacting individuals living in the same region and sharing the same culture?": Students will probably say "society" before you come to the end of the question. But how did they manage to find the word so quickly among the 50,000 to 75,000 in their working vocabulary?

2. What's George Washington's phone number? We immediately recognize the question is absurd. But how do we know so quickly, without more than a moment's thought? Do we mentally search the phone book of memory in a millisecond? Consult the encyclopedia of history in our head? Look up the dates of Washington and of the telephone and do some logical reasoning based on them?

3. ACORN is to OAK as INFANT is to _____. We know at once that the answer is ADULT. But how do we know? An analysis of this analogical reasoning would take 20–50 pages. In brief, we compare the attributes of the first two capitalized words, infer a rule that expresses their relationship, apply that rule to the third capitalized word, and extrapolate to get the missing fourth word.

4. In the place where you lived two residences ago, did your front door open at the left side or the right? To answer that question, says Hunt, you send a signal through the unseen branching network of your mind to exactly the right storage place, pluck out a reel of filed imagery, and project an image upon some inner screen, all in a moment.

5. Which word in the following group does not belong—rose, lily, hyacinth, potato, tulip? More mental work is involved in this simple example than we realize. By the time you read the second or third word you were already seeking a higher-level concept that would fit these items—perhaps "plant" or "flower." Knowing that the task was to find a category that included all but one of the terms, you had narrowed it down to "flower" by the time you reached the end of the list.

8. Memory Construction

In the fall of 1991, millions of television viewers tried to decipher what happened when Clarence Thomas and Anita Hill (pictured in the text) worked together a decade earlier. Law professor Hill accused her former employer of sexual harassment. Supreme Court nominee Thomas emphatically denied the accusation. At the time several leading researchers who specialized in memory suggested alternative theories of the conflicting reports (Barringer, 1991).

The first, and perhaps most obvious, was that one of the two was consciously lying. A second was that one of the two was suffering from a delusion. For example, Republicans supporting Thomas introduced an affidavit from a Hill acquaintance suggesting that she had the ability to "fabricate the idea that someone was interested in her" romantically. The third hypothesis, most relevant to the materials in this chapter, is that both were telling a version of the truth, and that both completely believed their own versions.

Bruce Sales of the University of Arizona suggested that "it could be they are each remembering a view or side of it that is partially true and then creating a memory" around this partial truth. Elizabeth Loftus of the University of Washington said, "How could Anita Hill have memories for things that are so detailed—Coke cans and Long Dong Silver and all the other very, very specific details unless it really happened?. . . In my own work I can inject these kinds of details into people's recollections, into the minds of people who are being as honest and sincere as possible. I could believe that her recollections could be, in part, things that happened to other people or things she read about." Another possibility, Loftus suggested, was that Judge Thomas's memory was selective, but not deliberately so. "He can be remembering his own past actions in ways that make him feel better about himself. In his case, that involves minimizing the conversations, or even denying they ever took place." Loftus concluded, "We're talking about completely normal people. If you start getting into delusional cases then you get into a group who are even more suggestible than most of us. But these are processes that characterize all of us."

9. Recovered or Constructed Memories of Abuse?

The text briefly mentions that some researchers (e.g., Loftus) believe that suggested misinformation may produce false memories of supposed child abuse. Module B of the text will discuss the possible role of the misinformation effect on eyewitness testimony.

The therapist's role in helping patients "recover" suspected repressed memories of childhood abuse is a hotly debated issue. Assuming that patients with a variety of symptoms may have been abused in childhood but have repressed memory of the experience, therapists use a variety of techniques including hypnosis and drugs to help them to recover it. In fact, in one recent survey of British and American doctoral-level therapists, 7 in 10 said they had used such techniques to help clients recover suspected memories of childhood sexual abuse (Poole et al., 1995). One much publicized case of recovered memory as a result of therapy is that of actress Roseanne Barr Arnold who claimed to recall sexual abuse beginning in infancy. The magnitude of the problem is reflected in the fact that since 1991 in the state of Washington alone 662 people who claim repressed memories of sexual abuse and other crimes have sought money for their therapy bills from the state's victim compensation fund.

Many psychologists believe that thousands of people are being falsely accused. Clearly accusations are tearing families apart. The False Memory Syndrome Foundation was established in 1992 to help the accused. It is presently tracking 700 suits against accused patients and 200 against therapists. Seven in ten accused persons report their accusers are women ages 31 to 50. Moreover, of those accusers, 71 percent have siblings who do not believe the accusation.

An excellent out-of-class assignment is to have students explore FMSF's huge Website (http://www.fmsfonline.org/) and report their findings back to class, e.g. What is FMS?, How did the FMS foundation start?, What is its purpose?, How does it seek to accomplish that purpose?

10. Overconfidence

The text cites several cases of overconfidence in political leaders. You might present the following additional examples of overconfidence among experts, most of which come from Russo and Schoemaker (1989):

"There is no reason anyone would want a computer in their home." (Ken Olson, president of Digital Equipment Company, 1977)

"Heavier-than-air flying machines are impossible." (Lord Kelvin—British mathematician, physicist, and president of the British Royal Society, 1895)

"Reagan doesn't have the presidential look." (United Artists executive when asked whether Ronald Reagan should be offered the starring role in the movie The Best Man, 1964)

"A severe depression like that of 1920–21 is outside the range of possibility." (Harvard Economic Society—Weekly Letter, November 16, 1929)

"Impossible!" (Jimmy "The Greek" Snyder when asked whether Cassius Clay could last six rounds in his upcoming bout with Heavyweight Champion Sonny Liston, 1964)

"They couldn't hit an elephant at this dist—" (General John B. Sedgwick—Union Army Civil War officer's last words, uttered during the Battle of Spotsylvania, 1864)

"We know on the authority of Moses, that longer ago than six thousand years, the world did not exist." (Martin Luther—1483–1546; German leader of the Protestant Reformation)

11. Searching for Confirming Information

You can illustrate our preference for information that confirms our beliefs in a variety of ways.

Eldar Shafir (1993) presented research participants with the following scenario:

> Imagine that you serve on a jury of an only-child sole custody case following a messy divorce. The facts of the case are complicated by a number of ambiguous considerations and you decide to base your decision entirely on the following few observations. To which parent would you award sole

custody of the child? Parent A, who has an average income, average health, average working hours, a reasonable rapport with the child, and a relatively stable social life, or Parent B who has an above-average income, minor health problems, lots of work-related travel, a very close relationship with the child, and an extremely active social life.

Most research participants picked Parent B. However, when a different group given the same scenario was asked to which parent they would deny custody, the majority also picked Parent B. Why? When asked who should be awarded custody, people look primarily for positive qualities and pay less attention to negative qualities. This perspective leads them to Parent B because of the close relationship with the child and the high income. When asked who should be denied custody, people look primarily for negative qualities and to pay less attention to positive qualities. This, too, would lead them to Parent B because of health problems and extensive absences due to travel.

In Why Children Fail, John Holt describes schoolchildren who were given 20 questions to identify an unknown number between 1 and 10,000. He reports they cheered when the teacher told them that "yes, it is between 5,000 and 10,000," but groaned when informed, "no, it's not between 5,000 and 10,000." The responses were equally informative, although the second had to be converted to the recognition that the number is between 1 and 5,000.

Still, a third example of our preference for confirming information comes from a study on the psychological basis of perceived similarity. Tversky and Gati (1978) found that when subjects were asked which countries were more similar to one another, East Germany and West Germany, or Sri Lanka and Nepal, most replied with East and West Germany. When a second group of subjects were asked which two countries are more different from one another, East Germany and West Germany, or Sri Lanka and Nepal, the majority also said East and West Germany. Gilovich suggests that people knew more about Germany than Sri Lanka or Nepal. When asked to assess the similarity of two entities, they paid more attention to the ways in which they are similar than to the ways in which they are different. Asked to assess dissimilarity, they became more concerned with differences than with similarities.

12. The Base-Rate Fallacy

Chapter 3 provides several practical examples of the base-rate fallacy. You can reinforce the text by providing more. For example:

A. Viewing the vivid movie Jaws gave many swimmers a fear of sharks, which no factual data on shark attacks would substantiate.

B. Many of us are more afraid of flying than driving (airplane crashes are vivid and memorable). But the truth is we are safer in commercial planes than driving to the same destination.

C. All physicians know about the statistical connection between smoking and lung cancer—and believe the connection to be causal. But it's radiologists and other physicians who treat lung cancer victims and who have seen the connection most vividly that are the least likely to smoke (Borgida & Nisbett, 1977).

D. Which method of generating electricity is more dangerous: with coal or with nuclear power? This question is, of course, more difficult to answer. Nuclear energy entails several risks, each of which are vivid and well-known (e.g., as a result of the disaster at Chernobyl). But the adverse effects of coal, currently the major alternative to nuclear power, are in the minds of some scientists, at least as great, though now less vivid (Brodansky, 1980). Burning coal puts carbon dioxide into the atmosphere. Eventually this could raise the earth's temperature, with disastrous consequences. And even if a nuclear accident claims hundreds of lives, coal mining will still have cost vastly more, through diseases and mining-related accidents.

E.   Let them eat anecdotes. How deserving are those who receive welfare? How rampant is welfare fraud? Careful studies have provided answers to such questions. But observers of former President Ronald Reagan have noted that when discussing such policy-related issues, he seemed more impressed by vivid anecdotes than by general statistics. Likewise, when the president told audiences about a young man who used food stamps to buy an orange, and then used the change to buy a bottle of vodka, he was exploiting the persuasive power of a vivid and memorable anecdote. One hopes that education in social psychology will enable students to better appreciate that such anecdotes may or may not be representative of what is generally true.

13. The Hot Hand: Finding Order in Random Events

Amos Tversky has demonstrated the everyday relevance of our inability to recognize a random sequence (see McKean, 1985). He notes that basketball players as well as fans believe that players tend to shoot in streaks. Presumably during a game a player may have a "hot hand" and thus can't miss. At other times he's cold and is hardly able to hit the backboard. Players may even attempt to work the ball to the hot hand.

Tversky and his colleagues interviewed Philadelphia 76ers coach Billy Cunningham and his players about shooting and then studied records of 48 of their games. While players estimated that they were 25 percent more likely to make a shot after a hit than after a miss, research found the opposite was true. The 76ers were 6 percent more likely to score after a miss than after a hit. Overall results indicated that the number of hot or cold streaks for four National Basketball Association teams was about what would be expected by chance. People forget, however, that random sequences often contain streaks simply by the laws of probability. Given that the average NBA player shoots about 50 percent from the floor, he has pretty good odds of making streaks of four, five, or even six due to the laws of chance alone.

14. Illusory Correlation

You can extend the text's discussion of illusory correlation with Gilovich's (1991) analysis of several folk beliefs including "It always rains right after you wash the car," "You always seem to need something just after you've thrown it away," "The phone always rings when you're in the shower," and "The elevator (or the bus) always seems to be heading in the wrong direction."

In analyzing these beliefs, Gilovich makes a useful distinction between "one-sided" and "two-sided" events. Events are two-sided if different outcomes produce the same intensity (if not the same kind) of emotion, or if they each necessitate further action on the part of the individual. Many times, however, events have only one outcome that arouses much affect or demands further action. As an example of a one-sided event, Gilovich cites how, in entering his office building through one of six possible doors, he often seems to find that the custodian has left that one and just that one locked. He writes, "I 'always' seem to select the locked door." The point is that a locked door arouses frustration and makes the event stand out in one's experience. Passing through an unlocked door gives rise to no emotion, requires no special effort, and goes unnoticed. Consequently, the locked doors stand out in one's memory and are the basis for the illusory correlation. If analyzed closely, the folk beliefs listed above have their basis in such "one-sided" events.

Gilovich also shows how this same process may work in close relationships, contributing, for example, to the common belief among couples that they are "out of sync." It seems one always wants to stay home when the other needs to socialize, or one wants to make love when the other "needs some space." Wanting to do something when the other doesn't can be frustrating and it can occupy one's mind for some time. When things go smoothly, events are less noteworthy. Even when they do stand out, they tend to do so by virtue of the quality of the events themselves, and not by virtue of the synchrony that produced them. They are remembered as instances of laughter, passion, or fun, and not as instances of synchrony.

15. Describe Original Illusory Correlation Research

The illusory correlation effect was first experimentally identified by Chapman (1967). Chapman exposed students to a series of word pairs. These words were paired so that each word was presented with several other words and all word pairs were seen equally as often. Given this organization, there was no built-in association between any word-pair. This methodology can be described rather easily in class. Simply generate two lists of five words (make them all about the same length for reasons I'll note later) and have "eggs" in one list and "bacon" in the other. Explain how each possible pair of words containing one word from list "A" and one word from list "B" were paired together and presented equally often to the participants (five times each). Then inform them that Chapman asked participants to estimate the percentage of total occurrences of all possible word pairs. Upon analysis, Chapman found that words having some form of inherent association between them (e.g., eggs-bacon) were perceived to occur together more frequently than the other word pairs—an illusory correlation. Another version of Chapman's experiment played on a different form of association. This time there were no inherent associations between word meanings, but rather in the length of the words. In each list, there was one word significantly longer than the others (e.g., blossoms and notebook in lists with other words with only four or five letters). When Chapman asked participants to estimate the percentage of total occurrence for each word pair, the percentage of pairing of the two unusually long words was overestimated. Again, an illusory correlation. In each case, it is regulable to explain the findings by suggesting different pairs of words were more or less memorable than other word pairs. For this reason, some have suggested that the illusory correlation is best understood as a result of the availability heuristic (some pairs are easier to remember than others).

16. Regression Toward the Average

The phenomenon of regression toward the average (or mean) was noted already by Sir Francis Galton in the nineteenth century (McKean, 1985). He observed that in any series of random clustering around an average, an extraordinary event is, by mere chance, more likely to be followed by an ordinary event. Thus very tall fathers will likely have slightly shorter sons and very short fathers somewhat taller sons. Regression to the average helps explain why great movies are often followed by poor sequels, why poor presidents have better successors, and why extremely intelligent women tend to have slightly duller husbands.

Regression to the average operates with regularity in sports, particularly where some luck is mixed with skill. While sports commentators recognize its effect, they often offer different explanations. Amos Tversky notes, "Listen to the commentators at the Winter Olympics. If a ski jumper has done well on his last jump, they say, He's under immense pressure, so he's unlikely to do as well this time.' If he did poorly, they say, He's very loose and can only improve.'"

Perhaps the so-called "Sports Illustrated Jinx" can also be understood in terms of regression to the average. Presumably if an athlete appeared on the cover of Sports Illustrated, his or her future would be clouded. Typically an athlete's performance became worse after this specific publicity. Some observers have noted, however, that athletes appear on the cover only after performing unusually well. Regression to the average would explain their poorer subsequent performance.

17. Self-Fulfilling Prophecy

The classic instance of self-fulfilling prophecy is probably the case of Clever Hans (Pfungst, 1965)—not to be confused with Freud's case of Little Hans! It's a delightful story that could be told to provide some historical background to the chapter section on self-fulfilling beliefs.

Robert Rosenthal (1994) provides an excellent overview of the research on self-fulfilling prophecy from the early laboratory studies, through Pygmalion effects in the classroom, to current research in management, the courtroom, and nursing homes. In this summary, Rosenthal also reviews his four-factor "theory" of how teacher expectations are communicated to students. One central factor is the "climate" in which teachers appear to create a warmer socio-emotional environment for their "special" students. This warmth is in part communicated through nonverbal cues. Another central factor is "input." Teachers seem to teach both more material and more difficult material to their "special" students. Additional factors include "output" and "feedback." That is, teachers appear to give their "special" students greater opportunities to respond. These are offered both verbally and nonverbally, e.g., giving students more time to answer a question. Teachers also seem to give their "special" students more informative feedback, again both verbal and nonverbal, as to how they are performing.

18. Applications of Research on Social Beliefs and Judgments

Hopefully the literature of this chapter will strengthen students' critical thinking skills. You can conclude this chapter by giving them some practice in applying what they have learned. One useful strategy for doing this is to present some popular yet questionable belief and ask them to analyze the possible sources of the belief and factors that maintain it. For example, they might examine the belief in facilitated communication, which is used in the treatment of autistic children. "Prisoners of Silence," a 1993 PBS production (Call 800-344-3337 to order), provides excellent coverage of the history and controversy surrounding the FC movement. Or they might examine belief in alien abduction. PBS's 1996 "Kidnapped by UFOs?" (Call 800-344-3337 to order) provides a fascinating survey of this belief including an interview with Elizabeth Loftus on memory construction. Still, a third possibility is the treatment called EMDR, or "eye-movement desensitization and reprocessing," in which counselors pass two fingers rapidly back and forth in front of the client's face. ABC's 20/20 segment entitled "When All Else Fails" and broadcast July 29, 1994 (Call 800-913-3434 to order), covers this therapy. It will stimulate a lively classroom discussion.

19. Popular Sources for Additional Classroom Material

Fiske, S., & Taylor, S. (1991). Social cognition, 2nd ed. New York: McGraw-Hill. A comprehensive, state-of-the-art introduction to how we form impressions and social beliefs and how we explain people's behavior.

Gilovich, T. (1991). How we know what isn't so. New York: Free Press. Discusses the fallibility of human reason in everyday life. Includes treatment of belief in ESP and in ineffective "alternative" health practices.

Kahneman, D., Slovic, P., & Tversky, A. (Eds.). (1999). Judgment under uncertainty: Heuristics and biases. Cambridge: Cambridge University Press. A classic collection of 35 articles on various topics including representativeness, attribution, availability, and overconfidence.

Levy, D.A. (1997). Tools of critical thinking: Metathoughts for psychology. Needham Heights, MA: Allyn & Bacon. Separate chapters explore biases described in the text including the fundamental attribution error, confirmation bias, and the belief perseverance. Emphasis is on applications and includes exercises that activate the learner.

Lynn, S. J. & Pyne, D. G. (Eds). (June 1997). <u>Current directions in psychological science</u>. This special issue of the helpful APS journal is devoted to the most recent research on false memories and includes articles by Elizabeth Loftus, Daniel Schacter, and Stephen Ceci.

Plous, S. (1993). <u>The psychology of judgment and decision making</u>. New York: McGraw-Hill. Examines heuristics, biases, and common traps in decision making. Introduces important principles of perception and memory, as well as models of decision making. Describes social influences on judgment.

Roese, N. J., & Olson, J. M. (Eds.) (1995). <u>What might have been: The social psychology of counterfactual thinking</u>. Hillsdale, NJ: Erlbaum. Surveys the work on counterfactual thinking. Examines its operation in judgments of causation and blame as well as in emotional experiences such as regret, elation, and sympathy. Considers the mechanisms underlying counterfactual thinking and its consequences for the individual.

Ross, L., & Nisbett, R. (1991). <u>The person and the situation</u>. New York: McGraw-Hill. Includes discussion of the attribution process and the fundamental attribution error.

Shermer, M. (1997). <u>Why people believe weird things: Pseudoscience, superstition, and other confusions of our time</u>. New York: W. H. Freeman. Describes fallacies of everyday thinking that lead to false beliefs. Examines belief in UFOs and various psychic phenomena as well as denial of the Holocaust.

DEMONSTRATION AND PROJECT IDEAS

Chapter 3 begs to be taught primarily through classroom demonstrations. Students will surely be intrigued by these cognitive biases once they have experienced them. Our own experience with these demonstrations triggers a note of caution: remember that these are not intended as an intellectual magic show designed to leave students feeling foolish. Rather, the overarching objective of the demonstrations—and of this chapter—is close to the heart of liberal education: to enable students to think more clearly and critically. We group these using the organizational scheme of the chapter.

1. Introducing Attribution Theory

Attribution theory can be introduced with Demonstration 3-1. We tend to attribute someone's behavior either to internal causes (for example, ability or effort) or <u>external</u> causes (for example, task difficulty or luck). The alternative forms come from Shirley Feldman-Summers and Sara Kiesler's (1974) research and can be used to consider the attributional differences for male and female success. Distribute each version to half the class. Females who succeed in traditionally masculine activities are often seen as less competent than a similarly successful male. However, their unusual luck or high motivation may offset their presumed lesser abilities.

Carole Wade and Carol Tavris suggest another simple, effective way of introducing attribution theory. Have students write down the first word or phrase that comes to mind in response to, "Most people are. . . ." After students have completed the exercise have volunteers share their answers. Next have students judge their own responses as positive (compassionate, cheerful), negative (hostile, stupid), or neutral (married, busy). By a show of hands have males and females separately indicate the category into which their response falls. Wade and Tavris report that females typically make more positive attributions. Ask students to indicate the possible consequences of making positive or negative attributions as well as to speculate regarding the factors shaping our judgments.

2. Explaining Unexpected Versus Expected Events

Chapter 3 mentions that people analyze and discuss why things happened the way they did especially when the event in question is either negative or unexpected (Bohner & others, 1988; Weiner, 1985). People's tendency to only ask the "why" questions when the event is negative or unexpected can be demonstrated in class. Simply prepare a small collection of event descriptions before class. Make some of them common place and expected (a young child swings from his mother's arm as they walk from the car to the store) and makes at least one or two negative and/or unexpected (a man calmly walks into the bookstore, draws a handgun and shoots the cashier). After each scenario, ask students to write down what questions they would like to ask you for the purpose of elaborating upon the scene. You should find that students will 1) generate many more questions for the unexpected events (suggesting the need to explain is high) and 2) these questions should be much more likely to be "why" questions (Why did he shoot the cashier?).

3. Introducing Person Perception

Although it may involve some personal risk and thus demands some courage, you can also introduce person perception and attribution theory by asking students to give their impressions of you. Distribute a copy of Demonstration 3-2 to each member of your class, inserting "your social psychology instructor" in the blank. You might also have students judge such characteristics as your age and marital status; favorite music, food, and color; ideal vacation and hobbies; place of birth; and number of siblings. Have your students turn in their judgments anonymously; prepare a summary table and use the next class period to discuss the results. Robin Lashley (1987) suggests you use the exercise to illustrate the following principles of person perception:

1. Students' responses often reveal strongly stereotyped thinking, specifically the "teacher stereotype." Lashley notes that students judge the typical teacher to be married, conservative, an introverted individual who prefers dark colors, sedentary hobbies, and structured vacations. Other stereotypes surface as well—for example, those based on age, gender, and physical attractiveness.

2. First impressions are often important. In justifying their judgments students will often refer to events occurring early in the semester. In fact, students may have already formed impressions from your reputation on campus. Furthermore, students may have selectively perceived and recalled your behavior to fit their initial impressions.

3. Responses may be used to demonstrate the actor-observer difference in perception. To illustrate, you will need to disclose your self-ratings on these characteristics. You probably will most frequently report, It depends on the situation." Differences between your ratings and those of your students may be examples of the fundamental attribution error (they are wrong) or, if your perceptions are more favorable, examples of a self-serving bias (you are wrong).

4. Agreements between you and your students' judgments serve as instances of successful perception. Many of these reflect inferences made from physical appearance (a wedding ring to infer marital status, facial wrinkles to infer age, clothes to infer favorite color, to name a few).

5. One result of this exercise is that students will become aware of their implicit personality theories. We all have theories about which traits are correlated; which traits characterize persons of a particular age, gender, or occupation; and what causes specific behaviors. Most generally, person perception is an active process in which we go beyond the information given.

Lashley notes several benefits of this exercise. Students acquire a better understanding of person perception, they come to appreciate the relevance of this process to their own social interactions, and last but not least, they get to know their instructor better.

4. Positivity Bias

A simple classroom replication of Yechiel Klar and Eilath Giiladi's (1997) recent study of the positivity bias provides a good introduction to the perception of others and to the biases that contaminate our social beliefs. It also provides an excellent link between the self-serving bias discussed in Chapter 2 and research on social perception discussed in Chapter 3.

In a series of eight studies Klar and Giiladi found that research participants judged an anonymous student as better than the average student, as above the group median, and as better than most students on a variety of desirable traits. Before the class, prepare as many slips of paper as you have students, numbering them consecutively. Put them in a hat or box, and have each student randomly draw out a number. Next tell your class that you are going to have them number off, and each student should notice the person with the number he or she has just drawn. Then ask each student to rate the "Intelligence" (politeness, consideration, friendliness, generosity could also be used) of that person relative to others in the class using a scale from 0 to 100. What score would they expect that person deserves if 0 is the least polite person in class, 50 is the average person, and 100 is the most polite person? Have them write down the number and then collect them. In class or between classes, calculate the mean of the ratings. If Klar and Giiladi are right, most people should rate their designee with a score above 50. The bias is clear—most people in the class can't be above the class average.

5. The Fundamental Attribution Error

The fundamental attribution error can be introduced by attempting to replicate Nisbett et al.'s (1973) finding that people often attribute others' behavior to their disposition, while giving environmental reasons for their own behavior. Thus, someone might say, "Judy is friendly and John is cool, but with me it all depends on the situation."

Distribute two copies of Demonstration 3-2 to each student. Have them complete the scale twice, once for some prominent personality (e.g., Jay Leno, Bill Clinton, George W. Bush), and once for themselves (for "you"). When finished, have them count the number of times they circled "depends on the situation" on each sheet. Are they more willing to ascribe traits to the prominent personality (which could be you, the instructor, or some other professor of their choice) than to themselves? If so, why? Relate their answers—for example, "I see myself behaving differently in different situations; you I see behaving the same everyday"—to the explanations of the fundamental attribution error.

You can also ask students to write a sentence or two describing "why you have chosen your particular major," and "why your best friend has chosen his or her major." Then ask students to classify each of the two explanations as more <u>external</u> (something about the subject—"chemistry is a high paying field" or <u>internal</u> (something about the person—"she loves working with numbers"). This will stimulate students' awareness of the distinction between these two categories of attribution. It should also demonstrate the fundamental attribution "error": external factors will more often be invoked when explaining one's own behavior than when explaining the choices of one's best friend.

6. The Correspondence Bias

Lovaglia (2000) suggests preparing opposing speeches on a controversial topic (e.g., abortion, gun control) before class. Then, find two volunteers and usher them out into the hall. Give them the prepared speeches and ask them to present the speeches to the class. Have the other students rate the true attitude of the presenter toward the controversial subject. You should find that the students will display the correspondence bias (Jones and Harris, 1967). This may be explainable because of the students' ignorance of who actually prepared the speeches.

Next Lovaglia suggests you ask for two more volunteers and have the two previous volunteers hand-over, in plain view, the scripts to these two new volunteers. Give the new volunteers a moment to read the speeches over and prepare, and then have them present the speeches as well. Again, have the other students rate the true attitude of the presenter. Will students still assume that speech content corresponds to the true attitudes of the speakers? Lovaglia says "yes."

7. Our Preconceptions Control Our Interpretations and Memories

A. <u>Expectations and interpretations</u>. Our expectations control our processing of information and can be demonstrated with a simple word game. Instruct students to shout in unison the answers to some questions: "What do these letters spell?" (Write FOLK on the board.) "What do these letters spell?" (Write CROAK.) "What do these letters spell?" (Write SOAK.) "What do we call the white of an egg?" The response will be a chorus, "YOLK."

Fisher (1979) makes two good suggestions for demonstrating how expectations may influence our perceptions. Ask your class to shout out the number that follows each of these: 29...72...372...2623...4099.... Many, if not most, will follow the last with 5000 rather than the correct 4100. Or, conduct a spelling bee in reverse. Spell out a word, which a volunteer in the class must then pronounce. "MAC DONALD... MAC HENRY... MAC MAHON... MACHINERY...." Most will be trapped by expectations into pronouncing the last word as a fictitious Scottish surname.

✓ B. <u>Fabricated memories</u>. Read the following list of 21 words:

Henry Roediger, III and Kathleen McDermott's (1995) research demonstrates how easily we form false memories. To begin, you might tell students that you are going to demonstrate the superiority of recognition over recall memory. Ask them to listen carefully as you read a list of words. Then present the following words at about 1.5 second intervals:

note
sound
piano
sing
radio
melody
horn
concert
instrument
symphony
jazz
orchestra
art
rhythm

After reading the words, ask students to write down as many as they can recall on a blank sheet of paper. Then distribute a copy of Demonstration 3-3 to the students and have them complete it. Students are certain to recognize words they did not recall, demonstrating the superiority of recognition over recall. Finally, for the false memory, ask how many recalled and wrote down the word <u>music</u>. Also ask how many gave <u>music</u> on the handout a "3" or "4?" As many as half are likely to have recalled music and even more will say they recognized it.

C. <u>Memory construction</u>. Allport and Postman's (1947) classic book, <u>The Psychology of Rumor</u>, provides many examples of memory construction, and of <u>assimilating</u> events (interpreting and recalling them in ways compatible with our existing beliefs). Explain to the class that you are going to hand out to the first person in each row a paragraph to read (Demonstration 3-4). After the first person in each row has read it, he or she is to turn it over and write down on paper what can be remembered. This description is then read by the second person who, after turning it face down, writes as much as he or she can recall on a second sheet of paper. The procedure is repeated until reaching the last persons—who then read their descriptions to the class after you have read the original. What types of changes have been introduced? Does the knife ever shift (as in Allport and Postman's research) into the hand of the black person? (If so, you may want to point out that the last person in the row is not necessarily responsible for any given change in the story.)

Sheldon Lachman (1984) suggests a similar demonstration that can be carried out during a regular classroom lecture. A short story is whispered from one student to another until everyone has participated. With a class of 35, the process is easily completed in a 50-minute session. At the start of the class session, students count off in order and place their number at the top of a blank sheet of paper. Take the first student out of the room (or out of earshot) and ask her to listen closely to the story because she will have to write down all she can recall on the sheet of paper. Proceed to read the following:

> A crowded city bus stopped at Belmont Park at 4:30 p.m. Among the passengers were two males who stood next to each other toward the front of the bus. One was a tall, well-dressed black carrying a briefcase. The other had a knife in his belt and was shaking his left fist.

After she had finished writing, she was to whisper her written report to the second student, who repeats the same steps. At the end of the period, write the story on the board beside the story written by the last student. Collect all of the story transcriptions and place them in order. You can analyze them for the distortions identified by Allport and Postman or, better yet, type and duplicate the protocols for analysis in class. In addition to assimilation, Allport and Postman identified two other common distortions: With leveling, perceivers drop certain details because they do not fit their cognitive categories or assumptions, and with sharpening, the details of the story that are consistent with the values and interpretations of the observer are emphasized.

8. The Monty Hall Three-Door Problem

The text discusses responses to the Monty Hall dilemma in the context of belief perseverance (See Focus box). Invite students to visit the Monty Hall Three Door Dilemma Web site at www.cut-the-knot.com/hall.html. The site explains the problem, asks visitors what they would do, and then invites them to test their strategy with a series of 10 choices. The tutorial vividly demonstrates that switching is the better strategy and offers several explanations for it.

The Monty Hall dilemma can also be easily demonstrated in class. Simply take three '4 × 6' cards and write 'WINNER' on one card and 'LOSER' on the other two (you may want to tape two cards together so that the writing cannot be seen through the other side of the card). Shuffle the cards and display them on the board or podium. Then have students pick a "door" (card). After they have chosen a door, privately look at the two "doors" not chosen and turn over one that has the word 'LOSER' written on it. Then ask the class if they'd like to switch. If they don't, they will only have a 1/3 chance of getting the 'WINNER' card. If, however, they switch, they will have 2/3 chance of getting the 'WINNER' card. You can explain that only if they originally picked the right card (1/3 chance) will they be better off staying put. Because the game forces one 'LOSER' card to be exposed after a choice has been made, the remaining unselected card now has a 2/3's probability of being the 'WINNER.' Once one trial is done, simply shuffle the three cards and do it again. It only takes about 10 to 15 trials to convert even the strongest skeptic.

9. We Overestimate the Accuracy of Our Beliefs

The exercises of this section will a) demonstrate the overconfidence phenomenon, and b) demonstrate the related bias toward confirming rather than disconfirming our beliefs.

A. <u>Overconfidence on exams</u>? As they leave an exam, do students tend to overestimate their exam performance? We have found they often do, particularly with the first test in the course. After your students have completed taking a social psychology test, have them predict their own score by writing their prediction on the top or back of the test or answer sheet. How many prove to be overconfident? The text reports that people who are given precise, repeated feedback on the accuracy of their judgments do <u>not</u> experience overconfidence. Weather forecasters and horse racing oddsmakers accurately estimate the likelihood of their predictions being fulfilled. Might we also expect that students' overconfidence will decline as they receive feedback on subsequent tests in the course?

B. <u>Overconfidence in the estimation of uncertain quantities</u>. In Demonstration 3-5, students attempt to provide a range that will include the true answer. If they correctly estimate their own likelihood of error, then the percentage of surprises should be two percent—one student wrong per item in a class of 50. The actual proportion of surprises will be more than 10 times that. Count the number of surprised students for each item after providing the answers:

1. 1,867,794 cars
2. 3.6 million square miles
3. 10.17 million people
4. 148,000 women lawyers and judges
5. 437 nuclear power plants

C. <u>Overconfident social judgments</u>. Our judgments of people are similarly vulnerable to overconfidence. A recent experiment by James Milojkovic and Lee Ross (1981) can be adapted to create an entertaining and memorable demonstration of this point (in fact, such an effective demonstration that, rather than report the experiment in the text, it has been reserved for your class use).

Distribute Demonstration 3-6 to the entire class and explain that, as a partial replication of Milojkovic and Ross (1981), you are going to test their ability to distinguish truths from lies. Further explain that you have put 10 slips in a hat, five of which say "tell the truth," and five of which say "tell a lie." Solicit a volunteer for each of the 10 topics, having each person draw one of these slips. Then invite each person to stand and tell his or her truth or lie, after which the remainder of the students are to guess whether it was a truth or a lie, and to indicate their confidence. When all the stories are told, have the volunteers reveal which statements were truthful and which were lies. Have the students then compute a) their percent correct out of 10, and b) their average confidence level. Finally, ask for a show of hands: "How many of you were more correct than confident?" (Few hands will rise.) "How many of you were more confident than correct?" (Most hands will rise.) You may further wish to compute the class average; Milojkovic and Ross report that their Stanford students were 52 percent correct and 73 percent confident, a result close to what we have obtained using the materials of Demonstration 3-6. Milojkovic and Ross also report that when people were 90 to 100 percent confident, they were not more correct than when they were only 50 to 65 percent confident.

D. <u>The bias to verify rather than falsify our beliefs</u>. The text suggests that one reason for the overconfidence phenomenon is that people search for confirming evidence rather than attempting to disconfirm their hunches. Demonstration 3-7 provides materials to replicate Wason's (1960) experiment described in the text. This demonstration would need to be conducted BEFORE students read the chapter, or perhaps by having the students each test several friends. Invite the students to generate sets of three numbers in an effort to discover the rule to which the first three numbers conform. (The rule is simply any three ascending numbers.) After they generate each set they should pause to let you indicate whether their set conforms or does not conform to the rule. After they are confident they have discovered the rule they should simply write it down and ask you to check it. Unless the class is very small, time will not permit you to get around to everyone a sufficient number of times. Nevertheless, most people will immediately begin generating sets of numbers that seek to verify rather than disprove their hunches. After enough such attempts at verification, many will have convinced themselves of a wrong rule—a mistake they could have avoided had they tested their hunch by seeking to falsify it.

E. <u>The four-card problem</u>. The confirmatory bias can also be illustrated in another demonstration, one not reported in the text. Put the following numbers and letters on four index cards:

	First side	Second side
Card 1	D	3
Card 2	3	D
Card 3	B	6
Card 4	7	D

Now place the cards with the first sides facing the class and pose the following problem:

Pretend someone were to show you four cards, each with a letter on one side and a number on the other. The sides facing up show D, 3, B, and 7. What cards would they need to turn over to test this rule [read slowly]: "If there is a D on one side of any card, there is a 3 on the other."

After students have written their answers you can invite verbal responses. Most people first want to turn over the D to attempt to verify the rule. That is fine, as you can demonstrate by turning the card. Then most people want to turn over the 3—again trying to verify the rule. So, since there is indeed a "D" on the other side, these students should be satisfied that the rule has been verified. (Actually, if the 3 had some other letter on the second side that would not have disproven the rule.) Ask finally: "How many of you chose card 7 as your first or second choice?" Reveal the "D" on the other side, which disproves the rule. Also, point out the deeper lesson that this has demonstrated: "By seeking only to <u>confirm</u> your idea, those of you who did <u>not</u> choose card 7 failed to detect a falsehood. Had you instead tested the idea by attempting to <u>disconfirm</u> it, you would have stepped closer to truth. In science, and in everyday life, we should find most credible those ideas that not only are seemingly confirmed by available evidence, but also withstand attempts to falsify them."

Peter Wason (1981), whose experiment that this demonstration is adapted from, reports that even after the falsifying card is revealed, most undergraduate students fail to see the error of their ways and correct their solution:

> The subject talks as if he were deluded; his attention is funnelled on his first decision; he contradicts himself in a way in which he would not do ordinarily; and he denies the very facts that confront him . . . . This incorrigible conviction that they are right when they are, in fact, wrong has analogies to real life crises of belief. Anyone who has campaigned for minority causes, such as unilateral nuclear disarmament . . . will know how ordinary people evade facts, become inconsistent, or systematically defend themselves against the threat of new information relevant to the issue.

Perhaps, however, your students are less incorrigible. You can test their ability to apply the principle just taught by using another of Wason's (and Johnson-Laird's, 1968) four-card problems. This time again present four cards: 1) a black circle (with a black triangle on the other side), 2) a red circle (with a black triangle on the other side), 3) a red triangle (with a black circle on the other side), 4) a black triangle (with a red circle on the other side). Questions: "Assuming that each card has a triangle on one side and a circle on the other, which card or cards need to be turned over to test the validity of this statement: Every card that has a black triangle on one side has a red circle on the other?" Most untutored people answer "black triangle" or "black triangle and red circle," thus looking for instances that would confirm the statement. The correct answer is black triangle (which would confirm the rule) and black circle (which would disprove the rule).

Your tutored students will likely generalize some of their learning on the first four-card problem to the second four-card problem, thus giving more correct solutions to the second. But can they generalize the general principle to a more dissimilar problem? Plan an inverted form of the game "Twenty Questions" in class (Penrose, 1962). In the ordinary game, a person asks questions of increasing specificity in order to discover a particular example. In the inverted game, a person thinks of a general class that others have to discover by finding out whether specific instances fall under it. For example, Penrose selected the general class of "living things" and gave as the initial example, "A Siamese cat." Questioners should be told to announce an answer to the class only when they are highly confident they have discovered it. Among untutored students, a tendency to verify rather than to disconfirm hypotheses occurs and it interferes with identification of the correct solution.

10. We Often Ignore Useful Information

A. <u>The impact of vivid events</u>. People typically overrecall vivid information that is more available to memory. Demonstration 3-8 provides a demonstration of the memorability of vivid events. It is also structured to provide yet another demonstration of overconfidence (since most students will be more confident than correct). On each question, Fischhoff, Slovic, and Lichtenstein (1977) report that the second cause of death—usually the more quiet cause—is actually far more prevalent:

<u>Deaths Per 100 Million Americans</u>

Homicide (9,200) vs. Diabetes (19,000)

Flood (100) vs. Infectious hepatitis (330)

All accidents (55,000) vs. Strokes (102,000)

All cancers (160,000) vs. Heart disease (360,000)

Tornados (44) vs. Asthma (920)

Drowning (3,600) vs. Leukemia (7,100)

Lightning (52) vs. Appendicitis (440)

Motor vehicle accidents (27,000) vs. Cancer of the digestive system (46,400)

Many people are <u>very</u> confident of their erroneous responses to these items. Why? Because they are insensitive to the invalidity of their "availability heuristic" (which uses ease of recall as one's clue to actual frequency).

B. <u>The availability heuristic and the news media</u>. Does the media sometimes lead us to distort frequency estimation by overexposing us to some events and underexposing us to others? Pose the following question to your students:

The FBI classifies crime in the United States into two categories—<u>violent crimes</u>, such as murder, rape, robbery, and assault, and <u>property crime</u>, such as burglary, larceny, or car theft. What percent of crimes would you estimate are violent rather than property crimes? What percent of accused felons plead that they are innocent by reason of insanity? What percent are acquitted? What percent of convictions for felony crimes are obtained through trial instead of plea-bargaining?

The answer to the first question is 13 percent. In 1995, there were 1,798,790 violent crimes reported and 12,068,400 property crimes. Less than 1 percent of all accused felons plead insanity and only a quarter of those are ultimately acquitted. Less than 10 percent of convictions for felony crimes are obtained through a trial; more than 90 percent result from plea-bargaining. However, aided by the news media's reporting, we tend to overestimate the number of violent crimes, pleas of insanity, and trials because they are more available to memory.

Demonstration 3-9 is based on a <u>Time</u> magazine report, January 13, 1986, p. 35. Give each student a copy to read. At some later point (e.g., end of class period or next class period) ask everyone to "assume that everything <u>Time</u> reported is true and continues to be true. Imagine, then, a frequent traveler who over the next five years showed up for 300 People's Express flights for which he or she had a reservation. Roughly how many times out of 300 attempts to board planes would you expect the traveler to be bumped because People's didn't have room?" Get a show of hands for answer. Explain that the correct statistical answer, assuming that everything <u>Time</u> reported is true, is 10/10,000 = 1/1000 - .33/300 = <u>0</u> times every 300 flights. Most students will answer more than 0, because the <u>vivid</u> tales of woe are, after a time, more <u>available</u> in memory than the dry statistical fact.

C. <u>Representativeness and probability judgments</u>. The text provides examples of how we judge the likelihood of things in terms of how well they represent or match a particular prototype. You can also demonstrate how representativeness leads to error by asking students to imagine they are offered a bet. A die with four green sides and two red ones will be rolled several times. They can be paid $25 if RGRRR or GRGRRR occurs. Write each on the chalkboard. Which sequence do they think is more likely to pay off? Most will choose GRGRRR. When Amos Tversky and Daniel Kahneman presented this choice, either hypothetically or by offering hard cash, at least two-thirds chose that sequence. While the sequence is more <u>representative</u> of a die with four green faces, in reality it is only two-thirds as likely because it is the same as the first alternative with the addition of a "G" (which has the probability of two-thirds on any given roll).

D. <u>The base-rate fallacy</u>. The text defines the base-rate fallacy as the tendency to ignore or underuse base-rate information, and instead to be influenced by the distinctive features of the case being judged. You can easily demonstrate this fallacy by posing the following problem Casscells and his colleagues (1978) gave to doctors and medical students: If a test to detect a disease whose prevalence is 1 in 1000 has a false positive rate of 5 percent (false positive rate is the percentage of times the test mistakenly indicates that the disease is present), what is the chance that a person found to have a positive result actually has the disease, assuming you know nothing else about the person? The researchers found that the most common answer was 95 percent. The correct answer is about 2 percent. Respondents tend to give too much weight to the case information and too little to the base-rate information. In explaining the correct answer, remind your students that only 1 in 1000 has the disease. When the test is given to the 999 who do not have it, it will identify about 50 as having it (.05 × 999). Thus of the 51 patients testing positive only one (approximately 2 percent) will actually have it. In brief, the base rate indicates that the overwhelming majority of people do not have the disease. Combined with a substantial false positive rate, this ensures that the vast majority of positive tests will be from people who do not have the disease.

11. Illusions of Causation, Correlation, and Personal Control

The "gambler's fallacy" is an example of illusory correlation. The gambler believes that later chance outcomes will balance early trends in the opposite direction, as if the early results somehow force or influence the later results. You can demonstrate the gambler's fallacy, if you are willing to temporarily deceive your students. You will flip a coin a number of times. Each time before you flip, have them record their guess. As you flip the coin five times record the following fake outcomes on the board: 1) tails, 2) heads, 3) tails, 4) tails, 5) tails. After they write their sixth guess, pause and ask them to agree that the outcome of the next toss is pure chance. Say, "Since it is 50-50 whether it will be heads or tails, half of you should predict each, right?" However, a show of hands will reveal that heads have been predicted by a 3 to 1 margin or more. Say, You folks don't seem to think this toss is a chance event. And that is called the 'gambler's fallacy.'"

Our flawed statistical intuition interferes with our recognizing chance events for what they are. If a sequence of events does not look random, then we will want to concoct some explanation for it. Thus if a family has four children—all girls—we may wonder whether the father is deficient in Y chromosomes.

The two versions of Demonstration 3-10 (adapted from Kahneman & Tversky, 1972) allow you not only to illustrate flawed statistical intuition, but also to teach two simple principles and to give students the satisfaction of knowing they have learned something. Give half of the class each version, asking them to complete only the first two items.

On Item #1, Kahneman and Tversky report that Israeli students are totally insensitive to the simple principle that statistical variability decreases as sample size increases. The odds of getting more than 60 percent girls in a sample of 1,000 babies (which are essentially zero) is not perceived as far less than the odds of getting more than 60 percent girls in a sample of 10 babies (roughly 40 percent). Believe it or not. To clarify by analogy, the odds of flipping six or more heads in 10 coin flips are reasonably good. The odds of getting 600 or more heads in 1000 tosses are infinitesimal. Point out that this dramatic failure to consider sample size leads people to be too confident of exact percentage results derived from small numbers of people, and not trusting enough of percentage results derived from large, representative samples of people.

On Item #2, people tend to see outcome "C" as more likely than outcomes "A" or "B." You can ask How many put answers less than 50 for 'A'? For 'B'?" (Most hands will likely rise.) How many put an answer of more than 50 to "C"? (Again, most hands will rise.) Actually, any given sequence is equally likely. The sequence that looks less random is actually no less likely than one that looks more random.

Now invite them to answer Items #3 and #4, which retest the sample principles. Kahneman and Tversky found that only 20 percent of their subjects realized that greater variability can be expected in the samples drawn from the smaller hospital. Do more than 20 percent of your students correctly answer "B" to Item #3? If so, you can congratulate them for apparently having learned something. And do students now recognize that any given sequence of cards is equally improbable?

Having learned that statistical variability decreases as sample size increases, your students should have little difficulty with these questions suggested by Gordon Wood (1984):

1. Assume you are playing tennis with a friend whose skill is a bit better than yours. Your friend suggests you play a little longer, with the loser buying dinner for the winner. If you want to increase your chances of winning, how much tennis should you play, given the choices of a single game, one set, or a match consisting of three sets?

2. Assume you are an above-average golfer and you have the opportunity to play the greatest golfer in the world. If you want to maximize your slim chance of winning should you elect to play 1, 18, 36, or 72 holes?

12. The Illusion of Control

Stephen J. Dollinger (1986) suggests a brief classroom demonstration for introducing the illusion of control and the overconfidence phenomenon. It provides an excellent introduction to Ellen Langer's research on gambling behavior and on how we are easily seduced into believing we can beat chance.

Ask for nine volunteers to participate in a brief card game. (You might inform the class that it's nonthreatening—they'll not even have to leave their seats.) Having identified the participants, present a standard deck of playing cards and announce that the student drawing the highest card will win $1.00. Distribute a sheet of paper to each student and tell the volunteers that after they have their cards, <u>but before looking at them</u>, they are to estimate their confidence in winning from 0 percent (absolutely no chance) to 100 percent (I'm certain I have the highest card). Tell them not to sign their sheets and indicate that you will not reveal their own individual estimate. For the first person, draw a card from the deck. For the second, and alternating thereafter, allow the student to select his or her own card. After all have a card and have indicated their probability estimates, collect the sheets of paper, carefully keeping the judgments of those given a card separate from those who have picked their own. After you have identified the winner and awarded the prize, calculate the mean estimates of the two groups. Dollinger reports that in his class those choosing their own card were significantly more confident of winning ($\underline{M}$ = 55 percent) than those whose card was assigned ($\underline{M}$ = 45 percent). Both groups were wildly overconfident given the base rate odds of about 11 percent.

13. Regression toward the Average

Jerzy Karylowski provides a simple classroom demonstration of regression to the average that will work with students having little or no background in statistics. Ask students if they will serve as your assistants in a study of aspiration level, a relatively stable personality dimension. Explain how both very low and very high aspiration levels are maladaptive. Also inform them that you believe you have a special psychic ability, which has therapeutic influence on those whose aspiration levels are either too high or too low. Go on to explain that although there are many ways to measure aspiration levels, none are perfect. A given test score will always be a function of at least two components: (a) the true score and (b) a combination of transient factors, such as the subject's mood, the subject's misunderstanding of some items, clerical errors in scoring, and so on.

Next, ask each student to think of three or four individuals they know well. A six-point scale will be used to test the subjects' aspiration levels. Scores 1 and 2 will indicate a tendency for aspirations to be lower than ability; scores 3 and 4 will indicate an appropriate aspiration level; and scores 5 and 6 will suggest an unrealistically high aspiration level. Testing proceeds as follows: First, each subject will be assigned a true score on the basis of any information or intuitions students have about him or her. Second, each subject will be assigned a transient-factor score based on die tossing or a number drawn out of a hat. Finally, assuming that true and transient scores are weighted equally, an average of the two will be the simulated test score.

After students have identified their subjects and obtained the simulated test scores, create a frequency distribution of all scores (they will range from 1 to 6) on the chalkboard. Select two extreme groups, the top 10 or 25 percent, and the bottom 10 or 25 percent. The top scores compose your high-aspiration group, the bottom scores your low-aspiration group. Have students note the scores, perhaps even calculating separate means for the entire distribution and for each of the extreme groups. Announce that one day has passed since you applied your psychic treatment and that students are to "retest" the subjects that fall into the extreme groups. Further, tell them that unless they believe in your psychic power, they should use the same true scores. Transient-factor scores, however, are to be assigned on the basis of a new round of die tossing.

Finally, tabulate the post-treatment results for both the low and high aspiration groups. Students will immediately see the regression toward the average effect. The post-treatment test scores for the high group will be lower and those for the low group will be higher.

14. Self-Serving and Self-Fulfilling Beliefs

Demonstration 3-11, suggested by John Brink, provides a replication of Steven Sherman's (1980) finding that people overestimate how desirably they would act were they to be approached unforewarned. You may want to modify the request to fit the specific needs of your department and attempt further replication of Sherman's finding that people tend to fulfill predictions they make of their own behavior. Of course, if the need is fictitious you will want to debrief your students immediately. Randomly distribute the two versions of Demonstration 3-11 to your class. Collect their responses and tabulate the percentage of volunteers in each group as well as the average number of hours they are willing to contribute. With a full replication also tabulate the number of volunteers who actually show and the hours they work. Are predictors of ourselves both self-serving and self-fulfilling?

15. Applying Research on Social Beliefs

Robert Abelson (personal communication) has suggested a project/paper that will give students practice in applying the social psychological principles of Chapters 2 and 3. Give students the following assignment:

> Take someone you know who holds what you regard as a ludicrous or at least false belief. Describe the belief. Then, drawing upon social psychological principles,

1. Indicate how it may have been formed.
2. Explain how it appears to be maintained.
3. Speculate how it might be changed.

16. The Social Connection Video Series

One of the entries in the video instructional supplement (The Social Connection Video Series), entitled "Eyewitness Memory," is pertinent to Loftus's pioneering work on the misinformation effect introduced in Chapter 3. Another entry, entitled "The Fundamental Attribution Error," is also highly relevant for discussions concerning Chapter 3. See the Faculty Guide accompanying the video series for program summaries, pause points, and classroom activities.

Demonstration 3-1

(with permission of S. Feldman-Summers)

Carefully read the following account of Dr. Mark Greer.

After finishing medical school, Mark Greer went to New York University Hospital where he completed both his internship and residency in general surgery. Though his obligations as a resident took up most of his time, Mark volunteered to work part-time in a Harlem health clinic, which was considerably understaffed. There he reorganized the surgery services to improve the post-operative care of the patients.

When his residency in surgery was completed, he returned to his hometown—Santa Clara, California.

After two years in Santa Clara, Dr. Greer has almost doubled the size of his practice, and is ready to hire another doctor as his partner. Mark's interest in good surgical care and his boundless energy have resulted in increased community activities to improve health care for the poor. This year he received an award naming him Santa Clara's Doctor of the Year. He is the youngest doctor to have received the award.

How much did each of the following factors contribute to Dr. Greer's success? Express your hunch by circling a number below each of the four factors.

1. Ability as a doctor:
   Not at all   0 1 2 3 4 5 6 7 8 9   To a great extent
2. Motivation to be successful as a doctor:
   Not at all   0 1 2 3 4 5 6 7 8 9   To a great extent
3. The ease of the goal:
   Not at all   0 1 2 3 4 5 6 7 8 9   To a great extent
4. Good luck:
   Not at all   0 1 2 3 4 5 6 7 8 9   To a great extent

Demonstration 3-1

(with permission of S. Feldman-Summers)

Carefully read the following account of Dr. Marcia Greer.

After finishing medical school, Marcia Greer went to New York University Hospital where she completed both her internship and residency in general surgery. Though her obligations as a resident took up most of her time, Marcia volunteered to work part-time in a Harlem health clinic, which was considerably understaffed. There she reorganized the surgery services to improve the post-operative care of the patients.

When her residency in surgery was completed, she returned to her hometown—Santa Clara, California.

After two years in Santa Clara, Dr. Greer has almost doubled the size of her practice, and is ready to hire another doctor as her partner. Marcia's interest in good surgical care and her boundless energy have resulted in increased community activities to improve health care for the poor. This year she received an award naming her Santa Clara's Doctor of the Year. She is the youngest doctor to have received the award.

How much did each of the following factors contribute to Dr. Greer's success? Express your hunch by circling a number below each of the four factors.

1. Ability as a doctor:
   Not at all   0 1 2 3 4 5 6 7 8 9   To a great extent
2. Motivation to be successful as a doctor:
   Not at all   0 1 2 3 4 5 6 7 8 9   To a great extent
3. The ease of the goal:
   Not at all   0 1 2 3 4 5 6 7 8 9   To a great extent
4. Good luck:
   Not at all   0 1 2 3 4 5 6 7 8 9   To a great extent

Demonstration 3-2

(with permission of R. Nisbett)

For each of the following 20 pairs of traits, circle the one trait in each pair, which is most characteristic of _____ . If neither of the traits in a trait pair is the most characteristic, indicate that by circling "depends on the situation."

serious	fun-loving	depends on the situation
subjective	analytic	depends on the situation
future oriented	present oriented	depends on the situation
energetic	relaxed	depends on the situation
unassuming	self-asserting	depends on the situation
lenient	firm	depends on the situation
reserved	emotionally expressive	depends on the situation
dignified	casual	depends on the situation
realistic	idealistic	depends on the situation
intense	calm	depends on the situation
skeptical	trusting	depends on the situation
quiet	talkative	depends on the situation
cultivated	natural	depends on the situation
sensitive	tough-minded	depends on the situation
self-sufficient	sociable	depends on the situation
steady	flexible	depends on the situation
dominant	deferential	depends on the situation
cautious	bold	depends on the situation
uninhibited	self-controlled	depends on the situation
conscientious	happy-go-lucky	depends on the situation

Demonstration 3-3
Bolt & Myers
©McGraw-Hill, 1999

Using the scale below, indicate whether you think each of the following words was read:

    4 = I'm sure I heard the word
    3 = I think I heard the word
    2 = I think the word is new
    1 = I'm sure the word is new

_____ 1. concert
_____ 2. rhythm
_____ 3. radio
_____ 4. art
_____ 5. orchestra
_____ 6. melody
_____ 7. music
_____ 8. note
_____ 9. jazz
_____ 10. symphony
_____ 11. sound
_____ 12. piano
_____ 13. horn
_____ 14. instrument
_____ 15. sing

Demonstration 3-4

Bolt & Myers

©**McGraw-Hill, 1999**

A crowded city bus stopped at Belmont Park at 4:30 p.m. Included among the passengers was a college student reading a magazine. Next to him a young woman wearing sunglasses talked to a small boy sitting in front of her. Across the aisle an elderly man with a cane and pipe carefully observed two other male passengers who stood next to each other toward the front of the bus. One was a tall, well-dressed black carrying a briefcase. The other had a knife in his belt and was shaking his left fist. Two signs above the windows read "Eat at Joe's" and "Vote for McGinnis."

Demonstration 3-5

Bolt & Myers

©McGraw-Hill, 1999

1. I feel 98 percent certain that the number of Japanese cars imported into the United States in 1990 was more than _____ but less than _____.

2. I feel 98 percent certain that the area of the United States is more than _____ square miles but less than _____ square miles.

3. I feel 98 percent certain that the population of Belgium is more than _____ but less than _____.

4. I feel 98 percent certain that in 1993 the number of women lawyers and judges in the United States was more than _____ but less than _____.

5. I feel 98 percent certain that in 1995 the number of operating nuclear plants in the world was more than _____ but less than _____.

Demonstration 3-6

(with permission of J. Milojkovic)

		Guess: Did the speaker tell the <u>truth or a lie?</u>	I am ___percent confident that my <u>guess is correct</u> *
1.	Something that happened to me during grade school	_____	_____
2.	My favorite meal	_____	_____
3.	My earliest memory	_____	_____
4.	My favorite vacation trip	_____	_____
5.	A high point of my high school days	_____	_____
6.	The most influential person in my life	_____	_____
7.	My favorite prof outside the psych department	_____	_____
8.	The part of the country in which I'd most like to live	_____	_____
9.	A surprising talent that I have	_____	_____
10.	Something interesting about a member of my family	_____	_____

*Estimates can range from 50 percent (I'm guessing—it's 50-50) to 100 percent (I'm absolutely sure).

Demonstration 3-7

Conforms to the Rule   Does Not Conform to the Rule

2, 4, 6

Demonstration 3-8

Which of the following are the more frequent causes of death in the United States?

1. Homicide or diabetes?
   I feel ___ percent sure of my answer*
2. Flood or infectious hepatitis?
   I feel ___ percent sure of my answer
3. All accidents or strokes?
   I feel ___ percent sure of my answer
4. All cancers or heart disease?
   I feel ___ percent sure of my answer
5. Tornados or asthma?
   I feel ___ percent sure of my answer
6. Drowning or leukemia?
   I feel ___ percent sure of my answer
7. Lightning or appendicitis?
   I feel ___ percent sure of my answer
8. Motor vehicle accident or cancer of the digestive system?
   I feel ___ percent sure of my answer

*Estimates can range from 50 percent (I'm guessing—it's 50-50) to 100 percent (I'm absolutely sure).

Demonstration 3-9

Airlines make a practice of overbooking their flights with the justification that many customers who make reservations do not show up. Overbooking, however, can result in some customers being bumped from their flights. Seats are assigned at the airport on a first-come, first-served basis to passengers with reservations. Time magazine recently reported that while all airlines overbook, People's Express is the worst offender. About 10 to 12 passengers per 10,000 are bumped from People flights, twice the industry average. It is not uncommon for veteran People flyers to arrive at least an hour in advance to make sure they get on board! Customers with reservations who fail to obtain a seat receive compensation—typically a place on a later flight and a free ticket for a future round trip on any of People's U.S. routes.

Demonstration 3-10

1. In a certain region, 1,000 babies are born every day. As you know, about 50 percent of all babies are girls. On what percentage of days will the number of girls be 60 percent or more of the 1000 babies?

2. Pretend that all families with six children in a city were surveyed. In 72 families, the exact order of births of boys and girls was G B G B B G. Given this much information, what is your estimate of the number of families in which the exact order of births was:

    _____a. B G B B B B

    _____b. B B B G G G

    _____c. G B B G B G

3. A certain town is served by two hospitals. In the larger hospital, about 45 babies are born each day, and in the smaller hospital, about 15 babies are born each day. The exact percentage of baby boys varies from day to day. Sometimes it may be higher than 50 percent, sometimes lower.

    In a period of one year, each hospital recorded the days on which more than 60 percent of the babies were boys. Which hospital do you think recorded more such days?

    _____a. The larger hospital

    _____b. The smaller hospital

    _____c. About the same (within 5 percent of each other)

4. On each round of a card game, the deck is shuffled and four cards are dealt each player. On one round, Ted was dealt a 3 of hearts, 8 of spades, queen of diamonds, and a 7 of hearts. Sharon was dealt the king of diamonds and the aces of diamonds, hearts, and spades. Which set of cards is the more improbable?

    _____a. Ted's

    _____b. Sharon's

    _____c. They are equally improbable

(From Kahneman, D., & Tversky, A. Subjective probability: A judgment of representativeness. Cognitive Psychology, 1972, 3, p. 430–454. Used with permission.)

Demonstration 3-10

1. In a certain region, 1,000 babies are born every day. As you know, about 50 percent of all babies are girls. On what percentage of days will the number of girls be 60 percent or more of the 1000 babies?

2. Pretend that all families with six children in a city were surveyed. In 72 families, the exact order of births of boys and girls was G B G B B G. Given this much information, what is your estimate of the number of families in which the exact order of births was:

    _____ a. B G B B B B

    _____ b. B B B G G G

    _____ c. G B B G B G

3. A certain town is served by two hospitals. In the larger hospital, about 45 babies are born each day, and in the smaller hospital, about 15 babies are born each day. The exact percentage of baby boys varies from day to day. Sometimes it may be higher than 50 percent, sometimes lower.

    In a period of one year, each hospital recorded the days on which more than 60 percent of the babies were boys. Which hospital do you think recorded more such days?

    _____ a. The larger hospital

    _____ b. The smaller hospital

    _____ c. About the same (within 5 percent of each other)

4. On each round of a card game, the deck is shuffled and four cards are dealt each player. On one round, Ted was dealt a 3 of hearts, 8 of spades, queen of diamonds, and a 7 of hearts. Sharon was dealt the king of diamonds and the aces of diamonds, hearts, and spades. Which set of cards is the more improbable?

    _____ a. Ted's

    _____ b. Sharon's

    _____ c. They are equally improbable

(From Kahneman, D., & Tversky, A. Subjective probability: A judgment of representativeness. Cognitive Psychology, 1972, 3, p. 430–454. Used with permission.)

Demonstration 3-11

(with permission of J. Brink)

The Psychology Department chairman would like you to know that some of our Psychology majors will need help in the somewhat tedious but necessary task of coding and collating data from their experimental projects. The Department is trying to get an idea as to whether these students can count on some of you for help. Will you volunteer some of your time to help these students in the near future? If so, you will be contacted within the next couple weeks.

_____ I'm sorry, but not this semester

_____ Yes, one or two hours

_____ Yes, three or four hours

_____ Yes, five or six hours

_____ Yes, seven or more hours

If yes, your name: _____

and your telephone: _____

Demonstration 3-11

(with permission of J. Brink)

The Psychology Department chairman would like you to know that some of our Psychology majors will need help in the somewhat tedious but necessary task of coding and collating data from their experimental projects. The Department is trying to get an idea as to whether these students can count on some of you for help. The Department is not asking for a commitment right now, but if you were to be asked, would you volunteer some of your time to help these students in the near future?

_____ I'm sorry, but not this semester

_____ Yes, one or two hours

_____ Yes, three or four hours

_____ Yes, five or six hours

_____ Yes, seven or more hours

If yes, your name: _____

and your telephone: _____

FILMS/VIDEOS

Are We Scaring Ourselves to Death? (ABC, 55 min., 1994). John Stossel's report is very good for introducing the availability heuristic. Describes how the media's vivid portrayal of specific cases leads us to overestimate relatively minor risks and underestimate more significant ones. (Order by calling ABC News 800-913-3434.)

Constructing Social Reality (ANN, 26 min., 1989). From the Discovering Psychology series, this video explores the factors that contribute to our interpretation of reality.

Eye of the Beholder (REY, 25 min., 1958). Illustrates how people can view the same individual very differently. Actor-observer differences are highlighted through a specific example. This film is divided into two parts. In the first segment, several people observe and each attributes different dispositions or traits to the central character, an artist. After this segment, stop the film and have students write a brief paragraph describing their own perceptions of the artist. They, too, will typically attribute particular traits to him. Then show the second part of the film, which deals with the artist's own explanation for his behavior. His perspective emphasizes situational determinants. This demonstrates 1) the subjectivity of perception, 2) the nature of attribution process, and 3) the fundamental attribution error.

From the Mouths of Babes (ABC, 16 min., 1993). Examines the reliability of young children's memories and reports of sexual abuse. Features Stephen Ceci's research on the misinformation effect. Simply repeating a leading question leads children to construct false memories. (Order by calling ABC News 800-913-3434.)

The Interpersonal Perception Task (UCE, 40 min., 1988). An excellent videotape for introducing social perception and attribution theory. Viewers are actively involved in interpreting nonverbal behavior. Comes with an instructor's guide prepared by Dan Archer and Mark Constanzo.

The Galatea Effect (CRM, 28 min., 1988). Presents the concept of self-expectation called the Galatea effect, describes the confidence born of high personal expectations and its importance to improved productivity.

Judgment and Decision Making (ANN, 30 min., 1989). Tversky and Kahneman are interviewed and illustrate both the availability and representativeness heuristics. From the Discovering Psychology series, this program examines the errors that contaminate individual and group decision-making.

Kidnapped by UFOs? (PBS, 60 min., 1996). From the Nova series, this film examines the belief in alien abduction and the biases that may underlie it. Includes interviews with Elizabeth Loftus and Carl Sagan.

Productivity and the Self-Fulfilling Prophecy: The Pygmalion Effect, 2nd Edition. (CRM, 28 min., 1987). Discusses self-fulfilling prophecy and its application, particularly to the manager-worker relationship.

Sensation and Perception (ANN, 30 min., 1989). From the Discovering Psychology series, this program portrays perception as involving an active construction of reality. Gives special attention to the role of expectancy and context effects. As eyewitnesses to a staged bank robbery, viewers learn their susceptibility to error.

Twelve Angry Men (UNA, 95 min., 1957). Deliberations of a jury demonstrate the different perspectives people have of similar events. Clearly demonstrates how personal factors influence social perception. (Available on videotape through many rental outlets).

CHAPTER 4
BEHAVIOR AND ATTITUDES

Do Attitudes Determine Behavior?
    Are We All Hypocrites?
    When Do Attitudes Predict Behavior?
    Minimizing Social Influences on Expressed Attitudes
    Minimizing Other Influences on Behavior
    Examining Attitudes Specific to the Behavior
    Bringing Attitudes to Mind
    The Potency of Attitudes Forged Through Experience
    Some Conclusions
Does Behavior Determine Attitudes?
    Role Playing
    Saying Becomes Believing
    The Foot-in-the-Door Phenomenon
    Evil Acts and Attitudes
    Interracial Behavior and Racial Attitudes
    Social Movements
Why Do Actions Affect Attitudes?
    Self-Presentation: Impression Management
    Self-Justification: Cognitive Dissonance
    Insufficient Justification
    Dissonance After Decisions
    Self-Perception
    Overjustification and Intrinsic Motivations
    Comparing the Theories
    Dissonance as Arousal
    Self-Perceiving When Not Self-Contradicting
Personal Postscript: Changing Ourselves Through Action

LECTURE AND DISCUSSION IDEAS

1. The ABCs of Attitudes

The text suggests that an attitude, one's favorable or unfavorable evaluative reaction toward something or someone, may be exhibited in beliefs, feelings, or intended behavior. Thus when assessing attitudes we tap one of the following dimensions: affect (feelings), behavior (intention), or cognition (thoughts).

Breckler's (1984) assessment of students' attitudes toward snakes provides a good classroom illustration of the ABCs of attitudes. Affect measures were taken while the subject was in the presence of a snake and included heart rate, adjective checklists of positive and negative mood, and a Thurstone scale with statements such as, "I feel tense," or "anxious," or "happy." Behavior measures included the average distance subjects maintained from a variety of pictured snakes, the extent of contact the subject was willing to have with a live snake, and a Thurstone scale with items like "I scream whenever I see a snake," and "I like to handle snakes." Cognitive measures included a Thurstone scale with statements such as "Snakes control the rodent population," and "Snakes will attack anything that moves," ratings of snakes on scales representing the evaluative dimension of the semantic differential, and the net proportion of favorable-to-unfavorable listed thoughts given in the presence of a snake. Breckler's analysis of responses to these various measures suggested the existence of three distinct components to attitudes that were moderately correlated.

2. Well-Known Examples of Attitude-Behavior Inconsistency

An excellent way to introduce the importance of understanding the nature of the attitude-behavior relationship is to provide well-known examples of attitude-behavior inconsistency, which have very obvious and negative repercussions. One example I use in class is the infamous Biblical story of Peter's denial of knowing Jesus. In Matthew 26:31-35 we read an account of Peter's expressed attitude toward Jesus. At the end of this passage Peter says, "Even if I have to die with You, I will not deny You!" (New King James Version). Later in the chapter, however, Peter denies knowing Jesus three times—twice to young servant girls! This can be found in Matthew 26:69-75. Additionally, this story can be used to introduce controlling features of the attitude-behavior relationship like 1) the role of external influences of attitude, 2) the role of external influences on behavior, and 3) the importance of attitude awareness (e.g., Snyder & Swann, 1976). For example, in every translation I have seen, verse 75 uses the word "remembered," clearly suggesting Peter was not aware of his attitude when he was acting until he heard the rooster crow—then he remembered his attitude. Other instructive questions for this example include "What external forces may have been influencing Peter's expressed attitude?" or "What external forces may have been influencing Peter's behavior?" After discussing well-known and important events, students will have a new appreciation for studying what is known about the attitude-behavior relationship.

3. Are We All Hypocrites?

The text notes that philosophers, theologians, and educators have long speculated about the connection between thought and action, character and conduct, private word and public deed. The question provides a good introduction to the literature on attitudes as well as to much additional theory and research in social psychology. Roger Brown (1986) once suggested that "Much of the content of social psychology concerns the factors that intervene between general principles of morality and moral action" (p. 85). What comes between principle and practice is an issue that can stimulate lively class discussion.

To start that discussion you might present some additional research findings that point to our hypocrisy. In each case ask students why they think discrepancy exists between what people say and do.

Representatives of the Roper Organization speaking at the American Demographics' Annual Conference on June 12, 1990, reported that 92 percent of Americans believe that pollution is a moderate or very serious threat, yet fewer than half do anything beyond recycling bottles or cans.

The overwhelming majority of Americans rate nutrition as moderately to very important. Nonetheless people are consuming more calories and consuming more fat than just a few years ago (Ahmad, 1998).

Surveys of Americans' values find "honesty" rising to the top. Yet when their respondents were guaranteed anonymity, Patterson and Kim (1991) found that 91 percent admitted to lying regularly.

By a margin of 3 to 1, Americans agree that "people should volunteer some of their time to help other people." When asked about their volunteer activity in the previous month, little more than a third report any activity at all and, of those, an even smaller percentage indicate that they have spend more than an hour per week in volunteering (Clary et al., 1994).

4. Hypocrisy and Change

Recently Elliot Aronson (1997) has used principles of cognitive dissonance theory to get sexually active teenagers to use condoms more regularly. Most teens know the benefits of condoms yet only a small percentage use them regularly. "Most of us engage in hypocritical behavior all the time because we can blind ourselves to it," argues Aronson. "But if someone comes along and forces you to look at it, you can no longer shrug it off."

In his study he recruited 72 sexually active college students to help design an AIDS-prevention program to be used in high schools. Students were asked to make videotapes explaining the dangers of AIDS and the benefits of condoms. Aronson told them they were role models and to help them prepare their presentations reminded them of the grim facts they had often heard before. Afterward some of the students were put in groups and asked to brainstorm why people don't use condoms when they should. They were encouraged to talk about the times they failed to follow their own rules. "In effect, what our research does is to rub people's noses in their own hypocrisy, and that's painful to confront," says Aronson.

The results were striking. Immediately following the experiment far more of those in the "induced-hypocrisy" group bought condoms than did those who just made the videos or who just brainstormed. Even more dramatic were the differences three months after the experiment. Aronson found that 92 percent of those in the hypocrisy group said they had been using condoms without fail. In contrast, only 55 percent of those who had just made the videotape and 71 percent of those who had only brainstormed reported doing so. "Because of self-reporting we can't be sure of those numbers," says Aronson, "but we can be sure of the relative difference."

5. The Theories of Reasoned Action and Planned Behavior

Introducing these popular theories extends the text's discussion of the conditions under which attitudes predict behavior. Fishbein and Ajzen's (1980) theory of reasoned action states that there are two major predictors of voluntary behavior: attitudes toward the behavior and subjective norms (beliefs about whether significant others approve or disapprove of the behavior). These two factors combine to influence behavioral intentions (the subjective probabilities of how a person intends to behave), which in turn determine behavior. The important point is that attitudes may or may not guide behavior on a given occasion depending on whether or not the subjective norm favors or does not favor the behavior, and whether it is the attitude or norm that is more important to the individual. The authors further specified three boundary conditions that can affect the magnitude of the relationship between intentions and behavior: (a) the degree to which the measure of intention and behavior correspond in their levels of specificity, (b) the stability of intentions between time of measurement and performance of the behavior, and (c) the degree to which carrying out the intention is under the personal control of the actor. Fishbein and Ajzen's summative model seems to predict behavior fairly well, including consumers' buying patterns, alcohol abuse, women's choices to be homemakers or to seek outside employment, and the level of educational attainment.

Ajzen's (1985) theory of planned behavior extends the model of reasoned action to incorporate a third variable, perceived behavioral control, as an antecedent to behavioral intentions. The development and testing of the theory of reasoned action assumed that the behaviors studied were under full volitional control. Obviously that is not always true and Ajzen argues that taking into account the actor's perceived ability to carry out the behavior of interest contributes to the accuracy of predicting behavior. Madden, Ellen, and Ajzen (1992) compared the theory of planned behavior with the theory of reasoned action for 10 behaviors chosen to represent a range with respect to personal control (from "getting a good night's sleep" to "taking vitamin supplements"). The results indicated that inclusion of perceived behavioral control enhanced the prediction of behavioral intention and behavior.

Finally, two recent lines of research further contribute to our understanding of how intentions get activated. Sheina Orbell and colleagues (1997) report that <u>implementation intentions</u> in which individuals identify precisely when and where the behavior is to be performed make enactment more likely. They assessed attitude, subjective norm, perceived behavioral control, and intentions before requiring participants to make implementation intentions concerning when and where they would perform breast self-examination during the next month. They found that goal intentions when supplemented by implementation intentions were more likely to be carried out. Their evidence suggests that implementation intentions are effective because they provide a mechanism that facilitates the retrieval of intentions in memory.

Deborah Kendzierski and Daniel Whitaker (1987) report that the self plays a critical role in linking intentions with behavior. Female undergraduates who had a self-schema that included "successful dieter," "disciplined at eating," or "careful about what I eat" were significantly more likely to act on dieting intentions than were those undergraduates who did not.

6. Attitude Functions

Recent research reflects renewed interest in the psychological functions of attitudes, an issue that first enjoyed popularity over 30 years ago. Katz (1960) suggested that attitudes serve (1) a knowledge function by helping us organize and structure our environment, (2) an instrumental function in helping us maximize rewards and minimize punishments, (3) an ego-defensive function by helping us deal with internal conflicts and defend against anxiety, and (4) a value-expressive function in helping us express ideals important to our self-concept.

Herek's (1987) research reflects the development of improved procedures for assessing and operationalizing attitude functions. In his first study Herek had college students write short essays beginning with one of two statements: "I have generally positive (or negative) attitudes toward lesbians and male homosexuals because. . . . " Content analyses produced evidence for three primary functions that resembled Katz's instrumental, ego-defensive, and value expressive goals. Herek next designed the Attitude Functions Inventory (AFI) as a less time-consuming, more objective measure of attitude functions. Likert-type items were constructed to represent the major functional themes in his subjects' essays. Four versions of the AFI were then administered to a new sample to assess the functional bases of attitudes toward homosexuals and toward each of three stigmatizing illnesses (AIDS, cancer, and mental illness). Factor analyses suggested the existence of four functions like those earlier identified by Katz. Herek argues that the AFI can be readily reworded to assess the motivational basis for almost any attitude.

7. A Case Study in Behavior and Attitudes

Neil Lutsky (1987) suggests the film Seeing Red as a rich source of case material for the study of attitudes. It presents the political biographies of those who composed the American Communist Party from the 1930s through the 1950s. Fighting for such causes as unionization, unemployment and Social Security benefits, and the eight-hour work day, these individuals committed themselves to what they believed was the best for America. The interviews with the former Communist Party members provide striking examples of the dynamics of attitude formation and change, attitude and action relationships, and cognitive dissonance.

8. Quiet Rage: The Stanford Prison Experiment

Philip Zimbardo has released a new 50-minute video of his now classic prison study. It includes original archival footage, flashbacks, post-experiment interviews with the prisoners and guards, and current follow-ups of the study's participants. The video documents the surprise arrests by City Police and graphically shows the pathology that developed and forced the two-week study to be terminated early. This video provides an excellent accompaniment to the text's treatment of the power of roles to shape self-identity. It can be ordered from Insight Media, 2162 Broadway, New York, New York 10024 (1-800-233-9910). Highly recommended!

9. Explain Attitude Measurement Techniques

You can provide a humorous introduction to some of the issues surrounding attitude measurement by showing the three-minute Candid Camera clip, "Space Doctor: Florida TV Survey." It is the last segment on McGraw-Hill's Candid Camera Classics for Social Psychology. People are asked their attitude toward "Space Doctor," a fictitious TV series. Their responses are often quite specific and emphatic. As the text indicates, we measure expressed attitudes, which, like other behaviors, are subject to outside influences.

Throughout the text, attitude measurement procedures will be taught by example. However, the text does not devote space to detailing Likert, semantic differential, and Thurstone scaling techniques. If you think such methodological detail necessary, this is the appropriate time to introduce it. (Note: Chapter 4 does introduce the Bogus Pipeline as an alternative self-report technique.) Consider also introducing behavioral measures of attitudes, such as the lost-letter technique (Milgram, 1972) and the wrong number technique (Gaertner & Bickman, 1972).

You might introduce alternatives to verbal report with examples provided by Lee Sechrest and Janet Belew (1983). For example, they note how a rather clever assessment of attitudes was elicited by a radio reporter who wished to predict the outcome of an upcoming presidential primary. He sat on top of a water tower and, as he announced each candidate's name, asked listeners to flush their toilets if they preferred that person. The reporter measured the drop in the water level after each candidate had been announced. The results of the "poll" paralleled election results surprisingly well. Eugene Webb and his colleagues (1981) report how the relative popularity of various television programs has been assessed by drops in water pressure and electricity surges during commercial breaks and half-times of football games. For example, the Michigan Daily (October 31, 1980) reported a 30-million gallon effect during breaks of the Superbowl telecast in Milwaukee, compared with a 14-million gallon effect of the Carter-Reagan debate.

Researchers have also attempted to use physiological measures of attitudes. For example, the galvanic skin response and pupil dilation have been used in studies of ethnic prejudice. Cacioppo and Petty (1981) have proposed use of the facial electromyograph (EMG) to assess attitudes. They recorded the electrical activity in subjects' facial muscles while they listened to a message with which they agreed or disagreed. Agreement was associated with the typical facial muscle pattern of happiness, disagreement with a pattern of sadness. Outside observers failed to detect these subtle changes. Findings suggest that the EMG can measure the intensity as well as the direction of an attitude.

10. Was Patricia Hearst "Brainwashed" Through Forced Compliance?

The most famous post-Korean war case of "brainwashing" is probably that of Patricia Hearst. Why did her attitudes change while under the influence of the SLA? Here is a sample discussion starter:

> February 3, 1974. Patricia Hearst, except for the wealth and power of her family, a quite typical 19-year-old student at the University of California at Berkeley, was kidnapped by some young revolutionaries who called themselves the Symbionese Liberation Army (SLA). On April 3rd, just two months after her kidnapping, she renounced her former life, her parents, and her fiance and announced that she had joined the SLA. "Try to understand the changes I've gone through," she asked. Much to everyone's surprise, Hearst (now "Tania") apparently meant business. Twelve days later her part in a bank robbery was videotaped and shown on national television. A month after that, bullets from her automatic rifle enabled two of her captors, William and Emily Harris, to escape after robbing a Los Angeles sporting goods store. The next day, all the SLA members except the Harrises and Patty Hearst were killed in a shootout. Still, she did not turn herself in, but instead managed, with the Harrises, to elude an FBI search for 20 months. When finally captured on September 18, 1975, Tania, the "urban guerilla," defiantly offered her clenched fist radical salute for all the world to see.

We will likely never completely understand Patricia Hearst's "thought reform." Many factors were no doubt involved—social isolation (which the Korean POWs had also faced), guilt aroused by her wealth and noninvolvement with the poor, and the close, controlled atmosphere of the SLA. In addition, the SLA successfully elicited her active participation. Her statements of public confession and her forced cooperation were not unlike those of the Korean POWs. "The trick," she wrote in Every Secret Thing, "was to agree with everything they said, to feign an interest in every one of their concerns—to be a model prisoner: subservient, obedient, grateful, and eager to learn . . . . In trying to convince them I convinced myself."

11. Self-Monitoring

Mark Snyder's Public Appearances, Private Realities is an excellent resource for lecture and discussion material on self-monitoring. According to Snyder, high and low self-monitoring reflect two characteristic interpersonal orientations. High self-monitors are sensitive and responsive to interpersonal cues to situational appropriateness. They seem to direct their social behavior by answering the question, "Who does this situation want me to be and how can I be that person?" On the other hand, low self-monitors seek to display their true dispositions and attitudes in every situation. Their social style seems to be shaped by this question, "Who am I and how can I be me in this situation?" Snyder suggests we exercise caution in making value judgments about one style over the other. For example, high self-monitors might be viewed as chameleons or "silly putty" creatures, but also as tactful and adaptable. Low self-monitors might be regarded as rigid and stubborn but also as honest and forthright.

You may go beyond the text, which describes the importance of this personality dimension in understanding the attitude-action relationship. Of particular interest to students may be the different friendship patterns of high and low self-monitors. High self-monitors seem to have an activity-based orientation to friendship. They pick friends because of their skills in particular areas, and thus have different friends for different activities. Low self-monitors have an affect-based orientation to friendship. They pick friends based on their similarity in values, attitudes, and personality. They are likely to have the same friends for many, if not most, of their activities.

High and low self-monitors may also respond differently to advertising appeals. For example, a set of advertisements for Canadian Club whiskey highlighted either the image associated with the product or the product's quality. Reactions to these advertisements indicated that high self-monitors thought the image-oriented ads were better, more appealing, and more effective. They were also willing to pay more for the product when the advertising appealed to image. In contrast, low self-monitors indicated a greater willingness to try the product and to pay a higher price when the advertising emphasized quality.

(See the "Demonstration and Project Ideas" in this chapter for the self-monitoring scale and related classroom exercises.)

12. The Justification of Effort

Cognitive dissonance theorists have predicted that if someone works hard to attain a goal, the goal will be more attractive than to the individual who achieves the same goal with no effort. Robert Cialdini (1988) applies the principle to the hazing ceremonies of school fraternities. During the traditional "Hell Week" held annually on college campuses, pledges are run through a variety of activities designed to test the limits of physical exertion, psychological strain, and social embarrassment. Too often, of course, the results are tragic. One pledge was told to dig his "own grave." After he complied with orders to lie flat in the finished hole, the sides collapsed and suffocated him before his prospective fraternity brothers could dig him out. Another choked to death after repeatedly trying to swallow a large slab of raw liver soaked in oil. A third was required to keep his feet under the rear legs of a folding chair while the heaviest fraternity brother sat down and drank a beer. Although the pledge refused to cry out, a bone in each foot was broken.

In spite of efforts to eliminate dangerous hazing practices, they persist. Why? It may be that they promote commitment to the group. As a result of their efforts, the new fraternity members may find the group more attractive and worthwhile. In the long run the hazing practices may insure group survival. Elliot Aronson and Judson Mills (1959) tested their observation that "persons who go through a great deal of trouble or pain to attain something tend to value it more highly than persons who attain the same thing with minimal effort." The researchers found that college women who had to endure a very embarrassing initiation ceremony in order to gain access to a sex discussion group convinced themselves that their new group and its discussions were extremely valuable. This was true even though the initial discussion was designed to be as dull as possible. Different coeds who went through no initiation were much less positive about the new group they had joined.

13. Action Identification Theory

Robin Vallacher and Daniel Wegner's (1985, 1987) action identification theory provides a good complement to the text's treatment of dissonance and self-perception theories. Vallacher and Wegner's theory focuses on how we interpret our own behavior and assumes that any given behavior can be described on different levels. For example, ask your students what they are doing at the present time. Some may describe their actions in low-level, mechanistic terms, e.g. they are sitting in class, listening to you speak, taking notes. Others may describe their actions in high-level terms, e.g. they are mastering a new theory, learning social psychology, preparing for a career. Similarly, painting a room can be described as "applying brush strokes" or "making the room look fresh." Locking a door can be identified as "putting a key in the lock" or as "securing the house." Making a list can be a matter of "writing things down" or "getting organized." Research suggests that some people consistently view their actions in either high-level or low-level terms.

Obviously, both high- and low-level accounts of behavior are accurate. However, higher-level explanations have more obvious implications for our self-concept. Moreover, those who identify their actions at higher levels seem to show more stable, consistent behavior over time. At the same time this may mean they have more difficulty changing maladaptive behavior patterns. For example, alcoholics who think of their drinking as "helping me relax in social situations" may find breaking the habit more difficult than those who identify drinking as "quenching my thirst."

A second interesting application of this theory involves interpretations of criminal actions. Wegner and Vallacher find that criminals tend to use low-level explanations of behavior. They are not "being dishonest' or "committing the crime of burglary." Rather they are "locating the money," "opening the safe," or "climbing the fence." In this way they need not confront the higher meaning of their act and it has few, if any, negative implications for their self-concept.

14. When Are Rewards Detrimental?

Robert Eisenberger and Judy Cameron's (1996) recent review suggests that the detrimental effects of rewards on intrinsic task interest may be more limited and conditional than is commonly supposed.

In addition to distinguishing between tangible and verbal rewards, Eisenberger and Cameron divide rewards into those that are performance-independent (given simply for taking part in an activity), those that are completion-dependent (given for completing a task or solving a problem), and finally those that are quality-dependent (given for meeting some normative standard of performance). Intrinsic motivation is typically measured either by the free time one spends on a task after withdrawal of a reward or by one's expressed attitude of interest, enjoyment, or satisfaction in the task. Eisenberger and Cameron's review indicated that verbal rewards actually increase intrinsic motivation whether measured by free time or attitude. Tangible rewards decrease intrinsic motivation as measured by free time only when they are expected and performance independent. Unexpected tangible rewards as well as tangible rewards that are completion dependent or quality dependent do not have detrimental effects. When one measures intrinsic motivation by expressed attitude one does not find detrimental effects of tangible rewards regardless of the form they take. Thus the sole reliable detrimental effect of rewards involves the reduction of time spent on an activity following the use of tangible rewards that are performance-independent.

Eisenberger and Cameron report that the detrimental effects of reward on creativity (the generation of novel behavior that meets a standard of quality or utility) are also limited and easily avoided. Here, doing their own research, the investigators distinguished between tasks involving high divergent thinking that require greater cognitive effort and those involving low divergent thinking requiring little cognitive effort. They further distinguish between small and large rewards as well as those that are salient or nonsalient. The results indicated that either a small reward or a large, nonsalient reward actually increased generalized creativity. Only reward for a low degree of divergent thought reduced creativity to a level less than that without reward.

15. "Attitudes Follow Behavior"—in Religion, Too

The social psychological evidence that action and attitude generate one another in an endless chain—like chicken and egg—parallels the interplay between people's rituals and their identity. Those who associate ritual with hocus pocus are unaware of the extent to which the natural rituals of our personal histories have shaped who we are. Many of the things we did without question in childhood have long since become an enduring part of our identities. Our lives are saturated with rituals—and not just those carried out at football games, weddings, and worship services. Our daily rituals are harder for us to recognize than the rituals of societies we call "primitive." This is why some sociologists have written books on the rituals going on right under our noses—the way we eat, the way we meet, the way we greet. As Tevye exclaims in Fiddler on the Roof, "Because of our traditions everyone of us knows who he is."

Tevye represents a Judaic religious tradition, which insists that we know reality not only by intellectual contemplation, but also through our acts of commitment. Pascal argued the same point. In his Pensees (Thoughts) he states his famous wager: We must wager either that God is or that God isn't; reason cannot prove which is true. Considering the potential gains and losses of both wagers should motivate any sensible person to bet that God does exist, or so Pascal thought. He recognized, though, that his calculating analysis probably wouldn't enable many people to really believe. What then? Pascal's advice:

> You would like to attain faith, and do not know the way; you would like to cure yourself of unbelief, and ask the remedy for it. Learn of those who have been bound like you, and who now stake all their possessions. These are people who know the way which you would follow, and who are cured of an ill of which you would be cured. Follow the way by which they began; by acting as if they believed, taking the holy water, having masses said, etc. Even this will naturally make you believe. . . .

Such convergence of thinking from different disciplines can be used to reinforce the concept of "levels of explanation." When we discover psychology, sociology, and theology expressing the same idea, each in its own words, we should not feel tension (as if one perspective competes with the others), but rather a sense of intellectual exhilaration at having uncovered a powerful idea.

16. Information and Attitude Change in the AIDS Dilemma

An article by Marie Helweg-Larsen and Barry E. Collins (1997) in "Current Directions in Psychological Science" (also available in the 01/02 issue of Annual Editions–Social Psychology) presents a wonderful opportunity for students to see the application of various theoretical models pertaining to the attitude-behavior relationship to the current debate surrounding AIDS education. This article acknowledges that most AIDS intervention programs designed to disseminate information about the transmission of HIV have not led to substantial behavior changes—in fact, there is some evidence that too much information may have negative consequences. Petty and Cacioppo's elaboration-likelihood model (introduced in Chapter 7), Ajzen's theory of planned behavior, and Festinger's cognitive dissonance theory are all brought to bear on this terrible problem.

17. Tie the "Educational Footnote" to Your Own Teaching Method

If you anticipate involving students by using demonstration activities and discussion questions, such as those suggested in this manual, you might use this chapter—especially its last section—to explain why you are doing so: Action stimulates thinking; experiencing phenomena first hand heightens understanding; active cognitive processing of concepts increases retention.

18. Popular Sources for Additional Classroom Material

Cialdini, R. B. (1993). Influence: Science and practice, 3rd ed. New York: HarperCollins. A captivating introduction to social psychological research on persuasion and its applications to everyday life. Includes a chapter on the consistency motive and how commitments to act shape attitudes.

Eagly, A. H., & Chaiken, S. (1993). The psychology of attitudes. Fort Worth: Harcourt Brace Jovanovich. This book is very advanced but is an excellent resource for those instructors who wish to beef-up their own understanding of the research on attitude formation and change. Also a relevant source for Chapter 7—Persuasion.

Festinger, L., Rieken, H., & Schacter, S. (1956). When prophecy fails. Minneapolis: University of Minnesota Press. The author of cognitive dissonance theory provides a fascinating account of the attitudes and behavior of a doomsday cult that predicted the end of the world and then coped with the failure of their prophecy.

Kraus, S. J. (1995). Attitudes and the prediction of behavior: A meta-analysis of the empirical literature. Personality and Social Psychology Bulletin, 21, p. 58–75. Reviews the link between attitudes and behavior. Examines the attitude-behavior relationship in terms of a variety of moderating variables. Good supplement to text coverage of this issue.

Petty, R. E., & Krosnick, J.A. (1995). Attitude strength: Antecedents and consequences. Hillsdale, NJ: Erlbaum. A scholarly book in which experts examine both the roots and fruits of persistent, influential attitudes.

Petty, R. E., Wegener, D. T., & Fabrigar, L.R. (1997). Attitudes and attitude change. In Spence, J. T., Darley, J. M., & Foss, D. J. (Eds.), Annual review of psychology, Volume 48 (p. 609–647), Palo Alto, CA: Annual Review, Inc. Overview of theory and research from 1992-1995. Covers work on attitude structure, attitude change, and the consequences of holding attitudes.

Snyder, M. (1987). Public appearances/private realities: The psychology of self-monitoring. New York: Freeman. Snyder introduces the concept of self-monitoring and its measurement. An excellent overview of research on this important personality variable.

Tesser, A., & Shaffer, D. (1990). Attitudes and attitude change. In M. Rosenzweig & L. Porter (Eds.), Annual review of psychology, Volume 41 (p. 479–523). Palo Alto, CA: Annual Reviews, Inc. Reviews recent research on attitude structure and functions. Includes a discussion of attitudes as predictors of behavior.

Zimbardo, P., & Leippe, M. (1991). The psychology of attitude change and social influence. New York: McGraw Hill. This book provides a basic introduction to attitudes, including how they influence, and are influenced by, our actions.

DEMONSTRATION AND PROJECT IDEAS

1. Measuring General Versus Specific Attitudes

The book points out that one reason attitude research has an interesting history results from the rather recent understanding of the importance of asking specific attitudinal questions for predicting specific behavioral responses. This important point made in the book can be easily highlighted in class by asking students to indicate their attitude toward some general personal attribute—say honesty or fairness. Then, have prepared a series of specific attitude questions, which are designed to result in a different response from the students. For example, most students will indicate that they have a very positive attitude toward being honest. However, when they are asked how they feel about returning money to a check-out clerk who gave them too much change, their attitude may not be as favorable. As a result of this exercise, students should clearly see the importance of asking specific attitude questions if they want to predict specific behavioral responses. As the book notes, the role of general versus specific attitude measurement seems so obvious to us now, but it took years of research to finally figure this out.

2. Saying Versus Doing

Wilbur Scoville (1981) provides a neat demonstration of the distinction between intentions and action. Begin by asking the class if any of them have ever eaten exotic foods like chocolate-covered ants, snails, or fried grubs. Turn to someone who didn't raise his or her hand and ask, "Well, now, would you consider eating a chocolate-covered ant?" While many will turn you down, you are likely to find someone who thinks they would. If necessary you can attach a price. "Well, would you for a dollar?" Do the same with a few more students.

When the bargaining is complete you will have identified three or four students who have publicly agreed to eat a chocolate-covered ant (or similar food) either for free or some nominal sum. At this point reach into your briefcase and pull out the nicely packaged delicacy (available from the gourmet food section of a large, metropolitan, department store). If you have selected your subjects carefully most of them will turn you down when it comes time to follow through (this preserves supplies). You are now able to introduce a meaningful discussion of the "What would you do if. . .?" question, which is the essence of many attitude surveys and opinion polls. Scoville notes that whether the student actually succeeds in eating the delicacy offered is not too important since the project lends itself to good discussion in either case.

3. Construct and Administer an Attitude Measure

If time allows, you might break the class into small working groups, and have each group devise items that would assess students' attitudes toward an interesting campus issue. This could be an issue decided upon by the whole class, or by each group separately. You can reinforce the distinction between cognitive, affective, and behavioral components of attitudes by instructing the group to define and assess each component. Group members could interview several people each, pool their findings, and then report their group findings to the class.

Demonstration 4-1 allows you to demonstrate the semantic differential technique, by having students judge the concept "social psychology." Point out that the first three scales load heavily on <u>evaluation</u>, the second three on <u>activity</u>, and the last three on <u>potency</u>. If this is administered very near the beginning of the course, and again near the end, it can also be used to assess changes in students' judgments of the discipline.

4. The Randomized Response Technique

The book mentions the bogus-pipeline as one method researchers have used to side-step the external influences on expressed attitude. Another technique used by researchers attempts to remove social desirability concerns by offering the respondent some degree of confidentiality. Warner's (1965) randomized response technique (RRT) consists of asking the participant a "yes/no" question and then having the participant privately generate a random event (e.g., rolling a die). Depending upon the outcome of this event, the participant answers according to previously given directions—either forced or truthfully. For example, using a single die, the participant might be told ahead of time that if the die is a "1," answer "no;" if it is a "6," answer "yes;" if something else, answer truthfully. By keeping the result of the random event to oneself, some level of confidentiality is achieved. This technique can be tried out in class. Simply bring some dice to class, distribute them and give them directions for how to answer (the mathematics are more efficient if you make only two out of six numbers forced responses). Then, ask some attitudinal questions, have them privately generate the random event, and answer accordingly.

If the instructor is daring, the sense of confidentiality felt by the RRT can be tested by asking a few very personal questions—it works best if these are not attitudinal questions per se, but rather past behavior questions (e.g., Have you ever been party to an abortion? Have you ever had a homosexual experience? Have you ever cheated on your income taxes?). If you gather up the responses and add them up, you may not find any "yes" responses. The conclusion should then be that either nobody rolled a 6 (very unlikely in a class of any size) or that the level of confidentiality offered by the random event is not great enough – a potential weakness of this methodology.

Of course, the inability to measure any one person's attitude is another limitation of the RRT. However, an estimate of population parameters can be accomplished through the use of elementary probability theory (see Fox & Tracy, 1980; Horvitz, Greenberg, & Abernathy, 1976; for more statistically efficient [and complex!] models.)

5. Illustrating Cognitive Dissonance

David M. Carkenord and Joseph Bullington (1993) suggest a classroom exercise that is very useful for introducing and explaining the concept of cognitive dissonance. Demonstration 4-2 is an adaptation of their specific suggestions. First, present the Attitude Survey (4-2a), which asks students to indicate their attitude by rating each item on a five-point scale ranging from strongly agree to strongly disagree. Then distribute the Behavior Survey (4-2b), which simply requests students to indicate whether or not they perform the stated behavior on a regular basis. Although you can collect student responses and report class results for each survey, it is not essential to the exercise. Carkenord and Bullington report that students' assessments of the demonstration indicate that they find it to be a useful learning experience in which they personally experience dissonance and self-insight.

6. Predicting Research Outcomes: Cognitive Dissonance and the Overjustification Effect

Timothy Osberg (1993) and Harry Hom, Jr. (1994) suggest classroom exercises that ask students to predict outcomes of research on cognitive dissonance and the overjustification effect, respectively. Using either or both of the exercises before students read the chapter will make the students eager to read this chapter and again demonstrate that psychology is not merely common sense. You might also use the opportunity to remind students of the danger of hindsight bias.

Introduce your students to cognitive dissonance by reading the following, adapted from Osberg's suggestion:

>Imagine that you are a participant in a psychological experiment.

On arriving at the laboratory, the experimenter seats you at a table and requires you to perform a dull task, such as turning wooden knobs again and again. After you finish, the experimenter tells you that, because his assistant couldn't make the next session, he needs you to tell the next subject that the tasks you have just performed are interesting and educational. After being paid either $1 or $20 to do this, you carry out the assignment. Finally, you are asked to privately rate your enjoyment of the initial task involving the turning of the wooden knobs. Under what condition, $1 or $20, do you believe your actual enjoyment rating of the tasks would be higher?

Students can provide their answers by a show of hands or by writing them down. Present a summary of the results. Osberg reports that almost all of his students vote for the $20 payment. Conclude by reporting that Festinger and Carlsmith found that those receiving $1 rated the task as more enjoyable than those paid $20. Introduce the concept of cognitive dissonance. Explain that those who received only $1 had insufficient justification for their behavior, which led to dissonance, which in turn produced a change in attitude about the task.

Hom suggests introducing the overjustification effect with a short discussion on whether preschool children enjoy drawing as well as receiving recognition in the form of "good player" badges or gold stars. Then have the class imagine they are conducting an experiment at a local preschool center. Instruct them to play close attention so they will be able to make predictions before learning the research outcome. Then give this synopsis of Mark Lepper and his colleagues's research:

Preschoolers who had earlier shown a strong interest in drawing during playtime were randomly assigned to one of three experimental conditions. In the "expected reward" condition, the experimenter showed the children a good player badge and then told them they could earn their own badge by drawing well. The preschoolers in this condition all earned badges. In the "unexpected reward" condition, children drew without promise of reward. However, at the end of the session, all the children were given badges for their work. In the third, or "control" condition, the preschoolers drew without expecting or receiving badges. Later children were observed during free playtime and the amount of time they spent drawing was assessed. Predict how much time each group spent in drawing.

Hom suggests drawing bar graphs of the time predictions on the chalkboard. Student predictions will be quite different from the actual results of the experiment. The correct prediction is that children from the expected reward condition later spent less time in drawing than those from the unexpected reward or control conditions. No significant differences were observed between the latter two groups. Explain to your class how an already justifiable activity can become "overjustified" by the promise of added reward. Interest can survive, however, when rewards are used not to bribe or to control, but to communicate a job well done.

7. The Self-Monitoring Scale

Mark Snyder and Steve Gangestad's (1986) Self-Monitoring Scale (Demonstration 4-3) provides a paper-and-pencil demonstration of a dispositional tendency, one that helps predict the extent of a person's attitude-behavior consistency. High self-monitors more readily adjust their behavior in response to external circumstances, and thus exhibit <u>less</u> consistency than do the more inner-directed low self-monitors.

The items are keyed for high self-monitoring:

1. False
2. False
3. False
4. True

5. True
6. True
7. False
8. True
9. False
10. True
11. False
12. True
13. False
14. False
15. False
16. False
17. True
18. True

Jeffrey Simpson (1988) and Melinda Jones (1994) suggest classroom exercises/student projects relating self-monitoring to dating patterns and advertising preferences. Among the questions Simpson asks his students are, "Are you currently dating someone exclusively (that is, one person and no one else)?" "If you are not dating one person exclusively at the present time, have you dated at least two different people in the past year?" Research suggests that exclusive daters tend to score lower in self-monitoring. Conversely, multiple daters tend to score higher in self-monitoring. Jones suggests collecting advertisements from newspaper and magazines that are either quality-oriented or image-oriented. Bring them to class and have students evaluate the effectiveness as well as the appeal of each ad. Low self-monitors seem to respond more favorably to quality-oriented appeals while high self-monitors react more positively to image-oriented appeals.

8. Attempt to Replicate the Forced Compliance Effect

Do people believe in what they have stood up for? Divide the class in half (for example, by distributing alternate forms of a blank page with instructions at the top), and instruct half to list arguments supporting some position (for example, that the legal drinking age should be 21 years) while the other half is instructed to support a contrasting position (for example, that the legal drinking age should be 18 years). You might ask them to pretend they were preparing for a debate. When they are finished, state that "I would also like an idea of your own personal attitude on this issue, since it may have affected the arguments you developed." For example, given the drinking age question, you might go on to say, "At the top of the page, just write the age at which you, personally, feel drinking should be legal."

You can use this demonstration to make several points. First, is there any tendency for compliance with the essay demand to breed acceptance of its stated position? Second, some of the students will have written counterattitudinal essays, some proattitudinal essays. Remind the class of the text's suggestion that dissonance seems to be triggered more by the former situation (little dissonance should be aroused by saying what you believe). Inquire whether those who wrote counterattitudinal essays did in fact feel some discomfort, discomfort (dissonance) that potentially could be reduced by believing what they wrote. Self-perception theory can apply to the proattitudinal essays, especially if one's feelings are ambiguous or ambivalent to begin with. Third, ask students whether they felt that you expected them to state opinions consistent with their essays. Did they sense that this was what you were looking and hoping for? If so, this demonstrates the problem of experimental "demand characteristics" described in Chapter 1.

9. Manipulate Facial Expressions

The experiments on facial feedback are easily illustrated with a demonstration that is usually good for laughs. Summarize the research and then say, "Let's try it. First, turn down the corners of your mouth. Furrow your brow. . . . Can you imagine that cartoons might seem less funny while wearing this expression? . . . But it's more fun to try the reverse effect. In the words of an old song, 'Put on a Happy Face.' Turn up the sides of your mouth. Lift up your eyes. Can you feel your mood improve?"

10. The Social Connection Video Series

One of the entries in the video instructional supplement (The Social Connection Video Series), entitled "Role Playing: The Power of the Situation," includes archival footage of the Stanford Prison Study and a conversation with Phillip Zimbardo. See the Faculty Guide accompanying the video series for a program summary, pause points, and a classroom activity.

Demonstration 4-1

Bolt & Myers

©McGraw-Hill, 1999

The purpose of this exercise is to measure the meaning of "social psychology" by having you rate the term against a series of descriptive scales. In completing this exercise, please make your judgments on the basis of what "social psychology" means to you at the present moment.

Here is how you are to use these scales:

If you feel that "social psychology" is <u>very closely related</u> to one end of the scale, you should place your check-mark as follows:

    old __X__ : _____ : _____ : _____ : _____ : _____ : _____ new

or

    old _____ : _____ : _____ : _____ : _____ : _____ : __X__ new

If you feel that "social psychology" is only slightly related to one side as opposed to the other side, then you should place your check as follows:

    old _____ : _____ : __X__ : _____ : _____ : _____ : _____ new

or

    old _____ : _____ : _____ : _____ : __X__ : _____ : _____ new

If you consider "social psychology" to be neutral on the scale, or if the scale is unrelated to "social psychology," place your check in the middle space.

Social Psychology

meaningless	____ : ____ : ____ : ____ : ____ : ____ : ____	meaningful
honest	____ : ____ : ____ : ____ : ____ : ____ : ____	deceitful
bad	____ : ____ : ____ : ____ : ____ : ____ : ____	good
fast	____ : ____ : ____ : ____ : ____ : ____ : ____	slow
passive	____ : ____ : ____ : ____ : ____ : ____ : ____	active
varied	____ : ____ : ____ : ____ : ____ : ____ : ____	repetitive
soft	____ : ____ : ____ : ____ : ____ : ____ : ____	hard
strong	____ : ____ : ____ : ____ : ____ : ____ : ____	weak
light	____ : ____ : ____ : ____ : ____ : ____ : ____	heavy

Demonstration 4-2a

ATTITUDE SURVEY

Please indicate the extent to which you agree with each of the statements below, using the following scale:

    1 = strongly disagree
    2 = disagree
    3 = neither agree nor disagree
    4 = agree
    5 = strongly agree

____ 1. Engaging in regular physical exercise three times a week promotes good health.

____ 2. Eating a variety of foods each day, including five or more servings of fresh fruits and vegetables, contributes to wellness.

____ 3. It is essential that all citizens exercise their right to vote if government is to effectively reflect the will of the people.

____ 4. Homelessness is a serious social problem that needs attention.

Demonstration 4-2b

BEHAVIOR SURVEY

Please indicate whether or not you have performed each of the following actions:

Yes No   1. I take time to engage in regular physical exercise at least three times a week.

Yes No   2. I regularly eat at least five servings of fresh fruits and vegetables each day.

Yes No   3. I voted in the last election for which I was eligible.

Yes No   4. Within the last year, I have personally done something to address the problem of homelessness (e.g., made a charitable contribution, talked with a homeless person, wrote my congressman regarding the problem of homelessness).

Demonstration 4-3

(with permission of M. Snyder)

The statements below concern your personal reactions to a number of different situations. No two statements are exactly alike, so consider each statement carefully before answering. If a statement is TRUE or MOSTLY TRUE as applied to you, circle the "T." If a statement is FALSE or NOT USUALLY TRUE as applied to you, circle the "F."

T F 1. I find it hard to imitate the behavior of other people.
T F 2. At parties and social gatherings, I do not attempt to do or say things that others will like.
T F 3. I can only argue for ideas, which I already believe.
T F 4. I can make impromptu speeches even on topics about which I have almost no information.
T F 5. I guess I put on a show to impress or entertain others.
T F 6. I would probably make a good actor.
T F 7. In a group of people I am rarely the center of attention.
T F 8. In different situations and with different people, I often act like very different people.
T F 9. I am not particularly good at making other people like me.
T F 10. I'm not always the person I appear to be.
T F 11. I would not change my opinions (or the way I do things) in order to please someone or win their favor.
T F 12. I have considered being an entertainer.
T F 13. I have never been good at games like charades or improvisational acting.
T F 14. I have trouble changing my behavior to suit different people and different situations.
T F 15. At a party I let others keep the jokes and stories going.
T F 16. I feel a bit awkward in public and do not show up quite as well as I should.
T F 17. I can look anyone in the eye and tell a lie with a straight face (if for a right end).T F 18. I may deceive people by being friendly when I really dislike them.

Note. From "On the nature of self-monitoring: Matters of assessment, matter of validity" by M. Snyder and S. Gangestad, 1986, Journal of Personality and Social Psychology, 51, p. 125. Copyright 1986 by the American Psychological Association. Reprinted by permission.

FILMS/VIDEOS

Conscience in Conflict (LCA, 35 min., 1973). From the feature film A Man for All Seasons. Explores the relationship between attitudes and behavior, and develops the theme that we come to know ourselves through our actions, we shape our identities through our acts of commitment.

Seeing Red (NEW, 100 min., 1982). Story of the American Communist Party that illustrated attitude formation and change, the attitude and action relationships, and cognitive dissonance.

CHAPTER 5
GENES, CULTURE, AND GENDER

Human Nature and Cultural Diversity
    Evolution and Behavior
    Culture and Behavior
    Social Roles

Gender Similarities and Differences
    Independence Versus Connectedness
    Social Dominance
    Aggression
    Sexuality

Evolution and Gender: Doing What Comes Naturally?
    Gender and Mating Preferences
    Gender and Hormones
    Reflections on Evolutionary Psychology

Culture and Gender
    Gender Roles Vary With Culture
    Gender Roles Vary Over Time
    Peer-transmitted Culture

Conclusions
    Biology *and* Culture
    The Great Lesson of Social Psychology

Personal Postscript: Should We View Ourselves as Products or Architects of Our Social Worlds?

LECTURE AND DISCUSSION IDEAS

1. Valuing Diversity

Teaching students to tolerate and even value cultural diversity has become an important objective at all levels of education. Clearly westerners ought to be more tolerant and even learn from customs different from their own. Surely this applies to the norms governing expressiveness, personal space, and individualism-collectivism, all discussed in the text.

However, ask your students, should there be limits to our respect for diversity? How should we react when another practice violates some deeply held value such as gender equality? For example, how about the Sudan law that requires a woman to obtain permission of her husband, father, or brother before she may leave the country? Or the law in Saudi Arabia that forbids women to drive?

Kaplan and colleagues (1993) provide an excellent overview of the debate between human rights activists and multiculturalists over what the former call "female genital mutilation" but the latter label merely "female circumcision." The procedure is one in which a girl, sometimes as young as an infant, has all or part of her external genitalia removed. That can mean excision of the clitoris and the labia minora. The practice is widespread in Africa, the Middle East, and Southeast Asia. Estimates are that from 85 to 114 million women, mostly Moslem, have endured some form of it. Should we view it as torture or tradition? Is it a violation of human rights requiring western intervention or none of our business? As Kaplan and his colleagues indicate, even critics who abhor the mutilations disagree about the means to end them. Some believe that westerners ought to work at the grass roots with African women to end the practice instead of grandstanding in the media. For example, Wilkista Onsando, chairperson for Kenya's largest and most influential women's rights group, argues, "Let indigenous people fight it according to their own traditions. It will die faster than if others tell us what to do."

2. Introducing Evolutionary Psychology

The text indicates that the underlying assumption of evolutionary psychology is that humans are gene-producing machines with the basic motivation of perpetuating their own genetic pool. Our genes predispose us to act in ways that enhance their chances of surviving and spreading. This fundamental motive underlies all behavior.

Bernard Weiner (1992) illustrates this important principle of evolutionary psychology by posing a number of questions. For example, suppose you were in a boating accident with your five-year-old and your one-year-old child, and you could save only one. Whom do you choose to save? Or, similarly, you are an older parent and the accident involves your 40-year-old and 20-year-old daughters, neither of whom can swim. Whom do you save? Most people choose the five-year-old and 20-year-old. Why? Since some children die between ages one and five, five-year-olds are more likely to reproduce, thereby perpetuating the gene pool. Similarly, a 20-year-old is more likely to reproduce than is a 40-year-old.

Ask your students, would they rather marry someone older or younger than themselves? And, what is most important in the selection of that mate? An exciting personality, industriousness, physical attractiveness, good financial prospects? It is mating that perpetuates the genetic pool. For women, reproductive capacities are limited to approximately 25 children. For men, reproductive potential is almost limitless. Because of a woman's greater investment in each child, she must be careful to select a mate who will help her in child-rearing. The male must simply choose females who can bear children. It follows that women should prefer older males because they typically have more resources to help in child care. Moreover, they should prefer mates with good financial prospects and industriousness. Men should prefer younger females because they are more likely to give birth. In addition, they should prefer physical attractiveness and an exciting personality, both reflecting their sexual preoccupation. This male-female distinction was also highlighted in a study in which both men and women were asked about the minimum level of intelligence they would accept in a person they were dating. Both males and females said, "average intelligence." But things changed when they were asked how smart a person would have to be before they would consent to sex. The women indicated much above intelligence; men said much below intelligence.

If you lecture on evolutionary psychology be sure to include some reference to the Coolidge effect. In certain animal species, a male that has become sexually exhausted from repeated copulation with the same female will demonstrate renewed vigor if presented with a succession of females. The phenomenon has been called the Coolidge effect because of a reported verbal exchange between President and Mrs. Calvin Coolidge. While touring a farm, the president's wife was impressed by the untiring sexual activity of one rooster. "You might point that out to Mr. Coolidge," she told the farmer. Hearing of her remark, the president asked the farmer whether a different hen was involved each time. When informed that this was true he replied, "You might point that out to Mrs. Coolidge." According to evolutionary psychology, the fundamental motive is to pass on genes, which occurs by having many offspring. Thus the genes of males who fertilize many females would be major winners in the genetic sweepstakes. Natural selection may have favored such males.

Another even more challenging question posed by Weiner concerns grandparents' reaction to a new child. Both sets of grandparents are ecstatic. But who might be kinder to the child and mourn more at the death of the child? Following the logic of evolutionary psychology, a female knows that any child she bears is hers. The male must determine that the female has really borne his child and not a rival's. The maternal grandparents, assured of 25 percent genetic carryover, should be especially happy.

3. Applying Evolutionary Psychology

Timothy Miller's (1995) How to Want What You Have (Avon Books) may be the only self-help book written from an explicitly evolutionary perspective. It provides one source for discussing some of the interesting practical implications of evolutionary psychology in class.

Miller provides a lucid account of the theory's emphasis on the importance of reproductive success and then shows how humans strive for its prerequisites: wealth, status, and love. He states, "The fundamental problem is that, from an evolutionary perspective, there is no such thing as enough reproductive success. We are instinctively driven to continue striving for more wealth, success, and love regardless of how much we have already achieved." This results in incredible suffering and unhappiness. However, Miller argues that we are not compelled to follow our instinctive cravings. He suggests, "We have sufficient intellectual capacity that we can ignore, or override our instinctual inclinations if we have good enough reason....People can learn to want what they have....Your best hope is to spit in instinct's eye." Miller's strategy for our coming to want what we have involves the deliberate, constant practice of compassion, attention, and gratitude.

4. Debating Gender Issues

Structured classroom debates provide a good way of introducing gender issues. Mary Roth Walsh's (1997) Women, Men, and Gender: Ongoing Debates (Yale University Press) provides an excellent resource for this purpose. It poses 18 different questions on which two experts take opposing sides. For example, "Should we continue to study gender issues?," "Do men and women have different ways of knowing?," "Is pornography harmful to women?" In addition to providing experts' short replies, there is an extensive list of references on each issue for students to consult in pursuing their own answer.

5. Gender Differences

Carol Ann Rinzler (1988) provides some delightful examples of gender differences that you can use to introduce or conclude the section in the text on gender roles. Rinzler notes that although men and women may be equal, they are not the same. For example, more boys than girls sleep walk. Women have only four-fifths as many red blood cells in each drop of blood. Men are more likely to hiccup. Women suffer more throbbing migraine headaches, men more piercing, cluster headaches. Ask your students some of the following:

1. Whose hands are warmer? Usually a man's because, at room temperature, healthy men have a larger flow of blood to their fingers than do healthy women. When a woman warms up, however, the flow of blood to her hands will exceed a man's because her blood vessels are more expandable. Thus her body can accept 40 percent more blood during pregnancy with no increase in blood pressure.

2. Whose forehead is more likely to feel warm? A woman's but it depends on the time of month. Normal temperature of either sex is 98.6°F. However, at ovulation a woman's temperature increases about one degree and remains there for 12 to 14 days until just before menstruation.

3. Whose armpits are smellier? A woman's. Men perspire most heavily on the upper chest from glands secreting only salts and water. Women sweat most heavily under the arms from glands that secrete fatty substances in addition to salts and water. Bacteria digest the fatty substances and their byproducts make this sweat smelly.

4. Whose nose knows this rose from that rose? Probably a woman's. The ability to smell, taste, and hear is influenced by a variety of hormones but especially the adrenal hormones. At almost every point in the cycle, a woman's senses are more acute. Her senses become even sharper as the monthly production of estrogen increases, peaking at ovulation.

5. Who's most likely to wake in the night with a stomachache? It's twice as likely to be a man. A gnawing pain in the middle of the night is a common symptom of a duodenal ulcer, still primarily a male affliction.

6. How Culture Bound is Social Cognition?

Ziva Kunda' (1999) article in Annual Editions–Social Psychology 01/02 (see Chapter 1 references) (see <u>Social Cognition: Making Sense of People</u> Chapter 11, p. 515–533 for original publication) presents a good opportunity to use the material from Chapter 5 to reflect upon the generalizability of material covered in the previous chapters—specifically Chapters 2 and 3. Kunda discusses in a very readable style East-West differences pertaining to the concept and structure of the self as well as attributional styles. Discussion questions might include "What other topics previously discussed in the text might have cultural limitations which challenge their usefulness in other cultural settings?" "What impact does the evidence that suggests we think differently as a function of our social/cultural context have on our ideas of which aspect of personhood is more central—social/cultural or cognitive?"

7. A World of Differences: Understanding Cross-Cultural Communication

As its title suggests, this new video produced by Dane Archer is designed to foster an awareness of the importance and nature of cultural differences. Only 30 minutes in length, it examines 14 key facets of cross-cultural miscommunication. Your class is certain to identify with the students who share their experiences from around the world.

Although some cultural differences are obvious and thus can be anticipated, for example differences in language, others are more subtle. They include differences in personal space, patterns of touching, emotional expression, gestures, courtship patterns, and parent-child relationships. These less obvious differences often prevent us from understanding people from other societies and cultures. A comprehensive instructor's guide offers a variety of strategies for using the video in the classroom. Rental is $75, purchase is $295. Order from University of California Extension Center for Media and Independent Learning, 2000 Center Street, Fourth Floor, Berkeley, CA 94704, Phone (510) 642-0460.

8. Cultural Differences

Roger E. Axtell's popular books <u>Do's and Taboo's Around the World</u> (1993, John Wiley) and <u>Gestures: The Do's and Taboo's of Body Language Around the World</u> (1998, John Wiley) are wonderful sources of lecture material on cultural differences. As Axtell illustrates, failure to recognize difference in cultural norms sometimes leads to conflict and embarrassment.

Axtell opens <u>Do's and Taboo's</u> with three delightful vignettes.

First, he tells of a banker who, before making an important business trip to Singapore, learned the names of his future clients. For example, the top man was Lo Win Hao. To make a good impression, he sprinkled his initial conversation with "Mr. Hao," "Mr. Chee," and "Mr. Woon." A note passed from a more experienced American read, "Too friendly, too soon." In Chinese, the surname comes first, the given name last. He had been calling the VIPS the equivalent of Mr. Ed, Mr. Charlie, and Mr. Bill.

A women in charge of family planning for an international human welfare organization bought some beautiful native beads on her arrival in Togo. Wearing them for the first time at a Saturday night reception, she was greeted with howling laughter. The beads she had purchased were normally worn around the waist and under a skirt to hold up a loincloth. To every Togelese eye, she had strutted out with a piece of underpants around her neck.

A third traveler arrived in Columbia with a bad head cold. Wheezing and blowing into a handkerchief at the airport was enough to get him arrested. The guards were convinced this visiting American was waltzing into their country snorting cocaine.

<u>Gestures</u> are equally illuminating. In the United States, nodding the head up and down means "yes;" shaking it signals "no." In Bulgaria, parts of Greece, Turkey, Iran, it is just the reverse. Americans, British, and Jewish cultures favor "face-to-face" relationships: "Look me in the eye, son." Among Native Americans and in parts of Africa respect is shown by avoiding the eyes. Rotating the forefinger around in front of the ear means "He's crazy" in the United States. In Argentina, it means, "You have a phone call." And how do men react to seeing a pretty girl? An American raises his eyebrows, an Italian presses his forefinger into his cheek and whistles, a Greek strokes his cheek, a Brazilian puts an imaginary telescope to his eye, a Frenchman kisses his fingertips, and an Arab grasps his beard.

9. Individualism Versus Collectivisim

This important cultural difference was introduced in Chapter 2 of the text. If you did not consider individualism-collectivism then, you may choose to do so now. Suggestions for discussing this value difference in the classroom can be found in Chapter 2 of this manual. See the relevant lecture/discussion topic and the Self-Construal Scale in the "Demonstrations and Projects" section of that chapter.

10. Assimilation or Multiculturalism?

Most nations today have become a diverse mix of people, forcing almost everyone to struggle with the tension between affirming diversity and seeking unity. In this context, you can generate an interesting classroom discussion by presenting two contrasting ideological positions regarding attitudes and policies toward immigrants and established ethnic minorities. Assimilation maintains that cultural minorities should give up their so-called "heritage" cultures and take on the "American" or "Canadian" way of life. Multiculturalism is the view that these groups should maintain their heritage cultures as much as possible while establishing themselves in the new culture. You might pose the question Lambert and his colleagues (1990) asked in their research: "Some people believe that cultural and racial minority groups should give up their traditional ways of life and take on the American (Canadian, French, etc.) way of life while others believe that these groups should maintain their traditional ways as much as possible when they come to America. What do you think?"

In a survey of Americans, Lambert and Taylor (1988) found surprising support for maintaining heritage cultures not only among immigrant minority groups but also among most majority "host" groups, black and white. Working-class whites were one exception. Conducting a similar study in France, Lambert et al. (1990) found that middle- and working-class families were neutral to slightly favorable to immigrants maintaining heritage cultures and languages rather than losing them through assimilation.

Classroom discussion is likely to include debate over whether pride in one's ethnic group competes with identification with the larger culture. More specifically, does a strong ethnic identification displace other social identities? Research suggests that a positive ethnic identity contributes to positive self-esteem, as does a positive mainstream social identity among those who have lost touch with their mixed ethnic roots. "Marginal" people who lack both an ethnic identity and a mainstream identity often have low self-esteem. Phinney (1990) finds that bicultural people, that is, those who identify with both the ethnic culture and the larger culture, typically have a strongly positive self-concept.

11. Proxemics

Proxemics, the study of the spacing between individuals, was pioneered by Edward T. Hall (1966). On the basis of his research Hall identified four zones, or distances, at which Americans interact with others.

The zone of <u>intimacy</u> ranges from actual body contact to a distance of 18 inches. This zone is reserved for a person's most intimate acquaintances. Thus, when strangers enter this zone, the person is likely to respond with suspicion.

The zone of <u>personal distance</u> extends from 18 inches–4 feet. Conversation between close friends or trusted acquaintances occurs at this distance.

<u>Social distance</u> ranges from 4–12 feet. This zone is appropriate for impersonal relationships, casual acquaintances, and work settings.

<u>Public distance</u> includes all space beyond 12 feet. Formal exchanges, such as a speaker addressing an audience, as well as interactions with strangers and those of high status occur at this distance.

Hall suggested that negative effects occur when people violate these "proxemic rules" in either direction, that is, by getting too close or remaining too distant.

Robert Sommer (1969) reports some of the best demonstrations of how people respond to a violation of these proxemic rules. For example, Sommer seated himself 6 inches from persons who were alone on a park bench. He then measured the time the stranger remained after he arrived. Compared to a control group of strangers who were left alone, those whose zone of intimacy was invaded left more quickly.

Evidence that one may react negatively to persons that remain too distant, as well as to those who get too close, comes from a study by Albert and Dobbs (1970). A persuasive message was delivered by an experimenter at the appropriate "social distance" of 5 feet, or within the less appropriate "personal" or "public" distance zones. Results indicated that attention to the message and the perceived expertness of the communicator were greatest at the medium distance. Recall of the content of the message also tended to be best when the communicator was in the appropriate zone of "social distance."

As the text suggests, differences exist between age groups, cultures, and the sexes in the size of personal space zones. At least two other factors may influence the size of this portable buffer as well. First, people with higher self-esteem seem to approach others more closely than do those with lower self-regard (Stratton, Tekippe & Flick, 1973). Second, in an interesting study of the spatial behavior of prisoners, Kinzel (1970) found that violent prisoners need at least three times as much space as do nonviolent prisoners in order to feel comfortable and free of threat. Equally intriguing was the finding that violent prisoners needed more space behind than in front of them, while nonviolent prisoners preferred a circular space.

A comical introduction to the negative reaction generated by violations of proxemic rules can be found in the movie Dumb and Dumber. Early in the movie (about five minutes) Lloyd Christmas imposes upon Mary Swanson by asking her to give him a big hug. This request is clearly a violation or proxemic rules since the two had just met a few moments earlier. The displeasure is easily seen on the face of Mary Swanson as she chooses to not offend Lloyd and gives a reluctant hug.

Discussion questions:

1. How may the study of proxemics be relevant to understanding social conflict?
2. What accounts for differences, for example, between males and females in spatial behavior?
3. How do we protect our personal space in crowded environments?

12. Social Time

All cultures have their own accepted ideas about appropriate behavior. One intriguing cultural difference involves the rules of time or "pace of life." Robert Levine and Ellen Wolff (1985) suggest that to understand a society we must learn its sense of time.

As a visiting professor at the Federal University in Niteroi, Brazil, Levine became acutely aware of cultural differences in social time. Teaching a two-hour class he found some students arriving more than an hour late. Similarly, staying late was of no more importance than arriving late in the first place. When Brazilian and Californian college students were asked what they would consider late or early for a hypothetical lunch appointment with a friend, the average Brazilian defined lateness as 33.5 minutes compared to only 19 minutes for the Californian students. Brazilians also allowed an average of about 54 minutes before they would consider someone early, while Californians drew the line at 24.

Levine and his colleagues attempted to clock the pace of life in various countries by looking at three basic indicators of time: the accuracy of a country's bank clocks, the speed at which pedestrians walked, and the average time it took a postal clerk to sell a single stamp. The very strong relationship that was found between the three measures suggests that we can speak of a unitary concept called "pace of life." For example, in comparing six countries on three continents Levine found the Japanese to have the most accurate clocks, the fastest walking time, and the most efficient postal clerks. The United States ranked second followed by England, Italy, Taiwan, and Indonesia. Levine and Wolff suggest that speed ought not be confused with progress. Perhaps looking carefully at the different paces of life around the world may help us distinguish more accurately between these two qualities.

13. Architects and Products of Our Social Worlds: The Shawshank Redemption

The chapter concludes with "the great lesson of social psychology" and a discussion of both the power of the person and situation. This is also a central theme in the wonderful feature film The Shawshank Redemption. You may want students to view the video outside of class and then hold a class discussion of how it demonstrates both the power of the person and the situation. (The film also provides the basis for a great term paper assignment.)

Alternatively, you may want to show a 15-minute clip that vividly illustrates the principle. Start the clip at approximately 57 minutes into the film where an inmate runs down the steps to inform the main characters, Andy and Red, that Brooks has gone berserk. As the story unfolds, Brooks has been granted parole after 50 years at Shawshank. He resists release (Red argues that, like most prisoners, Brooks has been "institutionalized"). Nonetheless, Brooks is set free and shortly thereafter takes his own life. This scene is immediately followed by Andy's success (after years of letter-writing) in receiving state funding of his proposed library. Euphoric over this success, he defies prison authorities, spends two weeks in solitary confinement, but returns to prison life nonetheless optimistic and determined. Over lunch Andy and Red debate the wisdom of hope in such an oppressive environment.

The scenes demonstrate both the power of the person and situation. In addition, they dramatically illustrate the three ways persons and situations interact as described in the text. A given social situation affects different people differently, people often choose their situations, and people often create their situations.

14. Popular Sources for Additional Lecture Material

Brislin, R. (1988). Increasing awareness of class, ethnicity, culture, and race by expanding on students' own experiences. In I.S. Cohen (Ed.), The G. Stanley Hall lecture series, Vol. 8, p. 137–180. Washington, DC: American Psychological Association. Excellent resource for classroom exercises and student projects on social class, ethnicity, culture, and race.

Bronstein, P. A., & Quina, K. (Eds.) (1988). Teaching a psychology of people: Resources for gender and sociocultural awareness. Washington, D.C.: American Psychological Association. Valuable resource for integrating gender and sociocultural issues into the curriculum.

Burn, S. M. (1996). The social psychology of gender. New York: McGraw-Hill. An excellent survey of the research on gender differences and gender roles. Examines gender as a social category and compares gender across cultures.

Canary, D. J., & Emmers-Sommer, T. M. (1998). Sex and gender in personal relationships. New York: Guilford. Reviews the empirical research on how the sexes communicate in close relationships. Considers how males and females communicate intimacy, control each other in conversation and conflict, and negotiate the division of labor in the household.

Enns, C. Z. (1994). On teaching about the cultural relativism of psychological constructs. Teaching of Psychology, 4, p. 205–211. Summarizes recent theory and research on how personality may be differentially shaped by individualistic and collectivistic cultures. Describes strategies for teaching about the impact of culture on personality.

Lipps, H. M. (1997). Sex and gender: An introduction (3rd ed.). Mountain View, CA: Mayfield Publishing. An overview of theories, research, and issues in gender studies. Examines similarities and differences between females and males. Shows how cultural perceptions of femininity and masculinity shape the questions surrounding gender research.

Lonner, W. J., & Malpass, R. (Eds.). (1994). Psychology and culture. Needham Heights, MA: Allyn & Bacon. Covers the entire range of cross-cultural psychology. A total of 43 short, easy-to-read essays, written by experts in the area, are arranged into seven major sections including basic psychological processes, social and developmental processes, and health psychology.

Matsumoto, D. (1996). Culture and psychology. Pacific Grove, CA: Brooks/Cole. Shows how culture affects a variety of psychological processes and issues including perception, thinking, language, intelligence, health, emotion, and work. Also cites many studies that demonstrate the discrepancies between traditional and cross-cultural interpretations of research.

Moghaddam, F. M., Taylor, D. M., & Wright, S. C. (1993). Social psychology in cross-cultural perspective. Introduces students to the important role of culture in social psychology. Examines research methods in cultural context and then applies a cultural perspective to the study of social cognition, social influence, social relations, and interactions between individuals and groups in applied settings.

Petrikin, J. S. (Ed.). (1995). Male/female roles: Opposing viewpoints. San Diego, CA: Greenhaven Press. Experts provide contrasting perspectives on how gender roles are established, whether women's and men's roles are improving, and on the future of female/male relationships.

Rainey, D. (1986). A gender difference in acceptance of sport aggression: A classroom activity. Teaching of Psychology, 13, p. 138–140. Provides an interesting activity that complements the text's treatment of gender differences in aggression. Students respond to six examples of sport aggression. Males and females disagree on what is acceptable.

Rose, H. R., & Rose, S. (Eds.). (2000). Alas, poor Darwin: Arguments against evolutionary psychology. New York: Harmony Books. A collection of 14 essays from noted authors such as Stephen Jay Gould attacking the extrapolation of evolutionary principles into the realm of social behavior.

Triandis, H.C. (1994). Culture and social behavior. New York: McGraw-Hill. Examines how humans are alike and different. Includes chapters on cultural influences on communication, aggression, helping, and conformity. Concludes with a chapter on intercultural training.

DEMONSTRATIONS AND PROJECT IDEAS

1. Identity Questionnaire

One way to help bridge the gap between topics discussed in the first part of the text (especially Chapters 2 and 3) with topics in the second section (especially Chapter 5) is to have students complete an identity questionnaire (adapted from a scale developed by Cheek, Tropp, Chen, and Underwood (1994). Demonstration 5-1 consists of 12 questions which can be used to generate a measure of personal identity (a person's perceived inner or psychological qualities), social identity (the way we think we are regarded and recognized by others) and collective identity (our sense of belonging to a larger social groups such as our race, ethnic heritage, or religious tradition).

To determine the student's personal identity score, average the responses from items 1, 4, 7, and 10; social identity score, average the responses from items 2, 5, 8, and 11; and collective identity, average the responses from items 3, 6, 9, and 12.

Brown (1998) suggests most European-American college students score highest on the personal identity items, while many Asian-American students score comparably higher on the collective identity items. You may also find a gender difference showing females to be higher in collective identity than males.

2. Intercultural Learning Activities

H. Ned Seelye's (1996) <u>Experiential Activities for Intercultural Learning</u> is a collection of 32 activities designed to foster cultural awareness and cross-cultural sensitivity. Each activity is intended to engender understanding and skill in some facet of intercultural contact. They include simulations, case studies, role plays, critical incidents, and individual and group exercises. Many activities are useful for the classroom; others can be assigned as individual projects to be completed outside of class. They range from basic introductory exercises to activities that explore intercultural activities in significant depth. Some examine intercultural activities in educational contexts; others address relatively complex workplace issues. This book is the first in a projected series and can be ordered in paperback for only $20.95 from Intercultural Press, Inc., P.O. Box 700, Yarmouth, ME 04096 (800-370-2665).

3, Cross-Cultural Dialogues

Craig Storti's (1994) <u>Cross-Cultural Dialogues</u> provides an excellent introduction to cultural diversity. It consists of a collection of 74 brief conversations between an American and someone from another culture. Each conversation includes at least one, often many, breaches of cultural norms that the reader is challenged to discover. Representing 10 cultures, the dialogues are organized by setting including social, workplace, and business. Answers along with analyses of the riddles are included at the end of each section. To illustrate: Ms. Smith asks Mrs. Kalas whether she knows Dr. Spetsos. The latter responds that she does. Ms. Smith follows up by noting that the doctor is an excellent surgeon. Rather surprisingly, Mrs. Kalas responds, "He's a very kind man." The answer to this riddle? Americans think of themselves in terms of what they do and accomplish. Thus they categorize by profession. In Mrs. Kalas's culture what a person does is not as defining as his or her personal qualities. This book can be ordered in paperback for only $15.95 from Intercultural Press, Inc., P.O. Box 700, Yarmouth, ME 04096 (800-370-2665).

4. Barnga: A Simulation Game on Cultural Clashes

Barnga is a simple card game, played in small groups, that simulates the effects of cultural differences on human interaction. Slightly different sets of rules are used and conflict occurs as participants move from group to group. In discovering that the rules are different, players experience culture shock. Sivasailam Thiagarajan, who designed the game, writes of his experience in a West African town named Barnga:

> I was working with some West African counterparts in preparing primary health education booklets. We shared the same basic principles and procedures related to health and to instructional development. Or at least it seemed so during our analysis of the curriculum and preparation of the materials. However, when I came down with a bout of malaria, my counterparts suggested that squeezing the juice of a tobacco leaf into my left nostril would relieve my symptoms. I never did check out this cure, but my perception of the other person's perception of the world underwent a major change. I had to understand and accept our cultural differences before we could function as a collaborative team.

Barnga is designed for nine or more participants and runs from 45 to 90 minutes. It is available for $16.95 from Intercultural Press, P.O. Box 700, Yarmouth, ME 04096 (207-846-5168).

5. Analyzing Critical Cultural Incidents

Richard Brislin and his colleagues have prepared a collection of 100 "critical incidents" (Brislin, R., Cushner, K., Cherrie, C., & Yong, M. [1986]. <u>Intercultural interactions: A practical guide</u>. Beverly Hills, CA: Sage) that are designed to help students understand the nature of culture as well as to prepare them to interact effectively with people from different ethnic groups. Case studies are presented for analysis, which effectively demonstrate how we take specific cultural norms for granted and how cultures differ in their perceived desirability of the same behavior. The examples are excellent for generating classroom discussion on cultural diversity.

6. Introducing Gender Norms

Introduce the topic of gender differences by having students take out a piece of paper and, making two columns, write down everything they think of when they hear the word "Man" and everything they think of when they hear the word "Woman." Encourage them to express their own ideas and feelings, not what others would expect them to write. After they have had five minutes to respond, divide your class into male and female subgroups of five students each and encourage them to share their lists. (To preserve anonymity, you may want to collect, shuffle, and redistribute lists within each subgroup.) After about 10 minutes of single-sex discussion, bring the class together and ask male volunteers to read from their list of male characteristics. Then ask females to do the same. Repeat the process for the list of female characteristics. Note on the chalkboard descriptions that are repeated frequently. Involve the class in a full discussion of gender differences. Ask if gender differences are due to biology, culture, or both.

7. Personal Space Norms

To illustrate cultural differences in personal space norms you might have students pair off and then carry on an informal conversation at varying distances. Anthropologist Edward Hall (see earlier lecture/discussion suggestion on proxemics) describes a cultural continuum of personal space. On the high-contact end, Mediterranean and South American peoples typically carry on social conversation that includes much eye contact, touching, and smiling at about a foot. On the other end of the scale, Northern European cultures conduct social chats at a distance of about two and a half feet. In the United States, a middle-of-the-road culture, people stand about 18 inches apart.

Ferraro (1990) suggests a small group project (four to six students each) in which students design and conduct their own field experiment testing effects of personal space invasions. Depending on time constraints and available subjects, students may want to include some investigation of individual differences. North Americans, British, and Scandinavians prefer more personal space than do Latin Americans, Arabs, and the French. Adults prefer more distance than children; men maintain more distance than do women. To avoid overlap in projects and to ensure that the research is both ethical and feasible, have groups briefly report their design before they conduct their study. Give students up to two weeks to complete their projects and then devote a class period to group presentations and discussion. Have students prepare a final written report.

Ferraro reports that the locations his students chose for data collection included the library, an elevator, a cafeteria, a bus stop, and a dormitory lounge. The most popular dependent variable was the time taken by subjects to respond to an invasion of their personal space. One group used a questionnaire. The members diagrammed a variety of personal space situations (e.g., a schematic of an elevator, varying the number of people in it) and asked respondents where they would stand in each case.

8. Norm Violation

Have students violate some implicit norm and report their experience to the class. Perhaps they could sing in the cafeteria, or sit directly next to a stranger, or face the rear in an elevator. Garfinkle (1967) had students take on an inappropriate role in a familiar setting, for example, by entering their own homes as if they were boarders. Not only will the exercise help students to appreciate the significance of norms but also the discomfort most people experience in violating them. Conformity literature is introduced in Chapter 6.

9. Language and Social Power

The text reports that the greater social power of men is expressed in their speech. "Men's speech" is supposedly direct ("That was fun"); "women's speech" is said to be more hesitating, more characterized by tag questions ("That was fun, wasn't it?"). Have each student observe the conversation of two or three male-female pairs. (Social norms will be more evident if the pair are not intimately acquainted.) Ask them to write down tag questions used by each speaker: Do males or females use tag questions more? The student observers might also count interruptions by men and by women. Who interrupts the most? Finally, they might listen for other differences (for example, who says "but" most often?).

10. Being Masculine is All Right

Instruct students to number one through six on a piece of paper and then to:

> Close your eyes and contemplate each side of your body separately. First, consider your right side. Assess its strengths, its weaknesses, its good points, its bad . . . . Now do the same with your left side . . . . Now answer the following question, opening your eyes only long enough to write your answer to each.

1. Which side is more active?
2. Which side is more passive?
3. Which side is more logical?
4. Which side is more intuitive?
5. Which side of you is more feminine?
6. Which side of you is more masculine?

Right handed students will likely answer "right" to the first, third, and sixth questions, and "left" to the others. That which is active and logical--the more dominant right side--is also perceived as more masculine. (Adapted from Fisher, 1979).

11. Male-Female Differences in Everyday Attitudes and Behaviors

Demonstration 5-2 asks questions that often reveal large behavioral differences between college age men and women. Put your students in small brainstorming groups and ask each group to hypothesize three or four more such behavioral differences and to propose a specific question to test their hypotheses. You can collate questions from the various groups into a second questionnaire to be administered to the whole class. Students should be eager to see how strongly their hypotheses are confirmed. To protect privacy, results should, of course, be tallied out of class.

12. Male-Female Differences in Empathy

The role of empathy in altruism is discussed more fully in Chapter 12. Demonstration 12-3 is the Davis (1980) Empathy Questionnaire and could also be used to introduce the male-female differences in expressed empathy. If your class is large and consists of both sexes, you can examine the gender difference by having your students complete the scale. Otherwise, have each student administer the scale to friends (both male and female), analyze data, and determine whether females express greater empathy. Davis reports significant differences on each of the four subscales with the largest difference occurring in fantasy scores.

13. Do Students Really Favor Equalitarian Marriages?

Gender roles norms are indeed changing, and today most students support marriages of "equally shared responsibilities." But it's one thing to favor the concept and quite another to favor the reality. Alternate the two forms of Demonstration 5-3 (from Bem, 1970) and distribute. Those who receive the description written from the husband's point of view will often perceive the marriage as equalitarian. If the marriage is truly equalitarian then it should remain so if one simply reverses the roles of husband and wife, as in the second version. Few, however, will perceive the reversed-roles marriage as fair to the husband.

This exercise could provide the stimulus for a lively discussion of what equalitarian marriage really is. Is it equality of vocations and incomes? Or is that materialistic—linking one's self-worth to one's income? Is personal androgyny the ideal? Or is it better to be "different but equal"? Should the ideal be "mutual submission in love?" No doubt you will uncover and perhaps help clarify diverse values.

14. Sex Role Scales

John P. Robinson and his colleagues devote an entire chapter to sex role inventories in <u>Measures of Personality and Social Psychology Attitudes</u> published in 1991 by Academic Press. Scales or sample items from the scales are included.

Bem's (1974) measure of psychological androgyny could be completed and scored in class. The test is commercially produced by Consulting Psychologists Press, Inc., 577 College Avenue, Palo Alto, CA 94306.

The Sex-Role Egalitarianism Scale (SRES), designed by Lynda and Daniel King, provides a particularly good introduction to gender roles and is certain to stimulate student discussion regarding traditional expectations of men and women. The instrument contains five subscales covering roles in marriage, parenting, employment, education, and social-linterpersonal relationships. It can be handscored in 5 to 10 minutes. An SRES Examination Kit, including manual, 10 question/answer documents, and 10 profile sheets is available for $27 from Sigma Assessment Systems, Inc., Research Psychologists Press Division, P.O. Box 610984, Port Huron, MI 48061-0984 (Telephone 1-800-265-1285).

Demonstration 5-1

(with permission of Jonathan M. Cheek)

These items describe different aspects of identity. Please read each item carefully and consider how it applies to you. Fill in the blank next to each item by choosing a number from the scale below:

        1 = Not important to my sense of who I am

        2 = Slightly important to my sense of who I am

        3 = Somewhat important to my sense of who I am

        4 = Very important to my sense of who I am

        5 = Extremely important to my sense of who I am

1. ____ My dreams and imagination.

2. ____ My attractiveness to other people.

3. ____ Being a part of the many generations of my family.

4. ____ My emotions and feelings.

5. ____ My popularity with other people.

6. ____ My race or ethnic background.

7. ____ My personal self-evaluations; the private opinion I have of myself.

8. ____ My reputation; what others think of me.

9. ____ My religion.

10. ____ My personal values and moral standards.

11. ____ The ways in which other people react to what I say and do.

12. ____ My feeling of belonging to my community.

(Adapted from Cheek, Tropp, Chen, & Underwood, 1994. Paper presented at the 102nd Annual Convention of The American Psychological Association, Los Angeles.)

Demonstration 5-2

1. Do you ever cry?
   ___ a. Yes, I do sometimes.
   ___ b. No, I seldom or never cry.
2. Do you think of yourself as overweight?
   ___ a. Yes
   ___ b. No
3. Right now, is your room neat?
   ___ a. Yes
   ___ b. No
4. In a locker room do you walk around in the nude?
   ___ a. Yes
   ___ b. No
5. Do you know your chest measurement?
   ___ a. Yes
   ___ b. No
6. In a relationship with someone of the other sex, would you like to be the dominant one?
   ___ a. Yes
   ___ b. No
7. Have you ever changed a tire?
   ___ a. Yes
   ___ b. No
8. Have you attended a worship service within the last month?
   ___ a. Yes
   ___ b. No

(Adapted from Jonides, J. S., and Rozin, P. Study guide for Gleitman's Psychology. New York: W. W. Norton, 1981. Used with permission.)

Demonstration 5-3

(with permission of Brooks/Cole)

Consider the following marriage relationship:

Both my wife and I earned Ph.D. degrees in our respective disciplines. I turned down a superior academic post in Oregon and accepted a slightly less desirable position in New York where my wife could obtain a part-time teaching job and do research at one of the several other colleges in the area. Although I would have preferred to live in a suburb, we purchased a home near my wife's college so that she could have an office at home where she would be when the children returned from school. Because my wife earns a good salary, she can easily afford to pay a maid to do her major household chores. My wife and I share all other tasks around the house equally. For example, she cooks the meals, but I do the laundry for her and help her with many of her other household tasks.

Would you say that this marriage

_____tends to favor the husband

_____is equalitarian

_____tends to favor the wife

Demonstration 5-3

(with permission of Brooks/Cole)

Consider the following marriage relationship:

Both my husband and I earned Ph.D. degrees in our respective disciplines. I turned down a superior academic post in Oregon and accepted a slightly less desirable position in New York where my husband could obtain a part-time teaching job and do research at one of the several other colleges in the area. Although I would have preferred to live in a suburb, we purchased a home near my husband's college so that he could have an office at home where he would be when the children returned from school. Because my husband earns a good salary, he can easily afford to pay a maid to do his major household chores. My husband and I share all other tasks around the house equally. For example, he cooks the meals, but I do the laundry for him and help him with many of his other household tasks.

Would you say that this marriage

_____tends to favor the husband

_____is equalitarian

_____tends to favor the wife

FILMS/VIDEOS

Brain Sex (INS, 150 minutes, 1993). Three volumes in this series examine gender differences. Videos explain how genes, hormones, and brain structure contribute to behavior differences. Helpful in presenting the evolutionary perspective.

Culture (INS, 30 min., 1991). This program portrays cultural diversity within the United States. It shows how different subcultures address human needs in different ways. Profiles the Cajun society of Louisiana, the Cherokee Indians, and Chinese settlements in the South.

Gender Development: Social Influences (ANN, 4 min., 1988). Module #9 from The Brain modules series. Clearly illustrates how we treat boys and girls differently and thereby encourage different abilities. For example, we talk more to girls but are more likely to encourage boys to explore their surroundings.

Gender Socialization (INS, 60 min., 1993). Examines how gender socialization affects self-esteem, emotions, behavior, and world view. Considers the intersection of gender socialization with race and class and how it might change.

Killing Us Softly: Advertising's Image of Women (Cambridge Documentary Films, P.O. Box 385, Cambridge, MA. 02139, 1980). A powerful, vivid, and witty analysis of how advertising reflects and shapes cultural stereotypes of women. (Rental—$46; Sale—$450). Highly recommended.

Still Killing Us Softly (DOC, 30 min., 1987). An updated version of the preceding film. Focuses especially on images of violence, sexuality, and objectification. Explores the relationship of media images to actual problems in society.

Man Oh Man—Growing Up Male in America (NEW, 18 min., 1988). Examines the forces that mold young boys into men. Explores personal definitions of masculinity, communication between genders, gender stereotyping, and changing roles.

Men, Women and Language (INS, 29 min., 1987). Examines origins of gender differences in the use of language and describes the female tendency to use weakening language such as non-specific adjectives and tag questions. Also looks at gender differences in the use of personal space.

Men, Women, and the Sex Difference: Boys and Girls Are Different (FHS, 43 min., 1997) A John Stossel ABC News special, which explores recent research on innate differences between males and females. Useful for introducing the evolutionary perspective.

Sex and Gender (ANN, 30 min., 1988). From the Discovering Psychology series, this video describes male-female similarities and differences and shows how gender roles reflect social values.

Stale Roles and Tight Buns (OAS, 30 min., 1985). Examines male stereotypes in magazine and newspaper ads. Negative images and themes include The Cowboy who is tough, unemotional, and alone, Competitive One-Upmanship, and Violence against women by men.

Theories of Gender Role Differences: The Biological Difference (INS, 60 min., 1994) Explores the theories that propose biological origins for differences in gender roles. Also considers the impact of social structure on gender role development.

Understanding Cultural Differences (INS, 30 min., 1996) Uses interviews with students of different cultures to examine diverse traditions and views. Focus is on overcoming cultural barriers in living in a multicultural environment.

A World of Gestures (UCE, 28 min., 1991). This humorous, entertaining program explores gestures from cultures worldwide. Examines the meaning and function of gestures as a form of nonverbal communication and studies their origins and emotional significance. Enhances appreciation of cultural diversity.

World Song (PYR, 15 min., 1993). This award-winning video celebrates our common humanity through a kaleidoscope of images and cross-cultural songs. It focuses on everyday events in the lives of people from different cultures around the world. Families witness love, marriage, birth, and aging.

CHAPTER 6
CONFORMITY

Classic Studies
    Sherif's Studies of Norm Formation
    Asch's Studies of Group Pressure
    Milgram's Obedience Experiments
    What Breeds Obedience?
    Emotional Distance of the Victim
    Closeness and Legitimacy of the Authority
    Institutional Authority
    The Liberating Effects of Group Influence Reflections on the Classic Studies
    Behavior and Attitudes
    The Power of the Situation
    The Fundamental Attribution Error
When Do People Conform?
    Group Size
    Unanimity
    Cohesion
    Status
    Public Response
    No Prior Commitment
Why Conform?
Who Conforms?
    Personality
    Culture
Resisting Social Pressure
    Reactance
    Asserting Uniqueness
Personal Postscript: On Being an Individual Within Community

LECTURE AND DISCUSSION IDEAS

1. Facilitated Communication: A Case Study in Social Influence

We are often unaware of the influence others have on us as well as we on them. Recent studies of facilitated communication (FC) with autistic children show how influence can be subtle, unnoticed, and yet powerful.

Facilitated communication was introduced as a revolutionary strategy that enabled autistic children to communicate their thoughts and feelings. The facilitator, trained in the technique, presumably steadies the arm of the autistic child who uses one finger to type words on a keyboard. In this way, thousands of children expressed their experiences in intelligible words, elaborate sentences, and sometimes poetry. In certain cases, the children even reported being sexually abused. However, Douglas Wheeler and his colleagues (1993) asked 12 autistic children to view pictures of common objects and then to type what they saw. When their facilitators saw the same objects, the children typed the correct label. However, when the facilitator saw a different object, or none at all, the children were never correct. Other findings have replicated these results, leaving both parents and teachers stunned. Until the controlled experiments were conducted, facilitators had no awareness of their influence on the children's movements. The use of facilitated communication in the treatment of autistic children receives critical appraisal in the 1993 PBS production Prisoners of Silence. It highlights Douglas Wheeler's research (Call 800-344-3337 to order).

2. Is Obedience Good or Bad?

The text notes that conformity is at times bad, at times good, and at times inconsequential. Michael J. Saks (1993) raises the question, "When is compliance bad and disobedience good, and when the reverse?" This is an excellent topic for small group as well as full class discussion. That question, as Saks notes, seems unavoidable in research and theory on obedience to rules.

Saks observes that an undertone of moral judgment accompanies most research on the topic. The work of Asch and Milgram suggests that conformity to group norms is wrong because it leads to error. Kelman and Hamilton's (1989) Crimes of Obedience implies that in some cases disobedience would be the noncrime. But, asks Saks, can we imagine being in the position of one who thinks that Milgram's subjects ought to have obeyed, perhaps because the short-term harm confers longer-term good? (That is both the law's and most parents' justification for punishment: We do harm when we punish, but do so in the service of a greater social good.)

Saks raises other provocative questions to wrestle with in the classroom. For example, should a physician perform an abortion on a patient who requests one? Does it make a difference whether abortion has been made criminal by democratic political process or by religious edict? What if, on the other hand, abortion is legal but the physician believes that the fetus has a moral entitlement to a full life span? Similarly, should a jury scrupulously follow the law to a conviction it feels is unjust? Or should the jury exercise its secret power to ignore the law and deliver an acquittal, which it believes to be just? Can one justify different answers to the doctor question and the jury question?

Certainly part of the dilemma in these situations is that people are presented with conflicting rules. The phrase "crime of obedience" implies that one violates one rule in the course of obeying another. In any given situation, how are we to know which rule to follow? A political protester who breaks the law may point to a higher principle that demands obedience. However, in a telephone panel study of 1575 Chicago residents, Tom Tyler (1990) found that 8 out of 10 respondents agreed that "people should obey the law even if it goes against what they think is right." Do your students agree? Saks relates how an administrator at a hospital once explained to him that whenever a conflict existed between federal law and an institutional law, the local rule controlled. While that would seem ludicrous to lawyers and judges, Saks notes it (a) makes good sense to those bound into the daily work of an organization whose task might be hampered by adherence to "government bureaucracy," and (b) is, as a practical matter, more enforceable within the hospital organization even though it is illegal.

3. Ordinariness of Goodness

What can we learn from the minority that resists authority in Milgram's studies of obedience? Rochat and Modigliani (1995) provide an interesting comparison of Milgram's disobedient participants with the people of the French village of Le Chambon (also discussed in the text) who, during World War II, resisted the efforts of authority to participate in the persecution of minority peoples. The authors reach the interesting conclusion that goodness can sometimes be expressed in quite ordinary ways that are mere extensions of common civility or basic decency.

Rochat and Modigliani found three main themes in disobedient participants' replies to the experimenter's prods that were suggestive of ordinary goodness. That is, those who resisted often articulated one or more of the following everyday rules of interpersonal relations:

1. One should not impose one's will on another. This was the most common reason given for disobedience. Subjects told the experimenter, "I'm not going to go against his will. If he doesn't want to do it I won't."

2. One is responsible for what one does to another. For example, one participant said, "Is this part of the contract? I'm not gonna continue unless he's willing to go along with the experiment. Legally I'm responsible for pushing his hand down. I'm the one responsible, and I can be sued as well as you can."

3. One is always free to choose not to obey harmful demands. In response to the experimenter's prod that "you have no other choice," one participant replied, "My choice is that I just walk right out of here. I can walk out any time I feel like getting out."

4. Suggestibility and Mass Hysteria

Among the most dramatic examples of suggestibility are cases of mass hysteria. In the text, Myers notes the "Seattle Windshield Pitting Epidemic." Potera (1988) cites examples of "Epidemic Psychogenic Illness" (EPI) that you might use in class. In a typical EPI outbreak, Potera notes, large numbers of people suddenly become ill, then recover within hours. No medical reason can be found. Schoolchildren and workers in routine, boring jobs seem to be the most frequent victims.

Psychiatrist Gary Small estimates that one in a thousand schools has an EPI episode each year. In one recent case, 41 Massachusetts grade-schoolers experienced nausea, shortness of breath, and abdominal pains during a concert rehearsal. Six children were hospitalized for several hours. The unexpected highlight of the evening's concert was the collapse of 29 children on stage. The children were "experiencing stress but were in situations that didn't allow for an emotional reaction like crying," explains Small. Instead, physical symptoms developed and "once one kid gets sick, it's OK for others to get sick."

Physician M. Joseph Fedoruk and a colleague describe how EPI can strike adults. In one dramatic incident an entire building of telephone operators was evacuated twice within two days. Headaches, shortness of breath, dizziness and nausea, symptoms, which the workers blamed on a strange odor, sent 81 percent of them to the hospital. An investigation of the building found nothing unusual. The workers performed simple, monotonous tasks for a low wage. Researchers suggest that stress built up waiting for an acceptable outlet. As with the schoolchildren, once someone reports symptoms, it provides a focus for other workers' anxiety and dissatisfaction, and the epidemic spreads like wildfire.

5. Destructive Obedience or Indecisive Disobedience?

Ross and Nisbett (1991) raise this question regarding Milgram's subjects. Their analysis reinforces the text's reflection on the power of the situation.

Ross and Nisbett note that relatively few of Milgram's subjects blindly obeyed. Most participants questioned the experimenter's wisdom in continuing and urged the experimenter to check on the learner's condition. In fact, at some point most refused to continue, some quite forcefully. Still in response to the experimenter's "The experiment requires that you continue....You have no choice," the subjects found it difficult to translate their intention to discontinue into actual termination.

From these findings, Ross and Nisbett argue that the Milgram experiments ultimately have less to say about "destructive obedience" than about ineffectual and indecisive disobedience. They suggest a thought experiment. What if the experimenter had announced from the start that, if at any time the teacher wished to terminate his participation, he could indicate his desire by pressing a button in front of him. If this "disobedience channel" had been opened up, very likely the obedience rate would have been sharply reduced. In short, it was the lack of a well-defined, legitimate channel to discontinue participation that condemned Milgram's subjects to their hapless fate.

Ross and Nisbett further suggest that the events that unfolded did not "make sense" or "add up." The teacher's task was that of administering severe electric shock to a learner who was no longer attempting to learn anything, at the insistence of an experimenter oblivious to the learner's cries, his warnings of a heart condition, and his ultimate refusal to continue responding. The experimenter made no attempt to explain why it was necessary to continue and even refused to "humor" the subject by checking on the learner's condition. Unless subjects grasped both the nature of the deception and the true purpose of the experiment, there was simply no way for them to arrive at a stable definition of the situation. How does one respond "when nothing seems to make sense," when one's own understanding of the actions and outcomes unfolding around one seems limited or deficient? Few people, suggest Ross and Nisbett, respond by acting decisively or asserting independence. Rather they become indecisive, unwilling, and unable to challenge authority, and highly dependent on those who calmly and confidently issue orders.

In conclusion Ross and Nisbett state, "We do not find evidence in Milgram's research that people are disposed to obey authority figures unquestioningly—even to the point of committing harmful and destructive acts. Rather what Milgram offered was a pointed reminder about the capacity of particular, relatively subtle situational forces to overcome people's kinder dispositions."

6. Obedience in Retrospect

Alan Elms was a graduate student of Stanley Milgram's who takes on various issues raised by other theorists concerning Milgram's famous obedience studies in an article entitled <u>Obedience in Retrospect</u> (1995). This article originally appeared in the <u>Journal of Social Issues</u> (Vol. 51, p. 21–31) but can also be found in the 01/02 edition of "Annual Editions–Social Psychology" edited by Davis (see Chapter 1 references). The issues raised include the ethical concerns, questions of whether the participants believed the manipulation, and the relevance of the findings. Some stimulus questions might include: In your opinion, were Milgram's shock studies helpful in understanding obedience and authority issues or were they so unrelated to real-life experiences that their results were basically meaningless? Was Milgram justified in deceiving his participants? How persuasive were the arguments mentioned that were targeted at discrediting Milgram's results? How would you have responded if you were one of Milgram's participants? What was the most surprising finding in this article?

7. Ethical Issues in Research: Deceiving Human Subjects

The literature on conformity, particularly Milgram's study of obedience, raises significant questions about the ethics of social psychological research. The controversy over the researchers' use of deception is reflected in an exchange between Diana Baumrind and Robert A. Baron (1981).

Baumrind maintains that the ethical, psychological, scientific, and societal costs of deception have been greatly underestimated.

Ethical costs are paid when the scientist acts to deceive those whose trust is based on the expectation of trustworthiness in return. When research subjects are given false or incomplete information, they are "deprived of their right to decide freely and rationally how they wish to invest their time and persons."

The psychological costs of deception are particularly severe when they reduce trust in legitimate authority, negatively affect subjects' ability to trust their own judgment, and impair their sense of self-esteem and personal integrity.

Deception also has scientific and societal costs. These include exhausting the pool of naive subjects, jeopardizing community support for scientific research, and undermining order and regularity in social relations, which are dependent upon truth-telling and promise-keeping.

Baumrind argues that debriefing subjects does not necessarily reverse these undesirable aftereffects of deception. For example, in Milgram's studies, debriefing did not restore the subject's self-esteem or willingness to trust authorities in the future. Studies that allow the researcher only the alternatives of a) deceptive debriefing (in which the full truth is not provided because it might lower the subject's self-esteem or adversely affect the research program) or b) "inflicted insight" (in which debriefing provides subjects with painful insight into themselves) should simply never be conducted. Baumrind concludes that investigators must consider "alternative research designs that would accomplish their worthy scientific objectives without violating the spirit and letter of informed consent by using intentionally deceptive or misleading instruction."

Baron responds that Baumrind overstates the potential costs of deception and underestimates both the necessity and potential benefits of such procedures. Moreover, researchers are sensitive to the use of deception and thus employ "informed consent" and "thorough debriefing" to mitigate the problem.

Informed consent involves the standard procedure of providing subjects with information about the nature of an experiment prior to their participation. Baron notes that this does not necessarily involve providing subjects with full information about all purposes, methods, and goals of a research project. If this were the case, investigators might have to give mini-courses on the theoretical bases of their research. Moreover, temporary deception about certain features is still feasible even within the context of informed consent. Subjects may be apprised that some information about the goals or purposes of a study is being temporarily withheld and that such information will be provided later. Such deception is essential in certain studies, for example, in investigating bystander reaction in emergency situations and in analyzing subtle forms of racial bias. The use of temporary deception in research has enabled important insights into why groups often make more extreme decisions than individuals, why humor may inhibit aggression, and why similarity rather than complementarity leads to marital satisfaction.

Debriefing, in which participants are provided with full information about all features of the study after their participation, renders any deceptions employed temporary in nature. Baron further argues that when subjects learn why the temporary deception was necessary, they do not seem to experience the negative reactions described by Baumrind. On the contrary, the vast majority responds positively. For example, in one study on the causes of aggression, subjects were led to believe that they could deliver shocks of varying strength to another person when in fact they could not. More than 95 percent of the participants evaluated this temporary deception as justified and worthwhile. This was true even when subjects completed an anonymous questionnaire and mailed it to someone other than the researcher. Finally, Baron maintains that the insight subjects gain into themselves as a result of debriefing is a valuable experience, even when the information is not flattering.

8. A Failure to Replicate

You may want to extend the text's report of the Hofling et al. (1969) study in which all but one of 22 nurses were ready to comply with a physician's order to administer an obvious overdose of a drug. Rank and Jacobson (1977) reported a much lower level of compliance when the drug in question was familiar to the nurses (Valium) and when they had an opportunity to consult with someone about the dosage. When people are more knowledgeable and when they have social support, they may be more likely to resist authority.

9. Kelman's Model of Social Influence

In discussing the reasons why people conform, the text distinguishes between <u>normative</u> and <u>informational</u> social influence. Herbert Kelman (1958) proposed a model of social influence, which extends this distinction by defining three responses to others' influence: compliance, identification, and internalization.

<u>Compliance</u> occurs when someone accedes to influence in order to achieve favorable reaction, to gain a tangible reward, or to avoid punishment. Thus workers may increase their productivity in order to receive a monetary bonus promised by the employer. Or a college student may study particularly hard to obtain an "A" on an upcoming examination. In each case, the individual <u>complies</u> with the influencing agent, not because of a belief that what is being done is right, but because the action is instrumental in obtaining some external reward or avoiding some external punishment. The result, of course, is that the attitude or action is expressed only so long as rewards and punishments are administered.

<u>Identification</u> occurs when people are influenced by another person because they want to establish or maintain a satisfying self-defining relationship with that person. Identification is like compliance in that the individual does not accept the influence of another person because its content is valid or intrinsically satisfying. However, identification differs from compliance in that the individual actually believes in the attitudes or actions, which he or she adopts. However, only when the individual is acting within the relationship upon which the identification is based will the acquired attitudes or actions be expressed.

<u>Internalization</u> occurs when the individual views a message as truthful and valid. The ideas and actions are intrinsically satisfying and are therefore integrated into the individual's value system. The most obvious examples of internalization are those that involve the evaluation and acceptance of a message on some rational grounds. One adopts the content of the message because it is found useful in solving some problem. Or one accepts the message of an expert simply because the expert is in a position to know what is right. Thus internalization is similar to informational influence.

Compliance, identification, and internalization are rooted in distinctly different types of power. To the extent that the agent's power to influence is based on <u>means control</u>, that is, on the ability to control the means whereby reward is achieved and punishment avoided, influence will take the form of compliance. To the extent that the agent's power is based on attractiveness, influence will take the form of identification. Attractiveness does not refer to those qualities, which make an influencing agent likeable, but simply to those qualities which make a self-defining relationship with him or her desirable. To the extent that the agent's power is based on his credibility, influence takes the form of internalization. An agent is credible when perceived as knowing the right answer and as being willing to communicate it.

A second important way in which the three processes of social influence differ is in terms of the conditions under which the acquired attitude or action is expressed. An individual will engage in an action that is based on compliance only when under the surveillance of the influencing agent. Thus people who comply with the 65 mph speed limit are likely to speed if they are certain no policemen are present. In contrast, an individual who has acquired an attitude through identification will express the attitude whenever his or her relationship to the influencing agent is salient. Since the individual may assume different roles at different times, however, the relationship to the influencing agent must be activated or brought into focus if the appropriate attitude is to be expressed. An attitude or action, which has been internalized, on the other hand, will be expressed regardless of the surveillance or salience of the influencing agent. The individual will express the attitude or perform the action whenever it is relevant.

10. Orientations to Political Authority

Herbert Kelman and Lee Hamilton's (1989) Crimes of Obedience provides a useful source of material for classroom lecture and discussion. Of particular interest is their description of rule, role, and value orientations to political authority. (These orientations are derived from the three processes in Kelman's model of social influence.) Rule-oriented citizens see their task as a matter of respecting authorities' demands, doing what is required of them, and staying out of trouble. In return they expect the government to uphold the rules and thereby protect their basic interests and security. Role-oriented citizens want to be, and indeed perceive themselves as, good citizens who meet their role obligations by active support of the government and faithfully obeying its demands. In return they expect the government to uphold the integrity of their roles by ensuring high status for the nation and relatively high personal status for themselves. They actively support policies that enhance their status within their roles as national citizens and their other roles in society. In contrast, value-oriented citizens are committed to the government because they share the cultural and institutional values on which they believe the state to be founded. They think they have the obligation to take an active part in formulating, evaluating, and questioning national policies. This includes opposing policies that violate fundamental values, even to the point of civil disobedience.

11. Introducing Conformity and Nonconformity Through Film

In addition to the other film resources identified below, it is possible to relate laboratory-based principles of conformity to graphic, filmed examples of conformity.

The 18-minute film, The Lottery, based on Shirley Jackson's short story, is a vivid study of conformity. A twentieth-century American community annually selects from among its membership a "winner" who becomes a sacrificial victim. Although questions are raised by some residents, all nevertheless conform. Why? Class discussion will highlight situational determinants. The concepts of conformity, compliance, acceptance, and normative and informational influence can all be illustrated through examples from the film.

The themes of conformity and resistance to social pressure are central in Dead Poets Society, a feature film starring Robin Williams. Williams portrays English professor John Keating who inspires his students to reject tradition and "seize the day, make your lives extraordinary." He has a profound impact on his students but eventually loses his job. Although there are many good scenes in this film on conformity and nonconformity, one of the most dramatic occurs at the very end of the film. You can introduce the literature on resistance to social pressure by showing the last five minutes 15 seconds of the film. Keating's elderly, authoritarian replacement walks into the classroom in an obvious effort to bring the students back in line. Keating enters shortly thereafter to remove his belongings. Many of boys in the class defy the strong social pressure being exerted by his replacement. First one, then another, and finally most of the class stand on their desks in saluting their former teacher.

The strength needed to be the lone opposition to a majority is well represented in the movie Twelve Angry Men (either 1957 or 1997 version). After the jury members get settled (about six minutes into the film), the powerful conforming pressure of 11 versus 1 is portrayed in the initial polling of the jury members. The minority position is maintained only because of an unusually strong character. Later in the movie, the minority position grows from one to two and the stranglehold of conformity pressures begins to loosen. Also, note the normative and informational reasons for conforming with the majority by the other jury members.

12. Does Power Corrupt?

David Kipnis (1984) attempts to answer that question. In research with his colleagues he has studied a number of dimensions of power including the strength of the tactics people use to get their way. He distinguishes between "soft tactics"—being nice, flattering, pleading; "rational tactics"—explaining, discussing, compromising; and "strong tactics"—ordering, threatening, getting angry. Strong tactics seem to trigger the following events: First, success seems to strengthen the powerholder's belief that he or she controls the other person. This is followed by devaluation of the people being influenced. Their behavior, no matter how good it is, is attributed to the orders rather than to their abilities or motivations. This typically sets the stage for subsequent exploitation.

Kipnis reports this sequence holds both in home and work settings. In research with 195 couples, he found that people who unilaterally controlled decision-making had a less satisfactory relationship than those who shared power. The dominant partners not only expressed less affection for their companions but also described them in less flattering terms in regard to intelligence, success, or skill. In another study, Kipnis and his colleagues instructed managers of small groups to influence in one of two ways. Authoritarian leaders were told to assert complete control over the assembly of model cars while democratic leaders were instructed to allow their employees to share in decisions about work. While employees working for both types of leaders did equally good work, authoritarian leaders complained their employees lacked motivation, evaluated their work less favorably, and rated them as less suitable for promotion.

13. Reactance and the Romeo and Juliet Effect

Does parental interference create reactance and thereby lead couples to commit themselves more firmly to the partnership and fall more deeply in love? Perhaps students can be encouraged to reflect on their own experiences in answering that question. Romeo and Juliet's passionate love affair took place against the background of total opposition from their two feuding families.

Driscoll, David, and Lipitz (1972) tested the hypothesis that parental opposition would deepen romantic love. In examining data from 140 Colorado couples, they found that parental interference and romantic love were positively and significantly related. The authors also reported that as parents began to interfere more in a relationship, the couple appeared to fall more deeply in love. Similarly, if the parents became resigned to the relationship and thus interfered less, the couples began to feel less intensely about one another.

14. Brewer's Optimal Distinctiveness Theory

The text notes that people feel uncomfortable when they appear too different from others. But, at least in western cultures they also feel uncomfortable when they appear exactly like everyone else. You can extend this theme in class by introducing Brewer's (1991) optimal distinctiveness theory.

Brewer argues that there is a fundamental tension between human needs for similarity to others on one hand, and a countervailing need for uniqueness on the other. Social identity theory provides one perspective on how these conflicting drives can be reconciled. Social identity (one's self-concept includes membership in some social category) can be viewed as a compromise where the need to be similar is met by belonging to some group, while the need for distinctiveness is met through inter-group comparisons. Brewer cites adolescent peer groups as providing a protypical case. She writes, "Each cohort develops styles of appearance and behavior that allow individual teenagers to blend in with their age mates while 'sticking out like a sore thumb' to their parents." Brewer hypothesizes that we avoid self-construals that are either too personalized or too inclusive and instead define ourselves in terms of distinctive category memberships. Social identity and group loyalty will be highest for those self-categorizations that simultaneously provide for a sense of belonging and a sense of distinctiveness. In two experiments Brewer and Weber (1994) found strong support for the theory.

15. Popular Sources for Additional Classroom Material

Fisher, C. B., & Fyrberg, D. (1994). Participant partners: College students weigh the costs and benefits of deceptive research. American Psychologist, 49, p. 417–427. Examines how research participants rate the scientific merits, psychological discomfort, and cost-benefit balance of three recently published studies utilizing deception.

Gibson, J. T., & Haritos-Fatouros, M. (1986, November). The education of a torturer. Psychology Today, p. 50–58. Argues that torturers are neither sadists nor deviants. Instead they are ordinary people conditioned to commit cruel, violent, and even fatal acts.

Johnson, M. A. (1989). Concern for appropriateness scale and behavioral conformity. Journal of Personality Assessment, 53, p. 567–574. Presents a measure of individual differences in susceptibility to peer pressure that could be used in class. In a test of validity, pressures to conform were exerted on four critical questions that subjects had identified as either personally important or unimportant.

Kelman, H. C., & Hamilton, V. (1989). Crimes of obedience. The authors analyze the Nazi war crimes, the My Lai massacre, Watergate, and the Iran-Contra affair and show "how responsibility may be 'lost' when it is most essential to retain it: in the military and bureaucratic hierarchies of the modern world."

Kerckoff, A. C., & Back, K. W. (1969, June). The bug. Psychology Today, p. 46–69. A description of a case of hysterical contagion in which employees in a textile factory became ill presumably because of insect bites. In fact, the victims were suffering from anxiety and the authors analyze the cause.

Milgram, S. (1974). Obedience to authority. New York: Harper and Row. This book provides a complete description of Milgram's controversial research on obedience. He reflects on the implications of his research and also considers the ethics of the obedience studies.

Milgram, S. (1992). The individual in a social world, 2nd ed. New York: McGraw-Hill. A collection of Milgram's essays and experiments including those on obedience and conformity. Includes the text of the address he gave on his last project, the Cyranic mode.

Miller, A. G. (1986). The obedience experiments: A case study of controversy in social science. New York: Praeger. Reviews the nearly two dozen obedience experiments conducted by Milgram and the ensuing replications, critiques, and controversies. Examines obedience and social destructiveness, the social psychology of authority, and intuitive beliefs about harmful obedience.

Miller, A. G., Collins, B.E., & Brief, D.E. (1995). Perspectives on obedience to authority: The legacy of the Milgram experiments. Journal of Social Issues, 51, p. 1–20. Provides the editors' introduction to an entire issue devoted to the Milgram studies and to the analysis of obedient and defiant behavior.

Remley, A. (1988, October). From obedience to independence. Psychology Today, p. 56–59. Describes changes in the traits parents value. At one time, parents trained their children to be obedient. Now they are raising them to be self-reliant.

Ross, L. & Nisbett, R. E. (1991). The person and the situation: Perspectives of social psychology. New York: McGraw-Hill. Although the book covers topics broader than conformity, chapters 2 and 3 may be particularly helpful for preparing lectures dealing with the classic studies of conformity (Milgram and Asch).

Sabini, J., & Silver, M. (1982). Moralities of every life. New York: Oxford University Press. Describes and analyzes phenomena such as envy, gossip, and procrastination from a social psychological perspective. Deals with Milgram's studies in a chapter entitled, "On Destroying the Innocent with a Clear Conscience."

Snyder, C. R., & Fromkin, H. L. (1980). Uniqueness: The human pursuit of difference. New York: Plenum Press. Draws from literature, advertising, and the laboratory to demonstrate the human concern with uniqueness. One chapter includes a scale to measure one's need for uniqueness.

Staub, E. (1989). The roots of evil: The origins of genocide and other group violence. New York: Cambridge University Press. Analyzes the social psychological roots of human torture and slaughter as practiced in Turkey, Nazi Germany, Argentina, Cambodia, Russia, and Greece.

DEMONSTRATION AND PROJECT IDEAS

1. Student Studies of Social Influence

Neil Lutsky (1993) suggests a very useful research paradigm for involving students in the study of social influence. It could also be used as the basis for classroom demonstration. Adapted from White (1975), student experimenters compare the responses of control subjects on a survey question to those of experimental subjects who have first been exposed to the contrived responses of others to the same question. For example, Lutsky's class created two forms of a survey containing the following question, "How much should you be expected to spend on all of your textbooks for three courses during an average term at Carleton?" On half the surveys, all 20 lines were left blank. On the other half, eight lines were filled in with signatures and with answers selected to be deviant from social norms. Student experimenters each recruited a set number of subjects and randomly assigned them to the two conditions. Robust influence effects were obtained. While control subjects gave a mean of $99.69, those first exposed to eight signatures giving a mean response of $180 gave their own mean of $145.94. In a second study, control subjects gave a mean of $105. Those exposed to eight bogus signatures averaging $80 gave a mean of $82.10.

As Lutsky points out, White's paradigm permits students to explore a variety of issues. Some student experimenters explored the significance of the survey question. For example, some respondents were told that their opinions would be shared with the Financial Aid Office and would be a factor that would go into students' financial aid packages. Even with this statement of importance, substantial influence effects were obtained. Other student experimenters used White's strategy to explore a question with moral meaning. Their survey included a background statement on euthanasia and then asked respondents to indicate at what chance of recovery, from 0–100 percent, they would recommend that a hypothetical patient's life support systems be discontinued. Social influence providing a mean of 50 percent elicited a recovery criterion of 35.9 percent, compared to the mean uninfluenced response of 20.1 percent.

2. Sherif's Studies of Norm Formation

Robert L. Montgomery (personal communication) suggests a classroom demonstration paralleling Sherif's studies of norm formation. It can serve as the point of departure for discussing conformity. The demonstration is based on research by Montgomery and Enzie (1971) and involves time interval estimation.

Make sure each student has a blank piece of paper and either pen or pencil. Have the students remove and hide their wrist watches and tell them not to look at the clock. They are also to avoid counting to themselves. Then say, "I am going to give you a time interval that I want you to estimate. I will say 'start' at the beginning, and 'stop' at the end of the interval. Then I want you to write down how long you think the interval was." (Montgomery suggests 45 seconds is a good interval, though several others may be used ranging from 15 to 75 seconds). After the judgments have been written down privately, a second trial begins. Say "start" and give the same interval (students rarely realize it's the same) as before. This time, however, ask students to give their responses orally, one by one, as you write them on the blackboard. After all have been recorded, collect the papers from the first trial (or have students read what they wrote). Record these on another section of the blackboard. Immediately students will see that the judgments written privately have much greater variation than those given orally (the social influence condition). Also, as was true in the Sherif study, when asked, many students will feel that they were not actually influenced that much by the others and that the second judgment given <u>actually</u> did seem more similar to the group norm that emerged.

Montgomery adds that the demonstration provides the opportunity for making distinctions between informational and normative influence, the difference between Sherif's and Asch's research, and for describing the overall design of the autokinetic studies. You might also ask, "Would subjects in this experiment be more likely to conform if they were with a group of friends instead of strangers? Would high status members of a "natural" group of friends influence middle and low status members more and be influenced less themselves?" Research by Pollis and Montgomery (1966, 1968) and Montgomery (1971) suggests that the answer to these questions is affirmative.

3. Suggestibility

John Fisher's fascinating book, <u>Body Magic</u> (Stein & Day, 1980), contains many simple demonstration ideas. Among the best are those that illustrate suggestibility.

For example, tell a friend that you see he has a scratch on his arm. Ask, "Does it itch?" Undoubtedly, he will be surprised, but you continue to look at his arm. You are certain you see a slight scratch on his arm. Eventually he is almost certain to feel a need to scratch the invisible mark out of a need for relief.

Stage hypnotists also present their audiences with the idea that they will begin to experience itching sensations on various parts of the body. In fact, the sensations will be so strong that they won't be able to keep from scratching them. Specific parts of the body are mentioned. The stage performer may even casually scratch herself. Before long the audience will be scratching imaginary itches. Does it work? Might you have felt the need to scratch as you read these words?

Another variation on this same theme is to suggest that the audience will feel a tickle in the throat, accompanied by an irresistible need to swallow. At this point, the performer himself, swallows. The suggestion proves irresistible. Reflexively the audience will do the same.

Finally, ask the audience to hold their hands in front of them about 16 inches apart, their index fingers pointing toward each other. Indicate to them that their fingers are becoming nervous in this position and consequently are not pointing together exactly. They will have difficulty in making the tips touch. Instruct them to bring their fingertips together quickly. They must do so quickly, without hesitation. Although this should be an easy assignment to carry out, the suggestion of doubt will cause the average person to miss. In fact, the more they try, the more difficult the task will become.

4. "Tell Me When You Smell It"

Different from those described above, this effective, hilarious demonstration of suggestion requires some practice and stage presence. Passed along and refined by Donald McBurney, he is uncertain of its origin. Although McBurney uses it in teaching sensation and perception, it works equally well for social psychology. (If you think you need a cover, present it as a brief diversion perhaps telling your class you just learned something remarkable about psychology from a colleague studying sensation and want to share it).

Explain how the nose is incredibly sensitive to odor. For example, as little as 10 parts per billion of ethyl mercaptan is detectable in air. Because of its low threshold, ethyl mercaptan is the chemical added to natural gas to gives it its familiar odor. Explain that chemicals like ethyl mercaptan smell very different depending on their concentrations. At higher concentrations, it smells quite foul. Odor thresholds are also highly variable because of such things as individual differences and the circulation of air. (Everything above is true.)

Now carefully remove a plastic lab bottle (of water!) from a box and place it on your front desk, preferably about 6 feet from the first row of students. Say something like, "Perhaps I shouldn't be doing this, but pure ethyl mercaptan was readily available from our chemistry lab. A single drop of it could render the room uninhabitable for the rest of the day." Avert you face and carefully remove the cap from the bottle. Go on to explain, "Because weak concentrations smell different, it may not smell like natural gas, but have some other smell. Also because of air currents in the room someone in the back may smell it before someone in front. Please raise your hand when you think you detect it." (Nod your head or say "okay" when someone raises their hand. If people are sitting in rows or you have a fairly large class, you can "recognize" nonexistent hands without being caught.) Back away from the bottle so you don't have to tolerate the odor.

When roughly a quarter of the people in class have raised their hands, return to the bottle to take a breath. In reaching for it knock it over in the direction of your students. They will cringe. Pick up the bottle, take a drink from it, sprinkle it over nearby students, pour it on yourself. After the howls of laughter have settled done, tell your class you have just demonstrated the power of suggestion. You might add that neighbors of crematoria often complain about the odor, but only because they see smoke coming out of the chimney. Conclude by noting that everything you said about smell was true; the only deception was using water instead of ethyl mercaptan. Although students may remember nothing else from your course, they will remember the day you spilled ethyl mercaptan in class!

5. Experiencing Conformity

Demonstration 6-1 invites students to recall experiences of conformity. If distributed, this could provide the basis for class discussion, or perhaps better yet, for discussion in small buzz groups.

6. Experiencing Nonconformity

The text suggests that one can sense the "awesome potency of social situations" by imagining oneself "violating some less than earth shaking norms: standing up in the middle of a class; singing out loud in a restaurant. In trying to break with social constraints one suddenly realizes how strong they are." Better even than imagining is doing such. Ask students each to do some wild norm-violating act—to dress atypically, to walk backwards across campus, to respond inappropriately to everyday greetings—and to record a) others' verbal and nonverbal responses and b) their own feelings. Students will enjoy discussing their experiences of nonconformity.

7. The Social-Emotional Price for Nonconformity

One powerful way to demonstrate the difficulty associated with nonconformity and deviating from established norms can be easily interjected into class. At the beginning of class—maybe even before the class begins, simply ask for a volunteer. Once one has been recruited, ask the volunteer to stand at their seat. While they are waiting for the next instruction from you, simply begin class. Conduct a normal class for as long as you'd like (at least three to five minutes) without making any reference to the standing student. By interviewing the student after the exercise the class can hear first-hand the social-emotional price paid by the student for this act of nonconformity.

A derivative of this exercise consists of passing out a form to every student which informs them of some cue you will give during class which will trigger the students to stand up at their seat (e.g., a word or gesture from you). One student (or more than one if you'd like), however, will not get this form. Instead, they will get a form, which tells them something totally unrelated to the upcoming classroom exercise (e.g., some unrelated demonstration form from this instructor's manual or some note suggesting a change in your office hours). After class has started, give the cue and see if all of the students stand up. A few will pick up on the trigger immediately and begin to stand. This will bring everyone else to their feet—even the person(s) who has no idea what is going on. If you don't gather up the forms individually, you may have a hard time determining which student(s) got the odd form. Once the nature of the exercise is revealed, the odd student(s) may not want to identify themselves as the one who chose not to pay the social-emotional price for nonconformity.

8. Would You Obey?

When Milgram described his study to psychiatrists, college students, and middle-class adults, and asked "How far would you go. . .?" the average estimated response of all three groups was about 135 volts. One way to introduce the Milgram obedience study is to have students predict how they would respond and, also, how the average college student would respond. Before students have read Chapter 6 distribute Demonstration 6-2. It lists the 30 voltage levels on Milgram's shock generator and identifies their level of intensity. Describe Milgram's procedure and then ask your students to estimate how they would respond. Virtually all will underestimate. You will also find evidence for self-serving bias (Chapter 2) as students will predict that they themselves would disobey earlier than would the average college student. Then report Milgram's actual results. One subject stopped at 135 volts; five at 150; one each at 165, 180, 285, and 300; three at 315, one each at 345 and 360; and 25 obeyed to the end.

9. Obedience and the Fundamental Attribution Error

Martin Safer (1980) reports that students who have read about Milgram's obedience experiments and have seen Milgram's film, <u>Obedience</u>, often mistakenly conclude that people are evil and would harm a stranger if given the opportunity. As the text says, "Cruelty is presumed to be inflicted by the cruel at heart."

But attributing cruelty to the subjects' evil dispositions misses the whole point of the experiment—which is that the subjects were sheep, not wolves. Demonstration 6-3 (courtesy of Martin Safer) asks students to estimate the shock level that subjects deliver when uncoerced by the experimenter. Under the conditions described, Milgram reports that only one subject in 40 set the maximum shock, and that over trials the shock level remained in the 45 to 60 volt range. Safer reports that University of Wisconsin-Madison students who are aware of Milgram's findings <u>overestimate</u> these freely chosen levels of shock. Will the same be true of students <u>who have read</u> the text discussion of attribution errors in people's explanations of obedience? You can find out.

Safer reports that this exercise helps students "understand how situational factors, rather than individual character, determine behavior in the obedience paradigm, as well as in the Zimbardo prison study." The exercise will also reinforce the Chapter 3 discussion of attribution.

10. Normative Versus Informational Social Influences

The chapter suggests that individualistic cultures may lead people to presume that being socially influenced is bad. That this is not necessarily so, and that people are influenced for informational reasons as well as in response to normative pressures, will be clear to those who experience Demonstration 7-4 (adapted from W. V. Haney, <u>Communication and Interpersonal Relations</u>, 4th ed., Richard D. Irwin, Inc., 1979, p. 250–251).

First, have each person complete Demonstration 6-4. Then form small groups, asking each to discuss each item to consensus. If, after a thorough airing of arguments it's clear that consensus is impossible, people may "agree to disagree" and circle their own current judgments.

After the discussions are complete, people may return to their original seats and you can announce the answers: "Question 3 is false; Question 6 is true; for all other questions the appropriate response is a question mark." There will be some incredulous students, but those groups that got the questioned-items correct will gladly explain their reasoning to those who did not. Now ask each student to calculate his or her number correct <u>before</u> group discussion, and the number correct <u>after</u> the group discussion. Then ask, "How many of you had more correct <u>before</u> the group discussion?" (Virtually no hands will rise.) "How many of you had more correct <u>after</u> the group discussion?" (Virtually every hand will rise.) Say, "It's obvious that nearly all of you were socially influenced—you changed one or more of your responses. Was this an example of what the text calls <u>normative</u> or <u>informational</u> social influence?" (Most will readily recognize that they have experienced informational influence—in this case, an Ah ha! insight or two as they were exposed to others' reasoning.)

This is a sure-to-work demonstration that is fun for students. It can easily be used in conjunction with Chapter 8's discussion of normative and informational influence in group discussion.

11. Reactance

Tell students that you "can easily demonstrate how predictable and compliant people are, especially in response to an authority figure. In some situations the average person really is quite predictable." Ask them to raise their pens and when you say DROP to drop them in unison.

Likely only a few will do so, whereupon you can open up a sealed envelope containing your actual prediction, which is that, given your denial of their freedom and individual uniqueness, most people would react opposite to your command and <u>not</u> drop their pen. This demonstration could introduce a discussion of reactance.

12. The Need for Uniqueness Scale

Demonstration 6-5 represents Snyder and Fromkin's (1977; 1980) Need for Uniqueness Scale.

To calculate the total Need for Uniqueness Scale score, reverse each of the individual scores on items 2, 3, 5, 7, 9, 11, 13, 14, 17, 19, 22, 23, 26, 27, 28, 31. That is, 1 to 5, 2 to 4, 3 to 3, 4 to 2, and 5 to 1. On these 16 reversed items, have students mark through their original score, and put the reversed score in the blank. Finally, add the scores for all 32 items. The higher the score, the higher the need for uniqueness as measured by the uniqueness scale. This scale was developed to measure not how different one actually may be but rather the magnitude of a person's desire or need to be unique.

Snyder and Fromkin (1980) report that among 1,404 students at the University of Kansas and Purdue University, a score of 100 was at the 50th percentile (i.e., an average, not very unique, need for uniqueness!):

Raw score	Percentile
70	2
80	10
90	26
100	50
110	74
120	90
130	98

13. The Psychological Reactance Scale

To introduce the research on "resisting social pressure" you might invite students to complete Dowd, Milne, and Wise's (1991) Therapeutic Reactance Scale (Demonstration 6-6). It is designed to measure individual differences in reactance potential or in the tendency to be oppositional. Dowd (in press) provides an excellent review of research utilizing the scale including a description of personality characteristics associated with psychological reactance and its likely developmental antecedents.

To calculate total reactance potential, reverse each of the individual scores on items 7, 11, 13, 14, 18, 21, 24, 25, and 28. That is, change 1 to 4, 2 to 3, 3 to 2, and 4 to 1. On these nine reversed items, have students mark thorough their original score, and put the reversed score in the blank. Finally, add the scores for all 28 items. The higher the score, the greater the tendency to be oppositional. For 150 introductory psychology students at a large mid-eastern university the mean was 68.86, and the range was 50 to 87.

14. The Social Connection Video Series

Several entries in the video instructional supplement (The Social Connection Video Series) provide additional information pertinent to Chapter 6. "Conformity and Obedience" reflects on Asch's and Milgram's famous studies as well as noting other non-experimental examples; "The Fundamental Attribution Error" discusses several ramifications dealing with this common tendency; and "Understanding Genocide" leads students to ponder the social forces involved in atrocities such as the Holocaust and Hussein's mass killings. See the Faculty Guide accompanying the video series for program summaries, pause points, and classroom activities for each of these videos.

Demonstration 6-1

When you were in high school, were there norms that dictated how you were supposed to look?

    Clothes: _____

    Shoes: _____

    Hair style: _____

Do you remember people who weren't groomed that way? How were they regarded and treated?

_____

At college, have there been things you've wanted to do, but haven't, because such activity would be socially disapproved?

_____

Or, under others' influence, have you done something that really wasn't your type of activity?

_____

Does this illustrate what the text terms <u>normative</u> or <u>informational</u> influence?

_____

Demonstration 6-2

Shock Level	Verbal designation and voltage level	Shock level at which I would disobey	Shock level at which the average college student would disobey	Percentage of subjects who would continue to the 450 volt level
	Slight Shock			
1	15			
2	30			
3	45			
4	60			
	Moderate Shock			
5	75			
6	90			
7	105			
8	120			
	Strong Shock			
9	135			
10	150			
11	165			
12	180			
	Very Strong Shock			
13	195			
14	210			
15	225			
16	240			
	Intense Shock			
17	255			
18	270			
19	285			
20	300			
	Extreme Intensity Shock			
21	315			
22	330			
23	345			
24	360			
	Danger: Sever Shock			
25	375			
26	390			
27	405			
28	420			
	XXX			
29	435			
30	450			

Demonstration 6-3

(with permission of M. Safer)

In the text, you read about the Milgram obedience experiment. In that experiment, the "teacher" was asked to shock a "learner" as part of an experiment. The shock generator looked like this:

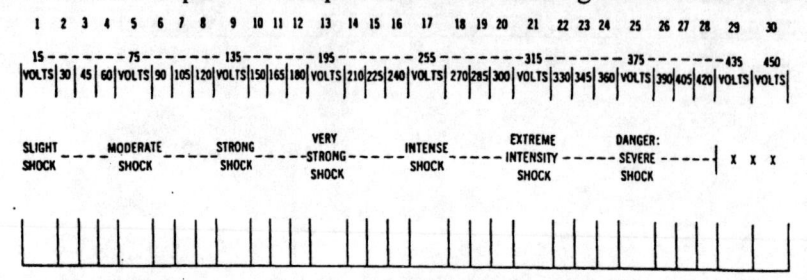

When ordered to do so, most "teachers" proceeded clear to the end of the shock generator, despite the "learners" protests.

Milgram also conducted the following experiment, using similar people. However, instead of increasing the shock after each error, the teacher was free to choose the shock level. Without any coercion from the experimenter, the teacher could use the highest levels on the generator, the lowest, or any in between. During the experiment, the learner made 30 errors, just like in the original experiment. After each error, the teacher had to choose a shock level. The teacher could stay at the same level after each error. Except for the teacher <u>choosing</u> the shock level, everything was exactly the same. Please answer the following questions, which ask you to predict how the teacher would respond in this version of Milgram's experiment.

On the average, what level of shock voltage do you think the teacher chose for the learner? Please look at the scale on the shock generator and then write down your answer (from 15 to 450 volts).

_____ volts

What shock level do you think the teacher chose for the learner's thirtieth (last) error? Use the same scale.

_____ volts

What percentage of teachers do you think eventually set the shock at 450 volts?

_____ %

Demonstration 6-4

<u>Directions</u>: Read the following story and answer the 12 questions, indicating true, false, or "?" if one cannot tell from the story whether the answer is true or false. You may refer back to the story while answering the questions—this is not a memory test.

A businessman had just turned off the lights in the store when a man appeared and demanded money. The owner opened a cash register. The contents of the cash register were scooped up, and the man sped away. A member of the police was notified promptly.

Statements about the story:

1. A man appeared after the owner had turned off his store lights.   T   F   ?
2. The robber was a man.   T   F   ?
3. The man did not demand money.   T   F   ?
4. The man who opened the cash register was the owner.   T   F   ?
5. The store owner scooped up the contents of the cash register and
   sped away.   T   F   ?
6. Someone opened a cash register.   T   F   ?
7. After the man who demanded the money scooped up the contents
   of the cash register, he ran away.   T   F   ?
8. While the cash register contained money, the story does not state how much. T   F   ?
9. The robber demanded money of the owner.   T   F   ?
10. A businessman had just turned off the lights when a man appeared
    in the store.   T   F   ?
11. The story concerns a series of events in which only three persons are
    referred to: the owner of the store, a man who demanded money, and a
    member of the police force.   T   F   ?
12. The following events in the store are true: someone demanded money, a
    cash register was opened, its contents were scooped up, and a man dashed
    out of the store.   T   F   ?

(From W. V. Haney, Communication and Interpersonal Relations, 4th ed. Richard D. Irwin, Inc., 1979, p. 250–252. Used with permission.)

Demonstration 6-5

(with permission of C. R. Snyder)

Directions: The following statements concern your perceptions about yourself in a variety of situations. Your task is to indicate the strength of your agreement with each statement, utilizing a scale in which 1 denotes strong disagreement, 5 denotes strong agreement, and 2, 3, and 4 represent intermediate judgments. In the blank preceding each statement, place a number from 1 to 5 from the following scale:

1	2	3	4	5
strongest agreement				strongest disagreement

There are no "right" or "wrong" answers, so select the number that most closely reflects you on each statement. Take your time and consider each statement carefully.

___ 1. When I am in a group of strangers, I am not reluctant to express my opinion openly.
___ 2. I find that criticism affects my self-esteem.
___ 3. I sometimes hesitate to use my own ideas for fear they may be impractical.
___ 4. I think society should let reason lead it to new customs and throw aside old habits or mere traditions.
___ 5. People frequently succeed in changing my mind.
___ 6. I find it sometimes amusing to upset the dignity of teachers, judges, and "cultured" people.
___ 7. I like wearing a uniform because it makes me proud to be a member of the organization it represents.
___ 8. People have sometimes called me "stuck-up."
___ 9. Others' disagreements make me uncomfortable.
___ 10. I do not always need to live by the rules and standards of society.
___ 11. I am unable to express my feelings if they result in undesirable consequences.
___ 12. Being a success in one's career means making a contribution that no one else has made.
___ 13. It bothers me if people think I am being too unconventional.
___ 14. I always try to follow rules.
___ 15. If I disagree with a superior on his or her views, I usually do not keep it to myself.
___ 16. I speak up in meetings in order to oppose those whom I feel are wrong.
___ 17. Feeling "different" in a crowd of people makes me feel uncomfortable.
___ 18. If I must die, let it be an unusual death rather than an ordinary death in bed.
___ 19. I would rather be just like everyone else than be called a "freak."
___ 20. I must admit I find it hard to work under strict rules and regulations.
___ 21. I would rather be known for always trying new ideas than for employing well-trusted methods.
___ 22. It is better always to agree with the opinions of others than to be considered a disagreeable person.
___ 23. I do not like to say unusual things to people.
___ 24. I tend to express my opinions publicly, regardless of what others say.
___ 25. As a rule, I strongly defend my own opinions.
___ 26. I do not like to go my own way.
___ 27. When I am with a group of people, I agree with their ideas so that no arguments will arise.
___ 28. I tend to keep quiet in the presence of persons of higher rank, experience, etc.
___ 29. I have been quite independent and free from family rule.
___ 30. Whenever I take part in group activities, I am somewhat of a nonconformist.
___ 31. In most things in life, I believe in playing it safe rather than taking a gamble.
___ 32. It is better to break rules than always to conform with an impersonal society.

Demonstration 6-6

(with permission of E. Thomas Dowd)

Personal Attitude Inventory

Respond to the statements below by using the following scale:

    1=strongly disagree
    2=disagree
    3=agree
    4=strongly agree

___ 1. If I receive a lukewarm dish at a restaurant, I make an attempt to let that be known.
___ 2. I resent authority figures who try to tell me what to do.
___ 3. I find that I often have to question authority.
___ 4. I enjoy seeing someone else do something that neither of us is supposed to.
___ 5. I have a strong desire to maintain my personal freedom.
___ 6. I enjoy playing "devil's advocate" whenever I can.
___ 7. In discussions, I am easily persuaded by others.
___ 8. Nothing turns me on as much as a good argument.
___ 9. It would be better to have more freedom to do what I want on a job.
___10. If I am told what to do, I often do the opposite.
___11. I am sometimes afraid to disagree with others.
___12. It really bothers me when police officers tell people what to do.
___13. It does not upset me to change my plans because someone in the group wants to do something else.
___14. I don't mind other people telling me what to do.
___15. I enjoy debates with other people.
___16. If someone asks a favor of me, I will think twice about what this person is really after.
___17. I am not very tolerant of others' attempts to persuade me.
___18. I often follow the suggestions of others.
___19. I am relatively opinionated.
___20. It is important to me to be in a powerful position relative to others.
___21. I am very open to solutions to my problems from others.
___22. I enjoy "showing up" people who think they are right.
___23. I consider myself more competitive than cooperative.
___24. I don't mind doing something for someone even when I don't know why I'm doing it.
___25. I usually go along with others' advice.
___26. I feel it is better to stand up for what I believe than to be silent.
___27. I am very stubborn and set in my ways.
___28. It is very important for me to get along well with the people I work with.

Dowd, E.T., Milne, C.R., & Wise, S.L. (1991). The Therapeutic Reactance Scale: A Measure of Psychological Reactance, Journal of Counseling and Development, 69, p.543. Copyright American Counseling Association. Reprinted with permission.

FILMS/VIDEOS

Conformity (PSU, 30 min., 1989). Identifies the pros and cons of conformity and examines its role in group decision making, the classroom, and the military. Explores the motives for conformity and suggests some individual differences.

Conformity and Independence (HAR, 23 min., 1975). Describes the classic studies of conformity—Asch, Sherif, and Milgram—as well as Moscovici's work on minority influence.

Conformity, Obedience, and Dissent (INS, 30 min., 1990). Explores the reasons for conformity, obedience, and dissent. Coverage includes Milgram's obedience study, research on styles of dissent and styles of leadership.

Disobeying Orders (FIL, 29 min., 1990). In focusing on G.I. resistance to the Vietnam War, this film highlights the conflict between obedience to authority and personal conscience. Includes cases of soldiers who suffered court martial and imprisonment for doing what they thought was right. Interviews with Vietnam veterans are interwoven with archival photos, film footage, and popular music of the 1960s.

The Lottery (EBE, 18 min., 1969). Based on the short story by Shirley Jackson. Explores conformity to tradition in a small, twentieth century American community.

McGraw-Hill Videodisc/Videotape in Social Psychology (McGraw-Hill, 4:12 and 1:10 min., respectively, 1993). The motion segment "Obedience" contains original footage from the first Milgram study and will provide students with an inside glimpse of what it was like to be a "teacher." The brief clip "Resisting Social Pressure" displays the famous incident at Tiananmen Square in Beijing, 1989, in which a single man halts a parade of tanks. CBS News reporter Richard Roth reflects on the man's possible motives.

Obedience (PSU, 45 min., 1963). Describes Milgram's research on compliance.

The Power of the Situation (ANN, 26 min., 1989). From the Discovering Psychology series, this video shows how our beliefs and behaviors can be influenced and manipulated by other people and by subtle situational forces.

The Wave (INS, 46 min., 1984). Based on an experiment carried out in a California high school in 1967. A teacher recreates the atmosphere of the Nazi Reich by drilling ideas of power, discipline, and superiority into his surprisingly willing students. Those who oppose "The Wave" are greeted first with disdain and finally with threats and violence.

Twelve Angry Men (UNA, 95 min., 1957) and (MGM, 117 min., 1997). Deliberations of a jury demonstrate the power of the situation. Many of the factors influencing conforming pressure are easily detected. (Available on videotape through many rental outlets).

CHAPTER 7
PERSUASION

The Paths to Persuasion
The Elements of Persuasion
    Who Says? The Communicator
    Credibility
    Attractiveness
    What Is Said? The Message Content
    Reason Versus Emotion
    Discrepancy
    One-Sided Versus Two-Sided Appeals
    Primacy Versus Recency
    How Is It Said? The Channel of Communication
    Active Experience or Passive Reception?
    Personal Versus Media Influence
    To Whom Is It Said? The Audience
    How Old Are They?
    What Are They Thinking?
Case Studies In Persuasion: Cult Indoctrination
    Attitudes Follow Behavior
    Compliance Breeds Acceptance
    The Foot-In-The-Door Phenomenon
    Persuasive Elements
    The Communicator
    The Message
    The Audience
    Group Effects
Resisting Persuasion: Attitude Inoculation
    Strengthening Personal Commitment
    Challenging Beliefs
    Developing Counterarguments
    Case Studies: Large-Scale Inoculation Programs
    Inoculating Children Against Peer Pressure to Smoke
    Inoculating Children Against the Influence of Advertising
    Implications
    Personal Postscript: Being Open But Not Naive

LECTURE AND DISCUSSION IDEAS

1. Introducing Persuasion

The motion segment "Persuading Voters" on The McGraw-Hill Videodisc/Videotape in Social Psychology contains five brief appeals for votes, all of which appeared at various times on national television. It provides a good introduction to the persuasion literature. Ask students, "Is the appeal effective? Why or why not?" In addition to introducing the four ingredients of persuasion studied in social psychology, namely the communicator, the message, how the message is communicated, and the audience, you can use the clips to discuss more specific questions addressed by the persuasion literature.

For example, do the appeals attempt to follow a central or peripheral route to persuasion? The first ad, probably familiar to many students, was run by the Clinton campaign in 1992. It motivates viewers to reflect on the claims versus the performance of George Bush and ends by asking how the viewer is doing. The second, run by the Reagan campaign in 1984, has been described as the subtlest, most allegorical political spot ever made. In addition to appealing to fear, it makes the viewer thoughtful about the issue it has raised, and is generally regarded as having had a strong impact on the public at large. The third, run by the 1988 Bush campaign, and the fourth, used by Clinton in 1992, are both obviously designed to elicit warm feelings. The fifth ad, used by Johnson against Goldwater in 1964, is perhaps the best known of all political spots. It aired only once: on NBC's Monday Night at the Movies on September 7, 1964. Some regard the ad as having indelibly branded Goldwater with a mad bomber image. It provides an excellent example of a fear appeal, and can lead to a consideration of the conditions under which such appeals are persuasive.

2. Influence Tactics for Sharing Ice Cream

A segment in Candid Camera Classics in Social Psychology (See Chapter 1 for reference) humorously introduces many of the features of persuasion. The 2nd "classic" is entitled "Influence Tactics for Sharing Ice Cream", and it features 3 children, only one of whom is given an ice cream cone. While the adult leaves the room to get the other cones the two other children push relentlessly upon the owner of the ice cream cone to share his good fortune. Some of the appeals work and some do not, but the entire 6six-minute segment is full of reference points for many of the concepts mentioned in the chapter—as well as a lot of laughs!

3. Mindless Versus Mindful Persuasion

In introducing the "two routes to persuasion," Pratkanis and Aronson (1992) give excellent examples of how people can be persuaded when they are in a mindless state as well as when they are thoughtful.

As consumers, we often don't think carefully about the purchases we make. In fact, research suggests that about half the purchases in a supermarket are impulse buys and that 62 percent of all shoppers in discount stores buy at least one item on an unplanned basis. The following principles effectively utilized by professional persuaders suggest less than mindful decisions:

-- Merchandise at eye level sells best. One study found that sales for products at waist level were only 74 percent as great and sales for products at floor level were only 57 percent as great as for those products placed at eye level.
-- Ads using animals, babies, or sex appeal are more effective than those using cartoon characters and historical figures.

-- Merchandise placed at the end of a supermarket aisle or near the checkouts is more likely to be purchased.
-- Bundle pricing, for example, selling items 2twofor $1 instead of 50 cents each, often increases the customer's perception of product "value."

In illustrating how we can be influenced when we are thoughtful, Pratkanis and Aronson present an intriguing contrast. A common response to being panhandled, that is, stopped by a passerby who asks for a quarter or any spare change, is to ignore the request and continue to walk mindlessly down the street. But what about a panhandler who asks, "Excuse me, do you have 17 cents that I could have?" The authors report that when that happened to them, their immediate thought was, "Why does this person need exactly 17 cents? Is it for bus fare? Is it for a specific food purchase? Maybe the person came up short at the market." The panhandler was a real individual with real needs, not someone they could mindlessly pass by. They complied with the request. Later they sent students out to panhandle for a local charity. Twice as many people contributed when asked for 17 to 37 cents compared to those who were asked for a quarter or any spare change.

4. The Need for Cognition

The text notes that people who are able and motivated to think through an issue are best persuaded through a central route to persuasion. For example, analytical people are more responsive to rational appeals than are less analytical people. Cacioppo and Petty's (1982) Need for Cognition Scale attempts to identify differences among individuals in their "tendency to engage in and enjoy thinking." Ask your students if the following are characteristic of them: "I tend to set goals that can be accomplished only by expending considerable mental effort," "I prefer watching educational to entertainment programs," and "I prefer my life to be filled with puzzles that I must solve."

Cacioppo and Petty reported total scores successfully discriminated between university faculty (people who presumably engage in and enjoy thinking for a living) and assembly-line workers (people who perform repetitive, monotonous tasks for a living). In addition, the authors found that scores were positively related to both field independence and general intelligence, and were negatively correlated with dogmatism. Those high in need for cognition preferred a complex problem-solving task over a simple one, whereas those low in need for cognition preferred the simple one.

Relevant to the persuasion literature is research showing that those high in need for cognition are more likely to desire and actively seek out issue-relevant information in forming their attitudes. For example, they were more likely to watch the 1984 presidential debates and to have more differentiated beliefs about the candidates. Research also suggests that those high in need for cognition demonstrate greater consistency between their attitudes and their behavior.

Finally, the need for cognition shows a positive correlation with self-esteem, masculine sex-role attitudes, various measures of curiosity, and effective problem-solving. It is unrelated to feminine or androgynous sex-role attitudes, sociability, shyness, or years of formal education.

5. Advertising and Classical Conditioning

The text notes that messages become more persuasive through association with good feelings. You may want to extend this principle by introducing advertisers' use of classical conditioning. Richard Perloff (1993) provides a good review of the literature along with a discussion of some important implications.

Begin by asking students to recount specific media ads that use the association principle. Perloff cites Marlboro ads showing a macho cowboy smoking a cigarette. You might refer to R. J. Reynolds' use of the cartoon character Joe Camel in its advertisements of Camel cigarettes. Joe is the epitome of "cool" and has proved particularly attractive to young children. Other examples include a perfume product associated with a young couple in embrace, and a soft drink linked with attractive young people enjoying a beach party. Are these ads effective? Research suggests that they can be.

One study paired a blue or beige pen with pleasant or unpleasant music. When subjects were asked to choose one of the colored pens, the overwhelming majority of the subjects selected the one associated with the pleasant music. Another study found that subjects developed significantly more favorable attitudes toward a brand of toothpaste when it was paired with beautiful nature scenes.

Perloff cites five practical implications of this literature for advertising. First, conditioned responses are hard to change. When Coca-Cola tried to introduce a new brand, the public was outraged. Perloff suggests that, at least in part, this may have been due to the fact that over the years Coke had been associated with some of the most powerful higher order stimuli in our culture. A Time magazine writer stated, "Changing the taste of the real thing was like tampering with motherhood, baseball, and the flag." Eventually the company brought back the old product. Second, concludes Perloff, one repetition is not enough. An advertisement linking a soft drink and a jingle must be presented many times to produce a change in preference. Third, associations must be crafted very carefully. There has to be a good fit between the higher order and conditioned stimuli. A stimulus that is too sexy may cause people to forget the product. On the other hand, if the image is lackluster, the association will fail. Researchers have suggested that advertisers should try to create situations that resemble the situations in which the person is likely to find the advertised product. Otherwise little generalization may occur. Fourth, celebrities must be chosen with care. Coca-Cola canceled ads featuring Madonna because it felt her new hit song was too sexy and controversial. When Magic Johnson announced he was HIV positive, and when O.J. Simpson was accused of murder, advertisers pulled their ads. Finally, writes Perloff, conditioning principles can be used in comparative ads. Discrimination occurs when one CS is paired with a UCS, and another is not. Based on this principle advertisers may wish to play music after their product, and then present a competitor's product not followed by a musical number. This strategy may lead consumers to develop a preference for the first product and prevent a preference from developing for the competitive product.

6. Six Principles of Influence

Robert B. Cialdini's (1993) very educational and entertaining Influence provides an excellent supplement to the chapter on persuasion. From experimental studies as well as his three-year immersion into the world of compliance professionals, Cialdini finds the majority of influence tactics fall within six basic categories: reciprocation, consistency, social proof, liking, authority, and scarcity. He discusses each of these principles in terms of their function in society and in terms of how their tremendous force can be utilized by a compliance professional in eliciting donations, votes, purchases, concessions, or assent. In addition, Cialdini examines each principle in terms of its capacity to produce a distinct kind of mindless compliance, that is, a willingness to agree without thinking first.

7. Legislating Seat Belt Use or a Twinkie Tax?

The text indicates that messages designed to persuade people to use seat belts have had little effect. Given that people fail to appreciate the cumulative risk and to protect themselves, some states have laws that require seat belt use. Perloff (1993) reports that at least one study has found that a message suggesting that failure to wear a seat belt could lead to a ticket significantly increased usage.

Do your students believe that legislation is the best strategy? Should we pass laws to protect people from themselves? To what extent should we legislate smoking, drinking, gambling, and prostitution? What are the likely effects of such legislation? Will compliance lead to acceptance? Does the theory of psychological reactance make any prediction?

Efforts to persuade people to choose a better diet and to exercise have also had little success. To combat the growing problem of obesity Kelly Brownell of Yale University's Center for Eating and Weight Disorders (see Ahmad, 1997) has suggested a "Twinkie Tax." This would mean slapping high-fat, low-nutrition foods with a substantial government "sin tax." There is some reason to believe it might work. For example, studies of the effects of price increases on tobacco and alcohol suggests a correlation between cost and consumption. However, small "snack taxes" in California and Maryland were quickly repealed after both food makers and consumers voiced strong objections. Critics argue that a federal version would be even less popular.

8. What Will It Take to Convince You?

Michael Lovaglia (2000) reflects upon research by Cialdini and others by providing several real-life examples of successful persuasion experiences in an article in Annual Editions–Social Psychology 01/02 (see "Popular Sources for Additional Classroom Material" for full reference) entitled Persuasion: What Will It Take to Convince You? (excerpted from Knowing People: The Personal Use of Social Psychology, p.118–125). This article lends itself to classroom discussion due to its brevity and the ease with which the material can be understood. Some possible discussion questions include: What recent experiences have you had where one or more of these techniques were being used on you? After reading this article, will you be more hesitant to say "yes" when someone asks you, "Will you do me a favor?" before they tell you what that favor is? Although Lovaglia's version of the Mustang transaction suggests that the principles of social psychology were being used by him on the car salesman, can the story be reinterpreted to suggest otherwise?

9. Interaction Effects in Two-Way Designs

Chapter 1 introduced experimental methodology, but left further discussion of experimental designs to later chapters. Chapter 7 presents several findings that are interaction effects rather than simple main effects. You may want to reinforce the concept of interaction, noting that the effect of one factor often depends on the level of another. We may talk in generalities ("credible sources are more persuasive"), but usually such simple effects are truer in some circumstances than in others. It is convenient to talk as if human nature is governed by simple effects. In reality, things are not so simple. Many research literatures begin with the revelation of some intriguing phenomenon. As research on the topic continues, later researchers qualify the initial finding with the discovery of interaction effects (e.g., the phenomenon occurs under condition X but not under condition Y).

10. The Appeal of Today's Cults

After members of the Heaven's Gate cult committed suicide, Philip Zimbardo (1997) reflected on the messages behind today's cults. His observations are provocative and worth sharing in class. In his essay Zimbardo elaborates the following five propositions:

1. Individuals do not join "cults." Rather they join groups that promise to meet their most pressing needs. Groups become "cults" only after we have concluded that they are deceptive, dangerous, and as challenging society's basic values. Cults promise instant friendship, identity, security, a healthy lifestyle, and an organized daily schedule. There is no crime or violence.

2. Cults reflect society's "default values," filling in its missing functions. In this way, cults tell us where and how society is failing its citizens. Our society is in a state of change and confusion in which its members find themselves isolated and alienated. The solution to cults is for our society to find ways to deliver on many of the cult's promises without its deception, distortion, and potential for destruction.

3. "If you don't stand for something, you'll fall for anything." The distortion and even loss of basic human values has made it difficult for many people to believe in anything or to trust anyone. In addition, people who are in a transitional phase of life, for example, those who have recently moved, lost a job, dropped out of school, divorced, or who have given up traditional religion as irrelevant are particularly susceptible to a cult's appeal.

4. All of us are vulnerable under the right (or wrong) conditions. Zimbardo writes, "The majority of 'normal, average, intelligent' individuals can be led to engage in immoral, illegal, irrational, aggressive and self destructive actions that are contrary to their values or personality—when manipulated situational conditions exert their power over individual dispositions."

5. Cult methods of recruitment are not different forms of mind control from those used by other compliance agents. Cults only show greater intensity and persistence in using tactics of social influence. One way in which this difference shows is in greater efforts to block any attempt by cult members to leave the group.

11. Becoming a Cult Leader

Pratkanis and Aronson's (1992) seven suggestions for "maintaining and creating a cult" provide a useful review and extension of the text's discussion of cult indoctrination. Their suggestions follow:

1. Create your own social reality. Remove all sources of information other than that provided by the cult. Mail should be censored and relatives should be prevented from visiting members. It's best if cult headquarters are isolated from the rest of the world.

2. Create a granfallon (coined by novelist Kurt Vonnegut to refer to proud and meaningless associations of human beings). Establish an ingroup of followers and an outgroup of the unredeemed. Constantly remind members: "If you want to be chosen, then you must act like a chosen one. If you are not chosen, then you are wicked and unredeemed."

3. Generate commitment through dissonance reduction. Insure obedience by establishing a spiral of escalating commitment (foot-in-the-door technique).

4. Establish the cult leader's credibility and attractiveness. Many cults have leader myths passed from member to member concerning the life and times of the cult leader.

5. Send members out to proselytize the unredeemed. This technique not only brings in new members but ensures that members are constantly engaged in self-sell, or self-generated persuasion.

6. Distract members from thinking "undesirable" thoughts. For example, never allow new recruits to be alone to think for themselves. Chanting and singing prevents thinking about anything else. Teach that any disagreeable thought is evil and from the devil.

7. Fixate members' vision on a phantom. Dangle the notion of the promised land and a vision of a better world before the faithful. By keeping members focused on a future phantom, you provide a powerful incentive to keep working. Phantoms also maintain hope by providing a sense of purpose and mission.

12. Evaluating Cults

Neal Osherow's (1984) careful analysis of People's Temple provides additional examples of the persuasion principles used by cults, and these can be used to extend the text's treatment. Osherow also raises the important question: In contemplating membership how do we distinguish between groups that might be safe and beneficial and those that could be dangerous? To determine whether we are being exposed to a potentially useful alternative way of living or being drawn into a dangerous one, Osherow suggests we seek answers to three more specific questions.

First, are alternatives being provided or taken away? People's Temple gave many a sense of purpose but it did so at a cost. It taught them to fear anything outside the Temple as "the enemy." Following Jim Jones was presented as the only alternative.

Second, is one's access to new and different information being broadened or denied? Jones controlled the information to which members would be exposed. He stifled all dissent and instilled distrust in each member for any outside messages.

Third, does the individual assume personal responsibility and control or is it usurped by the group and its leader? For most members, part of the Temple's attraction resulted from their willingness to relinquish responsibility over their lives. Personal autonomy was exchanged for security, the illusion of miracles, and the promise of salvation.

13. Popular Sources for Additional Classroom Material

Ball-Rokeach, S. J., Rokeach, M., & Grube, J. (1984, November). The great American values test. Psychology Today, p. 34–41. Shows how television can be persuasive when it challenges people to reflect on the consistency of their attitudes, values, and behavior.

Cialdini, R. B. (1984, February). The triggers of influence. Psychology Today, p. 40–45. Our automatic behavior patterns make us vulnerable to others who trigger these reactions for their own purposes. Examines several popular forms of social manipulation that persuade without appearing to manipulate.

Davis, M. H. (Ed.). (2000). Annual editions: Social psychology 01/02. Guilford, CT: Dushkin/McGraw-Hill. Updated annually, this volume provides convenient access to a wide range of current articles on social psychology appearing in magazines, newspapers, and journals.

Eagly, A., & Chaiken, S. (1993). The psychology of attitudes. San Diego: Harcourt Brace Jovanovich. Excellent treatment of 50 years of theory and research on attitudes and attitude change.

Perloff, R. M. (1993). The dynamics of persuasion. Hillsdale, NJ: Erlbaum. Excellent overview of the persuasion literature. Superb applications to everyday situations.

Petty, R. E., & Cacioppo, J. T. (1986). Communication and Persuasion: Central and peripheral routes to attitude change. New York: Springer-Verlag. Describes in detail the theory presented in Chapter 8. Introduces and integrates many separate findings from attitude change research.

Pratkanis, A., & Aronson, E. (1992). Age of propaganda: The everyday use and abuse of persuasion. New York: W. H. Freeman. Examines persuasion in everyday life and explains how we're tricked into persuading ourselves, why appeals to guilt and fear are effective, and how to resist being manipulated. Good coverage of the persuasion literature and of its applications.

Rotter, J. B. (1980, October). Trust and gullibility. Psychology Today, p. 35–42, 102. Rotter has devised a scale to measure how much confidence people place in others. Research with it suggests that high trusters are not more gullible than low trusters, but the former are happier, more likeable, and more trustworthy.

Schwartz, L. L. (1980). Tying it all together. Research, concepts, and fiction in an introductory psychology course. Teaching Psychology, 7, 192–193. Schwartz suggests the use of Ehrlich's novel The Cult to help students understand concepts in persuasion as well as other social psychological theory.

Shavitt, S., & Brock, T. C. (1994). Persuasion: Psychological insights and perspectives. Boston: Allyn & Bacon. Provides an excellent introduction to the persuasion literature. Unique in that prominent researchers relate their own stories of discovery.

Zimbardo, P., & Leippe, M. (1991). The psychology of attitude change and social influence. New York: McGraw-Hill. Introduces research on persuasion and behavior change. Examines subliminal messages as well as influence in the courtroom and in the promotion of health.

DEMONSTRATION AND PROJECT IDEAS

1. Persuasion Quiz

Demonstration 7-1 may be used to stimulate student interest and to show the value of persuasion research. The correct answers to most of these questions are not obvious, apart from research. As the chapter will reveal, statements 5, 8, and 9 are true; the rest are false. Naturally, this demonstration will be most effective BEFORE students have read the chapter.

2. Persuasion Attempts in Everyday Life

You may effectively introduce the persuasion literature as well as highlight its everyday relevance with a replication of Rule et al.'s (1985) research. Their purpose was to test Schank and Abelson's suggestion that people have at their disposal a persuasion package, a set of behaviors (or bag of tricks) they use whenever they need to persuade someone to do something.

Rule and colleagues first asked students to answer (a) "Who has tried to persuade you in the course of your everyday life?" (b) "Whom do you try to persuade in your everyday life?" and (c) "What kinds of things do people persuade other people (their friends, their fathers, or their enemies) to do?" Students generated a mean of 5.81 responses to "a," and a mean of 4.86 responses to "b." Students wrote more about being persuaded than about trying to persuade others. They generated a total of 12 reasons for the persuasive attempts: obtaining information, obtaining some object, obtaining permission, getting someone to do a favor, changing someone's opinion, getting someone to engage in some activity, buying or selling something, changing an existing relationship, changing someone's personal habit, helping the persuader, helping a third party, and getting someone to do something against self-interest.

In a second study, the researchers asked another group of students to list all the approaches they thought people would use to fulfill one of the goals from the list generated in the first study. The students generated a list of 15 different approaches ranging from asking directly to forcing the person.

In their final study, Rule et al. specifically asked a group of students to rank the 15 approaches as they might use them to persuade either their father or friend to do various things. Results indicated that regardless of who is persuading whom for what reason, there seems to be a standard order of persuasive strategies. That is, the rankings did not change as a function of the sex of the person providing the rankings, the target of the persuasive attempt, or the goal of the persuasive attempt. The strategies (from most to least preferred) follow: Asking (no reason for the request is given), invoking personal expertise (because the persuader is an expert, you should adopt the attitude), invoking personal need (that is, the persuader's need), buttering up (persuader makes the person feel wonderful or important), invoking role relationships ("you're not a true friend unless you do this for me"), bargaining for the favor, invoking a norm ("everybody's doing it"), invoking moral principle ("it's the right thing to do"), invoking altruism

("I'm not asking for myself, it's for the people I will be able to help if you grant the request"), offering a bribe (a rebate for a purchase), emotional appeals (persuader sulks hoping the target will feel guilty), personal criticism ("you're lazy, you never want to do anything"), deception (tricking the person into granting the request), threat, and finally, physical force.

3. Introducing Persuasion

Handout 7-2, designed by Bertram S. Allen, Jr. of Milligen College provides an excellent introduction to the literature on persuasion. Have students complete the exercise in small groups or, if you prefer, individually before the first class in which you discuss this chapter. Have volunteers share their answers with the full class. The discussion is certain to provide you with an opportunity to introduce the "two routes to persuasion" as well as the "the elements of persuasion" as described in the text.

4. Advertising Techniques

After briefly describing the two routes to persuasion ask students to bring to class one recent advertisement that uses a central route and one that uses a peripheral route. Explain that they can bring a magazine ad or describe a television commercial. Following Figure 7-1 in the text, have them explain what type of audience each ad appeals to, what kind of processing is required, and precisely how it attempts to persuade. Have volunteers present their ads to the entire class.

Vivian Parker Makosky (1985) suggests extending the persuasion literature, which is presented in the text, to a consideration of specific advertising techniques. To involve students you might ask them to bring in a favorite magazine ad and then use the ads to illustrate the more common advertising approaches.

For example, sometimes advertisers attempt to evoke a need and then represent their product as satisfying that need. Maslow's famous hierarchy provides one way of conceptualizing the range of human motivation. You might present the hierarchy—physiological needs, safety and security needs, needs for belonging and love, self-esteem and status needs, cognitive needs, aesthetic needs, and self-actualization needs—and then ask students what specific motive an ad appeals to. (Alternatively, you might present the hierarchy first and then ask students to bring in one ad appealing to each need level.)

Other advertisements are based on social and prestige suggestion. The essence of this approach is that one should buy or do X because someone else does. With social suggestion, that someone else is everyone else. As Makosky notes, the Pepsi generation, Wrigley's Spearmint Gum, and virtually every other product that features many people are relying on social suggestion. With prestige suggestion one should buy because some famous person says to do so.

Perhaps the most subtle advertising technique involves the use of loaded words and images. Certain buzzwords such as "natural" for beauty products and "light" for anything dietetic fall into this category. Attractive, athletic people who appear in advertisements for snacks also illustrate this approach. Loaded words and images are intended to enhance the impact of the message and sometimes to suspend reason (as when cigarettes are associated with outdoor scenes and "fresh" taste).

Makosky suggests additional student projects to accompany the discussion of advertising techniques. For example, you might ask students to bring to class the first five ads from an expensive magazine (e.g., Vogue) and the first five from an inexpensive magazine (e.g., Family Circle). Small groups of students then analyze the different needs appealed to in the magazines, the types of suggestion that are used, the different words and images that stand out. Students might also bring in the first five ads from a women's magazine and the first five from a men's magazine. The small group activity proceeds as above.

5. Persuasion Experiences

John Shaw (1977) reports that when University of Manchester (England) students described "one of the most influential persons in my life," their responses provided concrete examples of social influence variables. Demonstration 7-3 adapts Shaw's questions as a class exercise.

After students have completed the questionnaire, you could put them in small groups to compare their experiences, or you might tally their perceptions of the factors that made these relationships influential.

6. Generational Memories

The text suggests that age-related differences in social and political attitudes are likely due to the fact that the attitudes we develop when young persist largely unchanged. Because the attitudes developed by older people are different from those being developed by young people today, a generation gap occurs.

The text cites Schuman and Scott's (1989) research indicating that experiences during adolescence and early adulthood leave deep and lasting impressions. When they asked people to name the one or two most important national or world events over the last half century, most recalled events from their teens or early twenties. Replicating their findings makes for an interesting classroom exercise or student project. Ask respondents Schuman and Scott's central research questions: "There have been a lot of national and world events over the past 60 years—say, from about 1930 right up until today. Would you mention one or two such events or changes that seem to you to have been especially important? There aren't any right or wrong answers to the question—just whatever national or world events or changes that come to mind as important to you."

If your class includes different age groups, you may get vastly different responses. Alternatively, have each student ask the question of a person in their twenties, forties, and sixties. Pool the data in class. Compare the results with those of Schuman and Scott who found evidence for what they called generational "imprinting." The researchers report that most responses fell into the following categories (in descending order of frequency): World War II, the Vietnam War, space exploration, the assassination of John F. Kennedy, civil rights, the threat of nuclear war, communication/transportation, the Great Depression, computers, terrorism, moral decline, women's rights. Schuman and Scott conclude: "For the majority of 12 major national or world events that Americans recall as especially important, the memories refer back disproportionately to a time when the respondents were in their teens or early twenties....This supports a theory that adolescence and early adulthood constitute the primary period for generational imprinting in the sense of political memories."

More recently, Rubin and Schulkind (1997) asked 120 people in their twenties, thirties, and seventies to list their five most important memories (something your students could also replicate). In addition, they asked participants to describe memories triggered by a select group of words such as "house," "store," and "party." Results indicated that adults in their seventies listed events from their twenties as their most important and beloved memories. Specific words also triggered memories from early adulthood. In comparison, 20-year-olds tended to recall events from weeks or months ago, and 35-year-olds recalled events from the past several years.

7. Persuasive Appeals: Some Filmed Examples

The literature on emotional appeals can be introduced with a fear-arousing persuasive film perhaps <u>Scared Straight</u>, an antismoking film such as <u>Coach's Last Lesson</u> (produced by the American Lung Association), or an antinuclear war film, such as <u>The Last Epidemic</u> (produced by Physicians for Social Responsibility).

Elicit student reactions to the film. Is its use of vivid examples, fear, and emotion likely to arouse people's defenses, or is it persuasive?

Films from the Clio Awards series present award-winning commercials. You might ask students to analyze specific commercials in terms of the psychological research on persuasion, or you might show the film simply to introduce the materials and arouse interest in the topic of persuasion.

Finally, Fife & Drum Software's (316 Soapstone Lane, Silver Springs, MD 20905) Powers of Persuasion is a CD-ROM that includes newsreel footage and posters created by American propagandists during World War II. Have students analyze them in terms of persuasion principles.

8. Primacy Effect

Demonstration 7-4 allows you to test for order effects in impression formation. Distribute each form to half the class. Using these materials, A.S. Luchins (1957) reported primacy effects on rating scales A, G, I, and K.

9. Hiding a Persuasive Message Within an Attribution

Students can be shown the power of hidden messages (as discussed in Chapter 7) by modifying the research done by Miller, Brinkman and Bolen (1975). Miller et al. show that attributing qualities to a person or group can be more effective than outright persuasion. By repeatedly telling one group of fifth graders that they were neat and tidy (attribution) and repeatedly telling another group that they should be neat and tidy (persuasion), Miller et al. found that the former group displayed much better non-littering behavior than the latter.

This manipulation can be modified for classrooms by passing out one of two forms to each student at the beginning of class. One form reminds the student of how good of a note-taker they are while the other one informs the student that they should be a good note-taker. At the end of the class, simply have the students report how many pages (partial pages) of notes they have taken during the class period. If the class enrollment is big enough, you should get a measurable difference. After revealing the manipulation, have the students try and figure out why. Miller et al. suggest attribution tactics usually work better because the persuasive intent is hidden.

Demonstration 7-1
Bolt & Myers
©McGraw-Hill, 1999

True or False

1. T F Fear-arousing messages are generally ineffective.
2. T F Speakers who talk fast are viewed as less credible than those who talk with occasional hesitation.
3. T F In research to date, messages that acknowledge opposing arguments are always more effective than messages which are one-sided.
4. T F In a debate, it is usually advantageous to be the last to present your side of the issue.
5. T F Political advertising has little effect on voters in the general presidential election.
6. T F In actual fact, television commercials for toothpaste and aspirin have little effect on the buying habits of the general public.
7. T F People's attitudes change considerably during adulthood.
8. T F One way to strengthen existing attitudes is to challenge them.
9. T F Associating a message with the good feelings one has while eating or drinking makes it more convincing.
10. T F Under conditions studied so far, similar communicators are always more effective than dissimilar communicators.

Demonstration 7-2

(with permission of Bertram S. Allen, Jr.)

1. Describe an advertisement that has been effective in drawing your attention.
2. What method(s) was(were) used by the advertisers to draw your attention?
3. Which was spoken to more by the advertisement—your emotion or your reason?
4. What effect, if any, did the advertisement have in altering your attitudes or behaviors?
5. Describe an advertisement that has been ineffective in drawing your attention.
6. What method(s) was(were) used by the advertisers to draw your attention?
7. Which was spoken to more by the advertisement—your emotion or your reason?
8. What effect, if any, did the advertisement have in altering your attitudes or behaviors?
9. Compared to other individuals, do you consider yourself more, less, or equally affected by advertising messages in the media?
10. What is an effective public service announcement? What are the characteristics of the message, which makes it effective—the issue itself, the manner in which it is conveyed, or some other characteristic?

Demonstration 7-3

Consider: Who is one of the most influential persons in your life? Choose someone who has influenced you in the last 10 years, either positively or negatively. Make it someone other than your parents.

1. How old were you at the time? _____.
2. Why was this person influential? Was it more
   ___ the role the person occupied? (e.g., the person's power)
   ___ the knowledge and expertise the person possessed?
   ___ the person's personal qualities? (e.g., attractiveness)
   ___ something else?_____.
3. Did this person's influence upon you
   ___ tend to wear off with time?
   ___ endure?
   ___ grow even after the relationship ended? (sleeper effect)
4. Was the person's impact on you more based on
   ___ emotion, or
   ___ reason
5. Was the context for this relationship
   ___ personal friendship
   ___ a school relationship
   ___ a work relationship
   ___ some other setting?
6. Were this person's views
   ___ very discrepant from your own
   ___ not too discrepant from your own
7. How did this person influence you? What changed most?
   ___ your beliefs?
   ___ your feelings?
   ___ your behavior?
   ___ something else?_____.
8. Can you recall any new thoughts of your own ("cognitive responses") coming out of this relationship?

(From J. Shaw. Some "real-life" accounts of influential relationships. Human Relations, 1977, 30, p. 363-372. Used with permission.)

Demonstration 7-4

Directions. In everyday life we sometimes form impressions of people based on what we read or hear about them. Please read the following paragraph through once and answer the questions which follow about "Jim."

Jim left the house to get some stationery. He walked out into the sun-filled street with two of his friends, basking in the sun as he walked. Jim entered the stationery store, which was full of people. Jim talked with an acquaintance while he waited for the clerk to catch his eye. On his way out, he stopped to chat with a school friend who was just coming into the store. Leaving the store, he walked toward school. On his way out he met the girl to whom he had been introduced the night before. They talked for a short while, and then Jim left for school. After school Jim left the classroom alone. Leaving the school, he started on his long walk home. The street was brilliantly filled with sunshine. Jim walked down the street on the shady side. Coming down the street toward him, he saw the pretty girl whom he had met on the previous evening. Jim crossed the street and entered a candy store. The store was crowded with students, and he noticed a few familiar faces. Jim waited quietly until the counterman caught his eye and then gave his order. Taking his drink, he sat down at a side table. When he had finished his drink he went home. Rate "Jim" on the following scales by circling the appropriate number on each:

A.	friendly	1 2 3 4 5 6	unfriendly
B.	patient	1 2 3 4 5 6	impatient
C.	intelligent	1 2 3 4 5 6	unintelligent
D.	popular	1 2 3 4 5 6	unpopular
E.	warm	1 2 3 4 5 6	cold
F.	mature	1 2 3 4 5 6	immature
G.	aggressive	1 2 3 4 5 6	passive
H.	selfish	1 2 3 4 5 6	unselfish
I.	social	1 2 3 4 5 6	unsocial
J.	imaginative	1 2 3 4 5 6	unimaginative
K.	forward	1 2 3 4 5 6	shy

(From A. S. Luchins. Primacy and recency in impression formation. In C.I. Hovland et al., The order of presentation in persuasion. New Haven: Yale University, 1957. Used with permission.)

Demonstration 7-4

Directions. In everyday life we sometimes form impressions of people based on what we read or hear about them. Please read the following paragraph through once and answer the questions which follow about "Jim."

After school, Jim left the classroom alone. Leaving the school, he started on his long walk home. The street was brilliantly filled with sunshine. Jim walked down the street on the shady side. Coming down the street toward him, he saw the pretty girl whom he had met on the previous evening. Jim crossed the street and entered a candy store. The store was crowded with students, and he noticed a few familiar faces. Jim waited quietly until the counterman caught his eye and then gave his order. Taking his drink, he sat down at a side table. When he had finished his drink he went home. Jim left the house to get some stationery. He walked out into the sun-filled street with two of his friends, basking in the sun as he walked. Jim entered the stationery store, which was full of people. Jim talked with an acquaintance while he waited for the clerk to catch his eye. On his way out, he stopped to chat with a school friend who was just coming into the store. Leaving the store, he walked toward school. On his way out he met the girl to whom he had been introduced the night before. They talked for a short while, and then Jim left for school. Rate "Jim" on the following scales by circling the appropriate number on each:

A.	friendly	1 2 3 4 5 6	unfriendly
B.	patient	1 2 3 4 5 6	impatient
C.	intelligent	1 2 3 4 5 6	unintelligent
D.	popular	1 2 3 4 5 6	unpopular
E.	warm	1 2 3 4 5 6	cold
F.	mature	1 2 3 4 5 6	immature
G.	aggressive	1 2 3 4 5 6	passive
H.	selfish	1 2 3 4 5 6	unselfish
I.	social	1 2 3 4 5 6	unsocial
J.	imaginative	1 2 3 4 5 6	unimaginative
K.	forward	1 2 3 4 5 6	shy

(From A. S. Luchins. Primacy and recency in impression formation. In C.I. Hovland et al., The order of presentation in persuasion. New Haven: Yale University, 1957. Used with permission.)

FILMS/VIDEOS

The Ad and the Ego (RES, 57 min., 1996). A comprehensive documentary on the cultural impact of advertising in America. Challenges the notion that we are immune to advertising (Call 415-621-6196).

Advertising and the End of the World (MEDIA, 40 min., 1997). Presents advertising as the most persuasive message system in the consumer culture. We must attend not simply to isolated advertisements but to the way in which advertising functions as a cultural system (Call 800-897-0089).

Captive Minds: Hypnosis and Beyond (INS, 55 min., 1985). This program complements text coverage of cult indoctrination. Examines how groups command loyalty from their members. Methods include isolating recruits in unfamiliar environments, keeping them busy to the point of exhaustion, and weakening their sense of personal identity.

Communication: Negotiation and Persuasion (PSU, 30 min., 1989). Illustrates many techniques used to influence others' attitudes and behaviors. In highlighting nonverbal persuasive communications such as body language, facial expression, and the use of touch, this film extends the literature presented in the text.

Cults: Saying No Under Pressure (INS, 29 min., 1991). Explores the recruitment tactics of cults. Interviews with ex-cult members reveal the reasons why people join a cult and how people might resist the pressure to join.

Effective Persuasion (MCG, 11 min., 1968). Uses excerpts from speeches of Churchill, Kennedy, Stevenson, and King to illustrate the devices of effective persuasion, including direct speech, emotional appeal, and meeting the needs of the audience.

Faces of the Enemy (INS, 58 min., 1987). The program examines the dehumanizing images used in mass persuasion and propaganda. It draws from documentary footage, political cartoons, and interview, in an effort to analyze the psychological roots of enmity. (Powerful—preview before showing!)

Fight Spirit (INS, 50 min., 1986) Examines the mixture of persuasion and coercion used to convert raw recruits into a fighting force. Hierarchical structure, discipline, distinctive uniforms, and social support combine for effective persuasion.

The Heaven's Gate Cult: The Thin Line Between Faith and Reason (FHS, 20 min., 1997) An NBC Nightline program hosted by Ted Koppel. Prominent scholars and cult watchers discuss what might differentiate cults from the early days of today's major religions.

The Made for TV Election (NAA, 55 min., 1988). A provocative documentary on how national television news shapes presidential elections in the United States Media coverage is shown as an extension of network entertainment and marketing imperative.

The McGraw-Hill Videodisc/Videotape in Social Psychology (McGraw-Hill, 3:30 and 2.05 min., respectively, 1993). Two motion segments are relevant to this chapter. "Persuading Voters" presents five different presidential campaign ads. "The Waco Tragedy and Cults" is a CBS News segment that provides a good introduction to cult indoctrination.

Merchants of Cool (PBS, 55 min., 2000). The program talks with top marketers, media executives and cultural/media critics, and explores the symbiotic relationship between the media and today's teens, as each looks to the other for their identity. For a synopsis, go to: www.pbs.org/wgbh/pages/frontline shows/cool/etc/synopsis.html.

CHAPTER 8
GROUP INFLUENCE

What Is a Group?
Social Facilitation
    The Presence of Others
    Crowding: The Presence of Many Others
    Why Are We Aroused in the Presence of Others?
    Evaluation Apprehension
    Driven by Distraction
    Mere Presence
Social Loafing
    Many Hands Make Light Work
    Social Loafing in Everyday Living
Deindividuation
    Doing Together What We Would Not Do Alone
    Group Size
    Physical Anonymity
    Arousing and Distracting Activities
    Diminished Self-Awareness
Group Polarization
    The Case of the "Risky Shift"
    Do Groups Intensify Opinions?
    Group Polarization Experiments
    Naturally Occurring Group Polarization
    Explaining Polarization
    Informational Influence
    Normative Influence
Groupthink
    Symptoms of Groupthink
    Critiquing Groupthink
    Preventing Groupthink
    Groupthink and Group Influence
Minority Influence
    Consistency
    Self-Confidence
    Defections from the Majority

Is Leadership Minority Influence?
Personal Postscript: Are Groups Bad for Us?

LECTURE AND DISCUSSION IDEAS

1. Group Formation

You can extend the text's treatment of groups by asking your class why people form and join groups. Considerable literature addresses that question and can be introduced in class. Forsyth's (1999) Group Dynamics provides a good review distinguishing between the functional perspective that emphasizes the usefulness of groups for individual members and a second approach that traces group formation to the process of interpersonal attraction. Since the latter perspective is discussed at length in Chapter 11, at this point you may want to focus class discussion on the functional perspective.

For example, Schutz's (1958) Fundamental Interpersonal Relations Orientation stresses the relationship between psychological needs and group formation. Schutz suggests that the needs for inclusion, control, and affection may be satisfied by joining a group. Inclusion is the desire to be part of a group and to be accepted by a group. It is similar to the need for affiliation. Control is the need to guide the group by organizing and maintaining the group's processes. It corresponds to the need for power. Affection represents the need to establish and maintain open, positive relations with others.

Schutz argued that the three needs affect group behavior in two ways: they shape how we treat other people and how we want others to treat us. That is, inclusion refers to our need to join with other people and our desire to be accepted by them. Control refers both to our need to dominate as well as our willingness to allow others to dominate us. Affection includes our desire to like other group members as well as the need to be liked by them. Schutz's FIRO-B attempts to measure both the need to express and the need to receive inclusion, control, and affection.

2. Groups: Good or Bad?

The topic of group influence might be introduced or concluded with Buys' (1978) brief, tongue-in-cheek article, "Humans Would Do Better Without Groups." Students might be asked, on the basis of what they have already learned in social psychology, why someone might reach this conclusion. Included in Buys' summary is much of the literature pointing to the destructive effects of group influence on human functioning. In support of his thesis Buys cites research on conformity, diffusion of responsibility, deindividuation, panic, the risky shift, groupthink, and anonymity—most of which is discussed in the text chapter on social influence.

Is it true that groups are not good for humans? The psychologist's stock answer, "It all depends" seems most appropriate. Can your students think of any _positive_ functions that groups can serve?

Buys triggered the wrath of many social psychologists. A subsequent issue of the same journal (Personality and Social Psychology Bulletin, October, 1978) included responses entitled, "Groups Would Do Better Without Humans," "Humans Would Do Better Without Other Humans," and "Would Groups Do Better Without Social Psychologists?" The critics were quick to point out the positive functions of groups. For example, groups facilitate social, moral, and language development, provide the bases for a sense of membership and identity, and are a source of emotional comfort, support, and satisfaction. The respondents to Buys' review also noted that negative group influence is caused by the individuals who compose the group and that social psychology as a discipline may be biased against human group activities.

3. Individual Versus Group Problem-Solving

When should we use groups to solve problems? Stasson and Bradshaw (1995) make the following specific recommendations: First, for a single response/item task, group performance is likely to be worse than that of the best member. Thus, if the best member can be identified, assign the task to that person. Second, if the task consists of multiple items or subtasks, a group will outperform any one of its members when the members have nonoverlapping bases of knowledge or expertise. Finally, if it is unclear who is the best member, it is recommended that the task be assigned to a group regardless of whether the task has single or multiple parts because the group will likely outperform the average member and because it is likely that members will have some nonoverlapping areas of knowledge (in the multiple response type of task).

4. The Illusion of Group Effectivity

The illusion of group effectivity is the false belief that groups can stimulate creativity. Stroebe and his colleagues (1992) note that brainstorming is still widely used in business organizations and advertising in spite of consistent empirical evidence that people produce many more ideas when they work individually rather than in groups. In a review of previous studies the authors report how the productivity of brainstorming groups was assessed by comparing the quantity and quality of the ideas produced by real groups and those produced by nominal groups (i.e., subjects who worked individually and whose individual products are statistically aggregated). Results indicated that while the subjects produced fewer ideas when working in real groups than when working individually, 80 percent of these same subjects predicted that a person working in a group would be more productive than one working alone.

Stroebe and his colleagues suggest that one explanation for the illusion of group effectivity is that after a brainstorming session, group members are unable to differentiate between the ideas they had themselves and those that were suggested by other group members. When this difficulty is coupled with the self-serving bias, namely the tendency to see oneself favorably, group members are likely to attribute some of the ideas of other group members to themselves. This would explain why people who brainstorm in groups rate their productivity higher than people who generate ideas in individual sessions. In an experiment involving 92 female students, the authors replicated earlier studies, which found that subjects who brainstormed in groups were significantly less productive than subjects who brainstormed individually. As has been true in earlier studies, the female students were also more satisfied with their performance and felt more at ease in their brainstorming session. Those who worked individually believed that they would have had many more ideas if they had been in a group. Finally, when subjects were later presented with all the ideas that had been generated, those who had worked in groups were significantly more likely to indicate that while a particular idea may have been suggested by another group member, it had also occurred to them.

5. Calhoun's Behavioral Sink

You can introduce the topic of crowding by relating John B. Calhoun's (1962) classic studies of overcrowded rat colonies. Supplying his animals with plenty of food and water, Calhoun allowed them to breed freely in a quarter-acre pen. Most of the rats lived in smaller groups of 10 or 12 with the total population stabilizing at 150. He then divided the pen into four sections. Two of the largest males staked their claim to two pens in which they each kept a small harem of females. This arrangement forced the rest of the animals into the remaining pens. Sometimes as many as 60 rats would congregate around the feeding stations.

Calhoun reported that the crowding led to a general collapse of social behavior, what he termed a "behavioral sink." This was marked by a breakdown in mating, nest-building, and even eating of the young. Some animals displayed random and inappropriate aggression; others became passive and withdrawn. As conditions in the colony deteriorated, infant mortality exceeded 80 percent. Adult rats also showed a number of biological maladies typically associated with stress and tended to die prematurely. These findings led researchers to question the effects of human crowding.

6. Human Territoriality

The text's treatment of crowding can be readily extended to a consideration of territoriality. Territoriality, in which a specific space is marked out and defended against intrusion from others, is common in many animals. It serves important functions such as providing a place for food, shelter, and caring for the young. Furthermore it assures that animals will be dispersed more evenly over the environment.

Is territoriality present in humans? Altman (1975) has identified three common types of territory. Primary territories are places over which the occupant has exclusive control. Examples include homes, apartments, and private offices. Secondary territories are areas shared with others but over which regular users have considerable control. Examples include a classroom, church, or neighborhood bar. Public territories are uncontrolled areas that are used by whoever is the first to arrive. Examples include telephone booths, theaters, and parks.

In each type of territory, people may mark out space as their own and defend against intrusion. "No trespassing" signs, fences, or hedges are common markers used by homeowners. Leaving articles of personal clothing or books and magazines on tables or chairs serves to protect one's place in secondary or public territories.

Why do people want a territory? There are probably several reasons. It may give people a sense of security and make their lives more predictable and also seem more important. Some researchers have suggested that territoriality may protect people from those whom they fear or dislike. It may also foster the person's sense of self-identity and uniqueness.

People are more assertive and dominant when in their own territories. For example, one physician observed that patients who tended to be submissive in interacting with him in his office or in the hospital, could be quite assertive when visited at home. Studies comparing how dormitory residents interact in their own rooms versus those of others have revealed some interesting differences. Martindale (1971) assigned the roles of prosecutor or defense attorney to pairs of college students and had them debate the appropriate prison sentence for a criminal. Students who debated in their own rooms argued more persuasively and were more likely to win the negotiation. Conroy and Sundstrom (1977) studied conversation patterns of dormitory residents and their visitors. When the resident and visitor disagreed on an issue, the resident dominated the conversation. However, when attitudes were similar and the pair agreed, a so-called "hospitality effect" emerged in which the visitor was permitted to dominate the conversation.

Discussion Questions:

1. How do the concepts of personal space and territoriality differ? How is human territoriality different from that of nonhuman species?
2. Are there advantages to being the home team in sports?
3. How do people respond to invasions of their territory?

7. Experiencing Deindividuation

Ayala Pines and Christina Maslach (1979) suggest having students recall depersonalizing institutional experiences—in a hospital, a school, at the post office, or wherever. Then have them ponder: How did the structure or the procedure of that institution contribute to your feelings of depersonalization? What could be done to make that institution less depersonalizing?

8. Deindividuation and Intimacy

The text reports that anonymity can release positive as well as negative impulses. Have students imagine themselves as participants in a study conducted by Kenneth Gergen, Mary Gergen, and William Barton (1973).

The psychologist ushers you into a room that is fully lighted or totally dark, except for a tiny red light over the door so that, if you wish, you can leave at any time. He tells you, "You will be left in the room for no more than an hour with some other people, and there are no rules as to what you should do together. At the end you will leave the room alone and will never meet the other participants." You then spend the next 60 minutes with seven strangers.

What happens? Those in the lighted room sat around making light conversation. In contrast, participants in the dark talked less, but about more important things. Ninety percent intentionally touched someone and half hugged another. Very few disliked the experience; in fact, most volunteered to return without pay. Anonymity had released intimacy.

9. Collective Behavior

The text's discussion of the baiting crowd and the process of deindividuation can be readily extended in class to a discussion of other forms of collective behavior and their underlying processes. Brown (1965) provides excellent examples that can be presented in class, including panics of escape and acquisition, fads, crazes, lynchings, riots, and social movements.

In addition to deindividuation, Forsyth (1990) outlines contagion, convergence, and emergent norm perspectives on crowd behavior and then applies them to understanding the dynamics of the baiting crowd. For example, convergence theory argues that only certain types of people would be likely to bait victims to jump to their death. Their shouts spread to other members of the crowd through a process of contagion until everyone is infected by a norm of callousness or cynicism that seems to fit the requirements of the setting.

10. Rules for Effective Decision Making

What criteria should we use to determine whether the decision-making process is of high quality? From their extensive research on decision making in government, business, and private welfare organizations, Janis and Mann (1977) extract seven principles. To the best of their ability, effective decision makers:

1. Survey a wide range of objectives to be reached, always taking into account the multiplicity of values involved.
2. Consider a wide range of possible courses of action.
3. Intensively search for new information relevant to evaluating the alternatives.
4. Correctly consider and assimilate new information and expert judgments, even when they do not support the initially preferred course of action.

5. Reconsider both the positive and negative consequences of alternatives originally regarded as unacceptable, before making a final decision.
6. Carefully weigh the negative as well as positive consequences that could result from the preferred alternative.
7. Prepare detailed provisions for implementing and monitoring the chosen course of action, with particular attention to contingency plans that might be required if known risks were to materialize.

Janis and Mann suggest that each of these seven criteria can be viewed as a continuum such that the individual or group responsible for making a policy decision can be given a low, medium, or high rating. Any gross failure to meet one of the criteria can be regarded as a symptom of defective policymaking.

11. Constraints in Decision Making

Janis's (1989) Crucial Decisions is a useful resource for supplementing the text's treatment of groupthink and leadership. For example, Janis describes various constraints that inevitably require leaders to sacrifice something that reduces the quality of the decision-making process. For example, in order to meet a deadline, the search for relevant information may be short-circuited, or because of the need for acceptability among power factions in an organization, a very good alternative may have to be eliminated. Janis classifies these various constraints into three general types: cognitive, affiliative, and egocentric.

Cognitive constraints include all the salient external factors that restrict cognitive input (e.g., limited organizational resources for information gathering and analysis), as well as internal factors (e.g., the leader's own limited knowledge about complex issues) that limit the amount and quality of cognitive activity that executives can devote to working on a given policy decision.

Affiliative constraints include all the needs arising from the policymaker's affiliation with the organization as a whole, with a particular division or section of the organization, or with whatever face-to-face committees or informal work groups he or she belongs to. These include the needs for acceptability, consensus, and social support. Groupthink has its roots in affiliative constraints.

Egocentric constraints include the executive's personal and emotional needs such as the desire for prestige, the need to maintain self-esteem, the need to cope with stress, etc. Leaders may also have to cope with the anxiety, fear, or guilt that they may experience when dealing with decisional dilemmas.

12. A Closer Look at Groupthink: The Space Shuttle Challenger Tragedy

Gregory Moorhead, Richard Ference and Chris Neck (1991) offer students an opportunity to apply groupthink theory to the Space Shuttle Challenger tragedy in an article entitled "Group Decision Fiascoes Continue: Space Shuttle Challenger and a Revised Groupthink Framework" (also found in Annual Editions–Social Psychology 01/02). The authors take Janis' original criteria for groupthink and show how the situations and decisions leading up to the launch fit the criteria. In addition, Moorhead et al. suggest some additional features be added to the basic concept—namely time pressures and leadership style. The article is very digestible and its relevancy is easily seen by students. Some possible discussion questions include: What other recent events may have been influenced by the effects of groupthink? Do all of the eight criteria need to be present for the full effects of groupthink to be experienced? What can you do in the decision-making groups of which you are apart to diminish the tendency for groupthink? Hint: the book offers several valuable suggestions.

13. Fiedler's Contingency Model of Leadership

Fiedler's popular contingency model of leadership assumes that leadership effectiveness depends on—or is contingent upon—both the personal characteristics of the leader and the nature of the group situation. (Forsyth, 1983). First, the model distinguishes between two motivational styles of leadership. Relationship-motivated leaders seek to build strong interpersonal links with the other members of their groups and are more concerned with the maintenance of these relationships than with task completion. Task-motivated leaders concentrate on task completion as the primary goals of the group.

The leader's control or influence is the most important feature of the situation. Among the factors that are significant in determining situational control are leader-member relations (Are group members loyal to their leader and acknowledge his or her ability?), task structure (Is the goal and route to the goal clear?), and position power (Does the leader have control over rewards, punishment, salaries, hiring, and firing?).

According to the contingency model, motivational style and situational control interact to determine leadership effectiveness. Task-motivated leaders are presumably more effective in situations that are either highly favorable or unfavorable, while relationship-motivated are more effective in the middle-range situations. That is, a task-motivated style is more effective when leader-member relations are very good, when the task is well-structured and position power is very strong. Similarly, a task-motivated style is better when leader-member relations are very bad, the task is unstructured, and position power is very weak. In contrast, a relationship-motivated style is more effective when relations are good but the task is unstructured, and position power is weak, or when relations are bad, the task is structured, and position power is strong.

A good film to accompany the treatment of Fiedler's model is Leadership: Style or Circumstance described at the end of this chapter.

14. Questions About Leadership

You might begin a lecture/discussion on leadership by having students form small groups with the task of describing the most effective leader they have encountered. Students should describe both the characteristics and actions that they believe made the leader effective. Have the small groups look for commonalities in individual descriptions and report these back to the full class.

In an effort to make research on leadership more accessible and relevant to the lay public, Robert Hogan and his colleagues (1994) pose and answer questions that psychologists are often asked by persons who must choose and evaluate leaders. Their article, "What We Know about Leadership," provides an excellent source of material for classroom lecture and discussion. Among the questions and answers covered in the review are the following:

What is leadership? Hogan and associates suggest that leadership "involves persuading other people to set aside for a period of time their individual concerns and to pursue a common goal that is important for the responsibilities and welfare of the group." Furthermore, leadership is not domination; it occurs only when members willingly adopt the goals of the group as their own.

Does leadership matter? There are different ways to answer this question. One is anecdotal. For example, Lincoln's army was ineffective until Ulysses S. Grant assumed command. Some coaches can move from one team to another transforming losers into winners. Another way to answer this question is to ask the consumers of leadership. Several patterns of leadership behavior are associated with subordinates' performance and satisfaction. Among the most common complaints of failed leadership are, on one hand, managers' reluctance to exercise authority and, on the other hand, managers tyrannizing their subordinates, e.g., "treats employees as if they were stupid." A leader's credibility or trustworthiness may be the simple most important factor that influences subordinates' judgments of leadership effectiveness. Among the interesting findings that Hogan reports is evidence that, over the past decade, the failure rate among senior executives in corporate America has been at least 50 percent.

How are leaders chosen? Psychological research suggests that cognitive ability and normal personality measures, structured interviews, and simulations predict leadership success reasonably well. However, many organizations fail to take advantage of these selection services. Instead first-line supervisors are selected from the workforce on the basis of their technical talent rather than their leadership skills. Someone who is good at the activity of the unit is picked to be a supervisor on the basis of his or her proficiency.

How to forecast leadership? Hogan argues that empirical findings suggest that certain personality dimensions are consistently related to rated leadership effectiveness. The big-five model of personality traits helps to integrate this research. For example, one review indicates that surgency (i.e., dominance, assertiveness, energy or activity level, speech fluency, sociability, and social participation), emotional stability (i.e., adjustment, emotional balance, independence, and self-confidence), conscientiousness (i.e., responsibility, achievement, initiative, personal integrity, and ethical conduct), and agreeableness (i.e., friendliness, social nearness, and support) are related to leadership effectiveness. Another study found that the personality traits that best predicted managerial advancement were the desire for advancement, energy-activity level, and the readiness to make decisions (i.e., surgency); resistance to stress and tolerance for uncertainty (i.e., emotional stability); inner work standards (i.e., conscientiousness); and range of interests (i.e., intellect).

15. Seating Arrangements and Group Interaction ✓

Considerable research has examined the role of the physical environment in influencing group interaction. For example, seating arrangement has been addressed in a number of studies.

One obvious way to encourage interaction is to seat people facing each other. Robert Sommer and Hugo Ross (1958) noted that patients in a newly remodeled geriatrics ward seemed depressed—as they sat in chairs lined up along the walls, side by side. After the researchers rearranged the chairs in circles around tables, conversation almost doubled in a matter of a few weeks.

Typically classrooms seat students in straight rows and thus it's not surprising that students' public comments are directed to the teacher and rarely to other students. Actually students say little to the instructor either—two or three minutes worth during the average lecture class at one university, and only five or six minutes during the average seminar. Robert Sommer and Helge Olsen (1980) observed that in introductory psychology discussion groups held in straight-row classrooms at the University of California, Davis, only 48 percent of the students participated, averaging 1.4 statements per student during a class hour. After one of these classrooms was converted to a "soft" room with circular seating, 79 percent of its students contributed, averaging five comments per student per hour, one-fourth of which were directed to other students.

Bernard Steinzor (1949) attempted to determine whether people seated in certain positions in the group tended to speak at any particular time. Although initially he found few relationships, one day while observing a group he noticed that a participant changed his seat to sit opposite a group member he argued with at a previous meeting. In a reanalysis of the data Steinzor found that individuals tended to speak after the person seated opposite them spoke. This tendency, which has been dubbed the Steinzor effect, seems to occur primarily in leaderless discussion groups. When a strong leader is present, group members direct more comments to their closest neighbor.

The leadership role is closely associated with the chair at the head of the table (Forsyth, 1983). People appointed to lead small discussion groups tend to select seats at the head of the table. Other evidence indicates that those sitting at the head of the table tend to possess more dominant personalities, talk more frequently, and, in general, exercise greater interpersonal influence. Both perceptual prominence (the occupant at the head can maintain a great amount of eye contact with more group members) and the cultural meaning associated with sitting at the head of the table may explain this finding.

16. Popular Sources for Additional Classroom Material

Baron, R. S., Kerr, N. L., & Miller, N. (1993). Group process, group decision, and group action. Pacific Grove, CA: Brooks/Cole. Examines most of the group processes described in the text including social facilitation, social loafing, group polarization, and groupthink. Also reviews work on social dilemmas, group aggression, and the benefits of social support.

Brown, R. (1988). Group processes: Dynamics within and between groups. Cambridge, MA: Blackwell Publishers. Provides an excellent overview of research on group dynamics. Includes illustrations of group processes drawn from contemporary life. Coverage extends to crowd behavior, group productivity, ethnic prejudice, and conflict and cooperation between groups.

Forsyth, D. (1999). Group dynamics, 2nd ed. Pacific Grove, CA: Brooks/Cole. In addition to the topics discussed in the text, this introduction to group dynamics covers group formation, development, structure, and conflict. Includes separate chapters on collective behavior, and the group as an agent of change.

Hall, J. (1971, November). Decisions, decisions, decisions. Psychology Today, p. 51–54, 86–88. Group problem-solving can be superior to that of individuals. Guidelines for achieving solutions through consensus are provided.

Janis, I. (1982). Groupthink: Psychological studies of policy decisions and fiascos. Boston: Houghton Mifflin. Can be used to extend the text's treatment of groupthink. Examines the group decision processes that led to several historical fiascoes from Pearl Harbor to Watergate.

Janis, I. (1989). Crucial decisions: Leadership in policy making and crisis management. New York: Free Press. Attempts to answer when and why leaders of large organizations make avoidable errors that result in faulty policy decisions. Suggests strategies for preventing such errors.

Kephart, W. M., & Zellner, W. W. (1998). Extraordinary groups: An examination of unconventional lifestyles (6th ed.). New York: St. Martin's Press. Explores the inner workings of eight diverse groups including the Old Order Amish, the Oneida Community, the Gypsies, the Hasidim, and the Father Divine Movement. Emphasis is on illustrating major sociological principles.

Michener, A. H. (1998). Small group processes. Boulder, CO: Westview Press. Examines many group processes including minority influence, social loafing, group polarization, jury decision making, and groupthink. Group formation, group cohesiveness, and leadership are also treated.

Moscovici, S., Mucchi-Faina, A., & Maass, A. (Eds.). (1994). Minority influence. Chicago: Nelson-Hall Publishers. Both European and American researchers examine the power of minority influence to induce divergent thinking and to produce social change. Separate sections are devoted to theory and method in the study of minority influence.

Pfeiffer, J. W. (Ed.). (1989). The encyclopedia of group activities. San Diego: Pfeiffer and Co. Contains 150 experiential activities designed to help participants clarify values, increase self-awareness, and understand communication, conflict, and leadership in groups.

DEMONSTRATION AND PROJECT IDEAS

1. Who Am I?

Give students a couple of minutes to jot their responses to the question, "Who am I?" Then have them categorize their self-descriptions in terms of group and nongroup identifications. The importance of groups to our self-concepts will be obvious.

2. Is It a Group?

Chapter 8 begins by asking, "What is a group?" You can trigger discussion of this question by distributing Demonstration 8-1, which is adapted from an unknown source. Invite the class to vote yes or no for each situation and tally their votes. Draw out their criteria for judging each situation as a group or not. See if you can draw from their responses a definition similar to that in the text: "Two or more people who, for longer than a few moments, interact with and influence one another and perceive one another as 'us'." (A mere collection of individuals, such as passengers on a plane, was said not to constitute a group.)

Using this text definition, reexamine each situation:

1. The bus stop: This is a collection of individuals; they need not interact or influence one another in any way.
2. Worship: Do the members interact? Are they interdependent? Do they affect one another?
3. Fan club: If the members never see nor interact with one another, then they are not a group.
4. Seminar class: Assuming the students are not merely an audience to a lecturer, this is a group.

3. Social Loafing

Demonstration 8-2 is a modification of a classroom exercise created by Raymond Battalio and is based on an experiment designed by Charles Plott, Mark Isaac, and James Walker. The demonstration works with virtually any size class although it is best with fewer than 40 (Demonstration 8-2 was prepared for 30 but it is easily lengthened or shortened).

Distribute a copy of the demonstration as well as a small slip of paper to each student. Then read the following:

> Today I'm going to give you a chance to make some money. You are to write down either "1" or "0" on your slip of paper. How much money I pay you will depend on your choice as well as on that of everyone else in the room. Look at the chart in front of you. The total number of "1" votes will determine the payoff. For example, if 15 of you write down "1," the chart indicates that each of those voting "1" will receive 15 cents, while each person voting "0" will receive 27 cents. If only three of you write down "1," each of those voting "1" will receive 3 cents, while each person voting "0" will receive 15 cents. I'll give you a minute to think about the alternatives, but please don't discuss them with your neighbor.... Now please write down "0" or "1" without letting anyone see your choice. I do need your name (or student number) to prepare the payoff envelopes. Write it on the opposite side of the slip so that neither I nor anyone else in class need know how you voted.

After students have voted, collect the slips, count the number of "1" votes in front of the class and announce the payoff. The number of "1" votes are typically in the minority. Then put the slips in an envelope and distribute new slips for Round 2. Without any discussion, have them vote again. Typically, there will be even fewer "1" votes, because everyone now realizes that voting "0" always gives a bigger individual payoff than voting "1."

After the second tally students will be particularly eager to discuss the outcomes and to influence votes on the next round. Discussion often focuses on how the best collective outcome can be achieved. Someone is likely to suggest that the only "fair" outcome is for all to vote "1," with no one "free riding" on the rest. After allowing some time for discussion, take a third vote. As long as students are assured anonymity, "0" votes will continue. Three rounds are generally enough to introduce the dynamics of social loafing, but you can play as many rounds as your resources allow. Each time, however be sure to set the votes aside and record the payoff for "1" and "0" votes before continuing on the next round. While the payoff matrix is designed to keep the game relatively inexpensive (less than most film rentals), you can play with larger payoffs, as well as providing greater relative advantage for voting "0." Indeed, Battalio used 50 cents (instead of 12 cents) as the minimum payoff for "0" and 4 cents (instead of 1 cent) as the minimum payoff for "1." Increments of 4 cents for each additional "1" vote gave a consistent 50 cent advantage to those voting "0."

After class, you or your secretary can total each student's payoff and place it in a small envelope with the student's name or number on it. Distribute the envelopes.

4. Experiencing Evaluation Apprehension

The book suggests one of the reasons performance effectiveness changes when we are acting in public versus by ourselves is due to evaluation apprehension. The effects of evaluation apprehension can be demonstrated in class by simply having people perform tasks (answering math problems or solving anagrams) either at their desk or up in front of class on the board. Zajonc's (1965) theory suggests easy and well-learned tasks will be performed more efficiently in the presence of others, while difficult and unlearned tasks will be performed less efficiently. Of course efficiency can be operationalized as either time needed to complete the task or percent correct. Several variations can be explored: 1) changing the nature of the math problems, 2) changing the length of the anagrams, 3) changing the number of onlookers, and 4) altering the instructions of the onlookers (with or without instructions to evaluate the actor).

5. Deindividuation

David Dodd (1985) begins a discussion of deindividuation by asking students to write their response to this question: "If you could do anything humanly possible with complete assurance that you would not be detected or held responsible, what would you do?" Students turn in their answers anonymously. After the causes and consequences of deindividuation are briefly explained, the responses are read aloud to the class. The entire exercise requires about 15 minutes.

What responses can you expect? Dodd reports that the data obtained from several classes fell into 11 content categories: aggression, charity, academic dishonesty, crime, escapism, political activities, sexual behavior, social disruption, interpersonal spying and eavesdropping, travel, and a miscellaneous category. Answers were also categorized as prosocial, antisocial, nonnormative (violating social norms but without specifically helping or hurting others), and neutral (meeting none of the other three categories). The most frequent responses were criminal acts (26 percent), sexual acts (11 percent), and spying behaviors (11 percent). The most common single response was "rob a bank"—it accounted for 15 percent of all responses. Findings indicated that 36 percent of the responses were antisocial, 19 percent nonnormative, 36 percent neutral, and 9 percent prosocial.

6. Group Polarization

After eight years of using the choice dilemma items in classroom demonstrations, George Goethals and Amy Demorest (1979) concluded that the group polarization phenomenon is wonderfully involving and reliable, and that it provides a springboard for discussion of how one might explain it. The materials for Demonstration 8-3 have been used in more than 100 Hope and Calvin College classes. Never have results failed to confirm the experience of Goethals and Demorest.

The procedure is simple. BEFORE students read Chapter 8, reproduce, collate, and staple twice as many copies of the demonstration materials as you have students, so that you can distribute the materials to students for their individual responses, and then have them return these in exchange for fresh items prior to their discussions in groups of four or five. Introduce phase two by asking them to discuss each item to consensus, or to a point where, if consensus cannot be achieved, they have agreed to disagree. In either case, they should each mark their new items after discussion.

Before the next class, you can compute the average response to each item before and after discussion. (For simplicity, the group-by-group scores can be ignored.) The average response will nearly always be risk-prone (less than 5-in-10) for the Henry and Peter items before discussion and even more so after discussion. Students will initially be more cautious in their advice to Roger, a tendency that is usually accentuated by discussion. To show how the phenomenon generalizes to other materials, you can also administer the case of Mary N. (from Myers & Bishop, 1971). Students generally favor the field trip, and favor it even more strongly after discussion.

7. Informational Influence in Group Discussion

See Demonstration Idea #9 ("Normative Versus Informational Social Influences"), Chapter 6.

8. Are Six Heads Better Than One?

Marvin Shaw (1981) concludes that groups sometimes produce more and better solutions to problems than do individuals working alone. At least this seems to be true when there can be a division of labor (combining the contributions of several individuals), where it is possible for others to see and correct individual errors, or where the task involves creating ideas or remembering information. The following demonstration ideas embody one or more of these conditions, and thus will usually produce a group superiority effect.

A. Les Krantz's (1991) The Best and Worst of Everything (Prentice-Hall) provides an excellent source of information for formulating tasks comparing individual versus group performance. As one example, you might have students report, first as individuals and then in small groups, the most popular television programs of 1996–1997. Since this task involves the recall of information, groups are almost certain to perform better. In order of rankings, from first to tenth, the most popular 1996–1997 television programs were E.R., Seinfeld, Suddenly Susan, Friends, Naked Truth, Fired Up, NFL Monday Night Football, Single Guy, Home Improvement, and Touched by An Angel. (Source: Nielsen Media Research).

B. Demonstration 8-4 contains three problems that students should first attempt to solve on their own and then form small groups (say, of six members each) and arrive at a group decision. (Answers: 1. $20 as is evident if the farmer's expenditures are subtracted from his revenues. 2. Only two links must be cut, the fourth and the eleventh. These are given in payment on the first and second days. On the third day the three-link chain is given and the first two links are returned. These then are used for payment on days four and five. On the sixth day, the six-link chain is used, and the other links are returned in change. This process will work for a total of 23 days. 3. $60. The wholesale cost of the camera plus the $28 in change.)

Most college students are unlikely to come up with the right answers alone but are more likely to answer correctly after discussion. Chapter 8 reports the work of Patrick Laughlin and his colleagues, revealing that on more subtle cognitive tasks, truth still loses if but one person in a group of six is initially correct. But if a minority of two are initially correct, two thirds of the time they manage to convince all the others: truth <u>supported</u> wins. Look for this on Problems 1 and 3. Problem 2, however, is an "insight" problem. As Forsyth (1990) has observed, even if only one person comes up with the solution, it is generally so satisfying that everyone immediately agrees.

- C. <u>NASA Moon Survival, Lost at Sea, and Wilderness Survival Tasks</u>. All of these involve the remembering and application of information. The first is commercially available through Teleometrics Int'l., 1755 Woodstead Ct., The Woodlands, TX 77380. The others are available through Pfeiffer and Company, 8517 Production Avenue, San Diego, CA 92121-2280, and come with separate leaders' manuals. Groups nearly always do better than their average member, and often surpass even their best member. Hall reports that groups are most effective if the participants are instructed to: (1) present their positions as clearly as possible, yet be open to others' perspectives before pressing their own points; (2) look for the most acceptable alternative when in disagreement, rather than viewing the disagreement as a win-lose argument; (3) yield only to perspectives that appear sound and valid—don't change simply to avoid conflict; (4) do not avoid conflict by coin-flips, majority votes, and horse-trading deals; and (5) remember that differences of information and opinion are both natural and beneficial.

- D. <u>Twelve Angry Men</u>. Pfeiffer and Jones' <u>1972 Annual Handbook for Group Facilities</u> contains an excellent exercise to accompany the feature film <u>Twelve Angry Men</u>. The film itself highlights many social psychological principles and issues covered in the text, including the constructional nature of memory and perception, conformity, prejudice, and group influence, and particularly the effect of a minority on the majority. The film focuses on the deliberations of a jury in which all but one member initially vote for conviction. By the end of the film all jurors vote for acquittal. The exercise is introduced after 38 minutes of movie time. Viewers are each given a seating chart of the jury and asked to predict the order in which jurors will reverse their verdicts. After making individual judgments, they are instructed to reach consensus in a group. The rest of the film is then shown and the individual and group scores tallied by totaling error points.

9. Group Consensus Versus Independent Ratings

Thomas Rocklin (1985) describes a classroom exercise for comparing alternative group decision rules. As Rocklin observes, psychologists frequently use multiple judges to make assessments. For example, several judges may rate some dimension of a person's personality. In arriving at a final assessment, the raters may observe the stimulus person, hold a discussion and reach a consensus score. The diagnostic "staffing" used in mental health settings and university admissions committees typically follows this procedure. Alternatively, raters may observe the stimulus person, make independent assessments without discussion, and calculate the mean of their ratings. Which procedure is preferable? While the consensual procedure is commonly used, psychometricians do not recommend it. As Rocklin notes, the classical assumption that the expected value of the error components in a set of scores is zero holds only for independent scores. The discussion involved in the consensual procedure violates that assumption. However, when asked which of the two procedures they believe to be better, most students opt for the consensual procedure. They typically believe the discussion will uncover evidence that individual judges might overlook.

In introducing his demonstration Rocklin explains that since there is no clear way to determine the accuracy of personality ratings, the class will rate characteristics of a piece of string and a book instead. This class is divided into groups of three or four students each. Half of the groups are told that before forming a judgment they should have a thorough discussion, then write down their consensus. The other groups are told not to discuss the matter but to write down their individual judgments and compare a group average. A 109 cm string is then held up and students are asked to judge its length. In similar fashion, a 213 g book is held up and students are asked to estimate its weight. Rocklin reports that groups using the "independent" procedure were more accurate in making both judgments.

In explaining these results one can present the psychometric argument, namely, that positive and negative errors cancel each other out. Another tack is to suggest that any of a number of characteristics (e.g., assertiveness, age, sex) of an individual within the group could lead other members of the group to lend undue credence to that individual's judgment. Since these characteristics may bear no relationship to the ability to judge weight and length, the consensual procedure is less accurate than the independent procedure.

10. Experiencing Group Effects Firsthand

One way to wrap-up the section on group influence and review previous material at the same time entails picking an article which contains a variety of social psychological phenomenon covering many of the previous chapters (e.g., Muzafer Sherif's article on "Experiments in Group Conflict" or Neal Osherow's "Making Sense Out of the Nonsensical"—both articles found in Aronson, 1999). Have the students read it prior to the class and come prepared to discuss the material. Then arbitrarily break them up into small groups (four or five is ideal) and have them identify (and specify with a sentence or two of justification) on paper all of the social psychological concepts they can in the article. Give them about 15 minutes to list and defend as many as they can. In the meantime, identify each group with a number. Then have each group write their group number on their list and pass the list on to another group for evaluation (e.g., group 1 goes to 2, 2 goes to 3, and so on.). Inform the groups that they are now to inspect the forms they received from the other group and reject any concept, which they think was not sufficiently defended. At this point disclose that you will be rewarding the group who has the highest combined score. The combined score will be the number of accepted concepts plus the number of rejected concepts (from the other group's paper) minus the number of improperly rejected concepts (which you will determine after class). This requires that the inspecting group will also have to note their group number on the paper they are inspecting. Give the groups about 10–15 minutes to evaluate all of the concepts listed. Then gather up the papers and score them later. Note: there are many derivatives to this basic exercise.

At this point, you may ask the class what group-related concepts they just experienced as a result of the class exercise. There are many possibilities, but here are a few: the power of nominal groups, social loafing, evaluation apprehension, in-group/out-group thinking, group polarization, risky-shift, and groupthink.

11. The Social Connection Video Series

One of the entries in the video instructional supplement (The Social Connection Video Series), entitled "Role Playing: The Power of the Situation," can be used to introduce the process of deindividuation covered in Chapter 8. See the Faculty Guide accompanying the video series for a program summary, pause points, and a classroom activity.

Demonstration 8-1

Chapter 9 discusses "Group Influence." But what is a group? Consider each of the following: Is it a group, or not?

Yes   No

_____ _____   1. Five people waiting at the same corner for a bus.

_____ _____   2. People attending a worship service.

_____ _____   3. The Spice Girls Fan Club.

_____ _____   4. The students in a seminar class.

Demonstration 8-2

Number of People Picking "1"	Payout for Picking "1"	Payout for Picking "0"
0		$.12
1	$.01	.13
2	.02	.14
3	.03	.15
4	.04	.16
5	.05	.17
6	.06	.18
7	.07	.19
8	.08	.20
9	.09	.21
10	.10	.22
11	.11	.23
12	.12	.24
13	.13	.25
14	.14	.26
15	.15	.27
16	.16	.28
17	.17	.29
18	.18	.30
19	.19	.31
20	.20	.32
21	.21	.33
22	.22	.34
23	.23	.35
24	.24	.36
25	.25	.37
26	.26	.38
27	.27	.39
28	.28	.40
29	.29	.41
30	.30	.42

Demonstration 8-3

Bolt & Myers

©McGraw-Hill, 1999

Henry is a writer who is said to have considerable creative talent but who so far has been earning a comfortable living by writing cheap Westerns. Recently he has come up with an idea for a potentially significant novel. If it could be written and accepted, it might have considerable literary impact and be a big boost to his career. On the other hand, if he is not able to work out his idea or if the novel is a flop, he will have expended considerable time and energy without remuneration.

Imagine that you are advising Henry. Please check the <u>lowest</u> probability that you would consider acceptable for Henry to attempt to write the novel.

Henry should attempt to write the novel if the chances that the novel will be a success are at least:

____ 1 in 10
____ 2 in 10
____ 3 in 10
____ 4 in 10
____ 5 in 10
____ 6 in 10
____ 7 in 10
____ 8 in 10
____ 9 in 10
____ Place a check here if you think Henry should attempt the novel only if it is certain (i.e., 10 in 10) that the novel will be a success.

Demonstration 8-3

Bolt & Myers

©**McGraw-Hill, 1999**

Peter is an earnest young state representative who would like to run for governor of his state. Since he has a reputation as an able and conscientious legislator, several influential persons have pledged their support to him should he decide to run. But his opponent would be the incumbent governor who has a well-organized political machine behind him, so it would not be an easy campaign.

Imagine that you are advising Peter. Check the <u>lowest</u> probability that you would consider acceptable to make it worthwhile for Peter to run for the office.

Peter should attempt to run for office if the chances that he would win the election were at least:

___   1 in 10
___   2 in 10
___   3 in 10
___   4 in 10
___   5 in 10
___   6 in 10
___   7 in 10
___   8 in 10
___   9 in 10
___   Place a check here if you think Peter should run for office only if it is certain (i.e., 10 in 10) that he would win the election.

Demonstration 8-3

Roger, a married man with two children of school age, has a secure job that pays him about $26,000 per year. He can easily afford the necessities of life, but few of the luxuries. Except for a life insurance policy he has no savings. Roger has heard from reliable sources that the stock of a relatively unknown Company X might triple its present value if a new product currently in production is favorably received by the buying public. On the other hand, if the product is unfavorably received, the stock might decline considerably in value. Roger is considering investing his life insurance money in this company.

Imagine that you are advising Roger. Check the lowest probability that you would consider acceptable for Roger to invest in Company X stock.

Roger should invest in Company X stock if the chances that the stock will triple in value are at least:

___ 1 in 10
___ 2 in 10
___ 3 in 10
___ 4 in 10
___ 5 in 10
___ 6 in 10
___ 7 in 10
___ 8 in 10
___ 9 in 10
___ Place a check here if you think Roger should invest in Company X stock only if it is certain (i.e., 10 in 10) that the stock will triple in value.

Demonstration 8-3

Bolt & Myers

©McGraw-Hill, 1999

Mary N., a college junior, desires to spend her spring vacation on a biology field trip to another region of the country. Her parents, who have not seen her in several months, would like very much to have her home over vacation. Mary N. is unsure what to do. Since she is interested in becoming a biologist, she considers the field trip a rare opportunity for firsthand research experience. It would also help her test out her interest in becoming a biologist. On the other hand she knows that her parents have been looking forward for some time to having her home for a few days. Mary N. loves her parents and also appreciates the fact that they are financing her education.

Please put a check next to the ONE statement that best expresses your opinion:

____ I strongly favor that Mary N. go home for a vacation.

____ I moderately favor that Mary N. go home for a vacation.

____ I slightly favor that Mary N. go home for a vacation.

____ Undecided

____ I slightly favor that Mary N. go on the biology field trip.

____ I moderately favor that Mary N. go on the biology field trip.

____ I strongly favor that Mary N. go on the biology field trip.

Demonstration 8-4

1. A farmer purchased a horse for $70 and sold it for $80. He then purchased it back for $90 and sold it again for $100. How much money did he make in the horse business?

2. Shirley, a college student, has run short of cash and is unable to pay the rent on her apartment. Although she knows she will receive a final check from her former employer in 23 days, the apartment owner refuses to wait. Having recently received from her grandparents a valuable gold chain with 23 links, she proposes to pay for each day with one link. After she receives her check and pays cash, the apartment owner will return the links. Because of a history of mistrust, he wants payment every day, and Shirley does not want to pay any links in advance. She also wants to preserve the integrity of the chain to the degree that's possible. How many links must be cut while still paying the owner one link for each day?

3. A teenager purchases a camera for $62 by endorsing his paycheck of $90. Not having $28 change in his register the camera store owner runs across the street to the drug store and obtains $90 in cash for the check. He sells the teenager the camera and gives him his change. Later the check turns out to be fraudulent and the camera store owner must make good with the drug store. He originally paid $32 for the camera. What was his total out-of-pocket loss?

FILMS/VIDEOS

The Abilene Paradox (CRM, 27 min., 1985). Mismanaged agreement is as dangerous to organizational effectiveness as excessive conflict. Closely related to Janis's concept of groupthink.

Credibility (CRM, 42 min., 1994). James Kouzes and Barry Posner define leadership as a reciprocal relationship with constituents where respect must run both ways.

Group Decision Making and Leadership (PSU, 30 min., 1989). Depicts the strategies and interpersonal relationships among decision makers in a variety of situations. Suggestions are made for boosting group productivity and efficiency. Discusses the leadership role and shows that certain leaders can only be effective under the right circumstances.

Groups and Group Dynamics (INS, 30 min., 1991). Explores the centrality of groups in social life. Explains how groups function and how group membership is determined. Examines interactions within and between groups.

Groupthink, Revised Edition (CRM, 22 min., 1990). Discusses the symptoms of groupthink in the context of the Space Shuttle Challenger disaster.

The Leadership Challenge (CRM, 26 min., 1990) Best-selling authors James Kouzes and Barry Posner host this case study of five world leaders. The program suggests that leadership ability is not a special gift but a set of five key practices.

Leadership: Style or Circumstance (CRM, 28 min., 1974). Presents Fiedler's contingency model of leadership. Relationship-oriented and task-oriented styles are illustrated.

The Meeting Robbers (CRM, 20 min., 1983). Illustrates how an organization's time and money are "stolen" by well-intentioned employees because they lack the skills necessary to keep their meetings results-oriented.

Mob Psychology and Crowd Behavior: Disaster at Hillsborough (FHS, 52 min., 1991). Showing this program can extend the literature on deindividuation. It examines the causes of the riot at the 1989 soccer match in which 95 people were killed.

Twelve Angry Men (See Chapter 3.)

CHAPTER 9
PREJUDICE: DISLIKING OTHERS

The Nature and Power of Prejudice
    What Is Prejudice?
    How Pervasive Is Prejudice?
    Racial Prejudice
    Gender Prejudice
Social Sources of Prejudice
    Social Inequalities
    Unequal Status and Prejudice
    Religion and Prejudice
    Discrimination's Impact: The Self-fulfilling Prophecy
    Stereotype Threat
    Social Identity
    Ingroup Bias
    Conformity
    Institutional Supports
Emotional Sources of Prejudice
    Frustration and Aggression: The Scapegoat Theory
    Personality Dynamics
    Need for Status, Self-Regard and Belonging
    The Authoritarian Personality
Cognitive Sources of Prejudice
    Categorization
    Perceived Similarities and Differences
    Distinctiveness
    Distinctive People
    Vivid Cases
    Distinctive Events
    Attribution: Is It a Just World?
    Group-Serving Bias
    The Just-World Phenomenon
    Cognitive Consequences of Stereotypes
    Are Stereotypes Self-Perpetuating?
    Do Stereotypes Bias Judgments of Individuals?
Personal Postscript: Can We Reduce Prejudice?

LECTURE AND DISCUSSION IDEAS

1. SPSSI Curriculum Collection

The Society for the Psychological Study of Social Issues (SPSSI) (Division 9 of the American Psychological Association) has prepared an extensive collection of curriculum materials on prejudice and intergroup relations. Included are syllabi, reading lists, assignments, class activities, simulations, and video suggestions. Dr. Susan Goldstein of the University of Redlands has coordinated the project and it is of enormous help in teaching this chapter. To access the Curriculum Collection, send an e-mail with blank message to: spssi_pr@field.uor.edu. You will quickly receive a list of all available materials and directions on how to request specific files. The files you request will be forwarded to you immediately via "e-mail-on demand."

2. Modern Racism

The text reports that survey research shows a dramatic decline in prejudice against Blacks over the last few decades. Nevertheless indirect methods for assessing people's attitudes and behavior reveal disguised racial bias. The ABC PrimeTime segment "True Colors" (1993, 16 min.) provides an excellent introduction to modern racism. Two young adult males—a white American and an African-American—attempt to relocate in a large mid-western city. The story compares their interactions in a variety of settings with landlords, salespersons, and potential employers. Although most of us recognize that racial prejudice still exists, the contrasting treatment of these two men is dramatic and even shocking. In finding a job, renting an apartment, and even catching a taxi, the African-American is the victim of both subtle prejudice and overt discrimination. Anyone who thinks that racial prejudice in the United States has been eliminated should see this documentary. It is available for purchase at very reasonable cost by calling Core Vision at 1-800-537-3130.

James Patterson and Peter Kim's (1991) The Day America Told the Truth (Prentice-Hall) also discovers a racism that is subtler and more hypocritical than the blatant prejudice of 50 years ago. The authors suggest that white Americans today hold Blacks responsible for their current position in American society. "We tried to help," Whites say, "but Blacks wouldn't help themselves." It is a dramatic contrast to the attitudes of 1960s when many Whites from the president on down maintained that black people were owed compensation for the centuries of oppression. Patterson and Kim's survey also documents the phenomenon of greatest prejudice in the most intimate social realms, as described in the text. Have your White students reflect on their immediate reaction to the following:

Do you believe you could fall in love with a black person?

How do you think your friends would react if you married a black person?

You learn after an accident that you have received a blood transfusion from a black person. Would that bother you?

Does it make you uneasy to see a black man walking hand-in-hand with a white woman?

Do you believe that black persons are poor because they fail to take advantage of the opportunities open to them?

A Common Destiny: Blacks and American Society, a National Research Council study edited by black economist Gerald David Jaynes and white sociologist Robin M. Williams, Jr., provides what some regard as the most definitive report on race relations since the 1968 Kerner Commission. Among its important conclusions is that "the status of black Americans today can be characterized as a glass that is half full—

if measured by the progress since 1939—or as a glass that is half empty—if measured by the persisting disparities between black and white Americans since the early 1970s."

A Common Destiny reveals that overt discrimination continues with perhaps the clearest evidence being in housing. Since the 1960s there has been virtually no measurable progress in achieving integration. In New York, Chicago, and Detroit, black college graduates are almost as likely to live in segregated neighborhoods as are black high school dropouts. Moreover, the preference among Whites for segregated housing increases with their socioeconomic status. "The higher the white respondents' income," writes Jaynes, "the less they want to be in an integrated neighborhood."

Although in the abstract, Whites endorse the goal of achieving an integrated society, their support for specific governmental programs to achieve it is less than enthusiastic. A Common Destiny notes this inconsistency as one of the "important signs of continuing resistance to full equality of black Americans: principles of equality are endorsed less when social contact is close, of long duration, or frequent."

3. Four Principles of Modern Racism

To extend the text's treatment of racial prejudice, you might present McConahay's (1986) concept of modern racism in class. McConahay argues that the following four beliefs underlie modern racism:

1. Blacks now have the freedom to compete in the marketplace and enjoy those things they can afford. Discrimination is really a thing of the past.
2. Blacks push too hard, too fast, and into places where they are really not wanted.
3. Both the demands and tactics that blacks use are unfair.
4. Our social institutions are giving blacks more attention and status than they deserve.

McConahay notes that people who accept these ideas do not see themselves as prejudiced. In fact, they agree that racism is bad. Holding to the stereotypes that blacks are lazy, dishonest, or ignorant are wrong as are the practices of segregation and other acts of open discrimination. In the minds of modern racists, the four statements above are not racially inspired but empirical facts. Nonetheless, suggests McConahay, modern racism continues to generate negative racial affect, influences how people interpret new information, and perhaps, most importantly, how people interact with Blacks on a daily basis.

4. Racial Ambivalence and Value Conflict

The text notes that racial attitudes expressed by white Americans are far more liberal today than they were 40 years ago. Still racial prejudice is not extinct. Katz and Hass (1988) have attempted to explain Whites' conflicting racial attitudes in terms of two core value orientations.

Humanitarianism-Egalitarianism (HE) includes the democratic ideals of equality, justice, and concern for others' well-being. The Protestant ethic (PE) emphasizes devotion to work, individual achievement, and discipline. Katz and Hass hypothesized that HE likely strengthens a pro-Black (PB) attitude with the perception that black people, having a history of exclusion from the main society, are disadvantaged. In contrast, PE strengthens an anti-Black (AB) attitude with the view that Blacks' problems reflect their own shortcomings. The researchers predicted that the dual cognitive (i.e., value-attitude) structures would themselves, however, be independent.

Four scales, HE (e.g., "Those who are unable to provide for their basic needs should be helped by others"), PE (e.g., "People who fail at a job have usually not tried hard enough"), PB (e.g., "Blacks have more to offer than they have been allowed to show"), and AB (e.g., "Blacks should take the jobs that are available and then work their way up to better jobs") were devised and given to white students at eight colleges. As predicted, positive correlations were obtained between HE and PB, and between PE and AB. All other correlations tended to be much lower.

In a second study Katz and Hass used a priming technique (completing a particular scale made those specific cognitions salient) to test for causality. As predicted, priming a given value raised scores on the theoretically corresponding attitude but did not affect scores on the other attitude. Priming a single attitude influenced scores on the corresponding value, but not on the other value.

5. Ambivalent Sexism

As the text indicates, Glick and Fiske (1996) suggest that positive feelings toward women often go hand in hand with sexist antipathy. They have presented a theory of sexism formulated as ambivalence toward women. Although hostile sexism is readily understood, what is meant by benevolent sexism requires some explanation. Glick and Fiske define it as a set of interrelated attitudes in which women are stereotypically placed into restricted roles. Subjectively positive feelings tend to elicit behaviors typically categorized as prosocial (e.g., helping) or intimacy-seeking (e.g., self-disclosure). Benevolent sexism, however, is typically based on the notion that man is the provider, woman is his dependent.

According to Glick and Fiske, hostile and benevolent sexism are composed of three shared components: Paternalism, Gender Differentiation, and Heterosexuality. Paternalism literally means relating to others "in the manner of a father dealing with his children." Ambivalent sexism reflects both domination (women are not fully competent adults) and protection (women are weak and thus need to be provided for). Gender differentiation has both competitive and complementary elements to it. Gender is one of the earliest and strongest forms of group identity to be internalized. The competitive drive to differentiate (based in the desire to maintain social status) presents a social justification for male structural power. Only men have the traits necessary to govern important social institutions. Along with this, however, male dependency on women fosters the notion that women have many positive traits that complement those of men (e.g., sensitivity to others' feelings). Finally, heterosexuality is one of the most powerful components of men's ambivalence toward women. Men consider romantic relationships to be a top source of happiness. However, sex is a resource for which women act as gatekeepers. The belief that women use their sexual allure to gain dominance over men generates hostility toward them.

In recent research Glick and colleagues (1997) have demonstrated that, relative to nonsexists, ambivalent sexist men spontaneously categorize women into liked and disliked subtypes, traditional versus nontraditional, good sexy versus unattractive or "deviant" sexuality. Some women are put on a "pedestal" and others are put in the "gutter." The researchers also found that hostile sexism as measured by the Ambivalent Sexism Inventory (Demonstration 9-2) predicted less favorable attitudes toward women in a nontraditional role (career women), whereas benevolent sexism predicted favorable attitudes toward women in a traditional role (homemakers). By habitually placing women in two groups sexists can maintain both their positive and negative beliefs about women without experiencing conflict.

6. Stereotyping

To trigger discussion of stereotyping, ask students to:

Picture two people. Person A is adventurous, ambitious, logical, and independent. Do you have an image of this person? Person B is attractive, sensitive, gentle, and tender. Do you have an image of this person? How many of you pictured Person A as a male? How many of you pictured Person B as a male?

The differing show of hands demonstrates stereotyping, which the text defines as "a generalization about a group of people that distinguishes those people from others."

As a further example of stereotyping, students might enjoy offering their images of the owners of different makes of cars. Twenty-five years ago, Wells, Goi, and Seader (1958) found that Cadillac owners were described as rich, high class, famous, important, proud, and superior. Buick owners were characterized as brave, masculine, strong, modern, and pleasant. Chevrolet owners were seen as poor, ordinary, low class, simple, cheap, thin, and friendly. Ford owners were thought to be masculine, young, powerful, good-looking, rough, dangerous, and single. Plymouth owners were viewed as quiet, careful, slow, moral, fat, sad, thinking, patient, and honest. Do these stereotypes still hold? What about VW and Honda owners? Or, on your campus, do students have stereotypes of those who join particular fraternities and sororities, or who live in particular dorms? And how are music majors, business majors, and science majors perceived to differ from one another?

Ask: Are stereotypes objectionable? If yes, why? If someone says it's because they are false or inaccurate, ask if this is necessarily so. (Stereotypes, though sometimes grossly inaccurate, are also sometimes accurate.) If someone says it's because they are generalizations about groups that get applied to individuals, ask if this is necessarily bad. (If on the first day of camp, two captains choose up sides for a basketball game, would they not be wise to choose big, strapping people rather than wimpy-looking people, even if the stereotype that the former are better players is not always true?) If someone says it's because stereotypes are formed by hearsay, rather than direct experience, ask if this isn't true of many valid beliefs—that black holes exist in outer space, that Columbus discovered America. What is objectionable about stereotypes? Roger Brown (1965) argues it is a) the implicit <u>ethnocentrism</u>—the judgmental element that might lead one to label an outgroup as "clannish," in contrast to the "loyalty" of one's own group—and b) the implication that perceived differences are <u>inborn</u> and unalterable—for example, that the lower IQ scores of Blacks compared to Whites implies that Blacks are innately inferior.

7. Sexism in the Classroom?

Amy Saltzman (1994) provides an excellent summary of the conflicting research findings that address this issue. She raises and answers the following four questions:

<u>Do schools favor boys?</u> Saltzman notes that much of the case for a bias favoring males rests on Myra and David Sadker's claim that boys in elementary and middle school call out answers eight times more than girls. When boys call out, reported the Sadkers, teachers respond by giving them full attention and making constructive comments, while girls who call out are usually admonished to raise their hands. More recent studies have shown that the ratio of boys to girls who call out answers in class may be closer than 2 to 1. The fact that they do call out more often may result in teachers having greater opportunity to praise them. There seems to be little evidence that teachers respond differently to girls who do respond. On a somewhat different note, it appears that teachers pay more attention to boys because they act out more. Some experts believe that it is actually the misbehavior of boys and thus the attention they receive, rather than a pervasive bias against girls that may eat away at girls' self-esteem. One educator suggests that schools need to switch their focus from trying to eradicate sexism directed against girls to training teachers to better discipline boys.

<u>Does girls' self-esteem suffer more in early adolescence?</u> Most research suggests that it does but much of it relates to physical appearance. Studies suggest that boys and girls feel equally positive about their physical appearance in third grade, but every year after that, girls' opinion of their looks declines while boys' stays about the same.

<u>Is self-esteem related to academic success?</u> If there is a connection, it is elusive at best. Some studies have found self-esteem to be highest among African-American girls, considered among the groups most at-risk academically. One explanation for this has been that the black culture's emphasis on

independence and assertiveness gives black girls a greater sense of self-worth than white girls. As a result they are less likely to be influenced by concerns over physical appearance. The group with the lowest academic self-esteem consists of white girls who outperform virtually every other group, including white boys, in most academic areas. Even in math and science, boys no longer outshine girls by that much.

Does self-esteem affect career choice? The vast majority of women still flock to traditionally lower paying fields such as English literature, psychology, communications, and education. Men dominate in the higher-paying areas of engineering and science. Despite significant progress for women, 60 percent of law, medical, and dental students are men. In addressing the issue of whether self-esteem is behind this difference, Saltzman concludes that research has no clear answer.

8. Authoritarianism

In reviewing measures of authoritarianism, Christie (1991) suggests that the best short form of the F scale currently available for use in large cross-sectional studies of the population is Lane's (1955) four-item measure. In introducing this topic, you may want to read the following statements and simply have students write down whether they agree or disagree with each (percentage agreement is from a 1952 sample): 1. What young people need most of all is strict discipline by their parents. (agree: 76 percent) 2. Most people who don't get ahead just don't have enough will power. (agree: 64 percent) 3. A few strong leaders could make this country better than all the laws and talk. (agree: 51 percent) 4. People sometimes say that an insult to your honor should not be forgotten. Do you agree or disagree with that? (agree: 25 percent) These items provide a good introduction to the specific authoritarian tendencies cited in the text, namely, a submissive respect for ingroup authorities, an intolerance for weakness, and a punitive attitude.

Several points are worth making in lecturing on this topic. First, it is an excellent example of how psychological research can be closely tied to current events. Hitler's barbarous slaughter of millions of Jews provided a major stimulus for the study of authoritarianism. Second, the study of anti-Semitism quickly expanded to the study of ethnocentrism, because those who were hostile to Jews also expressed antagonism toward all groups other than their own. One researcher found that those scoring high on the F-scale tended to be intolerant of even Danerians, Pireaneans, and Wallonians. Third, the study of ethnocentrism expanded to the study of personality in general. The very existence of ethnocentrism suggests that attitudes may result from some characteristic of the people holding them rather than characteristics of the people toward whom they are directed. Finally, Adorno's <u>The Authoritarian Personality</u> is recognized as a classic work in social psychology in that it attempted to relate personality to ideology, that is, to one's social, political, and economic attitudes.

9. Enemies of Freedom

Bob Altemeyer's (1988) <u>Enemies of Freedom</u> provides a useful resource for classroom lecture and discussion on "right-wing authoritarianism." By right-wing authoritarianism Altemeyer means the combination of authoritarian submission, authoritarian aggression, and conventionalism. They are attitudes that seem to go together not just in North America but in a number of places throughout the world and seem to have become more common during the 1970s and 1980s.

Altemeyer notes that "highly submissive, conventional persons seem unusually fearful that the world is personally dangerous and that society is collapsing into lawlessness." It is this fear that produces aggressive impulses. The same submissive, conventional people also tend to be highly self-righteous and this self-righteousness disinhibits the aggressive impulse. The result is a considerable capacity for hostile behavior toward a bewildering array of victims.

Altemeyer argues that certain life experiences shape these attitudes more than do parents or peer groups. Higher education, particularly in the liberal arts, tends to lower authoritarianism. Interestingly, parenthood itself seems to increase it. The educational system, the media, and religion may be successfully enlisted in the control of authoritarianism.

10. Ever Been Labeled? Consequences of Stereotyping

The chapter's concluding section on the consequences of stereotypes could be introduced by asking students to reflect, privately and then in discussion, on several questions: Have you ever been "labeled?" Did you like being labeled? Did the label affect how other people perceived you? Did it affect how you acted?

As an alternative to this discussion, you might utilize a class exercise suggested by Susan Goldstein (1997). Prepare gummed labels with a trait that corresponds to a common racial or gender stereotype, e.g., lazy, impulsive, aggressive, or childlike. Have each student place a label on his or her forehead without knowing its descriptor. Using shifting dyads, have students discuss their "future plans" while treating each other based on the labeled traits. Finally, in preparation for discussion and before they have removed the label, have students reflect on how the exercise made them feel, what they believe their label to be, whether the treatment they received influenced their behavior, and how they approached the task of treating others based on the labeled trait.

Goldstein reports that students are typically surprised at how easy it is to treat another person according to stereotyped traits as well as the rapidity with which they find themselves acting according to their own trait label.

11. Where Bias Begins: The Truth About Stereotypes

Annie Murphy Paul (1998; also found in Annual Editions–Social Psychology 01/02; see Chapter 1 references) describes an argument for explaining negative stereotypes from recent research on unconscious information processing. The article describes several reaction-time studies, which manipulated good and bad adjectives paired with typical names of either black or white individuals (other similar studies are described as well). The results showed that people (even some African Americans) responded more quickly when a positive adjective was paired with a white name or a negative adjective was paired with a black name. This article is very brief digestible—ideal for class assignment. Here are some possible discussion questions: Does this article successfully challenge the notion that stereotyping is the act of some people but not others? Do you think the methodology used to investigate stereotyping was appropriate? (Is it fair to draw a link between "response times" on a test and a person's tendency to stereotype?) Is the presence of unconscious stereotyping a threat to our sense of freedom? Given the research, can society ever hope to eradicate prejudice and negative stereotyping?

Demonstration # 12 (Implicit Association Test) dovetails nicely with this lecture/discussion idea.

12. Popular Sources for Additional Classroom Material

Altemeyer, B. (1997). The authoritarian specter. Cambridge, MA: Harvard University Press. Examines the many ways authoritarianism undermines democracy. In presenting his latest research, Altemeyer shows how ordinary people may be psychologically predisposed to accept fascist policies.

Duckitt, J. (1992). Psychology and prejudice: A historical analysis and integrative framework. American Psychologist, 47, p. 1182–1193. The author argues that four causes of prejudice provide a relatively complete understanding of prejudice as both an individual and group phenomenon.

Furnham, A., & Procter, E. (1989). Belief in a just world: Review and critique of the individual difference literature. British Journal of Social Psychology, 28, p. 365–384. Examines the correlates between belief in a just world and other psychological and demographic variables.

Gaines, S. O., & Reed, E. S. (1995). Prejudice: From Allport to DuBois. American Psychologist, 47, p. 96–103. The authors suggest that racism is not a universal feature of human personality but a historically developed process. DuBois's "sociohistorical" view of personality challenges Allport's explanation of prejudice.

Jones, J. M. (1997). Prejudice and racism (2nd ed.). Theory, research, and case studies are interwoven in this excellent overview of the causes and consequences of prejudice and racism. Carefully traces the history of race relations in the United States from 1500 to the present.

Katz, P., & Taylor, D. (1988). Eliminating racism: Profiles in controversy. New York: Plenum. Experts document the reality of prejudice against Blacks, Hispanics, Japanese Americans, American Indians, and women, and examine the fruitfulness of various remedies, such as desegregation, cooperative behavior, and affirmative action.

Lee, Y., Jussim, L. J., & McCauley, C. R. (1995). Stereotype accuracy: Toward appreciating group differences. Washington, DC: American Psychological Association. This collection of essays offers a more positive view of stereotypes. Sometimes stereotypes are accurate and provide the basis for appreciating group differences.

Lerner, M. J. (1980). The belief in a just world. New York: Plenum. An excellent summary of the research on the just world hypothesis. The subtitle of the book suggests that belief in a just world is a delusion.

Office of Ethnic Minority Affairs. (2001). Communique. (Public Interest Directorate). Washington DC: American Psychological Association. Includes association reports and various updates on the recruitment, retention and training of psychologists of color, clinical practice and violence prevention in communities of color, and many other informational items.

Steele, C. (1997). A threat in the air: How stereotypes shape intellectual identity and performance. American Psychologist, 52, p. 613–629. Latest research on stereotype threat. In an academic setting, it has its greatest effect on the better, more confident students who belong to stereotyped groups.

Waller, J. (1998). Face to face: The changing state of racism across America. New York: Insight Books. This book makes the argument that American racism has moved from overt expression to more subtle expressions and discusses ideas for genuine solutions for racial discord.

DEMONSTRATION AND PROJECT IDEAS

1. Measuring Stereotypes

You can introduce the measurement of stereotypes with Demonstration 9-1. One popular approach is to ask respondents to estimate the percentage of people in the target group who possess a particular trait. Although you can identify any target group, "men" and "women" would be good initial choices because the specific items reflect communal (1, 4, 8, 10, 12, 15) and agentic (2, 3, 5, 6, 7, 9, 11, 13, 14, 16) factors (Eagly & Steffen, 1988). Have each student respond twice (once for "men," once for "women") and compare their ratings for specific items as well as their mean ratings for each factor. You can also compute the ratings for your class and present them at the next session. These might then be compared with Martin's (1987) research results as reported in the text. Reinforce the point made in the text that stereotypes (beliefs) are not prejudices (attitudes). Stereotypes may support prejudice, but then again one might believe, without prejudice, that men and women are "different yet equal."

If you use other target groups, e.g., ethnic categories, note McCauley and Stitt's (1978) suggestions that in addition to asking what percentage of a group possesses a specific trait, you must ask what percentage of <u>people in general</u> possess the trait. By dividing the subject's estimate of the target group by his or her estimate of the percentage of people in general who possess the trait, we obtain a <u>diagnostic ratio</u>. This tells us how much the respondent believes the trait distinguishes the target group from people in general.

An alternative approach to stereotype measurement is to have respondents use continuous scales to rate the extent to which groups (e.g., women) or prototypical group members (e.g., an average or typical woman) possess certain traits. Eagly and Steffen (1988) report evidence that these two approaches can be used interchangeably.

2. Gender Stereotypes

Demonstration 9-2 is adapted from the well-known research of Broverman et al. (1970). Note that it comes in three forms, each of which should be distributed to one-third of the class. In the 1970 report, items 1, 3, 6, 7, and 9 were more likely to be attributed to the healthy male; 2, 4, 5, 8, and 10 were more likely attributed to the healthy female; moreover, the mentally healthy adult was more similar to the healthy male than the healthy female. In a 1990s college classroom, are such results still obtained?

3. The Ambivalent Sexism Inventory

Demonstration 9-3 is the Ambivalent Sexism Inventory designed by Peter Glick and Susan T. Fiske (see the Lecture/Discussion Topic on "Ambivalent Sexism" earlier in this chapter). For use other than classroom demonstration, be sure to secure the permission of one of the authors (e-mail peter.s.glick@lawrence.edu).

To score, students should reverse the numbers (0 = 5, 1 = 4, 2 = 3. 3 = 2. 4 = 1, 5 = 0) they placed in front of items 3, 6, 7, 13, 18, and 21. An overall measure of sexism is found by simply finding the average of the numbers placed in front of all 22 items. The Hostile Sexism score is found by averaging the numbers in response to items 2, 4, 5, 7, 10, 11, 14, 15, 16, 18, and 21. The Benevolent Sexism score is found by averaging the numbers in response to items 1, 3, 6, 8, 9, 12, 13, 17, 19, 20, and 22. In each case, scores can range from 0 to 5 with higher scores reflecting greater sexism.

4. Mass Media Images of Women and Men

Mary Crawford (1994) suggests an exercise in which students read a typical Harlequin-style romance novel of their choice. Most are only about 200 pages and can be read very quickly. In a five-page paper, Crawford's students then analyze its plot and characters for the message it gives about femininity, masculinity, love, and relationships. The students are also asked to reflect on why these books are popular and why women choose to write them. This student project can be readily extended to the analysis of gender stereotypes in other media, for example, magazine advertisements, television commercials and programs, comic strips, and feature films.

5. Institutional Discrimination

Racism, according to the text's definition, refers to both an individual's prejudicial attitudes and institutional practices that subordinate people of a given race. Susan Goldstein (1994) suggests an exercise that is certain to promote students' critical thinking about institutional discrimination. Form small groups of four to six students and distribute copies of Demonstration 9-4. For each example have the students (1) determine if institutional discrimination is present, (2) identify groups against which the practice discriminates, (3) identify the intended purpose of each practice, and (4) if the intended purpose is legitimate, suggest how else this purpose might be achieved.

6. Understanding Sources of Prejudice

To give students practice in analyzing the social, emotional, and cognitive sources of prejudice, have them carefully examine a contemporary or historical case of prejudice and identify its possible causes. For example, you might provide details of the famous Emmett Till case (see below), which in 1955 caught the attention of the national news media, and played a role in galvanizing the civil rights movement. Have students analyze the case in terms of both personal prejudice and institutional racism and suggest what its social, emotional, and cognitive causes might have been.

On August 28, 1955, Emmett Till, a black teenager visiting from Chicago, was murdered in Money, Mississippi. His body was retrieved from a river three days later with an eye gouged out, a bullet in his skull, and his head crushed.

While visiting relatives in Money, the f14-year-old had made a remark to Carolyn Bryant, a white woman and wife of a local store owner. One report had him saying, "How about a date, baby?" Another said he merely whistled at her. Bryant's husband, Roy Bryant, and his half-brother, J.W. Milam, were charged with Emmett's murder. They admitted that they kidnapped him but left him alive. An all-white jury deliberated one hour before acquitting them.

A month later, in an interview with Look magazine, Milam admitted that he and Bryant had killed Till. Why? Milam explained, "What else could I do? He thought he was as good as any white man." Because they were acquitted in a murder trial, they could not be tried again for murder.

7. Gender Bias

Demonstration 9-5 allows you to replicate the Burstin, Doughtie, and Raphaeli (1980) study. BEFORE students read Chapter 9, administer each form of the demonstration to half the class. Do your students, like the Houston area people tested by Burstin et al., judge Mrs. Michaels more harshly than Mr. Michaels? If they do, before you present the results ask them if they believe in a double standard, or whether they believe they would judge similarly a father and a mother who behaved in this way.

8. Attribution for Male and Female Success

If you did not use Demonstration 3-1 to introduce attribution theory you may want to use it now. Randomly present each form to half the class. Females who succeed in traditionally masculine activities are often seen as less competent than a similarly successful male. However, their high motivation may offset their presumed lesser abilities.

9. Face-ism

Dane Archer and his colleagues' (1983) research on the media's portrayal of men and women reported that photos of men emphasize their faces while those of women emphasize their bodies. This was found not only in the American media but in publications from 11 other nations. An examination of artwork over six centuries confirmed the pervasiveness of this difference in the portrayal of men and women.

Your students can attempt to replicate these findings by examining current issues of their favorite magazines. They could also replicate another of Archer's studies in which subjects were asked to draw a man or a woman. The subjects were given a black sheet of paper with the following instructions:

> We are doing a study on drawing styles. Could you help us out by spending a few minutes to draw a woman (man)? The drawing can be as simple as you like—we are just interested in the ways people draw. If you can, please try to capture the character of a real person in your drawing.

The researchers report that both men and women prepared drawings in which the man's face was prominent but the woman's was not.

What are the possible consequences of "face-ism" in the media? In a final study, the researchers experimentally manipulated the degree of facial prominence in photographs. They found that the same person is perceived more favorably when the face is prominent than when it is not. Archer and his colleagues suggest that face-ism may perpetuate stereotyped conceptions of what's important about men and women.

10. Ingroup Bias

The favoritism found in perceptions of ingroups versus outgroups can be powerfully demonstrated in class. Jonathan Brown (1998) (see Chapter 2 references) has developed a classroom exercise where students make judgments regarding personality traits for themselves, other ingroup members and outgroup members. The forms contain eight positive and eight negative items. Simply have students complete all three versions of Demonstration 9-6 (counterbalancing the order of the forms is recommended). Then, determine the means for each of the 16 items for each of the three versions (this may require the demonstration to be split into two different class periods). The pattern you should find shows more favorable means for ingroup members (your college or university) compared to outgroup members (most other people) and more favorable means for the self compared to outgroup members and, to a lesser degree, ingroup members. The favorable self-ratings are reminiscent of the self-serving bias section found in Chapter 2. The favorable ingroup ratings compared to the outgroup should be universal, however, the favorable self-ratings may not be seen on every dimension (the talented, athletic and attractive items have often registered highest for the ingroup).

Brown reports the following data with a sampling of 87 undergraduates at the University of Washington.

		Target	
Attribute	Self	Others	UW
Positive Attributes			
Loyal	4.25a	2.59b	2.74b
Sincere	4.03a	2.63b	2.74b
Kind	3.99a	2.90b	2.86b
Intelligent	3.85a	2.90b	3.74a
Athletic	3.22a	2.61b	3.29a
Well-liked	3.58a	3.03b	3.23c
Talented	3.46a	3.08b	3.60a
Attractive	3.26a	2.91b	3.20a
M =	3.71a	2.83b	3.18c

Negative Attributes

Inconsiderate	1.43a	3.02b	2.70c
Phony	1.44a	2.91b	2.97b
Insensitive	1.46a	2.91b	2.53c
Unintelligent	1.25a	2.30b	1.70c
Dumb	1.10a	2.11b	1.48c
Unattractive	1.64a	2.43b	2.10c
Unwise	1.52a	2.42b	2.00c
Unpopular	1.82a	2.31b	2.09c
M =	1.46a	2.55b	2.20c

Within each row, means with different subscripts differ at $p<.05$ or less.

10. An Authoritarianism Scale

John Brink (personal communication) has designed a scale for classroom use that introduces students to the important components of authoritarianism. Handout 9-7 represents sample items from each of the subscales. Total score is obtained by summing the numbers in response to all 18 items. Total score can range from 18 to 126 with higher scores reflecting greater authoritarianism.

The specific items on the scale reflect the following components of authoritarianism: authoritarian submission—an uncritical submission to established social authorities and a suppression of dissent (Items 1–2); conventionalism—an overconcern with good manners or social propriety and a tendency to perceive odd or unusual behavior as somehow immoral (Items 3–4); destruction and cynicism—a cynicism regarding others' motives and an exaggerated tendency to view others as personally responsible for their own misfortune (Items 5–6); power and toughness—a preoccupation with the distribution of power in relationships, a loathing of weakness, and an identification with powerful individuals and groups so as to exaggerate one's own social status (Items 7–8); superstition and stereotypy—a susceptibility to unwarranted assertions or beliefs and a tendency to think in rigid oversimplified categories (Items 9–10); anti-intraception—a genuine distaste for inward reflection on private thoughts and feelings, and a discomfort with emotional expression (Items 11–12); projectivity—a tendency to minimize one's sense of personal responsibility for prejudice and injustice by attributing one's own hostile or otherwise unacceptable impulses to others (Items 13–14); authoritarian aggression—a self-righteous delight in the punishment of wrongdoers accompanied by a belief that authorities would approve of their suffering (Items 15–16); sexual concerns—exaggerated concern with sexual "goings-on" (Items 17–18).

11. The Just World Scale

Just world theory (Lerner, 1980) assumes that we all need to believe in a just world in which people get what they deserve and deserve what they get. As the text indicates, one result of this belief may be a tendency to derogate innocent victims. Rubin and Peplau (1975) reasoned that people vary in the degree to which they believe the world is just. To measure individual differences they designed the Just World Scale (JWS) (see Demonstration 9-8) and scores have been predictive of a variety of social attitudes and behaviors. To calculate the belief in a just world score, reverse each of the individual scores on items 1, 4, 5, 8, 10, 13, 16, 17, 20. That is, 0 to 5, 1 to 4, 2 to 3, 3 to 2, 4 to 1, and 5 to 0. Then on these reversed items, have students mark through their original score, and put the reversed score in the blank. Finally, add the scores for all 20 items. The higher the score is, the stronger the belief in a just world.

If students complete and score the JWS, presentation and discussion of research with it may prove particularly meaningful. For comparison purposes, the total scores of undergraduates at Boston University were slightly below the midpoint, indicating a tendency to reject belief in a just world. On the other hand, scores of Oklahoma State University students were above the midpoint on a 16-item revised scale, and indicated a tendency to accept the belief.

The first test of the scale was provided by the 1971 national draft lottery of 19-year-olds, which determined the order of induction into the armed forces. While most students expressed sympathy for the lottery "losers," high JWs ran counter to this pattern; they resented losers more than winners. Other studies have indicated that those with a strong belief in a just world may be most likely to derogate innocent victims. For example, in the Lerner and Simmons situation described in the text, high JWs derogate the innocent victim more than low JWs do. High JWs have also been shown to attribute more responsibility to rape victims, and have been more likely to derogate Blacks and women.

JWS scores have been positively correlated with authoritarianism, and with favorable attitudes toward the Congress, the Supreme Court, the military, and big business. Positive correlations also exist between JWS scores and trust in other people's sincerity, belief in an active God, and an internal locus of control.

Lerner has pointed out that the desire for justice is a two-edged sword. Belief in a just world may make one more sensitive to the reality of injustice. Several studies indicate that high JWs may be more likely to seek to restore justice. Not only do they advocate a stiffer sentence for the criminal offender, but under certain circumstances demonstrate greater prosocial behavior. For example, when victims have been portrayed as having relatively finite, manageable needs so that providing help will successfully restore justice, high JWs have been more willing to help than low JWs. Research has also indicated that when they themselves are in personal need, high JWs are more likely to respond positively to another's request for help. Presumably their greater willingness to help reflects an effort to make themselves more deserving of receiving assistance. Rugin and Peplau suggest that belief in a just world may motivate willingness to help when the help is relatively easy to give, when helping does not run counter to firmly entrenched social attitudes such as pre-existing prejudice against blacks or women, and when the altruistic behavior has the sanction of authority.

Discussion questions:

1. How does belief in a just world originate? Do the media play any role in promoting the belief?
2. Should we teach children that the world is not just? What would be the consequences?
3. How does one explain correlations between JWS scores and authoritarianism, religiosity, and an internal locus of control?

12. Implicit Association Test

A group of researchers at the University of Washington at Yale University (Greenwald, Banaji, and others) have created a web-site (www.yale.edu/implicit) where you and your students can take a variety of Implicit Association Tests designed to measure implicit attitudes and beliefs. The methodology involves reaction time tests pairing the labels "good" and "bad" with various names, faces and other stimuli. First the user will be asked to register their own ideas about what attitudes they have regarding topics such as (age, gender and race). Then, a series of images and words are flashed on the screen and the user is instructed how to register their responses on the keyboard. Each of the four tasks takes about 5–10 minutes to complete. Students will love this demonstration, which can be done on any computer with quality internet access.

Lecture/Discussion # 11 (Where Bias Begins: The Truth About Stereotypes) dovetails nicely with this demonstration.

13. The Social Connection Video Series

Several entries in the video instructional supplement (The Social Connection Video Series) provide additional information pertinent to Chapter 9. "The Fundamental Attribution Error" touches on the "just world" explanation for prejudice and discrimination; "Stereotype Threat" addresses Claude Steele et al.'s important work on this phenomenon; and "Understanding Genocide" may also be beneficial in a classroom session dedicated to the topic of prejudice. See the Faculty Guide accompanying the video series for program summaries, pause points, and classroom activities for each of these videos.

Demonstration 9-1

For each of the following characteristics, provide your best estimate or guess of the percentage of who possess the trait.

1. kind ___%
2. not easily influenced ___%
3. competitive ___%
4. aware of others' feelings ___%
5. dominant ___%
6. makes decisions easily ___%
7. independent ___%
8. understanding ___%
9. never gives up easily ___%
10. helpful ___%
11. aggressive ___%
12. warm ___%
13. self-confident ___%
14. stands up well under pressure ___%
15. able to devote self to others ___%
16. active ___%

Demonstration 9-2

(with permission of I.K. Broverman)

Circle the five characteristics that best describe a mature, healthy, socially competent adult male.

1. ambitious
2. tactful
3. adventurous
4. aware of others' feelings
5. need for security
6. self-confident
7. logical
8. gentle
9. independent
10. expresses tender feelings

Demonstration 9-2

(with permission of I.K. Broverman)

Circle the five characteristics that best describe a mature, healthy, socially competent adult female.

1. ambitious
2. tactful
3. adventurous
4. aware of others' feelings
5. need for security
6. self-confident
7. logical
8. gentle
9. independent
10. expresses tender feelings

Demonstration 9-2

(with permission of I.K. Broverman)

Circle the five characteristics that best describe a mature, healthy, socially competent adult person.

1. ambitious
2. tactful
3. adventurous
4. aware of others' feelings
5. need for security
6. self-confident
7. logical
8. gentle
9. independent
10. expresses tender feelings

Demonstration 9-3

(with permission of P. Glick)

Relationships Between Men and Women

Below is a series of statements concerning men and women and their relationships in contemporary society. Please indicate the degree to which you agree or disagree with each statement using the following scale: 0 = disagree strongly; 1 = disagree somewhat; 2 = disagree slightly; 3 = agree slightly; 4 = agree somewhat; 5 = agree strongly

____1. No matter how accomplished he is, a man is not truly complete as a person unless he has the love of a woman.
____2. Many women are actually seeking special favors, such as hiring policies that favor them over men, under the guise of asking for equality.
____3. In a disaster, women ought not necessarily to be rescued before men.
____4. Most women interpret innocent remarks or acts as being sexist.
____5. Women are too easily offended.
____6. People are often truly happy in life without being romantically involved with a member of the other sex.
____7. Feminists are not seeking for women to have more power than men.
____8. Many women have a quality of purity that few men possess.
____9. Women should be cherished and protected by men.
____10. Most women fail to appreciate fully all that men do for them.
____11. Women seek to gain power by getting control over men.
____12. Every man ought to have a woman whom he adores.
____13. Men are complete without women.
____14. Women exaggerate problems they have at work.
____15. Once a woman gets a man to commit to her, she usually tries to put him on a tight leash.
____16. When women lose to men in a fair competition, they typically complain about being discriminated against.
____17. A good woman should be set on a pedestal by her man.
____18. There are actually very few women who get a kick out of teasing men by seeming sexually available and then refusing male advances.
____19. Women, compared to men, tend to have a superior moral sensibility.
____20. Men should be willing to sacrifice their own well being in order to provide financially for the women in their lives.
____21. Feminists are making entirely reasonable demands of men.
____22. Women, as compared to men, tend to have a more refined sense of culture and good taste.

Glick, P., & Fiske, S. T. (1996). The ambivalent sexism inventory: Differentiating hostile and benevolent sexism. Journal of Personality and Social Psychology, 70, p. 512. Copyright 1995 by Peter Glick and Susan T. Fiske. Secure permission of one author before reproducing scale for any use beyond the classroom.

Demonstration 9-4

(with permission of S. Goldstein)

For each of the following examples, (1) assess whether institutional discrimination is present, (2) identify the group or groups against which the practice discriminates, (3) identify the intended purpose of each practice, and (4) if the purpose is legitimate, suggest how else it might be achieved.

1. A fire department requires that applicants for the position of firefighter be 5'8" or taller.
2. A Caucasian actor is chosen to play the part of an Asian man.
3. A corporation decides to fill a position opening "in-house" rather than to advertise.
4. Children of alumni receive preference for admission into a private college.
5. Persons accused of a crime who cannot post bail are imprisoned and thus appear in court dressed in prison clothes.
6. A health club offered a reduced family membership rate.
7. A teacher requires an oral presentation as part of the final grade.
8. A public meeting is held on the third floor of a building that has no elevator.

Demonstration 9-5

(with permission of E. Doughtie)

Tulsa, Okla.—"While the cat's away, the mice will play," says the old saying. However, for an Oklahoma woman, the mouse got caught at the game.

It seems that last month, Karl Michaels was away visiting relatives for a few days, leaving the two Michaels youngsters in the care of their mother, Kathy. Mrs. Michaels, however, took the opportunity to rendezvous with her secret lover, leaving the two children, Mark, 5, and Tommy, 3, as she had apparently done on several such occasions. This time, however, fear and hunger after many hours of neglect drove the Michaels children to the streets in search of their wayward parent.

A pair of city residents found the children wandering in the street almost three miles from the Michaels' home. The police were called in, and in the process of reuniting the children and their mother, the whole story came out.

"I don't see that what I did was too terrible," Kathy told an obviously upset spouse.

WOULD YOU AGREE THAT MRS. MICHAELS IS A POOR PARENT?

(CIRCLE ONE)

        1   2   3   4   5   6   7

Strongly disagree   Strongly agree

Demonstration 9-5

(with permission of E. Doughtie)

Tulsa, Okla.—"While the cat's away, the mice will play," says the old saying. However, for an Oklahoma man, the mouse got caught at the game.

It seems that last month, Kathy Michaels was away visiting relatives for a few days, leaving the two Michaels youngsters in the care of their father, Karl. Mr. Michaels, however, took the opportunity to rendezvous with his secret lover, leaving the two children, Mark, 5, and Tommy, 3, as he had apparently done on several such occasions. This time, however, fear and hunger after many hours of neglect drove the Michaels children to the streets in search of their wayward parent.

A pair of city residents found the children wandering in the street almost three miles from the Michaels' home. The police were called in, and in the process of reuniting the children and their father, the whole story came out.

"I don't see that what I did was too terrible," Karl told an obviously upset spouse.

WOULD YOU AGREE THAT MR. MICHAELS IS A POOR PARENT?

(CIRCLE ONE)

                1   2   3   4   5   6   7

Strongly disagree   Strongly agree

Demonstration 9-6

(with permission of J. D. Brown)

This scale consists of a number of words that describe some people. Read each item and then indicate to what extent you think each of the items DESCRIBES YOU. Use the following scale as your guide:

1	2	3	4	5
very slightly or not at all	a little	moderately	quite a bit	extremely

Inconsiderate	1	2	3	4	5
Dumb	1	2	3	4	5
Well-liked	1	2	3	4	5
Phony	1	2	3	4	5
Attractive	1	2	3	4	5
Unintelligent	1	2	3	4	5
Insensitive	1	2	3	4	5
Loyal	1	2	3	4	5
Athletic	1	2	3	4	5
Unattractive	1	2	3	4	5
Sincere	1	2	3	4	5
Intelligent	1	2	3	4	5
Unpopular	1	2	3	4	5
Unwise	1	2	3	4	5
Talented	1	2	3	4	5
Kind	1	2	3	4	5

Demonstration 9-6

(with permission of J. D. Brown)

This scale consists of a number of words that describe some people. Read each item and then indicate to what extent you think each of the items DESCRIBES MOST STUDENTS AT YOUR COLLEGE OR UNIVERSITY. Use the following scale as your guide:

1	2	3	4	5
very slightly or not at all	a little	moderately	quite a bit	extremely

Inconsiderate	1	2	3	4	5
Dumb	1	2	3	4	5
Well-liked	1	2	3	4	5
Phony	1	2	3	4	5
Attractive	1	2	3	4	5
Unintelligent	1	2	3	4	5
Insensitive	1	2	3	4	5
Loyal	1	2	3	4	5
Athletic	1	2	3	4	5
Unattractive	1	2	3	4	5
Sincere	1	2	3	4	5
Intelligent	1	2	3	4	5
Unpopular	1	2	3	4	5
Unwise	1	2	3	4	5
Talented	1	2	3	4	5
Kind	1	2	3	4	5

Demonstration 9-6

(with permission of J. D. Brown)

This scale consists of a number of words that describe some people. Read each item and then indicate to what extent you think each of the items DESCRIBES MOST OTHER PEOPLE. Use the following scale as your guide:

1	2	3	4	5
very slightly or not at all	a little	moderately	quite a bit	extremely

Inconsiderate	1	2	3	4	5
Dumb	1	2	3	4	5
Well-liked	1	2	3	4	5
Phony	1	2	3	4	5
Attractive	1	2	3	4	5
Unintelligent	1	2	3	4	5
Insensitive	1	2	3	4	5
Loyal	1	2	3	4	5
Athletic	1	2	3	4	5
Unattractive	1	2	3	4	5
Sincere	1	2	3	4	5
Intelligent	1	2	3	4	5
Unpopular	1	2	3	4	5
Unwise	1	2	3	4	5
Talented	1	2	3	4	5
Kind	1	2	3	4	5

Demonstration 9-7

(with permission of J. Brink)

Indicate the extent to which you personally agree or disagree with each of the items on this questionnaire. Respond to each item with a number from 1 to 7 using the following scale:

```
      1      2      3      4      5      6      7
```
Strongly disagree   Strongly agree

___1. Government censorship of the Internet may be necessary in order to protect our children.

___2. Students should be willing to give up some of their rights to privacy so that school officials can discourage drug abuse.

___3. The weird clothing and hairstyles of many rock musicians are clear signs of their immorality.

___4. It's unreasonable to ask our public schools to instruct non-English speaking children using the students' native language.

___5. It is human nature to do almost everything with an eye to one's own self-interest.

___6. Most people who are homeless today are simply not motivated to seek out the private and public welfare programs that are available to them.

___7. The most important qualities of a mature person are strength of will and ambition.

___8. A willingness to accept late papers only encourages students to take advantage of a teacher's weakness.

___9. The human capacity for extrasensory perception (ESP) has been greatly underestimated especially by nonreligious scientists.

___10. It's just as important to stop occasional marijuana use as it is to stop cocaine addiction.

___11. People who share their secrets are likely to lose their friends.

___12. The best way to deal with a problem or worry is simply to keep busy with cheerful activities.

___13. Individuals from racial minority groups usually want to live in neighborhoods populated primarily by members of their own race.

___14. Most welfare recipients today don't really appreciate the benefits they receive.

___15. School teachers should have the legal right to spank children who misbehave in the classroom.

___16. Those who worry about our deteriorating and overcrowded prisons seem to forget that prison life is supposed to be unpleasant.

___17. In public locker rooms and showers, gay men and lesbians must often experience fairly strong sexual temptations.

___18. Regardless of how they appear, men are interested in women for only one reason.

Demonstration 9-8

(with permission of Z. Rubin)

Directions: Indicate your degree of agreement or disagreement with each of the following statements in the blank space next to each item. Respond to every statement and use the following code:

5 = strongly agree
4 = moderately agree
3 = slightly agree
2 = slightly disagree
1 = moderately disagree
0 = strongly disagree

___1. I've found that a person rarely deserves the reputation he has.
___2. Basically, the world is a just place.
___3. People who get "lucky breaks" have usually earned their good fortune.
___4. Careful drivers are just as likely to get hurt in traffic accidents as careless ones.
___5. It is a common occurrence for a guilty person to get off free in American courts.
___6. Students almost always deserve the grades they receive in school.
___7. Men who keep in shape have little chance of suffering a heart attack.
___8. The political candidate who sticks up for his principles rarely gets elected.
___9. It is rare for an innocent man to be wrongly sent to jail.
___10. In professional sports, many fouls and infractions never get called by the referee.
___11. By and large, people deserve what they get.
___12. When parents punish their children, it is almost always for good reasons.
___13. Good deeds often go unnoticed and unrewarded.
___14. Although evil men may hold political power for a while, in the general course of history good wins out.
___15. In almost any business or profession, people who do their job well rise to the top.
___16. American parents tend to overlook the things most to be admired in their children.
___17. It is often impossible for a person to receive a fair trial in the USA.
___18. People who meet with misfortune have often brought it on themselves.
___19. Crime doesn't pay.
___20. Many people suffer through absolutely no fault of their own.

FILMS/VIDEOS

A Class Divided (PBS, 57 min., 1985). Updates Eye of the Storm with a reunion of the former third-graders and their teacher 15 years later. The young adults relate the profound and enduring effects of their lesson in prejudice.

America: In Black and White (ABC, 22 min, 2001). This Nightline episode (aired 3/28/01) examines the accusations of discrimination and racism regarding the "over-votes" in Florida for the Presidential election of 2000. Highlights how the same facts and situations are interpreted differently by black and white citizens of Duval County.

Beyond Hate (INS, 88 min., 1991). Hosted by Bill Moyers, this program examines the impact of hate on its victims. Interviews with Elie Wiesel, Jimmy Carter, Nelson Mandela as well as perpetrators of hate. Considers how hate can be reduced.

Can You See the Color Gray? (University of California, 54 min., 1997). Shows numerous people from diverse racial and ethnic backgrounds grapple with probing questions about their racial attitudes and feelings about their own ethnicity. Shows the subtle development of racial attitudes in children of varying ages. Video is divided into two parts of 27 minutes each.

The Fairer Sex (ABC News, 17 min., 1993). An ABC Prime Time Live segment that shows gender-based differences in treatment by exposing a male and a female to various experiences associated with moving to a new city. A perfect compliment to lecture topic #2.

Hate Crimes (INS, 22 min., 1996). Examines the problem of hate crimes and explains how stereotyping has fueled this violence. Shows how discrimination can lead to verbal abuse, vandalism, and physical violence.

Overcoming Prejudice (INS, 59 min., 1996). This documentary examines the origins of prejudice and its consequences. People who have overcome their prejudices share their experiences and suggest ways of finding common ground.

Prejudice (PSU, 30 min., 1989). Illustrates the stereotypes and emotions that typically underlie prejudice. Four different scenarios illustrate the nature of discrimination. Considers strategies for reducing prejudice and discrimination.

Prejudice, Discrimination, and Stereotypes (INS, 22 min., 1993). Examines the causes of prejudice and discrimination as well as the effects on both victim and perpetrator. Suggests ways to avoid stereotyping and to promote tolerance of others.

Prejudice: The Eye of the Storm (INS, 25 min., 1989). Children in a third-grade class are identified as superior or inferior on the basis of eye color and promptly demonstrate prejudice.

Racism in America (FHS, 26 min., 1989). Examines the resurgence of overt bigotry and racially-motivated acts of violence and explores the reasons for hostility against minorities. Looks at how one community successfully responded to its racial problems.

Racism 101 (MINN, 58 min., 1988). Examines racism on college campuses and suggests an unsettling return to the kind of racial prejudice that flared during the early days of the civil rights movement.

The Rift Between Blacks and Jews (ABC, 20 min, 1994). Recounts the partnership between Blacks and Jews in the blossoming civil rights movement in the '50s and '60s and concludes with a lively discussion about why the partnership has crumbled in recent years.

Sexual Stereotypes in the Media (FHS, 37 min., 1991). Examines how the media portray man as Superman, and woman as his slavish bride. The pervasiveness of these images leads women as well as men to accept them.

Understanding Prejudice: Gripes and Common Ground (INS, 55 min., 1996). Discusses the nature of prejudice and explores its sources. Multiculturalism, homosexuality, "politically correct" language, religious differences, and the media's role in promoting stereotypes are among the issues treated.

CHAPTER 10
AGGRESSION: HURTING OTHERS

What Is Aggression?
Theories of Aggression
    Is Aggression Biological?
    Instinct Theory and Evolutionary Psychology
    Neural Influences
    Genetic Influences
    Biochemical Influences
    Is Aggression a Response to Frustration?
    Frustration-Aggression Theory Revised
    Is Frustration the Same as Deprivation?
    Relative Deprivation
    Is Aggression Learned Social Behavior?
    The Rewards of Aggression
    Observational Learning
Influences on Aggression
    Aversive Incidents
    Pain
    Heat
    Attacks
    Crowding
    Arousal
    Aggression Cues
    Media Influences: Pornography and Sexual Violence
    Distorted Perceptions of Sexual Reality
    Aggression Against Women
    Media Awareness Education
    Media Influences: Television
    Television's Effects on Behavior
    Television's Effects on Thinking
    Group Influences
Reducing Aggression
    Catharsis?
    A Social Learning Approach
Personal Postscript: Reforming a Violent Culture

LECTURE AND DISCUSSION IDEAS

1. Introducing Research on Aggression

A vivid example of human aggression might be used either to introduce the social psychological literature or to provide students an opportunity to apply the theories discussed in the text. The film Crime and the Criminal (see below), which is adapted from the feature film In Cold Blood, provides one such vivid case. Narrated by Orson Welles, the film also raises the question of criminal responsibility in light of research on the causes of aggression.

2. Testosterone and Quality of Life

Salvador's (1997) study of 1709 men 40 to 70 years old provides a fascinating extension of the research linking aggressiveness with the male sex hormone testosterone. The higher a man's testosterone level, reports Salvadore, the less pleased he is with life and the less he looks forward to the future. Moreover, the less of the hormone a man has in his blood, the more emotional support he reports getting from family and friends. Salvador suggests that poor social relationships could account for the sadder feelings associated with possessing high levels of testosterone. Other research finds that men high in testosterone have roughly doubled the divorce rate of men low in the hormone. "They're very aggressive," observes Salvador, "so they may alienate people. Now they're getting older, and the future might not look so good."

3. Testosterone, Serotonin, and Frustration-Aggression Theory

Bernhardt's (1997) review of research findings connecting serotonin and testosterone to aggression provides an excellent example of how different theories of human social behavior are sometimes complementary rather than competing.

Bernhardt notes that high testosterone has been related to several types of aggression and dominance. Low serotonin activity has been associated with a hyper-responsiveness to aversive stimuli. Both testosterone and serotonin have been implicated in aggression through actions in the hypothalamus and amygdala.

According to Bernhardt's integrated model of aggression, high testosterone increases status-seeking behaviors (dominance seeking) which in turn increases the likelihood of a frustrating event. Low serotonin increases responsivity to aversive stimuli, which increases the likelihood of experiencing frustration with a negative mood. Berkowitz has argued that the important aspect of frustration that leads to aggression is negative mood. Bernhardt notes that the two theories from different domains of study are consistent. He observes that serotonin moderates the effects of frustration due to failed attempts at dominance by combined activity in the amygdala and hypothalamus. "The biological literature," concludes Bernhardt, "and the social psychological literature, respectively, converge to describe similar processes at different levels of discussion."

4. Regional Differences in Violence

The text's treatment of violence in the U.S. South and North can be readily extended in class. Homicide rates for white Southern males are substantially higher than those for white Northern males. Interestingly, survey research indicates that Southerners do not endorse violence in the abstract more than do Northerners. However, they are more likely to endorse violence as a means of self-protection, as an appropriate response to insults, and as a socialization tool in training children. For example, white Southern men are more likely than white Northern men to agree that a man has a right to kill to defend his home, that a violent response to an insult is justified, and that spanking is an appropriate discipline policy.

In one experiment, Nisbett (1993) recruited white male undergraduates whose permanent address was either in the South or North. All subjects filled out a brief questionnaire, which they were then asked to bring to a table at the end of a long narrow hall. In each case they had to crowd past a male undergraduate confederate who was working at an open file cabinet. The confederate was required to close the file cabinet to allow the subject to pass. When the latter returned a few seconds later, the confederate, who had just reopened the file drawer, slammed it shut, pushed his shoulder against the subject, and uttered, loudly enough to be clearly heard by the subject, "Asshole." The confederate then quickly entered a room with a locked door at the end of the hall. Nisbett reports that the reactions of Southern and Northern students were remarkably different. The former were more likely to show anger while the latter were more likely to express amusement.

A culture of honor, Nisbett argues, that is characteristic of particular economic circumstances, including the herding society of the early South, helps explain the regional differences. To reduce the likelihood of theft of their herds, pastoralists practiced extreme vigilance toward any act that might be perceived as threatening. They responded with sufficient force to frighten potential offenders into recognizing that they were not to be trifled with.

Recently Cohen and Nisbett (1997) reported field experiments that demonstrate the role of social institutions in perpetuating norms about violence. In one study, employers across the United States received letters from job applicants who presumably had killed someone in an honor-related conflict. Results indicated that southern and western companies were more likely than their northern counterparts to respond in an understanding way. In a second study, newspapers were given facts for a story concerning a stabbing in response to a family quarrel. Once again southern and western papers created stories that were more sympathetic toward the perpetrator.

5. Homicide Trends in the United States

One of the more prototypical forms of aggression is of course homicide. The U.S. Department of Justice has a web-page with a wealth of information regarding homicide in the United States (www.ojp.usdoj.gov/bjs/homicide/homtrnd.htm). One idea for an engaging class exercise consists of extracting various charts and tables from this web site and asking students to, on the basis of this data, theorize as to the causes of homicide. The question "So class, based on this data, why do you think people kill one another?" is sure to generate a lively discussion full of naïve theories put forward by students for consideration. Another suggestion would be to have a class discussion using this data before covering the text's material on aggression and then a second discussion after the material has been covered.

6. Self-Esteem and Violence

Chapter 2 of this manual includes a lecture topic on the role of the self-concept in violence. Contrary to the conventional wisdom, Baumeister and his colleagues (1996) report that high not low self-esteem underlies violent behavior, particularly "favorable self-appraisals that may be inflated or ill-founded and that are confronted with an external evaluation that disputes them." If you did not discuss this issue earlier, you could do so in connection with this chapter.

A series of three brief articles in the APA Monitor also address the relationship between self-esteem and aggression. First, Martin Seligman (1998) asserts that high self-esteem (not low self-esteem) is more determinative of aggressive acts. Ervin Staub (1999) responds by suggesting the relationship between self-esteem and aggression is much more complex than suggested by Seligman. Finally, Baumeister (1999) argues forcefully that low self-esteem does not cause aggression. These articles are also reprinted in the 00/01 printing of Annual Editions–Social Psychology (see Popular Sources of Additional Classroom Material in this chapter for reference). Following are some possible discussion questions: Were the articles successful in making you rethink the relationship between aggression and low self-esteem? How do you respond to Seligman's call to dismantle the school self-esteem movement? Does this discussion invoke ideas mentioned in Chapter 2 concerning people's enhancement needs? What do you think about Baumeister's idea of "self-control" programs versus "self-esteem" programs? How might you implement this information into your personal and professional life?

7. What Makes People Angry?

Surely this question, which you might pose to your students, is relevant to understanding the roots of hostile if not instrumental aggression. You might have your class attempt to replicate Averill's (1983) findings.

Averill asked his subjects to recall or keep careful records of their experience of anger. Most reported becoming mildly angry several times a week. Often the anger came in response to a relative or friend's misdeed. Anger was most likely when another person's act seemed willful, unjustified, and avoidable.

Using descriptions of everyday provocations, Ben-Zur and Breznitz (1991) investigated the effects of nine dimensions of self-reported anger. The main result was that the level of damage was the most important instigator of anger. Two other dimensions, the intentions of the harm-doer, and his or her ability to have prevented the damage, also had consistent, significant, and independent effects on the subjective feeling of anger.

Ben-Zur and Breznitz note that their results are surprising in light of the common claim that people should not become angry even if the damage is high, provided it occurred by mistake or was unavoidable. One possible explanation for the strong effect of damage may be that the subjective feeling of anger in certain cases may be determined by automatically-processed elements of the situation rather than by the cognitive evaluations of mitigating circumstances. Assessing damage is easier and faster than judging intentions or other causes behind the act. Once damage is determined, anger is proportionally aroused, and then its level may be difficult to change. The authors suggest that this analysis is not intended to imply that mitigating circumstances never affect anger. More importantly, mitigating circumstances may be crucial in determining anger's duration and mode of expression. The initial response, however, may be immediate, circumventing complex cognitive processes.

8. The Seville Statement

Surveys of adults including college students have found that 60 percent agree with the statement, "Human nature being what it is, there will always be war." In 1986, to counter the notion that peace is unattainable, 20 scientists from 12 nations met in Seville, Spain, to draft a statement on the issue. Reference is made to this statement in the text and you may want to expand on it in class. Below are some excerpts:

- It is scientifically incorrect to say we have inherited a tendency to make war from our animal ancestors. Warfare is a peculiarly human phenomenon and does not occur in other animals.
- It is scientifically incorrect to say that war or any other violent behavior is genetically programmed into our human nature. Except for rare pathologies the genes do not produce individuals necessarily predisposed to violence. Neither do they determine the opposite.

- It is scientifically incorrect to say that in the course of human evolution there has been a selection for aggressive behavior more than for other kinds of behavior. In all well-studied species, status within the group is achieved by the ability to cooperate and to fulfill social functions relevant to the structure of that group.

- It is scientifically incorrect to say that humans have a "violent brain." While we do have the neural apparatus to act violently, there is nothing in our neurophysiology that compels us to.

- It is scientifically incorrect to say that war is caused by "instinct" or any single motivation. The technology of modern war has exaggerated traits associated with violence both in the training of actual combatants and in the preparation of support for war in the general population.

- We conclude that biology does not condemn humanity to war, and that humanity can be freed from the bondage of biological pessimism. Violence is neither in our evolutionary legacy nor in our genes. The same species (that) invented war is capable of inventing peace.

The Seville Statement has not gone unchallenged. Fox (1988) called it a "shop worn denunciation of ideas that no one ever really had in the first place." More recently, Beroldi (1994) suggested that the Statement is likely "to cast a shadow of scientific and social disrepute on work done on war and violence from an evolutionary perspective." He finds it ironic that its authors seem to be much more biologically pessimistic about humanity than are evolutionary scientists. They seem, he argues, to believe that if research on the causes of violence includes biological and evolutionary perspectives, we will become hopelessly passive. In contrast, he maintains that a more complete knowledge of such factors would allow us to more scientifically study war so as to prevent it. Beroldi also argues that the Seville Statement suggests that evolutionary psychologists believe in the naturalistic fallacy—that what is, should be (thereby justifying the status quo). In fact, he writes, "Many evolutionary scientists include a disclaimer rejecting it in every work that touches on a sensitive topic."

9. Confronting the Aggressor

A good discussion topic related to the text's discussion of catharsis is the "victims' bill of rights," which gives crime victims the right to speak in court during sentencing. Some 40 states have now adopted the policy. Is it a good one? What effect will confrontation of the criminal have on the victim? Does it provide an example of how counterattack can have a calming effect when the target is the actual tormenter and is no longer intimidating so that the person does not afterward feel guilty or anxious? For some victims does it provide a nonaggressive way to express feeling and inform aggressors of the effects their behaviors have had?

Thigpen (1995) describes some of the dramatic face-offs that have occurred under the new let-the-victims-speak policy. In March 1995, two dozen people who sustained injuries or lost close relatives in the Long Island Rail Road massacre spoke at the sentencing of Colin Ferguson who was convicted of murdering six riders and wounding 19 on a commuter train in December, 1993. "The fear and pain I felt I will never forget," said Robert Giugliano, who was shot in the chest. Staring at Ferguson, he went on, "Look at these eyes! You can't! You're nothing but a piece of garbage!" Carolyn McCarthy, whose son was partially paralyzed and whose husband was killed in the massacre, said, "You are an evil person. You are not worthy of my time or thoughts or energy. You will be sentenced, and you will be gone from my thoughts forever."

In January 1995, Rose Falcone, the mother of an 18-year-old who was murdered during the carjacking of his Jeep, addressed the killer in a New York City courtroom: "I just want to ask you why didn't you just take the Jeep? Why? Why?" Prosecutor William Mooney concluded, "She seemed like a great weight had been lifted from her shoulders."

Stuart Kleinman, medical director of the Victims' Services Agency in New York City argues, "You can take action that makes you the powerful one, and that tends to counteract feelings of helplessness and can be very therapeutic." He describes a middle-aged man who came to him with insomnia and feelings of overwhelming rage after having been severely beaten in his office. After addressing the criminal in court, the victim reported that his rage had finally began to ebb and that he was sleeping more soundly.

10. Relative Deprivation: College Choice and Self-Concept

Herbert Marsh and John Parker's (1984) findings suggest that students of a given ability level will have higher self-esteem if they don't attend an elite school. This is true even though attendance at more prestigious schools is associated with a somewhat higher level of academic achievement. Ask your students to explain why this might be. The discussion will naturally lead to a consideration of how people's feelings of well-being are largely shaped by whom they compare themselves with. March and Parker's subtitle is instructive: "Is it better to be a relatively large fish in a small pond even if you don't learn to swim as well?" Not only social comparison theory but also the concept of relative deprivation can be readily introduced.

11. Relative Deprivation: Egoistic and Fraternal

Common sense tells us that those who are most dissatisfied and frustrated will be those who possess the least; those with more will be more satisfied. But to the contrary, there are now many documented instances where those who have more of a valued outcome (promotions, prosperity) are <u>less</u> satisfied than those who are objectively worse off (Martin, 1980). Researchers explain this puzzling phenomenon with the concept of "relative deprivation."

The text discussion of relative deprivation can be extended by distinguishing its two subtypes: egoistic and fraternal deprivation. <u>Egoistic deprivation</u> occurs when individuals compare their <u>personal</u> status to that of similar other people. An assistant professor might compare his or her salary raise to that awarded other assistant professors and feel egoistic deprivation.

<u>Fraternal deprivation</u> occurs when people compare their <u>groups'</u> outcomes to that of another group that has more. Professors at college X may compare their salaries to professors' salaries at college Y and feel fraternal deprivation.

Questions for discussion:

1. Would self-serving bias (Chapter 2) more likely contribute to egoistic or fraternal deprivation? Answer: Self-serving bias would feed egoistic deprivation, which requires that people not blame themselves for their failure to possess a desired outcome (Crosby, 1976). Not surprisingly, feelings of egoistic deprivation are more common than feelings of fraternal deprivation (Martin, 1980). However, to the extent that self-serving bias operates at the level of the group ("my group deserves better"), then it may also feed fraternal deprivation.
2. Which is the better predictor of collective violence and riot participation—egoistic or fraternal deprivation? Answer: fraternal, which involves dissatisfaction with an entire reward system (Martin, 1980).

12. Learning the Gender-Specific Ways to Aggress

One lecture topic might concern the interplay between gender and types of aggressive behavior. Alice Eagly and Valerie Steffen (1986) performed a meta-analytic review of the social psychological literature pertaining to aggression in an effort to find gender differences. Their analysis found that men, on average, are somewhat more aggressive than women. But arguably the most interesting findings concerned the different types of aggression displayed by different genders. They concluded that men, more than women, tend to aggress in ways that produce pain and physical injury and not in ways that result in psychological or social harm. Further, women were more perceptive of the products of aggression for both the victim (harm) and the aggressor (guilt, anxiety, and possible danger). Eagly and Steffen conclude the gender-based aggressive behavior differences are a result of learned aspects of gender roles as well as other social roles.

13. Children's Television Viewing

The American Psychological Association's nine-member task force on television, reporting in early 1992, noted the following facts, some of which you may want to present in class:

- The average child sees 100,000 acts of violence and 8,000 murders before the end of elementary school.
- The rate of violence on prime-time TV is five to six incidents per hour but on Saturday mornings, it's 20 to 25.
- Minorities are virtually absent and when they do show up, they are often victims or criminals.
- Men are major prime-time characters three times more often than women.
- Sex-stereotyped TV messages do increase children's sex-stereotyped beliefs.
- The probability of obesity in children increases by 2 percent with every hour per day of TV viewing.
- TV has no clear effect on school achievement or academic skills.
- Boys watch more TV than girls do—cartoons, action shows, news, sports.
- Girls who watch the most TV have the most negative attitudes toward women.

The second volume of the National Television Violence study released in March 1997 suggests that children's TV remains steeped in violence (Seppa, 1997). The study covered programming on 23 channels, seven days a week from 6 a.m. to 11 p.m. and explored the effect of ratings and public service announcements. Among the important findings were the following:

- Fifty-eight percent of TV programs contained violence.
- Seventy-three percent of these programs contained violence wiith no remorse, negative evaluation, or penalty for the violence
- Few programs showed the long-term consequences of physical aggression
- The TV-program warning "parental discretion advised" and the age-based motion picture ratings "PG-13" and "R" made many children more interested in watching a program rather than less.
- Anti-violence public service announcements are rarely useful, largely because they offer vague messages such as "Take control" and "Stay strong." Those that did show the real consequences of violence, for example, ending up in a wheelchair, seemed to have stronger effect on child viewers.

14. Advice for Parents on Television Watching

The 1992 APA task force on television that provided guidelines for parents in helping them regulate their children's viewing habits seem as relevant as ever. They include the following:

- Maintain an activities time-chart including TV viewing, playing with friends, and homework. Discuss what to eliminate and its substitute.

- Establish a weekly viewing limit. Have the child select programs from television schedules at the beginning of the week. Assign points to specific programs and give a point total for the week. Less desirable programs may cost more to watch.
- Rule out TV at certain times, e.g., mealtimes or on school nights.
- Encourage the entire family to have a program choice before turning the TV on.
- Remember that you provide a model. If you watch lots of TV, chances are your child will too.

In monitoring the violence children see, the report suggests that parents:

- Watch at least one episode of the programs their children watch to know its frequency and degree of violence.
- When viewing violence together, discuss why it occurs and how painful it is. Ask how conflict can be resolved without aggression.
- Explain how violence on programs is faked.
- Encourage children to watch programs with characters who cooperate and care for each other.

15. Does Educational Television Educate?

Chapter 10 discusses television's impact on people's social attitudes and behavior. A related question is whether educational programs succeed in teaching. Research on Sesame Street indicates the answer is yes: the program generally succeeds both in holding children's attention and in teaching. Sesame Street is given an inner-city setting, partly in hopes of appealing to children who often begin school with an educational disadvantage. Has it in fact closed the school-readiness gap between children from advantaged and disadvantaged backgrounds? Some research suggests that, ironically, the program may accentuate that gap (Cook et al., 1975; Rubenstein, 1978). Ask your students why this might be. Hint: Which children are most likely to have a parent who will sit them down in front of an educational program, such as Sesame Street?

16. Using a Feature Film to Introduce the Catharsis Hypothesis

A short clip from the feature film Fried Green Tomatoes provides an excellent opener for classroom discussion of the catharsis hypothesis.

The clip begins 77:12 minutes into the film and runs approximately 3:05 minutes. Evelyn Couch, a middle-aged, passive housewife, drives her car into the parking lot of a busy shopping mall. She waits patiently as another customer vacates his parking spot. Before Evelyn can drive in, however, two cocky teenagers take her spot. Their inconsiderate behavior and rude comments set her off and she repeatedly rams her car into the back of the teenagers' Volkswagen. For Evelyn there is clearly an immediate emotional release. In the scene that follows it is equally clear that the action has transformed her into an aggressive feminist. The hilarious scenes are more than entertaining. They demonstrate frustration as a cause of aggression and how venting aggression sometimes increases rather than decreases it.

17. Road Rage

Classroom discussion of aggressive driving provides an interesting extension of this chapter as well as the opportunity to review certain social psychological principles introduced earlier in the text.

Invite students to compare their driving habits with those of adults in a recent USA Today/CNN/Gallup Poll . Of those surveyed about their driving habits during the previous five years, 41 percent admitted honking at someone whose driving upset them, 39 percent shouted, cursed, or made gestures to other drivers whose driving upset them, 28 percent slowed down when someone behind them honked or flashed their lights, and 16% had a verbal exchange with another driver. Males and those of ages 18–29 admit to more aggressive acts. Self-serving bias was clearly evident in the poll as three-quarters reported that others were driving more aggressively today than five years earlier but only 13 percent admitted that they themselves were doing so (Puente & Castaneda, 1997).

Statistics on aggressive driving are difficult to compile because there is no consensus on definition and most cases go unreported. Nonetheless, the National Highway Traffic Safety Administration recently estimated that road rage causes two-thirds of highway deaths (O'Driscoll, 1997). Invite students to answer why aggressive driving occurs.

Among the answers psychologists have suggested (Sleek, 1996) are that the swelling congestion on highways is creating more frustration and stress. E. Scott Geller, a psychologist at Virginia Polytechnic Institute and State University, argues that urbanization, dual-income families, and workplace downsizing have left more people in crowded communities with more to do and less time to do it. People feel rushed and their stress is particularly noticeable when they drive. Other psychologists have suggested that cars promote deindividuation. The loss of self-awareness and evaluation apprehension reduces restraints on aggression.

Students may be interested in visiting psychologist Arnold Nerenberg's web site (www.roadrage.com) that deals with the problem of road rage including possible solutions to it.

18. Popular Sources of Additional Classroom Material

Baron, R., & Richardson, D. (1994). Human aggression, 2nd ed. New York: Plenum. Examines, in separate chapters, the biological, social, and personal causes of aggression. Explores the occurrence of aggression in natural settings.

Berkowitz, L. (1993). Aggression: Its causes, consequences, and control. New York: McGraw-Hill. An excellent summary of current research on the causes and control of aggression.

Davis, M. H. (Ed.). (2000). Annual editions: Social psychology 00/01. Guilford, CT: Dushkin/McGraw-Hill. Updated annually, this volume provides convenient access to a wide range of current articles on social psychology appearing in magazines, newspapers, and journals.

Englander, E. K. (1997). Understanding violence. Mahwah, NJ: Erlbaum. A survey of the causes and effects of violence. Includes consideration of special issues such as domestic and gang violence, and the role of substance abuse in violent behavior.

Felson, R., & Tedeschi, J. (Eds.). (1993). Aggression and violence: Social interactionist perspectives. Washington, DC: American Psychological Association. Situational and interpersonal factors that lead people to use coercion against another are reviewed in this recent APA publication. Scholars from different disciplines consider the use of aggression as a method of social influence, as an expression of grievances, and as an attempt to enhance identity.

Groebel, J., & Hinde, R. (Eds.). (1988). Aggression and war: Their biological and social bases. New York: Cambridge University Press. Prominent researchers summarize current understandings of the biological, psychological, and cultural sources of aggression.

Huston, A., et al. (1992). Big world, small screen: The role of television in American society. Lincoln, NB: University of Nebraska. Members of the American Psychological Association's Task Force on Television and Society consider television's influence on behavior.

Stoff, D. M., & Cairns, R. B. (Eds.) (1996). Aggression and violence: Genetic, neurological, and biosocial perspectives. Mahwah, NJ: Erlbaum. Surveys the biological bases of human antisocial, aggressive, and violent behaviors.

Tedeschi, J., & Felson, R. (1994). <u>Violence, aggression, and coercive actions</u>. Begins by reviewing traditional theories of aggression and then defines a social interactionist theory of aggression, which explores face-to-face confrontations and the intent of the aggressor's particular actions.

DEMONSTRATION AND PROJECT IDEAS

1. Aggression Quiz

Demonstration 10-1 may be used to stimulate student interest and to show the value of aggression research. The correct answers to most of these questions are not obvious, apart from research. As the chapter will reveal, statements 7, 8, 9, and 11 are true; the rest are false. Naturally, this demonstration will be most effective BEFORE students have read the chapter.

2. What is Aggression?

Social psychologists have offered differing definitions of aggression—as the delivery of noxious stimuli to another organism, as behavior that intends to injure an organism, etc. Both forms of Demonstration 10-2 may be distributed to assess a) students' agreements and disagreements about what aggression is, b) the reliability with which the text definition can be applied, and c) the extent of agreement between the students' own classification of aggressive acts and that implied by the text definition.

3. The Aggression Questionnaire

Demonstration 10-3 represents the Aggression Questionnaire designed by Arnold H. Buss and Mark Perry (1992). In scoring, the answers for items 15 and 24 must first be reversed (i.e., 1 = 5, 2 = 4, 3 = 3, 4 = 2, 5 = 1) and then the numbers for all 29 items are added to obtain a total score. When 1,253 introductory psychology students completed the questionnaire, mean scores for males and females were 77.8 and 68.2, respectively. Replicated factor analyses yielded four subscales. Items 1, 5, 9, 13, 17, 21, 24, 27, and 29 assess Physical Aggression; items 2, 6, 10, 14, and 18 measure Verbal Aggression; items 3, 7, 11, 15, 19, 22, and 25 tap Anger; and items 4, 8, 12, 16, 20, 23, 26, and 28 measure Hostility. Males scored higher than females on all subscales except on anger.

4. A Letter Writing Exercise

Dana Dunn (1992) describes an effective exercise in which students read the 1932 "Why War?" correspondence between Albert Einstein and Sigmund Freud (In J. Strachey, Ed., 1932/1964, <u>The standard edition of the complete psychological works of Sigmund Freud</u>, Vol. 22, p. 197–215, London: Hogarth) and then compose letters responding to it.

In his initial letter, Einstein pondered whether humanity can ever be free from the threat of war. He blamed war on both "the political power-hunger" of governments and humanity's "lust for hatred and destruction." He asked Freud for insights on how to eliminate armed conflicts. Freud's response emphasized culture and instinct. Violence evolved from conflict between individuals and could only be thwarted by laws created by communities. Organized communities, argued Freud, use violence to settle disputes because of humanity's self-preserving (erotic) and destructive (death) instincts. Freud concluded his letter by asking Einstein a question: "Why do you and I and so many other people rebel so violently against war?" In answering his own question, Freud pointed to the process of civilization, both its benefits (e.g., intellect) and constraints (e.g., repression), as leading to pacifism. However, he gave no recommendations on how to promote pacifism nor did he comment on the prospect of this philosophy being successful.

Students write a two-page letter responding to either or both authors. They are encouraged to express agreement or disagreement with their positions and to comment on the perspectives on human aggression that each offers. Are Einstein and/or Freud optimistic or pessimistic about our destiny? Are we destined to wage war because of avarice (nurture), some unfortunate disposition (nature), or a combination of both? Volunteers can be asked to read their letters in class.

An alternative, suggested by Dunn, is for you to briefly present a summary of Freud's and Einstein's ideas and then allow 10 minutes for free-writing. Students may write any response they choose. Typically the exercise encourages students to integrate the themes found in the letters with their own experience.

5. Relative Deprivation

Royce Singleton (1978) also provides a classroom demonstration of relative deprivation. He suggests that grade inflation in American colleges has probably raised students' expectations and thus also increased their dissatisfaction with what were once considered "good" grades. Since comparison with others is often the basis for self-evaluation, students assess the value of their own grades by comparing them with those of their classmates. The higher the grade relative to others, the more satisfying it will be. Thus as grades become inflated, good grades become less satisfying since they are not as "good" relative to others.

Singleton demonstrated this relative-deprivation effect by showing students past grade distributions that indicated he was either a "hard" or "easy" grader, and then asking them how satisfied they would be with final grades of A, B, and C. Students in the "hard grader" condition were more satisfied with all three hypothetical final grades than those in the "easy grader" condition.

If your students are still uncertain about the type of grader you are, you may be able to replicate Singleton's results. Of course, it is important to debrief students thoroughly as Singleton did. If you think your students already know how hard a grader you are, use Demonstration 10-4, which contains hypothetical grade distributions and asks for students' satisfaction with each grade. Randomly distribute an equal number of each form. Collect the forms, and, before the next class session, calculate any differences in satisfaction with grades under the two distributions. Report the results back to class and discuss in terms of relative deprivation.

6. Experiencing Media Violence

Showing the 14-minute film Violence Just for Fun is useful for introducing a number of issues raised in the text. The film is edited from Barabbas and its focus is on the savage and vicious battles of Roman gladiators. Asking students for their reactions to the film naturally leads to a discussion of the theory and research on the effects filmed violence has on the viewer. As a discussion starter pose the following questions:

1. Does the film produce catharsis (venting of one's pent-up hostilities), or is it arousing?
2. Do such depictions sensitize or desensitize one to violence?
3. How did the gladiator fights affect spectators? Were they more or less likely to behave aggressively after attending?
4. The film portrays an historical case of violence. What causes such aggression to occur?

7. Cultural Myths and Support for Rape

Martha Burt (1980) has reported that many Americans accept rape myths and thereby may be creating a climate hostile to rape victims. Demonstration 10-5 presents items from her Rape Myth Acceptance Scale. All are false except Item 2. Burt found that acceptance of these myths are strongly connected to other deeply held and pervasive attitudes such as sex role stereotyping, distrust of the opposite sex, and acceptance of interpersonal violence. Because rape myths are so closely interconnected with other strongly held attitudes, Burt believes they may be difficult to change. She suggests we begin by fighting sex role stereotyping at very young ages. In addition, she states, "Only by promoting the idea of sex as a mutually undertaken, freely chosen, fully conscious interaction, in contra-distinction to the often held view that it is a battlefield in which each side tries to exploit the other, can society create an atmosphere free of the threat of rape."

Acceptance of interpersonal violence was the strongest single predictor of rape myth acceptance. Burt maintains that while sex role stereotyping may be the precondition for targeting women as potential sexual victims, acceptance of interpersonal violence may be the attitudinal releaser of assaultive action. "Excessive violence has long been a theme in American life," writes Burt. "Rape is only one of its modes of expression."

8. Staging an Assassination

William Dragon has developed a classroom exercise in which students stage and videotape and instructor's assassination. For more information on the exercise and how to get a copy of the video or CD from Dragon, see "Demonstration and Project Idea" number 2 in Modular B.

9. The Social Connection Video Series

One of the entries in the video instructional supplement (The Social Connection Video Series), entitled "Understanding Genocide," pertains to discussions about the social determinants of aggression. See the Faculty Guide accompanying the video series for a program summary, pause points, and a classroom activity.

Demonstration 10-1

True or False

1. Data on war related deaths suggests we have reason for optimism in the twenty-first century.   T   F
2. Being accidentally shot by another hunter is an example of "cold aggression."   T   F
3. Strong evidence suggests the death penalty is a deterrent to homicides.   T   F
4. There is strong evidence suggesting human aggression is largely instinctively.   T   F
5. Violence and drinking alcohol are positively correlated.   T   F
6. Frustration always leads to aggression.   T   F
7. Carlos is more likely to be frustrated making $50,000 than Jack who is making $30,000 because Carlos' fellow workers are making $70,000 while Jack's fellow workers are making $30,000.   T   F
8. Merely watching others act aggressively can lead to aggressive actions.   T   F
9. Southern U.S. communities have higher homicide rates than northern U. S. communities.   T   F
10. Riots in the late '60s and early '70s were more likely to occur on cool days than on hot days.   T   F
11. Viewing scenes containing sexual coercion can change how men feel about violence toward women.   T   F
12. There is very little research suggesting the mere viewing of violence leads to more tolerant attitudes toward aggression.   T   F
13. Watching TV violence actually reduces pent-up violent urges.   T   F
14. People who watch a large amount of TV underestimate the frequency of violence in the world.   T   F
15. You are more likely to intensify your aggressive action when you are alone compared to when you are in a group.   T   F

Demonstration 10-2
Bolt & Myers
©McGraw-Hill, 1999

Is it aggression?

Yes No

___ ___ 1. A murderer is executed under Utah's capital punishment law.
___ ___ 2. A father spanks his disobedient six-year-old.
___ ___ 3. A woman shoots mace at her would-be rapist.
___ ___ 4. A batter's line drive hits the pitcher in the knee.
___ ___ 5. A frustrated wife yells at her "messy slob of a husband."
___ ___ 6. A smoldering destroyer in Pearl Harbor, 1941, manages to shoot down a Japanese plane.
___ ___ 7. A professor lowers a student's grade on a late paper.
___ ___ 8. A man passes along rumors about his rival's sexual transgressions.
___ ___ 9. A teenager tells his proud little sister that her art project is "dumb and ugly."
___ ___ 10. Two girls sneak out at night and "toilet paper" their mutual friend's front yard.

Demonstration 10-2
Bolt & Myers
©McGraw-Hill, 1999

The text defines aggression as "physical or verbal behavior that is intended to hurt someone." By this definition, is it aggression?

Yes No

___ ___ 1. A murderer is executed under Utah's capital punishment law.
___ ___ 2. A father spanks his disobedient six-year-old.
___ ___ 3. A woman shoots mace at her would-be rapist.
___ ___ 4. A batter's line drive hits the pitcher in the knee.
___ ___ 5. A frustrated wife yells at her "messy slob of a husband."
___ ___ 6. A smoldering destroyer in Pearl Harbor, 1941, manages to shoot down a Japanese plane.
___ ___ 7. A professor lowers a student's grade on a late paper.
___ ___ 8. A man passes along rumors about his rival's sexual transgressions.
___ ___ 9. A teenager tells his proud little sister that her art project is "dumb and ugly."
___ ___ 10. Two girls sneak out at night and "toilet paper" their mutual friend's front yard.

Demonstration 10-3

(with permission of A. H. Buss)

Rate each of the following items on a scale of 1 (extremely uncharacteristic of me) to 5 (extremely characteristic of me).

____ 1. Once in a while I can't control the urge to strike another person.
____ 2. I tell my friends openly when I disagree with them.
____ 3. I flare up quickly but get over it quickly.
____ 4. I am sometimes eaten up with jealousy.
____ 5. Given enough provocation, I may hit another person.
____ 6. I often find myself disagreeing with people.
____ 7. When frustrated, I let my irritation show.
____ 8. At times I feel I have gotten a raw deal out of life.
____ 9. If somebody hits me, I hit back.
____ 10. When people annoy me, I may tell them what I think of them.
____ 11. I sometimes feel like a powder keg ready to explode.
____ 12. Other people always seem to get the breaks.
____ 13. I get into fights a little more than the average person.
____ 14. I can't help getting into arguments when people disagree with me.
____ 15. I am an even-tempered person.
____ 16. I wonder why sometimes I feel so bitter about things.
____ 17. If I have to resort to violence to protect my rights, I will.
____ 18. My friends say that I am somewhat argumentative.
____ 19. Some of my friends think I'm a hothead.
____ 20. I know that "friends" talk about me behind my back.
____ 21. There are people who pushed me so far that we came to blows.
____ 22. Sometimes I fly off the handle for no good reason.
____ 23. I am suspicious of overly friendly strangers.
____ 24. I can think of no good reason for ever hitting a person.
____ 25. I have trouble controlling my temper.
____ 26. I sometimes feel that people are laughing at me behind my back.
____ 27. I have threatened people I know.
____ 28. When people are especially nice, I wonder what they want.
____ 29. I have become so mad that I have broken things.

(From "The Aggression Questionnaire" by Arnold H. Buss and Mark Perry, 1992, <u>Journal of Personality and Social Psychology, 63</u>, p. 454. Copyright © 1992 by the American Psychological Association. Reprinted with permission.)

Demonstration 10-4

(with permission of R. Singleton)

Assume that you have been given information about the distribution of final grades in a course you've just completed. The instructor has given 40 percent A's, 50 percent B's, and 10 percent C's, (D's and F's were not given). Knowing this, how satisfied would you feel if your final grade in the class:

were an A?

0% 10% 20% 30% 40% 50% 60% 70% 80% 90% 100%
completely   completely
dissatisfied   satisfied

were a B+?

0% 10% 20% 30% 40% 50% 60% 70% 80% 90% 100%
completely   completely
dissatisfied   satisfied

were a B?

0% 10% 20% 30% 40% 50% 60% 70% 80% 90% 100%
completely   completely
dissatisfied   satisfied

were a B-?

0% 10% 20% 30% 40% 50% 60% 70% 80% 90% 100%
completely   completely
dissatisfied   satisfied

were a C+?

0% 10% 20% 30% 40% 50% 60% 70% 80% 90% 100%
completely   completely
dissatisfied   satisfied

were a C?

0% 10% 20% 30% 40% 50% 60% 70% 80% 90% 100%
completely   completely
dissatisfied   satisfied

Demonstration 10-4

(with permission of R. Singleton)

Assume that you have been given information about the distribution of final grades in a course you've just completed. The instructor has given 10 percent A's, 30 percent B's, 40 percent C's, 15 percent D's, and 5 percent F's. Knowing this, how satisfied would you feel if your final grade in the class:

were an A?

0% 10% 20% 30% 40% 50% 60% 70% 80% 90% 100%

completely dissatisfied   completely satisfied

were a B+?

0% 10% 20% 30% 40% 50% 60% 70% 80% 90% 100%

completely dissatisfied   completely satisfied

were a B?

0% 10% 20% 30% 40% 50% 60% 70% 80% 90% 100%

completely dissatisfied   completely satisfied

were a B-?

0% 10% 20% 30% 40% 50% 60% 70% 80% 90% 100%

completely dissatisfied   completely satisfied

were a C+?

0% 10% 20% 30% 40% 50% 60% 70% 80% 90% 100%

completely dissatisfied   completely satisfied

were a C?

0% 10% 20% 30% 40% 50% 60% 70% 80% 90% 100%

completely dissatisfied   completely satisfied

Demonstration 10-5

(with permission of M. R. Burt)

Indicate your degree of agreement or disagreement with each of the following statements in the blank space next to each item. Respond to each statement by using the following code:

6 = Strongly agree
5 = Moderately agree
4 = Slightly agree
3 = Slightly disagree
2 = Moderately disagree
1 = Strongly disagree

____ 1. A woman who goes to the home or apartment of a man on their first date implies that she is willing to have sex.

____ 2. Any female can get raped.

____ 3. One reason that women falsely report rape is that they frequently have a need to call attention to themselves.

____ 4. Any healthy woman can successfully resist a rapist if she really wants to.

____ 5. When women go around braless or wearing short skirts and tight tops, they are just asking for trouble.

____ 6. In the majority of rapes, the victim is promiscuous or has a bad reputation.

____ 7. If a girl engages in necking or petting and she lets things get out of hand, it is her own fault if her partner forces sex on her.

____ 8. Women who get raped while hitchhiking get what they deserve.

____ 9. A woman who is stuck-up and thinks she is too good to talk to guys on the street deserves to be taught a lesson.

____ 10. Many women have an unconscious wish to be raped, and may then unconsciously set up a situation in which they are likely to be attacked.

____ 11. If a woman gets drunk at a party and has intercourse with a man she's just met there, she should be considered "fair game" to other males at the party who want to have sex with her too, whether she wants to or not.

____ 12. Many women who report being raped are lying because they are angry and want to get back at the men they accuse.

____ 13. Many rapes are invented by women who have discovered they are pregnant and want to protect their own reputation.

FILMS/VIDEOS

Aggression (PSU, 30 min., 1989). Social psychological research suggests that human aggression is primarily a learned activity. Various aspects of the physical and social environment reliably predict violent reactions. Examines strategies for reducing aggression.

Aggression, Violence, and the Brain (ANN, 7 min., 1986). One of the teaching modules (#30) from "The Brain" series, this brief clip shows Jose Delgado eliciting aggression in a bull through brain stimulation. Focuses on the case of Mark Larribus whose violence was traced to a brain tumor.

Born Bad (CNN, 57 min., 1996). Broadcast on CNN Presents, this program covers neuroscience research on the biological factors associated with remorseless violent crime. (Can be purchased for $19.95 by calling 1-800-799-7676 and asking for "Born Bad" broadcast March 17, 1996)

Crime and the Criminal (LCA, 33 min., 1973). Edited from the feature film In Cold Blood. Explores the criminal's personality and motives for murder. Raises question of personal responsibility.

Dreamworlds (INS, 56 min., 1991). This film uses footage from over 165 music videos to explore the relationship between the airing of objectified images of women and sexual violence. Images are intercut with the gang-rape scene from the feature film "The Accused."

Dreamworlds II (MED, 55 min., 1995). Update of Dreamworlds. Substitutes narrative for music and rearranges the videos to illustrate the story they tell about female sexuality.

The Effects of TV Violence on Children's Behavior (ABC, 5 min, 1993). A "World News Tonight" story about the new TV ratings system developed by the major broadcasting companies and some dialog about the degree of causality for childhood violence attributable to watching TV violence.

The Killing Screens: Media and the Culture of Violence (MED, 37 min., 1994). George Gerbner encourages the audience to think about the psychological, political, social, and developmental aspects of growing up and living in a culture marked by pervasive, ritualized violence images.

Rape: An Act of Hate (FHS, 30 min., 1989). Examines the history and mythology of rape, explains who are its most likely victims, and presents interviews with experts in sociology and law enforcement.

TV Violence and You (FHS, 30 min., 1997). George Gerbner analyzes one week of television programs to determine their level of violence. Effects of both blatant volence and subtle violent imagery are analyzed.

Violence Against Women (INS, 32 min., 1995). Explores the causes of violence against women and suggests ways of preventing these crimes. Features the personal stories of both victims and assailants. Examines how violence within a family shapes the child's concept of relationships.

Violence in the Home (INS, 30 min., 1989). Presents the devastating effects of domestic violence. Includes interviews with men and women in treatment. Uses dramatizations to show why violence occurs.

The Violent Mind (PBS, 90 min., 1988). The last program to appear in the PBS "The Mind" series. Emphasizes the biological influences in aggression and raises questions about criminal responsibility and punishment.

What Can We Do About Violence (FHS, 56 min. each, 1994). This four-part series, narrated by Bill Moyers, examines solutions to the problem of violence in America. Efforts to control violence include adult mentoring, conflict resolution, peer education, alternative sentencing, violence prevention counseling, and substance abuse rehabilitation.

CHAPTER 11
ATTRACTION AND INTIMACY: LIKING AND LOVING OTHERS

Friendships
    Proximity
    Interaction
    Anticipation of Interaction
    Mere Exposure
    Physical Attractiveness
    Attractiveness and Dating
    The Matching Phenomenon
    The Physical-Attractiveness Stereotype
    Who Is Attractive?
    Similarity Versus Complementarity
    Do Birds of a Feather Flock Together?
    Do Opposites Attract?
    Liking Those Who Like Us
    Attribution
    Self-esteem and Attraction
    Gaining Another's Esteem
    Relationship Rewards
Love
    Passionate Love
    A Theory of Passionate Love
    Variations in Love
    Companionate Love
Maintaining Close Relationships
    Attachment
    Attachment Styles
    Equity
    Long-Term Equity
    Perceived Equity and Satisfaction
    Self-Disclosure
Ending Relationships
    Who Divorces?
    The Detachment Process
Personal Postscript: Making Love

LECTURE AND DISCUSSION IDEAS

1. Introducing Attraction

Attraction research may be introduced by having students list factors they believe are important in the formation of <u>friendships</u> and of long-term <u>love</u> relationships. What similarities and differences exist between the two lists? Do males and females identify the same factors? Some of the variables discussed in the text (for example, similarity) are sure to be mentioned. Others (proximity, physical attractiveness) may be underestimated.

Ann Weber (1984) suggests a simple exercise for stimulating classroom discussion about interpersonal attraction. Ask students to answer this question:

> Suppose you had to spend the rest of your life on a small but fertile island—but with only <u>one</u> other human being. Further suppose you couldn't even choose the specific <u>individual</u> with whom you'd be sharing the island, but you <u>could</u> specify what this person's <u>sex</u> would be. What sex would you ask for your island-mate?

Weber reports that so far her students of both sexes have overwhelmingly responded, "female!" You can also substitute "age," "race," "educational level," or "religious preference," for "sex."

A related question you might pose for class or small group discussion would be: "What are the important qualities you look for in a friend?" The characteristics most often mentioned by 40,000 respondents to Parlee's (1979) survey were the following (in descending order): ability to keep confidences, loyalty, warmth or affection, supportiveness, frankness, sense of humor, willingness to make time, independence, good conversationalist, and intelligence.

Hill (1987) identified four dimensions that underlie affiliation motivation. These include emotional support (e.g., "One of my greatest sources of comfort when things get rough is being with other people"); attention (e.g., "I often have a strong need to be around people who are impressed with what I am like and what I do"); positive stimulation (e.g., "I think being close to others, listening to them, and relating to them on a one-to-one level is one of my favorite and most satisfying pastimes"); and social comparison (e.g. "When I am not certain about how well I am doing at something, I usually like to be around others so I can compare myself to them").

2. Exposure Effects: Payola

An interesting example of the power of exposure is the tendency for music companies to influence disk-jockeys (by secretly giving them money and other valuables) to play songs on the radio from groups they have signed to their label. Apparently record company executives are aware of the "familiarity breeds liking" idea. They know that the more airplay their song gets, the more records they're going to sell. This practice has taken on the name "payola." There are several web sites with plenty of information about how the bribery works. This site give a brief history: www.history-of-rock.com/payola.htm.

3. Desirable and Negative Qualities

Ask your students to write down the five attributes they most look for in a partner. Describing survey results in the United States, Robin Gilmour (1988) reports that men and women who were asked to select and rank potentially desirable attributes produced entirely different "top-10" lists. In order of importance, women most sought in a man the following: A record of achievement, leadership qualities, skill at his job, earning potential, a sense of humor, intellectual ability, attentiveness, common sense, athletic ability, good abstract reasoning. Most sought by men in a woman were the following: Physical attractiveness, ability in bed, warmth and affection, social skill, homemaking ability, dress sense, sensitivity to others' needs, good taste, moral perception, artistic creativity. As Gilmour indicates, some psychologists have argued that the classic studies of mutual attraction are actually better understood in terms of repulsion. That is, once we have screened others for disliked characteristics (such as an unattractive appearance, dissimilarity of attitudes, and disagreeable mannerisms) we tend to be attracted to them.

4. Love Styles

The text notes that Lee as well as Hendrick and Hendrick have identified three primary love styles—eros, ludus, and storge—which, like the primary colors, combine to form secondary love styles such as mania. You may want to describe this popular typology more fully in class as well as the efforts to assess the relative strength of each style (Hendrick, Hendrick, & Dicke, 1998).

A. Eros. Passionate love focuses strongly on physical attraction and sensual satisfaction. Erotic lovers look for rapidly developing, emotionally intense relationships and they tend to idealize their partners. They tend to agree that "Strong physical attraction is one of the best things about love."

B. Ludus. Ludic love is love practiced as a game or pleasant pastime for mutual enjoyment. Love is a series of challenges and puzzles to be solved. This type of lover dates several partners and moves in and out of love affairs quickly and easily. He or she refuses to mention any long-range plans and would be likely to agree, "I can get over love affairs pretty easily and quickly."

C. Storge. Friendship love is a caring, concerned love that is based on similar interests and pursuits. For those who love in this way, the most appealing aspect of the relationship consists in making a home and raising a family together. They desire a long-term relationship based on mutual trust and maintain that "Love is really deep friendship, not a mysterious, mystical emotion."

D. Mania. Possessive lovers are insecure, dependent, and tend to be fearful of being rejected. The typical manic yearns for love, yet anticipates that it will be painful. The manic lover tries to force the partner into greater expressions of affection, and agrees that "When my partner does not pay attention to me, I feel sick all over."

E. Pragma. "Pragma is the love that goes shopping for a suitable mate, and all it asks is that the relationship work well, that the two partners be compatible, and satisfy each other's basic or practical needs." Relationships are based on satisfactory rewards rather than romantic attraction. Practical lovers believe that "For practical reasons, I would consider what he or she is going to become before I commit myself."

F. Agape. Selfless lovers sacrifice their own interests in favor of their partner's and give without expecting a reward. They are not happy unless the partner is also happy. Prepared to share all they have, they are vulnerable to exploitation. The selfless lover states that "I would rather break up with my partner than stand in his or her way."

5. Sternberg's Love Triangle

As the test indicates, Robert Sternberg (1988) views love as a triangle whose three sides (of varying length) are passion, intimacy, and commitment. Commitment represents the cognitive side of the love triangle and represents both a short-term decision to love another person and a long-term commitment to maintain that love. As a relationship develops, commitment increases gradually at first and then grows more rapidly. Eventually it levels off or falls back to zero if the relationship fails. Intimacy is the emotional aspect of love and includes closeness, sharing, support, and communication. It grows steadily at first and then levels off. Moreover it may become hidden or latent in some successful relationships particularly if people come to know each other well and are thus predictable. However, if it disappears entirely, the relationship is likely to collapse.

Passion is the motivational side of the triangle, which leads to physiological arousal and an intense desire to be united with the loved one. It has a positive force that is quick to develop and a negative force that takes hold more slowly, lasts longer, and explains the heartache that remains when love has gone.

Alone and in combination the three components make possible eight kinds of love relationships. The absence of all three is nonlove and characterizes the majority of personal relationships. They are simply casual interactions. Intimacy by itself elicits liking and friendship. There is closeness and warmth but not the intense feeling that comes with passion or commitment. Passion alone is infatuated love. It can dissipate just as quickly as it arises. Commitment without intimacy or passion is empty love, sometimes seen in a 30-year-old marriage but also in arranged marriages. In the latter case empty love may precede other kinds of love. Romantic love combines intimacy and passion but lacks commitment. Passion plus commitment is fatuous love or Hollywood love. The pair is committed on the basis of their passion but without intimacy the relationship is unlikely to last. Companionate love is intimacy with commitment but no passion. It's seen in a long-term friendship or in a marriage where physical attraction is lost. Sternberg claims that only consummate or complete love possesses all three components. It is possible only in very special relationships.

6. Positive Illusions in Romantic Relationships

George Bernard Shaw cynically observed, "Love is a gross exaggeration of the difference between one person and everyone else."

Murray and Holmes (1997) wondered whether optimism about romantic relationships sustains those relationships or whether acknowledging partners' faults as well as one's own vulnerability from the start better prepares people to deal with the difficulties they are likely to encounter.

To answer that question they had both dating and married couples complete a measure of relationship illusions that assessed idealized perceptions of the partners' attributes, exaggerated perceptions of control, and unrealistic optimism. Results indicted that relationship illusions predicted greater satisfaction, love, and trust, as well as less conflict and ambivalence in both dating and marital relationships. In addition, a longitudinal follow-up of the dating sample indicated that relationships were more likely to persist the stronger were individuals' initial illusions. Relationship illusions predicted increases in later satisfaction but not vice versa.

7. Comparing Love and Friendship

Keith Davis (1985) suggests that love and friendship have a number of similarities. At the same time there are crucial differences that make love relationships "both more rewarding and more volatile."

Friendship includes the following elements:

1. Enjoyment—Friends enjoy each other's company most of the time.
2. Acceptance—Friends accept each other as they are and do not attempt to make the other into a different person.
3. Trust—Each assumes the other will act in light of his or her friend's best interest.
4. Respect—Friends respect each other in the sense of assuming that each exercises good judgment in making life choices.
5. Confiding—They share experiences and feelings with each other.

6. Understanding—They have a sense of what the other values and why the friend does what he or she does.

7. Spontaneity—Each feels free to be himself or herself in the relationship.

Love has all these same qualities as well as "passion" and "caring" clusters of characteristics. The "passion" cluster includes the following:

1. Fascination—Lovers are preoccupied with each other and tend to think about each other even when they should be involved in other activities.

2. Exclusiveness—Lovers have a special relationship that precludes having the same relationship with a third party.

3. Sexual desire—Lovers want physical intimacy with the partner.

The "caring" cluster includes the following:

1. Giving the utmost—Lovers care enough to give the utmost when the other is in need, sometimes to the point of extreme self-sacrifice.

2. Being a champion advocate—The depth of caring is reflected in the lovers' active championship of each other's interest and in a positive attempt to make sure that the partner succeeds.

8. Dealing with Dissatisfaction in Romantic Relationships

Introduce this topic with the assignment Rusbult and Zembrodt (1983) gave their subjects:

Think of a time in your life when you became dissatisfied with a romantic relationship in which you were involved. Describe the situation and your feelings, and especially your response to the situation. (What did you do about your unhappiness? What did you do about the relationship?)

In two studies Rusbult and Zembrodt identified four general categories of response to dissatisfaction: (a) exit—ending or actively abusing the relationship ("When I'm angry at my partner, I talk to him about breaking up"); (b) voice—actively attempting to improve conditions ("When we've had an argument, I work things out with my partner right away"); (c) loyalty—passively waiting for things to improve ("When I'm upset about something in our relationship, I wait awhile before saying anything to see if things will improve on their own"); (d) neglect—passively allowing the relationship to deteriorate ("When I'm upset with my partner I sulk rather than confront the issue"). Two dimensions were distinguished among the response categories—constructiveness/destructiveness and activity/passivity. Voice and loyalty were judged to be constructive behaviors while exit and neglect were seen as relatively more destructive. Exit and voice were viewed as fairly active; loyalty and neglect were judged to be more passive.

In further research Rusbult and her colleagues found that in comparison to their male partners, female subjects were more likely to engage in voice and loyalty and were somewhat less likely to neglect. They also found that destructive problem-solving styles were more powerfully predictive of couple distress and functioning than were constructive styles. That is, it appeared it is not so much the good, constructive things that partners do or do not do for one another in reaction to problems that determines whether a relationship works as it is the destructive things they do or do not do.

9. Another Theory of Attraction

The text uses reward theory as a simple principle for summarizing research on attraction. You might wish to present balance theory as an alternative.

Balance theory emphasizes the importance of human thought processes in understanding social behavior and more specifically assumes that people want to organize conceptions about others, themselves, and objects in the environment in a "harmonious, balanced, or symmetrical way" (Newcomb, 1961).

Newcomb's balance theory, sometimes called the A-B-X model, proposes that there is a natural inclination for an actor (A) to organize thoughts about a person (B) and thoughts about another person, object, or issue (X) in a way that is harmonious or "balanced." Such relationships will prove more satisfying than those characterized by imbalance.

For example, if <u>A</u>dam likes <u>B</u>ertha and they both like rock music, a balanced state is said to exist in their relationship. Where Adam likes Bertha but they disagree about rock music, there is imbalance. Such a state is unpleasant, and Adam will be motivated to change Bertha's attitude toward rock music, his own attitude toward them, or his attitude toward Bertha. Thus attitude similarity will produce attraction.

Examples of balanced relationships are provided below:

```
      1                 2                 3                 4
      A                 A                 A                 A
   +     +           +     -           -     +           -     -
  B   +   X         B   -   X         B   -   X         B   +   X
```

Examples of imbalanced relationships are the following:

```
      5                 6                 7                 8
      A                 A                 A                 A
   -     -           +     +           +     -           -     +
  B   -   X         B   -   X         B   +   X         B   +   X
```

One of the interesting tests of balance theory was provided by Aronson and Cope (1968). The title of their study was "My Enemy's Enemy Is My Friend" and was a specific test of Example 3 above. Subjects, presumably participating in a study of creativity, wrote stories that the experimenter then evaluated negatively. The evaluation was delivered very harshly to half the subjects and very kindly to the other half. A few seconds before completing his evaluation, the experimenter was called into the hallway by his supervisor and was himself given either lavish praise or a blistering condemnation for a report he had written. After the experimenter returned to the lab, he sent the subject to the departmental secretary to receive experimental credit. The secretary asked each subject to make phone calls to recruit subjects for a research project the supervisor was conducting. Subjects were willing to work harder for the supervisor who treated the harsh experimenter harshly (my enemy's enemy is my friend) than for a supervisor who treated a harsh experimenter kindly (my enemy's friend is my enemy) or for a supervisor who treated a kind experimenter harshly (my friend's enemy is my enemy). A large number of calls were also made for a supervisor who treated a kind experimenter kindly (my friend's friend is my friend).

10. What's Your Love Story

Robert Sternberg (2000) (also found in Annual Editions–Social Psychology 01/02; see Chapter 1 references) asks readers to identify their love story in an effort for them to find their perfect match. Sternberg, whose theory of love is recounted in the text, suggests his previous work, which dissected the components of love still leaves a couple rather foundational questions entirely open. That is, "what makes a person the kind of lover they are?" and, "what attracts them to other lovers?" Sternberg's suggests the answers to these questions are found in people's "love stories." In this easy to digest

"Psychology Today" article Sternberg suggests people's stories can be categorized into a limited number of types (e.g., the business story—"I believe close relationships are like good partnerships" or the travel story— "I believe that beginning a relationship is like starting a new journey that promises to be both exciting and challenging"). Once we realize our own story, Sternberg suggests, we can begin to recognize elements of that story in the stories of potential mates. At the end of the article, Sternberg asks the reader to choose between 12 different types of stories (Adapted from Sternberg, 1998). Some possible discussion questions include: Is this classification scheme too subjective to be called scientific? Can a theory of love be reduced to one story line? If we all have implicit theories of love, where do they come from? How well do the ideas expressed in this article fit with the theories mentioned in the text?

11. Proximity Effects

The importance of proximity in friendship formation may be highlighted by asking students to think of one close friendship formed since coming to college. Was proximity a factor? Did this person live nearby or sit nearby in some class?

Mady Segal (1974) examined the friendship patterns of Maryland State Police trainees and found proximity had a stronger effect on attraction than many other factors that conventional wisdom suggests are important. Proximity was a better predictor of friendships than similarity of religion, hobbies, age, marital status, or organizational memberships. Interestingly, Segal reported that the alphabetical order of surnames was significantly correlated with the formation of friendship. Trainees were assigned to classroom seats on the basis of the alphabetical order of their last names.

The following provides an excellent illustration of the "mere exposure" effect and could be presented in class. Ask students what might account for the attitude shift.

On February 27, 1967, the Associated Press carried this story from Corvallis, Oregon:

A mysterious student has been attending a class at Oregon State University for the past two months enveloped in a big black bag. Only his bare feet show. Each Monday, Wednesday, and Friday at 11 a.m. the Black Bag sits on a small table near the back of the classroom. The class is Speech 113— Basic Persuasion. . . . Charles Goetzinger, professor of the class, knows the identity of the person inside. None of the 20 students in the class do. Goetzinger said "the students' attitudes changed from hostility toward the Black Bag to curiosity and finally to friendship."

12. The Physical Attractiveness Stereotype in Bedtime Stories

Do the traditional bedtime stories and fairy tales read to children serve to perpetuate the physical attractiveness stereotype? Shari Thurer (Burtoff, 1980) believes that they do. She argues that physical deformity, chronic illness, and outer defects have come to symbolize inner defects, evil natures, and villainous behavior. The bad guy in Peter Pan, Captain Hook, wore a prosthesis; Cinderella's step-sisters were fat and ugly as well as mean; Hansel and Gretel were victims of an arthritic witch; Jack climbed the beanstalk only to find a wicked giant; Pinocchio's nose lengthened as his integrity slipped.

"It is hardly ever the arthritic nearsighted crone that is endowed with virtue and a sunny disposition, but the archetypal Snow White, the fairest of them all, who is blessed. It's almost as if the characters' moral temperaments were predetermined by the outcomes of a medical checkup," says Thurer, "Virtue is rewarded with physical grace, so that the ugly duckling turns into a swan and the frog into a prince. And would sighted mice be so foolish as to have their tails cut off?"

Other psychologists, including Freda Rebelski (Burtoff, 1980), a Boston University professor of psychology, have questioned the impact of fairy tales on children. She has argued that children distinguish reality from what they know to be fiction and claims no scientific data support the contention that fairy tales convey prejudice against the physically handicapped.

13. Sustaining Relationships

Notarius and Markman (1993) provide six truths for couples that are important in sustaining a happy marriage or in reviving an unhappy one.

First, each relationship contains a reservoir of hope. Even the most destructive conflicts start with good intentions, which provide some hope that a fully satisfying relationship can be achieved.

Second, one "zinger" will erase 20 acts of kindness. The constructive expression of criticisms and annoyances is very much a matter of learning how to express oneself and choosing the appropriate time and place for the conversation.

Third, little changes in oneself can lead to huge changes in the relationship. We tend to think changes have to be made by our partner, not by ourselves. However, often relationships can change dramatically by simply adding acts of thoughtfulness, for example, complimenting your partner on how he or she looks, or touching your partner's back when you walk by, and by subtracting thoughtless nastiness, for example, ignoring your partner when you are angry or calling your partner names.

Fourth, it's not the differences between partners that cause problems but how the differences are handled when they arise. Partners in happy relationships develop good listening skills, which involve understanding and acceptance of differences in personality and taste. Having a good listener is having a good friend.

Fifth, men and women fight using different weapons but suffer similar wounds. Men seem to have a harder time handling conflict while women have a harder time handling emotional distance. Thus men often withdraw while women may try to resolve every conflict through discussion. Both men and women share the need for acceptance, support, and affection.

Sixth, partners need to practice relationship skills in order to become good at them. Instead of continually changing partners in their quest for a happy relationship, people should learn to manage the conflicts, angers, and disagreements that are common to all relationships. People should enter into relationships with agreed-upon rules for handling the strong negative feelings that are an inevitable part of all relationships.

14. Jealousy

You might introduce this topic with the scenario Buunk, Angleitner, Oubaid, & Buss (1996) presented their research participants.

Ask your students to reflect on a serious romantic relationship they have had in the past, have currently, or might have in the future. They are to imagine that the person with whom they are seriously involved has become interested in someone else. What would be most upsetting—their partner forming a deep emotional attachment to that other party, or their partner enjoying passionate sexual intercourse with that other person?

In tests conducted in the Netherlands, Germany, and the United States, the researchers found that, consistent with evolutionary hypotheses, males exhibited more distress to sexual than to emotional infidelity, while females exhibited more distress to emotional than to sexual infidelity. Differences were large for the United States, medium for Germany and the Netherlands.

Ask your students if they have ever engaged in the following behaviors, all of which Peter Salovey and Judith Rodin (1985) found to be quite common. Have they ever called a lover unexpectedly just to see if he or she were there? Extensively questioned a lover about previous or present romantic relationships? Listened in on a telephone conversation of a lover or secretly followed him or her? Taken advantage of unplanned opportunities to look through a lover's belongings for unfamiliar names, phone numbers, etc? Salovey and Rodin define jealousy as the thoughts and feelings that arise when an actual or desired relationship is threatened.

Several investigators have suggested that jealousy is rooted in low self-esteem or insecurities about self-worth. People with poor self-concepts are more likely to fear that any existing relationship is vulnerable to threat. Jealousy is also more likely to occur when people believe they are putting more into a relationship than their partner is. They have serious doubts about their partner's commitment. Clinical observations suggest that males and females may respond differently to feelings of jealousy. Males seem less likely to admit they feel jealous but are more likely to express anger with themselves or toward the rival. Females are more likely to react with depression and with attempts to make themselves more attractive to the partner.

Salovey and Rodin report that people use three coping methods in dealing with jealousy and envy. (Envy is defined as the thoughts and feelings that arise when our personal qualities, possessions, or achievements do not measure up to those of someone relevant to us.) The first is "self-reliance"—a sort of stiff-upper-lip strategy that involves keeping a tight rein on expressions of sadness, anger, or embarrassment, and becoming even more committed to the loved one. The second is "positive comparisons and self-bolstering"—focusing on one's own good qualities and doing something nice for oneself. The third is "selective ignoring"—deciding that the desired person or object isn't that important.

Sharon Brehm has suggested that in controlling jealousy in society we need to abandon the notion that jealousy is a sign of "true love." It is first and foremost a reflection of our own desires, of our own self-interest. French philosopher La Rochefoucauld observed in the seventeenth century, "In jealousy, there is more self-love than love." Brehm further suggests that we need to work on reducing the connection between the exclusivity of a relationship and our own personal worth. She suggests attaching the following warning label to every intimate relationship.

> Warning: It is dangerous to your health and to your partner's if you do not know—surely, clearly, and beyond a doubt—that you are a valuable and worthwhile human being with and without your partner's love.

15. Popular Sources for Additional Classroom Material

Brehm, S. (1992). Intimate relationships, 2nd ed. New York: McGraw-Hill. Explores various aspects of intimate relationships including attraction, love, sexuality, communication, jealousy, conflict, and dissolution.

Harvey, J. (1995). Odyssey of the heart: The search for closeness, intimacy, and love. New York: Freeman. A good summary of social psychological research on love. Illustrates research findings on attraction and intimacy with actual case studies.

Hendrick, C., & Hendrick, S.S. (1993). Romantic love. Newbury Park, CA: Sage. An authoritative overview of what psychologists have learned about the types and stages of close personal relationships.

Marsh, P. (Ed.). (1988). Eye to eye: How people interact. Topsfield, MA: Salem House Publishers. A beautifully illustrated volume of 31 chapters explaining love, marriage, friendship, and family relationships.

Rutter, V., & Schwartz, P. (1998). The love test. New York: Perigee. Two sociologists have distilled research on social attraction into 32 romance and relationship self-quizzes that measure beliefs and attitudes regarding intimacy, commitment, and compatibility.

Sternberg, R. J., & Hojjat, M. (Eds.) (1997). Satisfaction in close relationships. New York: Guilford. Contributors explore models of love, close relationships across the lifespan, conflict in marriage, and clinical approaches to promoting relationship satisfaction.

Stewart, A. J. et al. (1997). Separating together: How divorce transforms families. New York: Guilford. Illuminates both the positive and negative aspects of divorce on family members and their relationships during the first year after parental separation.

Weber, A. L., & Harvey, J. H. (Eds.). (1994). Perspectives on close relationships. Boston: Allyn & Bacon. Summaries of research on sexuality, communication, support, attachment and other aspects of close relationships written by experts in these respective areas.

Werking, K. (1997). We're just good friends: Women and men in nonromantic relationships. New York: Guilford. Explores the challenges and rewards of cross-sex friendships, including their unique character, the cultural beliefs about them, and the influences of various social networks on them.

DEMONSTRATION AND PROJECT IDEAS

1. Attraction and Intimacy Quiz

Demonstration 11-1 may be used to stimulate student interest and to show the value of attraction research. The correct answers to most of these questions are not obvious, apart from research. As the chapter will reveal, statements 2, 3, 5, and 7 are true; the rest are false. Naturally, this demonstration will be most effective BEFORE students have read the chapter.

2. The Mere Exposure Effect

The text notes several examples of the mere exposure effect including the finding that people prefer the letters of their own names. You can replicate this finding in class by simply asking students to write down their five favorite letters of the alphabet. Then have them calculate whether the letters they picked constitute more than a fifth (actually 5/26th) of the letters in their first and last names (most easily calculated by having students write down their name and then cross out the letters they picked). By a show of hands, ask how many chose letters that constitute more than a fifth of the letters in their own name.

Harrison's (1969) study of mere exposure also provides the basis for another simple classroom demonstration or student project. Randomly select 50 names from your city's telephone directory. Have one group of students rate each name for how familiar it sounds, thereby reflecting how frequently they have been exposed to it in the past. Have another group indicate how much they think they would like or dislike the person bearing each name. Harrison found that those names that were rated as more familiar were also the best liked, and those that were rated as least familiar were the least liked. In fact, the overall correlation between the two sets of ratings was a remarkable +.87.

The text notes that advertisers and politicians regularly exploit the mere exposure phenomenon. Zajonc (1970) makes the same point by citing the case of Hal Evry who has a formula for political success. You make no speeches, take no stand on the issues, in fact, you don't appear in the campaign. Still Evry's organization guarantees your name will be as familiar as Tide or Ford. How can this work? Evry mounted a saturation campaign on behalf of one unknown candidate by flooding the city with signs saying, "Three cheers for Pat Milligan." The public saw these words on billboards, in full-page newspaper ads, on letters sent through the mails. The slogan appeared for months and on election day Pat Milligan was the clear winner.

3. Mate Preferences

The materials of Demonstration 11-2 have been used over several decades in research investigating mate preferences. Male and female responses for the characteristics were reported more than 50 years ago (Hill, 1945). Buss (1989, 1990) reports outcomes utilizing these items in a massive study of 37 cultures. He tested and found good support for the evolutionary hypotheses that "good looks" and "chastity" are rated more important by males than by females and that "good financial prospect" and "ambition and industrious" are rated more important by females than by males.

For the international sample, Buss (1989) reported that both sexes rated mutual attraction-love, dependable character, emotional stability and maturity, and pleasing disposition as most important and chastity, similar religious background, and similar political background as least important.

4. Personal Want Ads and Interpersonal Attraction

Gregory Cutler (1998) has students analyze personal want ads from newspapers to illustrate motivations underlying interpersonal attraction and romance. In replicating Gonzales and Meyers (1993), students examine the traits males and females believe are important to possess in attracting companions as well as the qualities they seek in potential partners. Gonzales and Meyers identified six important content categories: attractiveness (both physical attractiveness, e.g., cute, slender and social attractiveness, e.g., classy, sophisticated); financial security (e.g., established, accomplished, professional); expressive (e.g., affectionate, caring, nurturing); instrumental (e.g., intelligent, ambitious, competitive); sincerity (e.g., considerate, faithful, dependable) and sexual references (e.g., physical contact, sex-related physical characteristics). Extending this list, Cutler's tallied references to age, religiosity, and interests such as outdoor activity as separate categories. Students examine both offers and appeals for traits as they are made by males and females. In summarizing the relevant research, the text indicates that men typically offer wealth or status and seek youth and attractiveness; women more often do the reverse.

5. Similarity Versus Complementarity

Demonstration 11-3 is adapted from K. Blau (1974). Have students check those adjectives that describe themselves. Second, they should think of a close friend and check the traits they believe describe that friend. Finally, they should do the same for someone they know but with whom they could never become close friends.

To test the similarity hypothesis, ask students to tabulate the number of traits in common between "self" and "friend" as well as the number in common between "self" and "nonfriend." Students will find they have more characteristics in common with the their "friends" than with their "nonfriends." The complementarity hypothesis would suggest that with a pair of friends one might be high and the other low on the same needs. Do the students note any traits for which the "self" and "friend" lists show one with a check and the other without a check?

Complementarity occurs when two people are high on complementary traits. Two types of complementary traits are included in the list. Assertive and meek traits are one set and protective and dependent traits are the other. The key to these traits is below. Put the key on the blackboard and have the students count the number of each type of trait on the "self" and "friend" lists and note them on the bottom of the checklist. Is there evidence supporting the complementarity hypothesis for any of the "self" and "friend" pairs? You could collect the data and perform correlational analyses to answer the questions more systematically. Does one score high on assertive and low on meek, while the other scores high on meek and low on assertive?

Key to Complementary Traits

Assertive Traits: 1, 2, 7, 18   Meek Traits: 8, 13, 14, 21

Protective Traits: 5, 9, 15   Dependent Traits: 6, 11, 16

6. Generating Interpersonal Closeness —Experimentally

Aron and associates (1997) developed a rather involving (but very enjoyable for the students) classroom exercise, which increases interpersonal closeness between pairs of students by using tasks that prompt self-disclosure. As students arrive to class, they are placed into predetermined pairings (based on responses to previously administered attitude and attachment-style questionnaires) and seated together at a moderate distance from other pairs. Each pair then carries out a series of self-disclosure and relationship building tasks or small talk and nondisclosure tasks for about 45 minutes (here is the manipulation). Finally, the students are separated and are asked to complete a post-interaction questionnaire (Aron suggests Aron et al.'s [1992] Inclusion of Other in the Self Scale). Aron found significant results suggesting those in the closeness condition forged a much more meaningful interpersonal relationship than those in the "small-talk" condition. Aron's methodology suggests getting informed consent approval from students before doing the exercise.

7. Passionate Love Scale

Demonstration 11-4 consists of Elaine Hatfield's Passionate Love Scale (PLS). Passionate love is defined as:

> A state of intense longing for union with another. Reciprocated love (union with the other) is associated with fulfillment and ecstasy. Unrequited love (separation) with emptiness; with anxiety or despair. A state of intense physiological arousal.

The scale was designed to tap the cognitive, emotional, and behavioral components of passionate love (Hatfield and Sprecher, 1985).

A. Cognitive components:
1. Preoccupation with the partner (Items 5, 19, 21)
2. Idealization of the other or of the relationship (Items 7, 9, 15)
3. Desire to know the other and be known (Items 10, 22)

B. Emotional components:
1. Attraction to other, especially sexual attraction (Items 16, 18, 29)
2. Negative feelings when things go awry (Items 1, 2, 8, 20, 28, 30)
3. Longing for reciprocity (Item 14)
4. Desire for complete union (Items 11, 12, 23, 27)
5. Physiological arousal (Items 3, 13, 17, 26)

C. Behavioral components:
1. Actions toward determining the other's feelings (Item 24)
2. Studying the other person (Item 4)
3. Service to the other (Items 6 and 25)

Hatfield and Sprecher (1985) report that PLS scores are significantly correlated with both Rubin's Love and Liking scales, satisfaction with the overall relationship, and satisfaction with the sexual aspect of the relationship. No overall gender differences were found in passionate love although men do seem to love more passionately in the early stages of the relationship. For both genders passionate love increases as the relationship goes from early states of dating to deeper levels of involvement but then levels off.

8. Attachment Styles

Demonstration 11-5a provides Hazan and Shaver's (1986) measure for retrospective assessment of childhood attachment. Demonstration 11-5b consists of Hazan and Shaver's (1987) measure of adult attachment types. The measures provide an excellent introduction to the text's discussion of close relationships.

Demonstration 11-5a measures childhood attachment style and is based on the categories outlined by Mary Ainsworth and her colleagues who suggested that the mother's sensitivity to her infant's needs during the first year of life is a crucial determinant of whether the infant forms secure attachment relationships. Ainsworth delineated three types of attachment: secure, anxious/ambivalent (insecure), and avoidant. If the mother is slow or inconsistent in responding to her infant's cries or if she regularly intrudes on the infant's desired activities, she is likely to produce an infant who cries more than usual, explores less than usual, and seems generally anxious. If, on the other hand, the mother consistently rebuffs or rejects the infant's attempt to establish physical contact, the infant may learn to avoid her. Attachment style has a profound impact on the child's developing personality. John Bowlby argues that the nature of this early relationship shapes beliefs about self and others that influence social competence and well-being throughout life.

Hazan and Shaver (1987) examined adult love relationships in terms of these early attachment styles. Demonstration 11-5b asks students to choose a category that best describes themselves presently. About half of all respondents categorize themselves as secure, and the other half are evenly split between avoidant and anxious, which parallels the distribution found in research on infant attachment types. Research suggest that secure lovers have relationships characterized by happiness, trust, and friendship. They are able to accept and support their partner despite their partner's faults. Their relationships tend to endure. Avoidant lovers are marked by fear of intimacy, emotional highs and lows, and jealousy. Anxious/ambivalent lovers experience love as involving obsession, desire for reciprocation and union, emotional highs and lows, and extreme sexual attraction and jealousy. As expected, the nature of adult attachment is correlated with early attachment style.

9. The Trust Scale

Demonstration 11-6 is the Trust Scale designed by John Rempel and John Holmes (1986). According to the authors, trust is one of the most important and necessary aspects of any close relationship. They argue that there are three fundamental elements of trust: predictability, dependability, and faith.

Predictability is the ability to foretell our partner's specific behavior including both things we like and dislike. Predictability implies consistency. At the same time, consistency is not enough for confidence to grow if the other's behavior is negative. A sense of predictability must be based on the knowledge that your partner acts in consistently positive ways.

The feeling that your partner is a dependable person is based on the emerging sense that he or she can be relied on when it counts. These judgments depend heavily on how your partner responds in situations in which you might feel hurt or rejected. Has he or she been a supportive and understanding listener in the past?

Faith enables a person to go beyond the available evidence and to feel secure that, regardless of how the partner changes, he or she will continue to be responsive and caring.

In scoring the scale, responses to items 3, 5, 6, 8, 12, 13, 15, 16, and 17 are reversed. That is, 1 is changed to 7, 2 to 6, 3 to 5, 5 to 3, 6 to 2, and 7 to 1. A score of 4 is unchanged. For a "predictability" score add 1, 3, 8, 11, 13, and 18. For "dependability," add 2, 5, 7, 9, 15, and 17. For "faith," add 4, 6, 10, 12, 14, and 16.

Rempel and Holmes suggest that an overall score exceeding 110 indicates a very trusting person. Such people feel they are involved in a very successful relationship and that their love for their partner is very strong. Even when a partner does something negative, it is not taken as evidence of a lack of love or caring. People who score below 90 fall into the low-trust category. In particular, people scoring low on faith express less love for their partner and are less inclined to see their relationship as one of mutual giving. Those scoring between 90 and 110 are described as having "hopeful" trust. They expect their partner to act in a relatively pleasant, helpful, and accepting manner, though they are less confident than the trustful group. The hopeful person is someone who wants to see the best but is perhaps afraid to believe it.

10. The Social Connection Video Series

One of the entries in the video instructional supplement (The Social Connection Video Series), entitled "Social Ostracism," addresses Kipling Williams research on people's intense need to belong and connect with others. See the Faculty Guide accompanying the video series for a program summary, pause points, and a classroom activity.

Demonstration 11-1

True or False

1. People who are very different from each other often form meaningful relationships on the basis of those differences (opposites do indeed attract).   T   F
2. One of the most powerful predictors of whether any two people will be friends is how often their paths cross (how often they see each other).   T   F
3. Prolonged thinking about an upcoming blind date will increase your chance of liking that person.   T   F
4. Familiarity with a person tends to breed contempt.   T   F
5. Most people prefer mirror images of themselves to accurate pictures.   T   F
6. As it turns out, physical attractiveness is a relatively minor factor in predicting attraction. T   F
7. Evidence suggests that the preferences we have for physically attractive people show up early in development.   T   F
8. For males, viewing pornography increases their judgments of attractiveness regarding their mate or girlfriend.   T   F
9. Falling in love, it seems, is really about knowing who you are and then finding someone to be your complement.   T   F
10. Paying someone compliments after they have recently been "dumped" by their dating partner will tend to get you nowhere. Your chances will improve if you wait.   T   F

Demonstration 11-2

Rate the following characteristics in terms of their importance to you in choosing a mate. Use the following scale:

3 = indispensable
2 = important but not indispensable
1 = desirable but not important
0 = irrelevant

___ 1. ambition and industriousness
___ 2. chastity (no previous experience in sexual intercourse)
___ 3. dependable character
___ 4. desire for home and children
___ 5. education and intelligence
___ 6. emotional stability and maturity
___ 7. favorable social status or rating
___ 8. good cook and housekeeper
___ 9. good financial prospect
___ 10. good health
___ 11. good looks
___ 12. mutual attraction—love
___ 13. pleasing disposition
___ 14. refinement, neatness
___ 15. similar education
___ 16. similar religious background
___ 17. similar political background
___ 18. sociability

Demonstration 11-3

CHECKLIST

	Self	Friend	Not Friend
1. active	___	___	___
2. aggressive	___	___	___
3. ambitious	___	___	___
4. belligerent	___	___	___
5. brave	___	___	___
6. dependent	___	___	___
7. dominant	___	___	___
8. gentle	___	___	___
9. helpful	___	___	___
10. independent	___	___	___
11. needs sympathy	___	___	___
12. obliging	___	___	___
13. passive	___	___	___
14. peaceful	___	___	___
15. protective	___	___	___
16. seeks protection	___	___	___
17. self-centered	___	___	___
18. self-confident	___	___	___
19. sociable	___	___	___
20. tactless	___	___	___
21. timid	___	___	___
22. unconventional	___	___	___

Leave Blank:

Total assert	___	___	___
Total meek	___	___	___
Total prot	___	___	___
Total dep	___	___	___

(From Instructor's manual for Secord and Backman's Social Psychology by K. Blau. Copyright © 1974 by McGraw-Hill, Inc. Used with permission of McGraw-Hill Book Company.)

Demonstration 11-4

(with permission of E. Hatfield)

In this questionnaire you will be asked to describe how you feel when you are passionately in love. Some common terms for this feeling are passionate love, infatuation, love sickness, or obsessive love.

Please think of the person whom you love most passionately <u>right now</u>. If you are not in love right now, please think of the last person you loved passionately. If you have never been in love, think of the person whom you came closest to caring for in that way. Keep this person in mind as you complete this questionnaire. (The person you choose should be of the opposite sex if you are heterosexual or of the same sex if you are homosexual.) Try to tell us how you felt at the time when your feelings were the most intense.

All of your answers will be strictly confidential. Use the following scale, placing a number in the blank to the left of each statement.

1	2	3	4	5	6	7	8	9
Not at all true				Moderately true				Definitely true

___ 1. Since I've been involved with ___, my emotions have been on a roller coaster.

___ 2. I would feel deep despair if ___ left me.

___ 3. Sometimes my body trembles with excitement at the sight of ___.

___ 4. I take delight in studying the movements and angles of ___'s body.

___ 5. Sometimes I feel I can't control my thoughts; they are obsessively on ___.

___ 6. I feel happy when I am doing something to make ___ happy.

___ 7. I would rather be with ___ than anyone else.

___ 8. I'd get jealous if I thought ___ were falling in love with someone else.

___ 9. No one else could love ___ like I do.

___ 10. I yearn to know all about ___.

___ 11. I want ___—physically, emotionally, mentally.

___ 12. I will love ___ forever.

___ 13. I melt when looking deeply into ___'s eyes.

___ 14. I have an endless appetite for affection from ___.

___ 15. For me, ___ is the perfect romantic partner.

___ 16. ___ is the person who can make me feel the happiest.

___ 17. I sense my body responding when ___ touches me.

___ 18. I feel tender toward ___.

___ 19. ___ always seems to be on my mind.

___ 20. If I were separated from ___ for a long time, I would feel intensely lonely.

___ 21. I sometimes find it difficult to concentrate on work because thoughts of ___ occupy my mind.

___ 22. I want ___ to know me—my thoughts, my fears, and my hopes.

___ 23. Knowing that _____ cares about me makes me feel complete.
___ 24. I eagerly look for signs indicating _____'s desire for me.
___ 25. If _____ were going through a difficult time, I would put away my own concerns to help him/her out.
___ 26. _____ can make me feel effervescent and bubbly.
___ 27. In the presence of _____, I yearn to touch and be touched.
___ 28. An existence without _____ would be dark and dismal.
___ 29. I possess a powerful attraction for _____.
___ 30. I get extremely depressed when things don't go right in my relationship with _____.

Demonstration 11-5a

(with permission of C. Hazan)

Read the following paragraphs and check the one that best describes your relationship with your mother when you were growing up. Then do the same for your relationship with your father.

Mother   Father

_____   _____   1. Warm/Responsive—She/he was generally warm and responsive; she/he was good at knowing when to be supportive and when to let me operate on my own; our relationship was almost always comfortable, and I have no major reservations or complaints about it.

_____   _____   2. Cold/Rejecting—She/he was fairly cold and distant, or rejecting, not very responsive; I wasn't her/his highest priority, her/his concerns were often elsewhere; it's possible that she/he would just as soon not have had me.

_____   _____   3. Ambivalent/Inconsistent—She/he was noticeably inconsistent in her/his reactions to me, sometimes warm and sometimes not; she/he had her/his own agendas which sometimes got in the way of her/his receptiveness and responsiveness to my needs; she/he definitely loved me but didn't always show it in the best way.

From Hazan, C., & Shaver, P. (1986). Parental caregiving style questionnaire. Unpublished questionnaire

Demonstration 11-5b

(with permission of C. Hazan)

Which of the following best describes your current feelings? Read the descriptions below and choose the one that best summarizes your feelings and behavior in romantic love relationships.

___ 1. Secure—I find it relatively easy to get close to others and am comfortable depending on them. I don't often worry about being abandoned or about someone getting too close to me.

___ 2. Avoidant—I am somewhat uncomfortable being close to others; I find it difficult to trust them completely, difficult to allow myself to depend on them. I am nervous when anyone gets too close, and often, love partners want me to be more intimate than I feel comfortable being.

___ 3. Anxious/Ambivalent—I find that others are reluctant to get as close as I would like. I often worry that my partner doesn't really love me or won't want to stay with me. I want to get very close to my partner, and this sometimes scares people away.

From "Love and Work: An Attachment-Theoretical Perspective," by C. Hazan and P. Shaver, 1987, Journal of Personality and Social Psychology, 52, p. 515. Copyright © 1987 by the American Psychological Association. Reprinted with permission.

Demonstration 11-6

Read each of the following statements and decide whether it is true of your relationship with your partner. Indicate how strongly you agree or disagree by choosing it in the space provided in the left-hand margin.

1 = strongly disagree
2 = moderately disagree
3 = mildly disagree
4 = neutral
5 = mildly agree
6 = moderately agree
7 = strongly agree

___ 1. I know how my partner is going to act. My partner can always be counted on to act as I expect.

___ 2. I have found that my partner is a thoroughly dependable person, especially when it comes to things that are important.

___ 3. My partner's behavior tends to be quite variable. I can't always be sure what my partner will surprise me with next.

___ 4. Though times may change and the future is uncertain, I have faith that my partner will always be ready and willing to offer me strength, come what may.

___ 5. Based on past experience I cannot, with complete confidence, rely on my partner to keep promises made to me.

___ 6. It is sometimes difficult for me to be absolutely certain that my partner will always continue to care for me; the future holds too many uncertainties and too many things can change in our relationship as times goes on.

___ 7. My partner is a very honest person and, even if my partner were to make unbelievable statements, people should feel confident that what they are hearing is the truth.

___ 8. My partner is not very predictable. People can't always be certain how my partner is going to act from one day to another.

___ 9. My partner has proven to be a faithful person. No matter who my partner was married to, she or he would never be unfaithful, even if there was absolutely no chance of being caught.

___ 10. I am never concerned that unpredictable conflicts and serious tensions may damage our relationship because I know we can weather any storm.

___ 11. I am very familiar with the patterns of behavior my partner has established, and he or she will behave in certain ways.

___ 12. If I have never faced a particular issue with my partner before, I occasionally worry that he or she won't take my feelings into account.

___ 13. Even in familiar circumstances, I am not totally certain my partner will act in the same way twice.

___ 14. I feel completely secure in facing unknown new situations because I know my partner will never let me down.

___ 15. My partner is not necessarily someone others always consider reliable. I can think of some times when my partner could not be counted on.

___ 16. I occasionally find myself feeling uncomfortable with the emotional investment I have made in our relationship because I find it hard to completely set aside my doubts about what lies ahead.

___ 17. My partner has not always proven to be trustworthy in the past, and there are times when I am hesitant to let my partner engage in activities that make me feel vulnerable.

___ 18. My partner behaves in a consistent manner.

FILMS/VIDEOS

Attachment (INS, 24 min., 1996). Examines the attachment process in infants. Uses "The Strange Situation Test" to explore the infants' development of relationships with caregivers.

Facial Disfigurement: Two Stories of Pride and Prejudice (FHS, 30 min., 1997). A BBC documentary that examines the lives of two people—an adult and child—who live with severe facial deformity. The adult woman describes the social stigma associated with disfigurement and a psychologist describes the emotional implications of facial deformity.

The Familiar Face of Love (INS, 47 min., 1989). John Money introduces the concept of a "love map"—a mental blueprint of one's ideal relationship that develops through early childhood experiences. Program examines how people fall in love and choose a mate.

Face Value: Perceptions of Beauty (FHS, 26 min., 1994). Considers whether perceptions of attractiveness are universal and biological, or rooted in time and fashion.

Friendship (PSU, 30 min., 1989). Examines determinants of attraction including proximity and similarity. Suggests that strong friendships combine mutual self-disclosure, the expression of compassion toward one another, and the willingness to commit time and energy to the union.

Gender and Relationships (INS, 30 min., 1990). Considers the factors that influence peoples' feelings of love, affection, and sexuality. Presents recent research findings on the nature of love, sexual orientation, and gender differences in sexual attitudes, motives, and behaviors.

Looks! How They Affect Your Life (MTI, 51 min., 1984). An excellent video on the importance of appearance in our personal and social lives. Reviews basic research findings.

Love, Lust, and Marriage: Why We Stay, Why We Stray (ABC, 55 min. 1997). This ABC John Stossels' special, broadcast October 21, 1997, explores many aspects of social attraction including three stages of human love: lust, infatuation, and attachment. The evolutionary significance of physical beauty and of marriage are presented as are four major predictors of divorce. Order by calling 1-800-913-3434.

The Secrets of Staying Together (ABC, 18 min., 1993). This ABC 20/20 report looks at John Gottman's research on signs of failing marriages. The results are somewhat surprising and very interesting to students; many of whom are asking marriage-related questions to themselves for the first time.

Sex and Marriage (INS, 30 min., 1994). Explores differences in customs relating to sex and marriage across different cultures. Explains that marriage customs often evolved for economic reasons.

CHAPTER 12
ALTRUISM: HELPING OTHERS

Why Do We Help?
    Social Exchange
    Helping as Disguised Self-Interest
    Empathy as a Source of Genuine Altruism
    Social Norms
    The Reciprocity Norm
    The Social-Responsibility Norm
    Evolutionary Psychology
    Kin Protection
    Reciprocity
    Comparing and Evaluating Theories of Altruism

When Will We Help?
    Situational Influences: Number of Bystanders
    Noticing
    Interpreting
    Assuming Responsibility
    Situational Influences: Helping When Someone Else Does
    Situational Influences: Time Pressures
    Personal Influences: Feelings
    Guilt
    Negative Mood
    Exceptions to the Feel Bad-Do Good Scenario
    Feel Good, Do Good
    Personal Influences: Personality Traits
    Personal Influences: Religiosity

Whom Do We Help?
    Gender
    Similarity

How Can We Increase Helping?
    Undoing the Restraints on Helping
    Reduce Ambiguity, Increase Responsibility
    Guilt and Concern For Self-Image
    Socializing Altruism
    Teaching Moral Inclusion

Modeling Altruism
Attributing Helpful Behavior to Altruistic Motives
Learning About Altruism
Personal Postscript: Taking Social Psychology Into Life

LECTURE AND DISCUSSION IDEAS

1. Introducing Altruism

Case studies in helping can provide a good introduction to the literature on altruism. The last motion segment on the McGraw-Hill Social Psychology Videodisc/Videotape presents CBS news footage of the rescue of Jessica McClure (2:05 min.). The text includes a photograph of the event and suggests Jessica's rescuers were driven by a sense of social responsibility.

Jessica's rescue occurred in October 1987. A Pew Research Center poll after Princess Diana's death found that in the last decade only Jessica's rescue rivaled the Paris car accident in worldwide attention (Babineck, 1997). Sympathetic observers from around the world inundated the little girl with homemade gifts, cards, and cash. The money, estimated at $1 million or more, has been placed in a trust fund awaiting her 25th birthday. Today Jessica makes A's and B's in school, plays the piano and French Horn, and loves to rollerskate. Her parents, Chip and Missy McClure (portrayed in the videoclip), divorced in 1990. Rescuer Robert O'Donnell shot and killed himself in 1995. His brother Ricky reported that O'Donnell's life "fell apart" because of the stress of the rescue, the attention it created, and the anticlimactic return to everyday life.

Additional case studies to present in class include the annual awardees of the Carnegie Hero Fund Commission. Established in 1904 by Andrew Carnegie, the commission has recognized more than 8,000 acts of heroism since its founding. In addition to a medal, awardees receive $2,500. Among the 1997 recipients were Patrick O'Toole, 47, of Wall Township, New Jersey, who pulled Linda Johntry out of her wheelchair just before it was hit by an oncoming train, Shannon "Shane" Williams, 28, of Wauseon, Ohio, who pulled two people out of a burning plane moments before it exploded at the airport he managed in Wauseon, and Randy Joe Boswell, 33, of Wilmington, North Carolina, who drowned after successfully pushing an 11-year-old girl toward shore in a strong Atlantic Ocean current off Kure Beach, North Carolina After presenting the case studies, ask students to define "altruism" and reflect on what motivates it.

2. Models of Helping

How do we decide when to offer aid? Brickman and his colleagues (1982) suggest that whether help is offered as well as the form it takes is largely dependent on how we answer two questions. First, who is responsible for the problem? Second, who is responsible for the solution? The answers to these two questions form the basis for four models of helping.

In the moral model, actors are held responsible both for problems and solutions and are believed to need proper motivation. Historically, we have viewed criminality and alcoholism in this way: "You got yourself into this mess, now get yourself out." Helpers simply exhort people to assume responsibility for their problems and to work their own way out.

In the compensatory model, people are not seen as responsible for problems but they are responsible for solutions. Jesse Jackson once stated, "You are not responsible for being down, but you are responsible for getting up." People need power and the helper may provide resources or opportunities that the recipients deserve. Nonetheless, the responsibility for using this assistance rests with the recipient.

In the medical model, individuals are seen as neither responsible for the problem or for the solution. Helpers say, "You are ill, and I will try to make you better." This approach, of course, characterizes the health care system in all modern societies. Helping involves providing treatment and care.

In the enlightenment model, actors are seen as responsible for problems but as unable or unwilling to provide solutions. They are viewed as needing discipline. Helping means earning their trust and giving them guidance. Alcoholics Anonymous explicitly requires new recruits both to take responsibility for their past history of drinking (rather than blaming it on something or someone else) and to admit that it is beyond their power to control the drinking without the help of God and the community of ex-alcoholics.

Brickman suggests that the wrong choice of model in a given situation will undermine effective helping and coping. For example, the potential deficiency of the moral model is that it can lead its adherents to hold victims of leukemia and rape responsible for their fate. Those advocating the compensatory model may alienate the people they help. The recipients may come to see themselves as having to solve problems they did not create, thereby developing a rather negative, even paranoid view of the world. The deficiency of the medical model is that it fosters dependency, and people may lose the ability to do even something that they once did well. The possible drawback of the enlightenment model is that it can lead to a fanatical or obsessive concern with certain problems and a reconstruction of people's entire lives around the behaviors or the relationships designed to help them deal with these problems.

3. A Taxonomy of Helping

Pearce and Amato (1980) propose a classification scheme that categorizes helping along three important dimensions. You can use the taxonomy to introduce the literature on altruism. First, helping can be rated in terms of the degree to which it is planned and formal (e.g., volunteering to serve as a "Big Brother" or "Big Sister") versus spontaneous and informal (e.g., helping a secretary by picking papers she has dropped). Helping can also vary according to the severity of the problem (e.g., giving change to someone for a bus ride versus giving aid to someone in a serious automobile accident). Finally, Pearce and Amato argue that helping can vary in terms of whether it involves the indirect giving of assistance (e.g., donating to charity), or doing something directly to help a person in need (e.g., helping a child learn to ride a bicycle).

You might ask your students to list the different kinds of help they have received and given to friends, acquaintances, and strangers in the last three months. Ask for volunteers to share their answers. On the basis of college students' responses to the question, McGuire (1994) created an alternative classification scheme of helping. She describes four kinds of assistance that include (1) casual helping—doing a small favor for an acquaintance such as lending the person a pen; (2) substantial personal helping—helping a friend move into a new apartment; (3) emotional helping—providing emotional or personal support to a friend, such as listening to his or her personal problems; and (4) emergency helping—giving assistance to a stranger who is a victim in an automobile accident. (Helping with a homework assignment or schoolwork was the most frequently mentioned assistance, classified as a form of "casual helping.")

4. Evolutionary Psychology and Kin Selection

Kin selection is the idea that evolution has selected altruism toward one's close relatives to enhance the survival of mutually shared genes. The opening lecture/discussion of Chapter 5 discusses evolutionary theory and poses several questions, which illustrate how specific acts of helping can reflect concern for gene survival. If you did not use them earlier, you can do so now.

5. The Reciprocity Norm

Cialdini (1993) provides wonderful illustrations of the reciprocity norm that you can cite in class. For example, he describes the university professor who sent Christmas cards to perfect strangers. Holiday cards came pouring back from people who had never met or heard of him. The majority never even inquired into his identity.

Sometimes the reciprocity rule is used to exploit us. For example, many people who receive free samples in the supermarket find it difficult to return only the toothpicks or the empty cups. Instead they buy the product even if they did not particularly like it.

Cialdini suggests that part of President Lyndon Johnson's initial success in getting so many programs through Congress was due to many legislators owing him favors. In contrast, Jimmy Carter's difficulty may have been partially due to his being a newcomer to whom no one was indebted.

The Hare Krishna Society's effective use of reciprocity led to huge increases in contributions. In airports and other public places, they approach the target person with a gift—a book, a magazine, but most often a flower. The unsuspecting passers-by are under no circumstances allowed to return them. Only after the Krishna member has brought the force of reciprocation to bear, is the target asked to provide a contribution to the society.

6. Egoism Versus Altruism

In <u>The Brighter Side of Human Nature,</u> Alfie Kohn identifies several dangers in viewing people as primarily selfish and seeing altruism as rare, as associated only with that one odd self-sacrificing individual we know, or with the short list of Carnegie heroes we read about annually.

First, argues Kohn, it does each of us an injustice by putting part of human nature beyond our reach. In <u>The Plague,</u> Camus deliberately has his narrator refrain from praising the noble efforts of the residents of the disease-infected town because "by attributing overimportance to praiseworthy actions one may, by implication, be paying indirect but potent homage to the worse side of human nature. For this attitude implies that such actions shine out as rare exceptions, while callousness and apathy are the general rule."

Second, to dwell on saintliness communicates the reassuring message that a few larger-than-life characters have become specialists in helping others. The effect may be to relieve us of the responsibility of having to do the same. We may call them exemplary but they are not models for us. Kohn cites one experiment, which showed that subjects who read about people who did an exceptional amount of volunteer work subsequently rated themselves as slightly less altruistic than did those who read about individuals who were less helpful.

Finally, altruism may be turned into an all-or-nothing proposition. If our private definition of the word ends with: "See 'Mother Teresa,'" and if we are sure we could never be like her, then we may comfortably practice a lifestyle of self-aggrandizement. In effect, our understanding becomes a self-fulfilling prophecy: If I know altruism is not within my reach, why bother to attempt to act that way or to cultivate it in my children?

Malka Drucker also points to the need to see the rescuers of Jews in Nazi Germany as ordinary human beings. To treat them as normal is to argue that altruism is accessible to anyone—saints and sinners alike. "It tells you that you don't have to be Mother Teresa," says Drucker. "You don't have to be a better person than you already are in order to do good." Turning the rescuers into paragons lets the rest of humanity off the hook.

7. Volunteerism

A recent Gallup poll indicates that approximately 100 million Americans are involved in some sort of voluntary helping behavior on a regular basis. What motivates them? In researching that question, Snyder (1992) reports that volunteering can serve four primary functions. (1) Volunteerism is <u>value-expressive</u> when it reflects the personality characteristics and convictions that are central to the volunteer's self-concept ("I am concerned about people less fortunate than me.") (2) Volunteerism is socially-adjustive when it is motivated by a response to social pressure ("People I am close to want me to volunteer.") (3) Volunteer work is ego-defensive when it helps volunteers deal with inner conflicts and anxieties concerning their personal worth and competence ("Doing volunteer work relieves me of some of the guilt over being more fortunate than others.") (4) Volunteer work serves a knowledge function when it provides the volunteer with the opportunity to learn new skills and competencies or improve existing ones ("Volunteering allows me to gain a new perspective on things.")

Omoto and Snyder (1990) studied volunteers who helped people with AIDS and found that those who were motivated by a value-expressive function showed greater willingness to have direct contact with AIDS patients than were those motivated by socially-adjustive or ego-defensive functions. However, people whose initial motivations were to improve their own self-esteem and to develop personally were more likely to remain volunteers than were those who were motivated by their desire to help others. Snyder (1992) suggests this may have been because those who helped for selfish reasons had fewer illusions about the unpleasant aspects of helping AIDS patients. He states, "Ironically it may be those volunteers who themselves are motivated by the most selfish of motivations who, in the long run, end up offering the greatest benefits to other people and making the most altruistic contributions to society."

8. Good Samaritan Laws

Most European countries have "good Samaritan" laws that make it a crime not to summon aid or help someone in serious distress (Benac, 1997). These laws were operative in the investigation of photographers at the scene of Princess Diana's car crash in August 1997. In contrast, only a handful of states require people to help strangers in an emergency. Some legal experts suggest the difference is partly due to cultural differences in values in which American individualism contrasts with European social solidarity.

Vermont, Minnesota, and Wisconsin are among the states that have the strongest laws but even these laws are narrowly written, infrequently used, and when applied, carry light punishment for violation. For example, in Vermont, failure to help someone "exposed to grave physical harm" is punishable by a fine of up to $100. The Minnesota law makes it a petty misdemeanor to fail to help someone at the scene of an emergency who "is exposed to or has suffered grave physical harm." Violation of Wisconsin's law carried one of the most severe penalties—up to 30 days in jail and a $500 fine. However, the law has been difficult to enforce, partly because it includes broad exceptions.

Ask your students if they think helping should be compelled through legislation? R. Lance Shotland (1985) discusses some of the potential benefits as well as problems with such legislation. It might reduce diffusion of responsibility by making bystanders realize they will be held personally responsible for their inaction. Furthermore, it could tip the balance toward intervention if bystanders find the situation ambiguous. They might feel it safer to guard against a penalty by intervening rather than walking away.

Shotland argues that these benefits will come only if the duty-to-assist legislation can be strongly enforced. Clearly that has been difficult. Often ambiguity does surround those in distress. People fear intervening on the wrong side of a dispute, they may wonder what they're getting into when they pull off the road, and they worry about doing the wrong thing for someone who has been injured. Should a witness be penalized for an innocent mistake, and how can it be distinguished from deliberate shirking of civil duty? The laws also have an implicit time frame within which the authorities must be notified. In the famous case of Kitty Genovese, one person called the police after considerable soul-searching about what action to take. His response was too late. Should he have been prosecuted? Could it ever be determined, without his cooperation, how soon he knew of the attack? Is it possible that witnesses may actually be discouraged from reporting information because they fear legal reprisal?

9. "The Sweet Smell of Helping"

You can extend the text's discussion of feelings and helping with Baron's (1997) interesting study on the relationship between odors and helping. Baron found that passersby in a large shopping mall were significantly more likely to assist a stranger by retrieving a dropped pen or providing change for a dollar when these helping opportunities occurred in the presence of a pleasant fragrance (e.g., baking cookies, roasting coffee). Findings further suggested that the effects of pleasant odors on positive social behavior resulted at least in part from odor-induced increases in positive affect.

10. The Altruistic Personality

Samuel and Pearl Oliners' (1988) The Altruistic Personality: Rescuers of Jews in Nazi Europe reported that rescuers were motivated by three primary factors. About 11 percent were motivated primarily by a commitment to the justice principle. These people had strong beliefs about how others ought to be treated. In the process of helping they often also became strongly attached to those they rescued. Fifty-two percent were motivated by social norms. Helping was seen as obligatory by friends, family, or church. In offering help they did what they felt was expected. The remaining 37 percent were moved by empathy, by the suffering of those whose lives were in danger. It was not first of all principle nor social obligation that motivated this group but their feelings of connection to the victim.

11. Bystander "Apathy?"

Bring to class a recent newspaper report, which either involves people's willingness or unwillingness to help and ask students to explain their behavior. Or, read the following brief report of the Kitty Genovese murder from the New York Times, March 27, 1964, and ask why people were unwilling to help.

> For more than half an hour 38 respectable, law abiding citizens in Queens watched a killer stalk and stab a woman in three separate attacks in Key Gardens.
>
> Twice the sound of their voices and the sudden glow of their bedroom lights interrupted him and frightened him off. Each time he returned, sought her out and stabbed her again. Not one person telephoned the police during the assault; one witness called after the woman was dead.

Few will mention the possible role of situational factors. Most will view another's willingness or unwillingness to help in terms of dispositions, such as apathy or callousness. Research on the importance of situational factors can then be presented.

You might also contrast the Kitty Genovese case with that of Reginald Denny in 1992.

> On April 29, 1992, during one of the worst civil disturbances in U.S. history, Reginald Denny was forced to stop his truck at an intersection in south central Los Angeles. Four African-American youths forced him out of his truck and began to beat him mercilessly. He was near death when four strangers, also all African Americans, risked their lives to come to his aid. Having watched the scene broadcast live on television, they had left the safety of their homes and driven to the scene. Fighting off his assailants, they lifted Denny into the cab of his truck and brought him to the hospital. Doctors reported that had he arrived five minutes later, he would have died.

In addition to asking why Denny was helped, ask your students what is the more normal human response, nonintervention or helping?

12. Cause of Death: Uncertain(ty)

Bob Cialdini (2001; Chapter 4 p. 111–119. Also available in Annual Editions–Social Psychology 01/02, see Chapter 1 references) revisits the infamous Kitty Genovese story mentioned in the text and tries to explain it using social psychological principles. Cialdini makes a compelling argument regarding both the power of diffusion of responsibility and, more interesting, the power of uncertainty. Cialdini discusses how people look for social proof and the notion of pluralistic ignorance. Cialdini concludes with a bit of advice regarding how the reader can help remove uncertainty and increase feelings of responsibility if they ever find themselves in a situation requiring help. This brief essay is easily read and very interesting. Some possible discussion questions include: Why do people, when they first here stories like the Kitty Genovese story, always tend to conclude the culprit is callousness on the part of the individual bystanders? Are you aware of any stories where help was needed and people were present but help was not offered? Based on the research in Chapter 12, what could Kitty Genovese have done to improve her chances of getting help?

13. Bound and Gagged

One of the selections in the McGraw-Hill Videotape of Candid Camera Classics in Social Psychology is entitled "Bound and Gagged." This four-minute clip shows Allen Funt tied up to an office chair and blindfolded sitting in an office suite. Several lunch-delivery companies are then called to delivery some food to this office. The first three delivery-men offer little to no help, but finally on the fourth try the person tries to offer genuine help. Funt helps to confuse the delivery-men about the proper interpretation they should make (Darley and Latane's second step) by conversing with them in a usual manner. This clip can easily lead to a discussion on the misinterpretation of helping situations, bystander apathy, and helping when it violates norms.

14. Socializing Altruism

Alfie Kohn's (1988) recommendations for raising a helpful child complement the text's treatment of socializing altruism. Kohn makes the following six suggestions:

1. Focus on the positive. Telling a child what not to do is insufficient. One must teach the child how (and why) to help.

2. Explain the reason. Children should hear why altruism is desirable as well as why aggression is not. For example, "When you share your toys, Josh gets to play, too, and that makes him feel good."

3. Set an example. Especially before three years of age, children are strongly influenced by adult models. In general, showing how to be helpful is more effective than telling.

4. Let them help. Taking care of a younger sibling or a pet enables the child to experience what it means to be prosocial. Children should have the opportunity to practice what they've learned about being sensitive to others.

5. Promote a prosocial self-image. Children should be taught to think of themselves as caring people even though their prosocial tendencies were initially shaped by a parent.

6. Be a warm, empathetic parent. Children who form a secure attachment to their parents are likely to feel that the world is a safe place. They are also likely to feel good about themselves and well-disposed toward other people. Being responsive to children's needs, including their occasional preference for distance from you, is also important.

15. Responses to Being Helped

Most of the research in social psychology on altruism has been on the giver rather than the receiver of help. The text reflects this emphasis in discussing a variety of factors that influence a person's willingness to help.

How does the recipient respond to the assistance he or she is given? With gratitude? Research indicates that is not always the case. Kenneth Gergen and his associates (Gergen et al., 1975) conducted a cross-cultural study of those receiving aid. While the researchers found no major differences among the countries in recipients' evaluations of the donor, subjects were found to prefer donors who expected them to repay the aid. A greater liking was found for poor than wealthy donors, and subjects also indicated a greater desire to repay the poor than the wealthy donor, even when repayment was not demanded.

Why might people dislike free gifts? First, we may prefer relationships, which are equitable, in which giving and receiving are in balance. Then, too, we may suspect that the donor who apparently wants nothing in return is attempting to manipulate or use us in ways not clear at the moment.

Receiving aid may also have an effect on one's level of self-esteem (Fisher, Nadler, & Whitcher-Alagna, 1982). Help from another may make one feel incompetent; that is, the recipient's feelings might be, "I should have been able to do it myself." When aid lowers recipients' self-esteem, they are more likely to dislike the aid and the donor and to avoid seeking such help again. Fisher and Nadler (1974) found that when the donor is very similar to oneself, receiving aid is likely to reduce one's self-esteem. Being tutored by a fellow student can be deflating; being tutored by an expert is not.

How recipients respond to help is also influenced by their present level of self-esteem. Nadler, Altman, and Fisher (1979) manipulated subjects' self-esteem by providing positive or negative evaluations of their personalities. Later, when the subjects performed poorly on a laboratory task, their partners either provided help or did not. When the recipients' self-esteem was high, the aid made them feel worse; in contrast, when their self-esteem was low, the aid made them feel better, as if the support showed that others care.

Discussion Questions:

1. What implications does this research have for the giving of international government aid?
2. Does the research have implications for social welfare policies established by the government?
3. Have you ever received a gift that made you feel uncomfortable? Are you suspicious of businesses that offer free gifts?

16. Popular Sources for Additional Classroom Material

Darley, J. M., & Latane, B. (1968, December). When will people help in a crisis? Psychology Today, p. 54–57, 70–71. The classic work on the bystander phenomenon is presented. The authors describe their decision tree to explain conditions under which a person will intervene.

Fogelman, E. (1994). Conscience and courage: Rescuers of Jews during the Holocaust. New York: Doubleday Anchor. What prompted a small number of people during World War II to risk their lives to save the Jews? Some were motivated by deeply held moral values. Others' motivation was mainly emotional and based on personal attachments or identification with the victim.

Hunt, M. (1990). The compassionate beast. New York: William Morrow. Describes evidence for the human side of humankind. In addition to considering the biological and social roots of prosocial behavior, Hunt examines how altruism is socialized and suggests specific strategies for increasing it.

Kohn, A. (1990). <u>The brighter side of human nature</u>. New York: Basic Books. Suggests that we need to revise our assumption that people are innately selfish and aggressive. Examines the work on prosocial behavior giving special attention to the literature on empathy.

Monroe, K. R. (1996). <u>The heart of altruism: Perceptions of a common humanity</u>. Princeton, NJ: Princeton University Press. Discusses altruism from a variety of perspectives. Concludes that altruists view themselves as strongly linked to others through a shared humanity.

Rose, H., & Rose, S. (Eds.). (2000). <u>Alas, poor Darwin: Arguments against evolutionary psychology</u>. New York: Harmony Books. A collection of 14 essays from noted authors such as Stephen Jay Gould attacking the extrapolation of evolutionary principles into the realm of social behavior.

Schroeder, D. A., Penner, L. A., Dovidio, J. F., & Piliavin, J. A. (1995). <u>The psychology of helping and altruism</u>. New York: McGraw-Hill, Inc. Provides both an overview and integration of the research literature on prosocial action. Considers when and why people help as well as the characteristics of the prosocial personality.

DEMONSTRATION AND PROJECT IDEAS

1. Helping Quiz

Demonstration 12-1 may be used to stimulate student interest and to show the value of helping research. The correct answers to most of these questions are not obvious, apart from research. As the chapter will reveal, statements 3, 4, and 8 are true; the rest are false. Naturally, this demonstration will be most effective BEFORE students have read the chapter.

2. Defining Altruism

Chapter 12 suggests that the definition of altruism is debatable, because seemingly self-giving acts may have an underlying selfish motive. Demonstration 12-2 invites students to classify various acts as altruistic or not. On each item ask people to explain their answer. See if from their agreements and disagreements you can fashion a <u>definition</u> of altruism, and a list of some of the <u>motives</u> that might underlie helping behavior.

3. Revisiting the Fundamental Attribution Error

One of social psychology's contributions to the study of altruism has been the identification of situational influences on helping, which are often ignored or underestimated. As the text indicates, Darley and Batson's (1973) Good Samaritan study revealed the powerful effect of time pressures. Not reported in the text was their contrasting finding that religious orientation, a dispositional variable, had no effect on helping rates.

Before students read the text describe Darley and Batson's study, clearly identifying time pressure and religious orientation as the critical independent variables. To assess the latter, the researchers used measures of intrinsic versus extrinsic religiousness. For intrinsics, religion is an end in itself (e.g., "My religious beliefs are what really lie behind my whole approach to life"); for extrinsics, religion is a means to some other end (e.g., "A primary reason for my interest in religion is that my church is a congenial social activity").

Ask students to predict any difference the levels of each independent variable had on helping rates. Consistent with the fundamental attribution error, they are likely to predict that the dispositional variable had greater impact than the situational. However, results indicated otherwise. Sixty-three percent of participants who were not in hurry stopped to assist while only 10 percent of those in a hurry offered help. Religious orientation had no significant impact on helping rates.

4. The Reward-Cost Model of Helping

Kenneth Kerber (1980) suggests a classroom test of the reward-cost model of helping that can also be used to demonstrate the complementary nature of correlational and experimental research. Demonstration 12-3 provides materials for a) an analysis of the correlation between willingness to help and perceived rewards and costs, and b) a 2 × 2 manipulation of the rewards (other person willing to return the favor or not) and costs (test tomorrow or Thursday morning). Since each student should be given only one of the five versions of Demonstration 12-3, using all five versions requires a fairly large class. The data are probably best analyzed between class sessions.

5. Smile and the World Smiles with You: The Reciprocity Norm

Efforts to replicate Hinsz and Tomhave's (1991) findings can provide the basis for an interesting student project. Student pairs went into public settings (shopping centers, grocery stores, library, sidewalks) and simply observed how passers-by responded to a smile or a frown. The student displayer walked about 5 feet in front of the coding student and made eye contact with a single oncoming subject. The displayer then signaled the student following (e.g. a slight wave of the hand from the wrist down or an arm held behind the body) to observe the respondent's facial expression.

Over half the subjects responded to a smile with a smile, whereas few subjects responded to a frown with a frown. The authors suggest that the reciprocity norm may govern responses to smiles: We should respond in degree and kind to the rewarding actions, in this case, greetings, of others. In contrast, a frown on the face of an approaching person does not serve as a form of greeting but generally represents unfriendly or negative affect. Frowns occur rarely in brief encounters and have ambiguous implications for the observer. Understandably, passers-by seemed to respond to a frown with a look of bewilderment. Additional findings indicated that females were more likely to smile than males, and people were more likely to smile at a female than at a male.

6. Are Helpful People Happy?

A classroom exercise suggested by Bernard Rimland addresses that question. Distribute a sheet of paper to each student and ask the class to list 10 people they know well, using only initials or nicknames. Beside each name the students should write an "H" if the person tends to be happy or an "N" if not. Then they should go through the list a second time writing "S" for selfish and "U" for unselfish. Rimland describes selfishness as a stable tendency to devote one's time and resources to one's own interest and welfare and an unwillingness to inconvenience oneself for others.

Draw a 4 × 4 table on the board with happy/unhappy on one axis and selfish-unselfish on the other. Ask students to reproduce the table on their own sheets and count the number of people among the 10 names that fall into each cell. Then have each student read off the number in each cell and tally on the chalkboard. The results will be dramatic. The happy/selfish cell will have few cases; virtually all the happy people will be in the "unselfish" cell. Ask students if they know anybody who is both selfish and happy. Few will. As Rimland points out, the finding may represent an interesting paradox: selfish people are those whose activities are devoted to bringing themselves happiness. As judged by others, however, these selfish people are far less likely to be happy than those who are devoted to making others happy.

Alan Feingold has suggested that selflessness and happiness may be associated because they are both socially desirable characteristics; we may see people we like as possessing both traits and those we dislike as having neither. Using self-rating scales of happiness and selflessness, Feingold reported a positive correlation between the two variables for males, but not for females.

7. Analysis of Charity Appeals

Appeals for donations are frequently placed in popular magazines by charitable organizations. You might collect several (or have students do the same) for presentation in class. Ask students what motive is assumed by each appeal and how effective they suspect it would be.

For example, on my campus a collage of posters was recently used to attract blood donors. Read the following in class and ask, "What does each assume about motives for helping?... Is it an effective appeal?"

1. "It is one of the most beautiful compensations of this life that no man can sincerely help another without helping himself"—Ralph Waldo Emerson. Donate blood.
2. Donate Blood! It's an Uplifting Experience!
3. Hug a Blood Donor! (A giant teddy bear wears a sweatshirt with the words, "We Care.") Please donate.
4. Stand Out in the Crowd. Give Blood.
5. Don't Be Chicken! Donate Blood.
6. Blood Is Like a Parachute...If It's Not There When You Need It, Chances Are You Will Never Need It Again. Donate Blood.
7. They Operate on Him Tomorrow. You Should Be There. (Closeup of a young child sitting on a hospital bed) Blood. Give a Little So Someone Can Live.
8. (Profile of a smiling, middle-aged African American Male holding up a small card with a "B-" printed on it) We Need All Types. Somewhere, Someone Is Counting on You. Please Give Blood Regularly.
9. How Do You Tell a 4-Year-Old She May Never Be 5? (Closeup of a particularly attractive young girl) Blood. Give a Little So Someone May Live.
10. Give Blood Today. Someone You Love May Need It Tomorrow.

8. Field Experiment on Helping

Many of the experiments described in Chapter 12 lend themselves to replication, or better yet, to having their methods applied to some <u>new</u> question proposed by the class. For example, are some types of people, some situations, or some types of appeals, more likely to elicit help (e.g., when papers are dropped)?

Specifically, students could be placed into groups and assigned to replicate one of the five ways (leave out the United Way measure) Levine, Simon, Brase, & Sorenson (1994) measured helping. Levine et al. looked at helping across 36 cities, but your students could compare different areas of the same city, different times of day, or even differences in the person needing help. Different groups could be assigned different measures. Groups should include at least three people (victim, recorder, and organizer).

9. Empathy Questionnaire

Demonstration 12-4 is the Empathy Questionnaire designed by Mark Davis (1980). Davis suggests that empathy is a complex multi-dimensional concept that includes both the ability to assume the perspective of another and emotional reactivity.

The 28-item measure consists of four seven-item subscales. Questions 1-7 constitute the "fantasy" scale and tap the tendency to transpose oneself imaginatively into fictional situations. To calculate scores, students should reverse their scores on items 3 and 6. That is, change 0 to 5, 1 to 4, 2 to 3, 3 to 2, 4 to 1, and 5 to 0. Then they should add the scores on the seven items for their total "fantasy" score.

Questions 8-14 compose the "perspective-taking" scale and reflect an ability to shift perspectives, to step "outside the self" when dealing with other people. Scores on 9 and 12 should be reversed, and then the scores on questions 8 through 14 added.

Questions 15-21 reflect the "empathic concern" scale and assess the degree to which the respondent experiences feelings of warmth, compassion, and concern for another. Items 16, 19, and 20 should be reversed, and then responses for all seven items added.

Questions 22-28 measure "personal distress"—the respondent's own feelings of fear, apprehension, and discomfort at witnessing the negative experiences of others. Items 25 and 28 should be reversed, and then the scores on the seven items totaled.

Davis reported the mean score for undergraduates on the fantasy scale was 18.75 for women and 15.73 for men, which is a significant difference. Significant differences were also obtained on the other three subscales. Mean scores for women and men, respectively, were as follows: perspective-taking scale, 17.96 vs. 16.78; empathic concern scale, 21.67 vs. 19.04; and personal distress scale, 12.18 versus 9.46.

How does empathy develop? One idea is that early in development the child cannot differentiate well between the self and others. When seeing another in distress, the child typically experiences it as his or her own distress. With time, however, this "empathic distress" gives way to what is called "sympathetic concern." The child exhibits feelings of compassion and sympathy for the person in trouble. One important factor contributing to this shift is the development of role-taking skills in the child. Davis suggests that the negative correlation between the "perspective-taking" and "personal distress" scale supports this developmental perspective. That is, with adults, greater perspective-taking tendencies seem to be associated with less personal distress and more concern for the other.

10. The Social Connection Video Series

One of the entries in the video instructional supplement (The Social Connection Video Series), entitled "The Bystander Effect," presents Darley and Latane's classic research on the bystander phenomenon. Another entry, entitled "Understanding Genocide," deals with reconciliation and forgiveness, topics central to altruism. See the Faculty Guide accompanying the video series for program summaries, pause points, and classroom activities.

Demonstration 12-1

True or False

1. If you are going to offer something in return for a donation, you'd better make it something people want or you might as well offer nothing at all.   T   F
2. Today, there are virtually no social scientists who believe genuine altruism really exists.   T   F
3. Our tendency to help, it appears, varies based on our judgments of how personally responsible the victim is for their situation.   T   F
4. Many psychologists believe that a substantial amount of the helping behavior we see can be accounted for by evolutionary theory.   T   F
5. After much research, it is now very clear: As the number of people who see a person in distress increases, the likelihood the person will be helped increases.   T   F
6. When requesting help at an emergency, it is best to ask people in general to call 911 as opposed to singling one person out and assigning that responsibility.   T   F
7. We tend to shed our feelings of responsibility and forego helping once we've seen someone else offer help in an emergency.   T   F
8. Being in a hurry decreases our tendency to help.   T   F
9. Compared to a neutral mood, adults experiencing a mild negative mood are less likely to help.   T   F
10. Contrary to the stereotype, religious people are less likely to do charitable volunteering than non-religious people.   T   F
11. Surprisingly, a person's decision to help others has little to do with the perceived similarity between themselves and the person in need of help.   T   F

Demonstration 12-2
Bolt & Myers
©McGraw-Hill, 1999

Is It Altruism?

Yes   Maybe   No

___ ___ ___ 1. Bob, a college student, spends three hours per week as a "Big Brother" to an eight-year-old boy whose father has died.

___ ___ ___ 2. Mary, an attorney, stops to aid the victim of an automobile accident.

___ ___ ___ 3. Bill notifies the bookstore manager when he sees a college student attempt to shoplift some notebook paper.

___ ___ ___ 4. John, a firefighter, rescues an elderly woman from an apartment building fire and is overcome by smoke, but later receives a hero's award.

___ ___ ___ 5. Millie anonymously donates $500 to a local charity.

___ ___ ___ 6. Sam attempts to save his three-year-old from drowning.

___ ___ ___ 7. Sally buys a raffle ticket from a charitable organization.

___ ___ ___ 8. Jim agrees to donate his eyes for transplant in the event of his death.

___ ___ ___ 9. Jill, a college student, gives a pint of blood in exchange for $7.50.

___ ___ ___ 10. Wanda, a police officer, arrests a bank robber who is fleeing the scene of the crime.

___ ___ ___ 11. Believing that "those who give shall receive great blessings in return," Ralph and Doris contribute their family's monthly paycheck to their church fund drive.

Demonstration 12-3

One evening, just as you settle down to study for an important test, an acquaintance from down the hall in your dormitory enters your room. He/she asks you for assistance with some homework, which is due the next morning. It turns out that you have already taken the same course in which your acquaintance needs assistance.

Indicate how much help you would give the person who needs assistance by circling the appropriate number.

1	2	3	4	5	6	7
no help at all						very much help

When helping a person, we sometimes experience <u>rewards</u> as a result of our behavior. For example, we may feel better about ourselves, we may receive thanks from the person we help, we may receive praise for our behavior, we may receive assistance at a later time from the person we helped.

Indicate the rewards, which are likely to come from helping in the situation described above.

1	2	3	4	5	6	7
no rewards at all						very high rewards

When helping a person, we sometimes experience <u>costs</u> as a result of our behavior. For example, we may lose valuable time, we may receive no thanks for our help, we may have to expend a lot of effort.

Indicate the costs, which are likely to come from helping in the situation described above.

1	2	3	4	5	6	7
no costs at all						very high costs

(From Kerber, K. W., Rewards, costs, and helping: A demonstration of the complementary nature of experimental and correlational research. <u>Teaching of Psychology</u>, 1980, *7*, p. 50–52. Adapted with the permission of the author.)

Demonstration 12-3

It is 8 o'clock on a Monday evening, and you have just begun to study for a very important examination. The examination is scheduled for tomorrow morning at 10 o'clock. You need an excellent performance in order to make up for a poor showing on the previous test in this class.

Just as soon as you settle down to work, an acquaintance from down the hall enters your room and asks for assistance with his/her mathematics homework, which is due the next morning. You took the same mathematics course last semester.

Before responding to his/her request, you ask if your acquaintance will do a favor for you in return for your help. Your acquaintance says that he/she is willing to do a favor of your choice in return for your assistance with the homework.

Indicate how much help you would give to the person who needs help by circling the appropriate number.

   1   2   3   4   5   6   7
no help at all   very much help

(From Kerber, K. W., Rewards, costs, and helping: A demonstration of the complementary nature of experimental and correlational research. <u>Teaching of Psychology</u>, 1980, <u>7</u>, p. 50–52. Adapted with the permission of the author.)

Demonstration 12-3

It is 8 o'clock on a Monday evening, and you have just begun to study for a very important examination. The examination is scheduled for Thursday morning at 10 o'clock. You need an excellent performance in order to make up for a poor showing on the previous test in this class.

Just as soon as you settle down to work, an acquaintance from down the hall enters your room and asks for assistance with his/her mathematics homework, which is due the next morning. You took the same mathematics course last semester.

Before responding to his/her request, you ask if your acquaintance will do a favor for you in return for your help. Your acquaintance says that he/she is willing to do a favor of your choice in return for your assistance with the homework.

Indicate how much help you would give to the person who needs help by circling the appropriate number.

  1   2   3   4   5   6   7
no help at all   very much help

(From Kerber, K. W., Rewards, costs, and helping: A demonstration of the complementary nature of experimental and correlational research. Teaching of Psychology, 1980, 7, p. 50–52. Adapted with the permission of the author.)

Demonstration 12-3

It is 8 o'clock on a Monday evening, and you have just begun to study for a very important examination. The examination is scheduled for tomorrow morning at 10 o'clock. You need an excellent performance in order to make up for a poor showing on the previous test in this class.

Just as soon as you settle down to work, an acquaintance from down the hall enters your room and asks for assistance with his/her mathematics homework, which is due the next morning. You took the same mathematics course last semester.

Before responding to his/her request, you ask if your acquaintance will do a favor for you in return for your help. Your acquaintance says that he/she is not willing to do a favor of your choice in return for your assistance with the homework.

Indicate how much help you would give to the person who needs help by circling the appropriate number.

    1   2   3   4   5   6   7
no help at all   very much help

(From Kerber, K. W., Rewards, costs, and helping: A demonstration of the complementary nature of experimental and correlational research. <u>Teaching of Psychology</u>, 1980, <u>7</u>, p. 50–52. Adapted with the permission of the author.)

Demonstration 12-3

It is 8 o'clock on a Monday evening, and you have just begun to study for a very important examination. The examination is scheduled for Thursday morning at 10 o'clock. You need an excellent performance in order to make up for a poor showing on the previous test in this class.

Just as soon as you settle down to work, an acquaintance from down the hall enters your room and asks for assistance with his/her mathematics homework, which is due the next morning. You took the same mathematics course last semester.

Before responding to his/her request, you ask if your acquaintance will do a favor for you in return for your help. Your acquaintance says that he/she is not willing to do a favor of your choice in return for your assistance with the homework.

Indicate how much help you would give to the person who needs help by circling the appropriate number.

   1   2   3   4   5   6   7
no help at all   very much help

(From Kerber, K. W., Rewards, costs, and helping: A demonstration of the complementary nature of experimental and correlational research. Teaching of Psychology, 1980, 7, p. 50–52. Adapted with the permission of the author.)

Demonstration 12-4

Respond to each of the following items by circling the appropriate number.

1. When I am reading an interesting story or novel, I imagine how I would feel if the events in the story were happening to me.

    0   1   2   3   4
    does not describe me well   describes me very well

2. I really get involved with the feelings of the characters in a novel.

    0   1   2   3   4
    does not describe me well   describes me very well

3. I am usually objective when I watch a movie or play, and I don't often get completely caught up in it.

    0   1   2   3   4
    does not describe me well   describes me very well

4. After seeing a play or movie, I have felt as though I were one of the characters.

    0   1   2   3   4
    does not describe me well   describes me very well

5. I daydream and fantasize, with some regularity, about things that might happen to me.

    0   1   2   3   4
    does not describe me well   describes me very well

6. Becoming extremely involved in a good book or movie is somewhat rare for me.

    0   1   2   3   4
    does not describe me well   describes me very well

7. When I watch a good movie, I can very easily put myself in the place of a leading character.

    0   1   2   3   4
    does not describe me well   describes me very well

8. Before criticizing somebody, I try to imagine how I would feel if I were in their place.

    0   1   2   3   4
    does not describe me well   describes me very well

9. If I'm sure I'm right about something, I don't waste much time listening to other people's arguments.

    0   1   2   3   4
    does not describe me well   describes me very well

10. I sometimes try to understand my friends better by imagining how things look from their perspective.

    0   1   2   3   4
    does not describe me well   describes me very well

11. I believe that there are two sides to every question and try to look at them both.

    0   1   2   3   4
    does not describe me well   describes me very well

12. I sometimes find it difficult to see things from the "other guy's" point of view.

    0   1   2   3   4
    does not describe me well   describes me very well

13. I try to look at everybody's side of a disagreement before I make a decision.
    0   1   2   3   4
    does not describe me well   describes me very well

14. When I'm upset at someone, I usually try to "put myself in his shoes" for a while.
    0   1   2   3   4
    does not describe me well   describes me very well

15. When I see someone being taken advantage of, I feel kind of protective towards them.
    0   1   2   3   4
    does not describe me well   describes me very well

16. When I see someone being treated unfairly, I sometimes don't feel very much pity for them.
    0   1   2   3   4
    does not describe me well   describes me very well

17. I often have tender, concerned feelings for people less fortunate than me.
    0   1   2   3   4
    does not describe me well   describes me very well

18. I would describe myself as a pretty soft-hearted person.
    0   1   2   3   4
    does not describe me well   describes me very well

19. Sometimes I don't feel very sorry for other people when they are having problems.
    0   1   2   3   4
    does not describe me well   describes me very well

20. Other people's misfortunes do not usually disturb me a great deal.
    0   1   2   3   4
    does not describe me well   describes me very well

21. I am often quite touched by things that I see happen.
    0   1   2   3   4
    does not describe me well   describes me very well

22. When I see someone who badly needs help in an emergency, I go to pieces.
    0   1   2   3   4
    does not describe me well   describes me very well

23. I sometimes feel helpless when I am in the middle of a very emotional situation.
    0   1   2   3   4
    does not describe me well   describes me very well

24. In emergency situations, I feel apprehensive and ill-at-ease.
    0   1   2   3   4
    does not describe me well   describes me very well

25. I am usually pretty effective in dealing with emergencies.
    0   1   2   3   4
    does not describe me well   describes me very well

26. Being in a tense emotional situation scares me.
    0   1   2   3   4
    does not describe me well   describes me very well

27. When I see someone hurt, I tend to remain calm.
    0   1   2   3   4
    does not describe me well   describes me very well

28. I tend to lose control during emergencies.
    0   1   2   3   4
    does not describe me well   describes me very well

NOTE: From "A multidimensional approach to individual differences in empathy" by M. H. Davis, 1980, <u>Catalog of Selected Documents in Psychology</u>, 10, p. 85. Reprinted by permission of the author and Select Press.

FILMS/VIDEOS

Brother's Keeper (NBC, 15 min., 1996) Broadcast on NBC's Dateline on April 30, 1996, this brief segment featuring John Darley provides excellent coverage of the bystander phenomenon. Covers the tragic case of Deletha Word who was savagely beaten on the Belle Isle Bridge over the Detroit River while dozens of observers did nothing. To order, call 1-800-420-2626.

The Courage to Care (PBS, 30 min., 1986). With commentary by Elie Wiesel, this program examines those individuals in Nazi Germany who intervened on behalf of the Jews.

Helping and Prosocial Behavior (PSU, 30 min., 1989). Considers motives for helping, including the reciprocity and social responsibility norms. A community "Park Pride Day" scene exemplifies the remarkably altruistic behaviors of the typical citizen.

Silent Witnesses: The Kitty Genovese Murder (INS, 50 min, 1999). This video grapples with the disturbing question of human apathy in the face of atrocity—in this case, the infamous Kitty Genovese murder.

SOS: Action or Apathy (BOS, 7 min., 1976). An animated illustration of the problem of social responsibility. Features a man's response to an SOS message discovered on the beach.

When Will People Help? The Social Psychology of Bystander Intervention (HBJ, 25 min., 1976). Daryl Bem describes research on the bystander phenomenon. Reenactment of several laboratory studies.

CHAPTER 13
CONFLICT AND PEACEMAKING

Conflict
- Social Dilemmas
- *The Prisoner's Dilemma*
- *The Tragedy of the Commons*
- *Resolving Social Dilemmas*
- Competition
- Perceived Injustice
- Misperception
- *Mirror-Image Perceptions*
- *Shifting Perceptions*

Peacemaking
- Contact
- *Does Desegregation Improve Racial Attitudes?*
- *When Does Desegregation Improve Racial Attitudes?*
- Cooperation
- *Common External Threats*
- *Superordinate Goals*
- *Cooperative Learning*
- *Generalizing Positive Attitudes*
- *Group and Superordinate Identities*
- Communication
- *Bargaining*
- *Mediation*
- *Arbitration*
- Conciliation
- *GRIT*
- *Applications In The Real World*

Personal Postscript: Communitarianism

LECTURE AND DISCUSSION IDEAS

1. Prisoner's Dilemma and Collective Panic

After students have played some version of the Prisoner's Dilemma in class, you might draw further parallels between the laboratory game and events outside the laboratory. Roger Brown (1965) used the Prisoner's Dilemma to provide insight into the dynamics of collective panic. This application is an excellent illustration of how group irrationality, say people rushing exits in a theater fire and thereby greatly increasing the potential loss of life, is the result of individuals rationally pursuing their own self-interest.

The payoff matrix for a panic escape is presented below with P representing any person in the building at the time of the fire and G, the group of individuals nearby P.

	G Take Turns	G Rush Exit
P Take Turns	+ for P; + for G	--for P; ++for G
P Rush Exit	++for P; --for G	-or P; - for G

If both P and G take their turns in leaving the building, both may expect to escape, perhaps with minor burns or some smoke inhalation. This is a favorable outcome (+) for each. If both P and G decide to rush the exit, they risk more serious injury, perhaps even loss of life. This constitutes a negative outcome (-) for each. If P waits while G rushes the exit, P faces certain death (--), while G may escape without injury (++). On the other hand, if P rushes the exit while G waits, the outcomes are reversed with P being the first one out (++) and G certain of facing doom (--).

What is the individual's rational solution to the dilemma? It is to rush the exit. Regardless of what G does, P is better off by rushing the exit. Ironically, this produces the greatest loss of life and injury. Media reports are certain to comment on how "irrationally" the people behaved, and may even suggest that all could have escaped if they had only remained calm and taken their turns. A replication of Mintz (1951) would simulate the escape panic. A bottle with a narrow neck (about an inch) and several aluminum or wooden cones (about 3/4" in diameter) with attached strings are necessary for this demonstration. Place the cones in the bottle and give each student in the group a string and either "competitive" or "cooperative"" instructions. For the former, promise a small reward to the person who is the first to get his or her cone out in the allotted time, and for the latter, promise each member of the group a reward if they all get their cones out in the allotted time. Discuss the results and draw the analogy to panic.

Brown provided additional examples of how the laboratory dilemmas discussed in the text are useful in understanding the dynamics of various sorts of collective behavior including the acquisitive panic and the lynching mob.

Discussion Questions:

1. In what ways is the model of panic provided by Prisoner's Dilemma unrealistic?
2. From the research presented in the text on laboratory dilemmas, how might panics of escape be avoided?
3. What would the payoff matrix for a "run on the bank" look like? What would be the matrix for the arms race (arming versus disarming) between the United States and the Soviet Union?

2. The Tit-for-Tat Strategy

The text notes that in laboratory games the most successful strategy has proved to be simple "tit-for-tat," which begins with a cooperative opening play and then always matches the other player's last response. Axelrod (1980a, 1980b) asked experts in game theory from a variety of disciplines to submit strategies for a Prisoner's Dilemma computer tournament. The first tournament was run as a round robin so that each of 14 entries (some provided very complex strategies) was paired with every other entry. A game consisted of exactly 200 moves. The best strategy (the one that accumulated the most points) proved to be simple tit-for-tat, which had been submitted by Anatol Rapoport. After these results were announced Axelrod called for a second round. This time the 62 entrants were able to design strategies based on the lessons learned from the first round. Once again, however, tit-for-tat won. Axelrod's analysis of the results indicated that three factors seemed to be important to a successful strategy. First, it pays to be "nice." A nice rule is one which will never be the first to defect. Being the first to defect is costly. Tit-for-tat cooperates on the first move and defects only after the other player defects. Second, a successful strategy is "provocable." A rule is provocable if it immediately defects after an "uncalled for" defection from the other. Provocability discourages the other side from persisting whenever defection is tried. Third, a successful strategy is "forgiving." It does not hold a defection against the other player but seeks to restore mutual cooperation.

3. Misperception in the Persian Gulf Conflict

Nelson (1991) discusses various psychological factors in war and peacemaking. Of particular interest is his discussion of misperception in the Gulf War.

Extending Piaget's concept of egocentric perception, Nelson describes sociocentric perception as adults' tendency to perceive events in the world only from their own society's perspective. Saddam Hussein misperceived how other countries would view his invasion of Kuwait, hostage-taking, use of Scud missiles, and release of oil into the Gulf. He erroneously believed that the U.S. public would not support the president in a war against him, and he had mistaken expectations about the actions of other Arab countries. Newsweek magazine concluded that "Saddam has little idea how his actions are seen outside his borders."

The United States and its allies also demonstrated sociocentric perceptions in underestimating Saddam's grievances against Kuwait and the deeply held Iraqi view that much of Kuwait is rightfully part of Iraq. They believed that Saddam would not invade Kuwait even after he deployed 100,000 troops along the border. After the invasion they seemed convinced that deployment of huge military forces would cause Saddam to back down and remove his army from Kuwait.

Hussein's perceptions were tainted by self-serving and ingroup bias. He grossly exaggerated his own military power. He boasted about the "Mother of All Battles," and about destroying Israel with a rain of fire. He exaggerated his enemies' perversity in maintaining that Kuwait was conspiring with the United States and other nations to wage an economic war against his own country.

Misperception was also evident in the United States' belief that Saddam would respond to ultimatums, threats, and insults. President Bush's comparison of Saddam to Hitler was certainly exaggerated if it implied that Iraq posed a military threat analogous to Hitler's Germany.

In addition to discussing the role of misperception, Nelson shows how, in the Gulf War, threats and counterthreats escalated the conflict making it psychologically difficult for either side to back down and thereby lose face. Both sides appeared to be motivated by anger, pride, and power as well as by their own nation's interests. In particular, Saddam Hussein seemed more concerned with personal pride than the survival and well-being of his people.

4. Exaggerating the Other's Position

The text notes that each side to a conflict overestimates the extremity of the other's views. Keltner and Robinson's (1996) review provides many everyday examples of this phenomenon. They report that both sides to a conflict typically assume that the difference between the two sides' attitudes is one and one half to four times greater than is the actual difference.

Keltner and Robinson's study of the Western Canon debate, which involves revisionists' and traditionalists' attitudes toward literature and a liberal arts education illustrates there point. From a list of 50 literary works, which included works of traditional authors (e.g., Shakespeare) and revisionist authors (e.g., Douglass), English professors selected 15 books they would teach in a hypothetical introductory English course and 15 books they believed their opponents would teach. Revisionists and traditionalists actually chose seven of the same books. Both sides, however, underestimated how many books they actually selected in common. This phenomenon was also found for pro-choice and pro-life partisans' attitudes toward abortion, students' attitudes toward cuts in the U.S. goverment budget, and liberals' and conservatives' attitudes toward the events surrounding the Howard Beach incident in which a young black man was killed on a freeway while escaping white pursuers.

Keltner and Robinson found two additional biases. First, a consistent perceiver effect emerged. That is, partisans in power exaggerated the magnitude of the conflict more than partisans seeking change. For example, traditionalists polarized the Western Canon dispute more than revisionists. Secondly, a consistent target effect occurred. Those partisans seeking change were judged to be more extremist than their counterparts by both sides to the dispute.

5. Conflict Strategies and the Dual Concern Model

Pruitt and Rubin (1986) describe five specific strategies for dealing with conflict. They present the options in the hypothetical case of Peter Colger who has been looking forward to a two-week vacation at a quiet mountain lodge. His wife, Mary, however, has expressed her preference for a busy seaside resort. Peter, argue Pruitt and Rubin, can respond by contending, that is, arguing for the merits of a mountain vacation, even threatening to go alone if Mary does not agree. He can take a problem-solving approach and attempt to find a vacation spot that satisfies both sets of interests. He can yield to Mary's preference and go to the seashore. He can be inactive (do nothing) in the hope that their disagreement will go away. Finally, Peter can withdraw from the controversy by deciding not to take any vacation.

Pruitt and Rubin suggest that a dual concern model specifies the conditions under which a specific strategy is followed. Concern only about one's own outcomes and needs in the realm under dispute is likely to lead to contending. Concern only about the other's outcomes likely leads to yielding. Although the two concerns in the dual concern model are sometimes reduced to a single dimension, with selfishness (concern about own outcomes) on one end and cooperativeness (concern about the other's outcomes) on the other end, this is an improper simplification. Both concerns can be strong at the same time and when they are, problem-solving is the preferred strategy. When both concerns are weak, inaction is the likely approach. The model makes no prediction about the antecedents of withdrawing.

6. Conflict and Coalition Formation

Intergroup conflict often involves the formation of coalitions in which subgroups marshal forces against one another. As Forsyth (1990) indicates, researchers have often used a "convention" or "legislative" role-playing format to study the factors influencing coalition formation. For example, in one typical study 17 votes were distributed unevenly among the four members of a group with one person given eight votes, another seven, and the remaining two, one vote each. A majority of votes, that is, at least nine, was required to earn a monetary payoff. In this particular situation, four winning coalitions are possible:

8-7, 7-1-1, 8-1, and 8-1-1. Although the nature of communication varies from study to study, subjects typically use written messages, make suggestions to the researcher, or bargain face to face. Two dependent variables are of special interest: the nature of the coalition formed (e.g., 8-1 or 7-1-1) and the division of the payoff by the winners.

Forsyth's review of the literature suggests the following conclusions:

A. In most cases, coalitions contain the minimum number of individuals necessary to win, what is sometimes called the cheapest winning solution. Thus, a coalition of 8-1-1 is highly improbable because an 8-1 alone guarantees success.

B. Coalitions of two tend to be more stable and cohesive than larger coalitions. Surely, part of the reason for this is that information can be exchanged more rapidly and accurately in smaller coalitions. In addition, confidence and trust are more uncertain in larger coalitions.

C. Individuals with fewer resources are often preferred partners. The person who has just enough to tip the balance is a popular partner. The weaker individual may be more likely to realize that combining forces with the more powerful is the only route to success, and stronger individuals may find weaker partners more attractive because they may be satisfied with a smaller fraction of the payoff. In a sense, then, weakness is strength, and strength is weakness. Time and again, research finds that the most powerful get excluded from coalitions. Not only are they less likely to see their need for others but others are more fearful of being exploited by the powerful.

D. Two norms tend to dominate the division of payoffs. The equity norm suggests that coalition members receive payoffs in proportion to their inputs. The equality norm recommends everyone share equally regardless of input. Stronger members of coalitions tend to argue for equity, weaker members for equality.

E. Gender differences are clearly evident. Women don't always form the cheapest winning solution, they are less likely to exclude the powerful member, they refrain from taking full advantage of the weak, and they divide up payoffs based on equality. In short, women may be more likely to adopt an anticompetitive norm.

7. Does Threat Promote Cooperation?

Is threat an effective strategy for eliciting cooperation? Deutsch and Krauss (1960) designed the trucking game in an attempt to answer that question.

Pairs of participants were asked to imagine that they were owners of two trucking companies, Acme and Bolt. Their task was to move merchandise from one location to another over a road drawn on a board in front of them. Their profits in the game would be determined by the speed with which they completed this assignment.

Each player had the choice of a long route or a short one. However, the short route had a stretch of one-lane road through which only one truck could pass at a time. If both selected the route simultaneously, the truckers would be unable to pass and both would lose money. The best strategy, of course, was to take turns on the shorter route.

To determine whether providing truckers with threat capability would promote cooperation, the researchers established three conditions. In the bilateral threat condition, Acme and Bolt each had a gate they could close to block the other's transit across the short route. In the unilateral threat condition only one of the players had a gate. In a no-threat condition, neither company possessed a gate.

The results indicated that participants were better off when they could not threaten each other. If threat was available both players lost money. Moreover losses were greater when both had gates. They earned money only when neither had threat capability.

Some research (e.g., Shomer, Davis, & Kelley, 1966) suggests that under certain limited conditions threat may promote cooperation. For example, when threat is the only form of communication possible, and when it can signal one's intent without actually producing a negative outcome for the opposing party, it may facilitate cooperation. In most cases, however, threat increases rather than decreases tension.

Discussion Questions:

1. What are the implications of these research findings for the arms race?
2. Can the capability of each superpower to destroy the other ever be a deterrent to conflict? Is it important that a military balance, in which neither power has superiority, be maintained?
3. What would be the consequences if the United States or the Soviet Union began unilateral disarmament?

8. Common Mistakes in Negotiation

Max Bazerman (1986) describes five common mistakes negotiators make and suggests some strategies for avoiding them.

1. Expanding the fixed pie. Too often negotiators assume there is only a fixed amount of profit or gain and that to win something, the other party must necessarily lose it. Sometimes this is true, of course, but too often we assume it is without trying to think integratively. For example, purchasing goods is usually thought of in win-lose terms. However, another approach may be possible. A retailer may be willing to cut the price if payment is made in cash.

2. Dehexing the winner's curse. In some negotiations we may find that the other party accepts our offer more quickly than we anticipated, and we wonder if we've been taken. A key factor in the winner's curse is that one side may have much better information than the other. To protect ourselves in negotiations of any sort we may need to borrow expertise. For example, before buying a used car, we may be wise to get a mechanic's evaluation.

3. De-escalating conflict. Often both sides in a conflict start with extreme demands, expecting to compromise somewhere in the middle. However, they get caught up in the conflict and take a hard line instead of a conciliatory or problem-solving approach. To prevent this kind of escalation, negotiators must constantly evaluate the benefits of continuing along the same course. Also negotiators should avoid pushing opponents into a corner, getting them angry, or making them feel they can't afford to give up the struggle.

4. Undercutting overconfidence. Bazerman notes that negotiators consistently expect the other side to concede more than objective analysis would suggest. Also, in final-offer arbitration, negotiators overestimate the likelihood that their final offer will be accepted. Wherever possible, negotiators should try to obtain objective assessments from outside experts to temper overestimation.

5. Reframing negotiations. Research has shown that there are important differences in how people respond to problems depending on whether they are framed in terms of gains or losses. For example, given a choice between a small sure gain and a risky larger gain, most people take the sure thing. However, if the same situation is presented as a choice between a sure small loss and a possible larger loss, most will prefer to gamble. This framing effect suggests that if you are evaluating a settlement in terms of what might be lost, you should also consider what can be gained. It also suggests that a negotiator emphasize what the opposition has to gain from a risk-free settlement. Finally, when mediators are trying to reach a compromise, they should frame suggestions in ways that show what both sides have to gain.

9. Problem-Solving Workshops

The text's reference to Herbert Kelman's workshops that have brought together Arabs and Israelis, and Pakistanis and Indians can be readily extended in class. Workshop participants are typically politically involved but unofficial representatives of conflicting parties. Discussions in which the opposing parties speak directly with each other are completely private and confidential. Results indicate that both sides typically come to understand the other's perspective and also how the other side reacts to their own group's action. Kelman (1997) explains that while most of the work takes place in small groups the focus is on promoting change in the larger system. He describes five ways in which workshop group serves as a vehicle of change at the macrolevel.

First, the group is a microcosm of the larger system in which the forces of the larger system may manifest themselves. Dynamics of the larger conflict are acted out and can be analyzed at the very moment they occur. Third-party interventions help in this analysis. Second, the group provides a laboratory in which the opposing parties may engage in a process of open, noncommittal exploration of different alternatives. It is a process that can produce solutions to be brought back into the two communities. Third, the group provides a setting for direct interaction. Certain processes central to conflict resolution such as empathy, learning and insight, and creative problem solving necessarily take place at the individual level. Fourth, the workshop constructs a coalition across conflict lines. It typically strengthens the hands of the pronegotiation elements on each side in their struggle within their own communities. Finally, the group forms the nucleus for a new relationship. Two groups destined to live together in a small space must ultimately establish a cooperative and mutually enhancing relationship. Interaction in the workshop group both promotes and models a new relationship between the parties.

10. Building Cooperation, Empathy, and Compassion in the Classroom

Elliot Aronson (2000) addresses the conflict and tension that so often accompanies high school classrooms in this exerpt from his book Nobody Left to Hate: Teaching Compassion After Columbine (Chapter 6, p. 125–153; this excerpt is also found in Annual Editions–Social Psychology 01/02; see references Chapter 1). This piece creatively introduces the problem, discusses ways to reduce competition and foster cooperation, and concludes with a thorough examination of Aronson's idea of the "jigsaw classroom." This exerpt makes for an excellent reading assignment to be followed-up with classroom discussions. This exercise is good for producing classroom discussions and usually results in promoting understanding between students as well as validating students' own high school experiences— by hearing others recount experiences that they thought only they had had.

11. Psychological Traps

Jeffrey Rubin's (1981) treatment of psychological traps can be used to extend the discussion of laboratory dilemmas in the text. Sometimes we invest time and money in an interpersonal relationship or a career that is yielding diminishing returns. Even when it no longer makes sense, we continue to spend our resources on an aging automobile, a risky stock investment, or a doubtful poker hand. Rubin and Brockner (1975) labeled the kind of entrapping situation in which we wait for a goal that never arrives the "Rosenkrantz and Guildenstern effect." Perhaps the simplest example of such a trap is placing a phone call and being put on hold. After waiting for some time, one experiences conflict over whether to hang up or not. More time may be wasted by continuing to hold. On the other hand, waiting a bit longer seems justified in light of the investment already made. So a person frequently continues to hold.

To study this kind of entrapping situation, Rubin and Brockner designed a simple laboratory experiment in which college students could win $8 by solving a crossword puzzle. Although the puzzle consisted of only 10 words, some were so difficult that the use of a scarce resource, a crossword dictionary, was required. In order to obtain the use of this resource the students had to wait in line until it became available—which it never did. Moreover, the longer subjects waited for it the less money they could win. Each student was given an initial stake of $2.40 and three ""free"" minutes to work on the puzzle. After that, students were charged for each additional minute they worked. Moreover, after requesting the dictionary they had to turn their puzzles face down and could merely wait for the dictionary to become available. Most students became entrapped. In fact nearly 20 percent stayed in the experiment the full 15 minutes. Entrapment was greatest (a) when the sum to be won decreased slowly rather than rapidly, (b) when subjects were not shown a chart describing how their payoffs were affected by the passage of time, and (c) when subjects were told they were first rather than third in line for the dictionary.

On the basis of his research and that of others Rubin gives some advice on how to avoid entrapment:

1. Set limits on your involvement and commitment.
2. Once the limit has been set, stick to it.
3. Do not look to other people to see what you should do.
4. Be conscious of your desire to impress others.
5. Remind yourself of the costs involved.
6. Remain vigilant. Avoiding one trap does not guarantee you will successfully avoid the next.

Discussion Questions:

1. What motivates people to persist in a self-defeating course of action? Do motives change as people become entrapped?
2. What kinds of people are most likely to become entrapped?
3. How does the study of psychological traps help us to understand why labor strikes or wars between nations continue beyond the point where either party can gain enough to offset its losses?

12. The Dollar Auction

Another non-zero-sum game not described in the text is the Dollar Auction (Shubik, 1971). The auctioneer offers to sell a dollar to the highest bidder, with one simple rule: The two highest bidders must both pay their bids, although only the highest bidder gets the dollar.

While initially many people join in, the first moment of truth occurs as the bidding passes 50 cents. The participants realize the auctioneer will get $1.05. As the trap becomes apparent, the bidding narrows to two people. The next moment of truth comes as the bidding passes $1. The lower bidder realizes that raising to $1.05 will produce a loss of a nickel. Failing to do so, however, will produce a much greater loss.

Allan Teger (1980) has played the Dollar Auction with 40 groups. He reports the bidding always went over a dollar. Once, it even went as high as $20. When Teger later asked the bidders why they bid beyond $1, many replied that they were forced to by the bids of their opponents (a situational explanation). But when asked why their opponents continued to bid, most expressed bewilderment. Some even implied their opponents were crazy (a dispositional explanation).

You might point out to your students that as the bidding progresses, participants' motives usually change. The desire to make some easy money shifts to a struggle to minimize loss. Finally, participants seek merely to save face and defeat the other person.

13. Analyzing Current Events

At any given time, there are (or have recently been) current events (national or local) ,which deal with the issues discussed in Chapter 13. For instance, at the time of this writing, the U.S. is negotiating with

China for the release of several U.S. Navy personnel as well as the return of a crippled spy plane, which, due to a mid air-collision with a Chinese jet, had to make an emergency landing on Chinese territory. Instances like this one are excellent opportunities for students to put their new-found knowledge pertaining to conflict and peacemaking to work. Simply take the amount of class time needed to properly describe the current situation (or describe a recent situation when it was at the peak of uncertainty), form small groups (3-5 students per group) and ask students to 1) analyze the current situation (identify dilemmas, perceived injustices, and misperceptions), and 2) create an exit strategy which takes into account concepts such as cooperation, bargaining, superordinate goals, mediation and conciliation. Reconstituting the class for the purpose of sharing each groups' ideas will usually result in a variety of creative solutions guaranteed to spark further discussion.

14. Popular Sources for Additional Classroom Materials

Brembs, B. (1996). Chaos cheating and cooperation: Potential solutions to the Prisoner's Dilemma. OIKOS, 76, p. 14–24. A thoughtful review of the literature through 1995.

Christie, R. (1970, November). The Machiavellis among us. Psychology Today, p. 82–86. Christie describes the characteristics of Machiavellianism, provides a sample 10-item test the reader can take, and presents research on how Machiavellians relate to others.

Etzioni, A. (1969, September). Kennedy's Russian experiment. Psychology Today, p. 42–45, 62–63. A consideration of Kennedy's strategy for peace in which the President sounded the dangers of nuclear war and took a conciliatory attitude toward the Soviet Union. The unilateral gestures were reciprocated.

Fisher, R., & Ury, W. (1991). Getting to yes: Negotiating agreement without giving in, 2nd ed. New York: Penguin Books. Provides a concise, step-by-step strategy for reaching mutually acceptable agreements in interpersonal, intergroup, and international conflicts.

Glance, N. S., & Huberman, B. A. (1994, March). The dynamics of social dilemmas. Scientific American, p. 76–81. An excellent introduction to social dilemmas. Explains how global cooperation among individuals with conflicting choices can be secured.

Herzberger, S. (1996). Violence Within the Family: Social Psychological Perspectives. Examines child, partner, sibling, and elderly abuse. Includes a discussion of prevention and treatment strategies.

Kohn, A. (1986). No contest: The case against competition. Boston: Houghton Mifflin. Contrary to the conventional wisdom, cooperation rather than competition leads to superior performance. Trying to beat others and to do well work at cross-purposes.

Pruitt, D. G., & Rubin, J. (1986). Social conflict: Escalation, stalemate, and settlement. New York: Random House. Identifies sources of conflict, describes five strategies for dealing with conflict, and presents the process of conflict in terms of a three-stage model.

Rabow, G. (1988, January). The cooperative edge. Psychology Today, p. 54–58. Describes how Scrabble, bridge, and basketball can be played as cooperative, non-zero-sum games. Cooperation works in play and everyday life.

Rubin, J. Z., Pruitt, D. G., & Kim, S. H. (1994). Social conflict: Escalation, stalemate, and settlement. New York: McGraw-Hill. Identifies the sources of conflict, the strategic choices made in conflict, factors affecting escalation of conflict as well as de-escalation and problem solving.

Rubin, J., & Rubin, C. (1989). When families fight: How to manage conflict with those you love. New York: Arbor House/William Morrow. Identifies the reasons families fight and how they can manage conflict more constructively.

Theobold, P. (1997). Teaching the commons: Place, pride, and the renewal of community. Boulder, CO: Westview. A good complement to the text's discussion of the commons dilemma. Examines philosophical assumptions about how human beings should meet their needs, govern themselves, and educate their children.

Worchel, S., & Simpson, J. A. (Eds.). (1992). Conflict between people and groups: Causes, processes, and resolutions. Chicago: Nelson-Hall. This book treats interpersonal, intergroup, and international conflict in separate sections. Experts examine how conflict originates and how and why it frequently becomes amplified over time.

DEMONSTRATION AND PROJECT IDEAS

1. Conflict and Peacemaking Quiz

Demonstration 13-1 may be used to stimulate student interest and to show the value of conflict and peacemaking research. The correct answers to most of these questions are not obvious, apart from research. As the chapter will reveal, statements 3, 4, and 8 are true; the rest are false. Naturally, this demonstration will be most effective BEFORE students have read the chapter.

2. Competition and Conflict

Linden Nelson (1991) has designed a useful classroom activity that demonstrates how competition generates conflict. Adapted from Kelley and Grzlek's (1972) research, it effectively shows how competitive assumptions and motives coupled with poor communication can interfere with effective problem solving when cooperation is desirable.

Preparation

A. Before class, copy the following chart onto the chalkboard:

TRIAL	# White	Dollars for White	# Green	Dollars for Green
1				
2				
3				
and so on to 20				

B. Have each student number from 1 to 20 on paper in order to keep track of money earned.

C. Distribute to each student one green and one white index card.

Instructions

You are about to participate in a simulation situation where we will pretend that real money is involved. Act as though real money were involved. The amount of money you will receive on each trial will depend in part on which card you raise up when I say "now." It will also depend in part on which color cards others hold up. After each trial I will write on the board the numbers of people raising white and green and the values for white and green. The values for white and green depend on the numbers of people raising white and green. People who raise one color, always the same color, will get more money than those who raise the other color. However, the more of you who hold up the color with the higher value, the lower the values will be for both colors. You are not allowed to talk or ask questions. After each trial, write down the amount of money you have earned, depending on whether you raised white or green. Try to make as much money for yourself as possible. [Repeat the instructions a second time, but do not answer questions.]

Conducting the Exercise

After each trial, count the number who raise a green card and fill in the chart on the chalkboard using the following values:

NUMBER WHO RAISE GREEN

	0	1	2	3	4	5	6	7	8	9	10	11	12	13
Dollars for White	1	4	7	10	13	16	19	22	15	28	31	34	37	40
Dollars for Green	0	2	5	8	11	14	17	20	23	26	29	32	35	38

	14	15	16	17	18	19	20	21	22	23	24	25	26	27
Dollars for White	43	46	49	52	55	58	61	64	67	70	73	76	79	82
Dollars for Green	41	44	47	50	53	56	59	62	65	68	71	74	77	80

	28	29	30	31	32	33	34	35	36	37	38	39	40	41
Dollars for White	85	88	91	94	97	10	103	106	109	112	115	118	121	124
Dollars for Green	83	86	89	92	95	98	101	104	107	110	113	116	119	122

After the tenth trial, announce that communication <u>will</u> be allowed for the remaining trials. If students wish to speak to the group, they should speak up so all can hear. Before beginning each trial, ask "does anyone else wish to address the group?" Remind students to "act as though real money were involved."

Conclusion

Usually, nearly all students raise green by trials 13 or 14. The simulation may be ended at that point.

1. Allow class discussion. Why were most raising white on trials 8-10?
2. Point out that a student made $1 more by raising green than white, regardless of what other students did. For each person who raised white, the values for both colors were reduced by $3. Thus, getting $2 more than others resulted in getting one dollar less for oneself (for raising white rather than green).
3. Communications after trial 10 usually give evidence of competitive thinking. Competitive thinking can blind a person to cooperative problem-solving possibilities.

4. During trials 1-10, most students assumed that "getting more than others means getting the most for myself." That competitive assumption is true for many situations in our society, but it was false in this situation. What are some real life situations where "trying to get more than others""is not a good idea? Point out how competitiveness can be good or bad depending on the situation and one's values. Apply to athletic teams, family relationships, management and labor, the nuclear arms race, etc.

5. Raising the green card was cooperative in that it increased the values for everyone. Why did cooperation increase after trial 10? For situations where people need each other's help to get what they want, improving communication usually increases cooperation. Why is that so and why is that important?

3. Individual Gain or Common Good?

The APA has posted a class exercise revised by Carol Dean (www.apa.org/ed/dilemma.html), which puts students into a social dilemma over the allocation of bonus points. The exercise can be used to demonstrate the cumulative negative effect of several people acting selfishly. The system tolerates some selfishness, but not too much. The execution is simple and the results are sure to promote discussion. Simply inform the students that they can receive either 5 or 15 bonus points on their next test depending merely upon which allocation they ask for (see the sample form on the web-site). However, notify the students that the points will only be doled out if less than 15 percent of the class asks for the 15 points—otherwise, no points are given. Dean suggests trying this exercise just before a test—when competitive drive is at its highest. Dean also notes that she had used this exercise many times and has yet to give out bonus points!

4. Individual Rationality, Group Irrationality

The dilemma of individual versus group well-being can be experienced through one of several games.

A. Prisoner's Dilemma. Demonstration 13-2 presents the Prisoner's Dilemma in an expanded form. Compose the class into pairs of groups (do not reveal the pairings), allowing each group to be a player. (Composing groups makes the experience more fun and minimizes your record keeping.) To heighten students'' involvement, let each profit unit on the matrix correspond to one cent, to be collected by each individual in the group at the end of the simulation. The total cost for a class of 40 students will generally be less than a single film rental.

The game can be played by simply using the decision categories 0 to 6. Or to increase students' awareness of real life parallels, you can impose a terminology that simulates the business world (e.g., by having two gas stations across the road from one another in an out-of-the way town, each of which every day must decide whether to lower its gas price 0 to 6 cents below the recommended retail price. Doing so lowers the profit margin, but increases volume, at the competitor's expense. No communication between the stations is permitted—that would be illegal price fixing.) The same matrix might also simulate an arms race, using the following instructions:

This is an exercise that simulates international relations. Each group will act as a country and will be interacting with <u>one</u> of the other countries. Each month your country gains through taxation enough money to build up the six missiles, thus strengthening your military defenses against the threatening neighbor country, or up to six factories, which will provide more goods for your people. If you build four missiles, then you will have money left for two factories, and so forth.

The simulation will consist of up to 15 months. At the start of each month both your country and the other country must decide <u>how many missiles</u> you wish to build that month. Record your group's decision on one of the slips provided. A courier will carry your decision to the U.N. table, where I will record your action and give you feedback on the other country's action.

Your outcome will depend on what action you take and what action the other country takes. If you will look at the payoff matrix, I will explain this with a few examples. If you both decide to build three missiles some month, then you will both gain three profit units for that day, as you can see at the center. Note that if both of you have the same number of missiles, you both gain as much profit as you have new factories—which in this case is three. If you both built zero missiles (meaning six factories) then you would both gain a profit of six. At the end of the simulation you can each, individually, sum your country's units for the months and I will then give you each (as a cash tuition rebate) one cent for each unit you profited.

Let's try a couple more examples. Ask yourself, what would be the payoff in profit units if your country on month 5 built six missiles while the other country built none? Can you see (in the upper right corner) that you would have gained 12 profit units while they lost 6? This is because in addition to gaining a profit unit for every new factory (of which you had none) you also gain, and they lose, two units for every missile you have built in excess of the number they built. Since you built six missiles more than they did, this military advantage gains you 12 profit units.

To summarize, each month you must decide how many missiles to build, with the understanding that more missiles means fewer factories. After your group has recorded its decision, bring it to the U.N. table and I'll return your slip with feedback on the other country's decision. You can then each record these outcomes on your record sheet, and proceed to discuss your decision for the next month. Questions?

You can terminate the simulation at any point (such as when it begins costing you too much money). Announce the termination three trials ahead and observe the exploitative behavior on the last couple trials. The terminology (building missiles vs. lowering gas prices) may itself be a significant variable; people may behave more cooperatively when it avoids an "arms race" than when it means higher consumer prices. Nevertheless, an arms race or two is likely to occur, despite everyone's awareness of how mutually detrimental it is. Cooperative solutions are often achieved following a GRIT-like strategy by one party (which initiates small cooperative gestures and waits for them to be reciprocated). Communication (allowing an exchange of written messages after about eight trials) often boosts cooperation.

B. Commons Dilemma. An excellent, simplified introduction to the concept of a social trap and specifically to the logic of the Commons Dilemma is to replicate William Allman's (1984) hypothetical offer to the readership of Science 84. Each reader was invited to mail in a small card, asking for either $20 or $100. Everyone would receive what was requested with this important stipulation; if more than 20 percent asked for $100, the deal was off and no one would get anything. Replicate the offer in class by distributing 3 × 5 cards to your students and pose either Allman''s hypothetical question or a real social trap based upon it. We've tried both. For the latter, we offered students a choice of a cookie or a can of soda pop, with the requirement that if more than 20 percent asked for the soda, no one would receive anything.

First, Allman''s results. 21,753 readers chose $20; 11,758 chose $100. The $100 responses were 35 percent of the total. In two sections of social psychology we obtained responses to the hypothetical dilemma that were close to Allman''s: 42 picked $20 and 17 selected $100. For the cookies and soda pop? 35 picked a cookie, 24 the soda. The exercise naturally leads to consideration of other social traps, particularly, to the "tragedy of the commons," which is described in the text.

C. <u>Sell-a-Dime</u>. The detrimental effect of competition can be illustrated by holding a dime auction. Select two students to bid against each other for a dime, using the procedure discussed in the text, except starting with a one cent bid. Repeat the auction with succeeding pairs of students. Keep a running total of the winning bids on the board. As students observe the costs of noncooperation, does cooperation (leading to lower bids) increase with repeated trials?

5. **Prisoner's Dilemma on the Web**

Invite students to play Prisoner's Dilemma at http://serendip.brynmawr.edu/~ann/pd.html and prepare either an oral or written report on their experience. They should describe their strategy (or strategies) and how it may have changed in the course of playing the game. They will play with a partner who follows a tit-for-tat strategy. The site also provides additional information on Prisoner's Dilemma that complements the text's treatment of social dilemmas.

Another internet site (www.princeton.edu/~mdaniels/PD/PD.html) stays true to the name and invites players to consider a situation in which they and another person awaiting trial are questioned by investigators (the other person is played by the computer). This program also involves four different possible strategies used by the computer player.

There are many other sites where students can play various versions of the Prisoner's Dilemma game in a variety of contexts. For example at http://netrunners.mur.csu.edu.au/~osprey/prisoner.html students can match up with real opponents. Finally, many other sites provide historical, mathematical, and theoretical information regarding the Prisoner's Dilemma game (e.g., www.aridolan.com/ad/adb/PD.html).

6. **Simulation Games**

a. <u>Starpower</u> provides 18 to 35 students a memorable experience of several dynamics of conflict, including mirror image perceptions and the justification of inequity by those with wealth and power. The game is fun and its quality materials are reasonably priced at $35 plus $2 shipping from Simile II, Box 910, Del Mar, CA 92014.

b. <u>Baf'a Baf'a</u>, another simulation kit from Simile II ($39.50 plus $2), socializes one group of students into the relaxed, intimate, sexist culture of the Alphans, and another group into the competitive culture of the Betans. Once all participants feel comfortable in their own culture, they begin sending representatives to visit the other culture. The observers typically have difficulty communicating with those whose language and customs are culturally different, and report these difficulties when returning to their home culture.

c. <u>Barnga</u> simulates the effects of cultural differences on human interaction. Participants play a simple card game in small groups where conflicts begin to occur as players move from group to group. Players learn that people from different cultures perceive things differently and they must resolve these differences in order to function effectively in a cross-cultural group. As few as nine players or large groups can play it. Price is $22.95 from Intercultural Press. Call 1-800-370-2665.

7. **The Machiavellian Bargainer**

The Machiavellian scale was designed by Richard Christie to measure the degree to which people believe others can be manipulated. A short form of the scale appears as in <u>Psychology Today</u>, November 1970, p. 82–86, and could be read in class.

Christie and his associates speculated that the perfect manipulator would:

1. be cool and detached with other people

2. lack concern for conventional morality since rules often stand in the way of successful manipulation
3. have low ideological commitment since means are more important than ends
4. have no pathological disturbance or symptoms of neurosis or psychosis. A good manipulator must have an undistorted view of reality.

Do people with high Mach scores behave differently from those with low scores? In one fascinating bargaining study (Christie & Geis, 1970), ten $1 bills were placed on a table in front of three subjects. They were told that the $10 would belong to the first two who could agree on how to divide it. The only restriction was that the money had to be divided between only two; that is, one person had to be left out. One of the three persons in the group was a high Mach, one was a medium scorer, the third a low Mach. The average winning for high Machs was $5.57, for middle Machs, $3.14, and for low Machs $1.29.

This study could be illustrated in a classroom bargaining demonstration. Select three students to participate. Present 10 candy bars and tell the students that you will give the candy to the first two who can agree on how to divide them. Emphasize that the candy bars can only be divided between two; that is, one person must be left out. If the Mach scale is first administered, you might select a high Mach, moderate Mach, and low Mach to participate in the exercise.

Research indicates that high and low Machs behave differently when the situation (1) allows for improvisation—that is when there is ambiguity or a lack of structure, (2) involves face-to-face interaction, and (3) is emotionally arousing. Under these three conditions, high Machs are more successful than low Machs in achieving their ends.

The behavioral difference is very likely due to a number of factors. First, high Machs tend to concentrate on a task and their own private goal. Low Machs get carried away with interpersonal relationships that may have little to do with the task at hand. Secondly, high Machs resist social influence while low Machs accept it. Finally, high Machs control the group while low Machs accept the structure defined by others. Other findings:

1. Males are generally more Machiavellian than females.
2. High Machs do not do better on measures of I.Q. or ability.
3. Machiavellianism is not correlated with authoritarianism.
4. Lawyers, psychiatrists, and social psychologists are more Machiavellian than accountants, surgeons, or natural scientists.
5. High Machs are likely to come from urban rather than rural backgrounds.

8. Conflict Styles

Paul Wehr offers Demonstration 13-3 as a way to stimulate discussion of different responses to conflict. After students have ranked the conflict behaviors, discuss each one in terms of its underlying motivation and its conflict resolving potential. Wehr classifies the behaviors as follows:

1. negotiation
2. issue proliferation
3. placating
4. avoidance
5. confrontation, expression of feelings
6. Ventilation & withdrawal
7. submission
8. displacement

9. Role Reversal

Chapter 13 indicates that role reversal can sometimes boost understanding of another party's point of view. You can demonstrate the process by forming the class into groups of four and having each person wear a name tag. Give them a provocative topic to discuss--some campus or national issue that will elicit opposing views--and ask them all to participate in the discussion. After 10 minutes of discussion have each person trade name tags with someone whose point of view is somewhat different. Now ask them to continue talking as if they were the person whose name tag they are now wearing. After five minutes, ask them to discuss how it felt to reverse roles, and how accurately their point of view was expressed by their partner.

10. Argumentativeness Scale

Do your students vary in argumentativeness? Demonstration 13-4 is Dominic Infante and Andrew Rancer's (1982) scale of argumentativeness. According to the authors, argumentativeness is a stable trait which predisposes an individual to advocate a specific position on controversial issues and to attack alternative positions. Presumably the argumentative person views debate as an exciting intellectual challenge. Feelings of excitement and anticipation precede an argument and feelings of satisfaction and accomplishment follow it. In contrast individuals who score low on the scale try to keep arguments from happening and feel relieved when they are successfully avoided. When induced to argue, the low argumentative person has unpleasant feelings before, during, and after the argument.

Scoring instruction:

Tendency to approach argumentative situations: add scores on items 2, 4, 7, 9, 11, 13, 15, 17, 18, 20.

Tendency to avoid argumentative situations: add scores on items 1, 3, 5, 6, 8, 10, 12, 14, 16, 19.

Argumentativeness trait: subtract the total of the 10 "tendency to avoid" items from the total of the 10 "tendency to approach" items.

11. The Social Connection Video Series

One of the entries in the video instructional supplement (The Social Connection Video Series), entitled "Social Ostracism," includes some of the work done by Elliot Aronson on the jigsaw classroom. Another entry, entitled "Understanding Genocide," deals with reconciliation and forgiveness, topics central to peacemaking. See the Faculty Guide accompanying the video series for program summaries, pause points, and classroom activities.

Demonstration 13-1

True or False

1. Studying conflict is virtually impossible to do in the laboratory due to ethical concerns. As a result, researchers are only left with the option of analyzing actual events after the fact. T F
2. The oft-occurring arms races between nations can be justified by the research that suggests threatening enemies with massive military strength has traditionally deterred the breakout of war. T F
3. Those resources common to many people (air, water, energy) are the resources that tend to get exploited for personal gain. Why? Because the negative impact of any one person's misuse of these resources is minimal to themselves and others. T F
4. Groups of people who share common resources are more likely to self-regulate their use of the common resource if they feel connected to their group and are strongly associated with their group. T F
5. Unfortunately, mere communication with others seldom results in cooperative action. T F
6. Thanks to the increase in the number of professional opportunities offered to women, perceptions of gender equality has significantly improved over the last 30 years. T F
7. Merely increasing the contact or exposure between conflicting parties has uniformly improved efforts to head-off future conflicts. T F
8. Helping conflicting parties to realize superordinate goals has been shown to be a very successful strategy for minimizing future clashes. T F
9. Unfortunately, there is little evidence to suggest that becoming friends with one racially different person will soften a person's negative attitude towards people of that race in general. Apparently it takes a lot more than one different-race friend to breakdown a negative racial attitude. T F
10. Research suggests starting a negotiation with a good faith offer will almost always prove more effective than beginning with a tough bargaining stance. T F

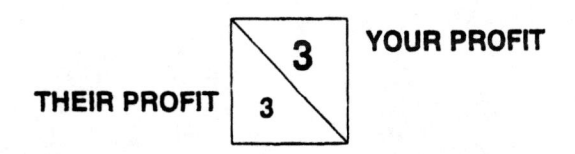

Demonstration 13-2
Bolt & Myers
©McGraw-Hill, 1999

YOUR DECISION

	0	1	2	3	4	5	6
0	6 / 6	7 / 4	8 / 2	9 / 0	10 / -2	11 / -4	12 / -6
1	4 / 7	5 / 5	6 / 3	7 / 1	8 / -1	9 / -3	10 / -5
2	2 / 8	3 / 6	4 / 4	5 / 2	6 / 0	7 / -2	8 / -4
3	0 / 9	1 / 7	2 / 5	3 / 3	4 / 1	5 / -1	6 / -3
4	-2 / 10	-1 / 8	0 / 6	1 / 4	2 / 2	3 / 0	4 / -2
5	-4 / 11	-3 / 9	-2 / 7	-1 / 5	0 / 3	1 / 1	2 / -1
6	-6 / 12	-5 / 10	-4 / 8	-3 / 6	-2 / 4	-1 / 2	0 / 0

(Rows labeled **THEIR DECISION**. Each cell shows: YOUR PROFIT / THEIR PROFIT.)

Legend: cell displays **3** (YOUR PROFIT) upper-right, **3** (THEIR PROFIT) lower-left.

Demonstration 13-2

Your Country _____
Your Decision _____
Feedback: Their Decision _____ (leave blank)

Demonstration 13-2

Your Country _____
Your Decision _____
Feedback: Their Decision _____ (leave blank)

Demonstration 13-2

RECORD SHEET

Your Country Number: _____

Month	Your Country's Profit	Other Country's Profit
1	_____	_____
2	_____	_____
3	_____	_____
4	_____	_____
5	_____	_____
6	_____	_____
7	_____	_____
8	_____	_____
9	_____	_____
10	_____	_____
11	_____	_____
12	_____	_____
13	_____	_____
14	_____	_____
15	_____	_____

Your country's total profit: _____

Demonstration 13-2

Instructor's Record Sheet

	Group 1	Group 2	Group 3	Group 4	Group 5	Group 6
1						
2						
3						
4						
5						
6						
7						
8						
9						
10						
11						
12						
13						
14						
15						

Demonstration 13-3

Joan had nearly reached the end of her rope. School was cancelled and she has been irritated by her children all day. Her environmental action group (which had to meet at her house since she couldn't get a sitter) had a long and frustrating afternoon meeting.

Tom has been looking forward all day to relaxing at home and having a leisurely drink with Joan. His subordinates have been remarkably inept in carrying out an important assignment, and he has been blamed. One of his best friends at work is being fired, and now he is considering quitting his job as well. He arrives home, looks around at the noise and disorderliness, and snaps at Joan: "With nothing else to do all day long, I can't understand how you can be such a sloppy housekeeper!"

Assume that you are Joan, and rank the following responses in order of your preference for them, marking your most preferred response as 1, etc.

____ 1. "Well, why don't we clean up together if it makes you so uptight?"

____ 2. ""I'd be neater if you acted more like a real father and took the kids off my hands every once in a while.""

____ 3. "Did you have a hard day at the office, dear?"

____ 4. (Say nothing; assume it will all blow over.)

____ 5. "I get angry when you accuse me unfairly; I've had as rough a day as you have. I think it's time we discussed sharing household responsibilities more."

____ 6. "If that's the nicest thing you can say, I'm leaving! I'll be next door at Sharon's until you cool off."

____ 7. "Give me another 10 minutes and it will be all cleaned up."

____ 8. "Timmy! Will you get off that floor and wash your filthy hands before dinner?"

(Reprinted by permission of Westview Press from <u>Conflict Regulation</u> by Paul Wehr. Copyright (c) 1979 by Westview Press, Boulder, Colorado.)

Demonstration 13-4

The questionnaire contains statements about arguing controversial issues. Indicate how often each statement is true for you personally by placing the appropriate number in the blank to the left of the statement. If the statement is <u>almost never true</u> for you, place a "1" in the blank. If the statement is <u>rarely true</u> for you, place a "2" in the blank. If the statement is <u>occasionally true</u> for you, place a "3" in the blank. If the statement is <u>often true</u> for you, place a "4" in the blank. If the statement is <u>almost always true</u> for you, place a "5" in the blank.

___ 1. While in an argument, I worry that the person I am arguing with will form a negative impression of me.

___ 2. Arguing over controversial issues improves my intelligence.

___ 3. I enjoy avoiding arguments.

___ 4. I am energetic and enthusiastic when I argue.

___ 5. Once I finish an argument I promise myself that I will not get into another.

___ 6. Arguing with a person creates more problems for me than it solves.

___ 7. I have a pleasant, good feeling when I win a point in an argument.

___ 8. When I finish arguing with someone I feel nervous and upset.

___ 9. I enjoy a good argument over a controversial issue.

___ 10. I get an unpleasant feeling when I realize I am about to get into an argument.

___ 11. I enjoy defending my point of view on an issue.

___ 12. I am happy when I keep an argument from happening.

___ 13. I do not like to miss the opportunity to argue a controversial issue.

___ 14. I prefer being with people who rarely disagree with me.

___ 15. I consider an argument an exciting intellectual challenge.

___ 16. I find myself unable to think of effective points during an argument.

___ 17. I feel refreshed and satisfied after an argument on a controversial issue.

___ 18. I have the ability to do well in an argument.

___ 19. I try to avoid getting into arguments.

___ 20. I feel excitement when I expect that a conversation I am in is leading to an argument.

<u>Note</u>. From "A Conceptualization and Measure of Argumentativeness" by D. A. Infante and A. S. Rancer, 1982, <u>Journal of Personality Assessment</u>, <u>46</u>, p. 76. Reprinted by permission.

FILMS/VIDEOS

An Acquired Taste (NEW, 26 min., 1986). A filmmaker turns 40 and looks back at the school, work, and media influences that shaped his life. His reflections pose critical questions about competition and American fixation with being "number one."

Agreeing to Agree: A Film about Negotiating Skills (MINN, 31 min., 1988). Humorously illustrates four specific steps to successful negotiation. Students tour the fictitious International School of Negotiation where a deal is made behind every door, from trading a football player to negotiating the release of a spy.

Avoiding Conflict: Dispute Resolution Without Violence (FHS, 47 min., 1996). Shows how ordinary problems can ignite into violence and how the problems can be resolved peacefully. Details ways of stemming the rising tide of violence in our schools, streets, and homes.

Children of the Third Reich (FHS, 50 min., 1997). Children of the Nazis meet with children of the Holocaust. This BBC production shows how individual acts of reconciliation and healing help to transcend the heinous nature of the crimes committed.

Conflict on the Line (MINN, 15 min., 1982). Portrays a case study in conflict within an organizational setting. Provides a superb introduction to a classroom discussion of the causes of conflict and its possible management.

Dealing with Conflict (MINN, 20 min., 1992). Presents five key positions people take when in conflict. Explains the choices people have for constructive or destructive outcomes.

Faces of the Enemy (INS, 58 min., 1987). Uses enemy images taken from documentary footage, propaganda posters, and political cartoons of different nations to show how we dehumanize our opponents in justifying war. A powerful film that you may want to preview before showing in class.

In Space, Toward Peace (ANN, 26 min., 1989). From the Discovering Psychology series, this video program includes a discussion of the psychology of peace, from the complexity of arms negotiations to our responses to the possibility of nuclear war.

Resolving Conflicts (CRM, 22 min., 1981). Interpersonal conflict is a part of our daily routines. Two basic approaches to resolving conflict are considered.

MODULE A
SOCIAL PSYCHOLOGY IN THE CLINIC

Making Clinical Judgments
    Illusory Correlations
    Hindsight and Overconfidence
    Self-Confirming Diagnoses
    Clinical Versus Statistical Prediction
    Implications
Social Cognition in Problem Behaviors
    Social Cognition and Depression
    Distortion or Realism?
    Is Negative Thinking a Cause or a Result of Depression?
    Social Cognition and Loneliness
    Social Cognition and Anxiety
    Social Cognition and Illness
    Reactions to Illness
    Emotions and Illness
    Stress and Illness
    Explanatory Style and Illness
Social-Psychological Approaches to Treatment
    Inducing Internal Change Through External Behavior
    Breaking Vicious Cycles
    Social Skills Training
    Explanatory Style Therapy
    Maintaining Change Through Internal Attributions for Success
Social Support and Well-Being
    Close Relationships and Health
    Confiding and Health
    Poverty, Inequality, and Health
    Close Relationships and Happiness
    Friendships and Happiness
    Marital Attachment and Happiness
Personal Postscript: Enhancing Happiness

LECTURE AND DISCUSSION IDEAS

1. Evaluating Clinical Judgment and Therapy

The first section of Module A deals with clinical judgment and concludes that psychotherapists, like other professionals, are vulnerable to illusory thinking. To reinforce this point as well as to help students strengthen their critical thinking skills, you might introduce some popular yet unproven therapy in class for evaluation. Chapter 3 of this manual suggested two good possibilities. The use of facilitated communication in the treatment of autistic children receives critical appraisal in the 1993 PBS production "Prisoners of Silence" (Call 800-344-3337 to order). This program provides excellent case material for classroom analysis. There are good examples of how illusory correlation, vivid cases, belief perseverance, and overconfidence contribute to unshakable belief in the therapy's efficacy in the absence of clear scientific support. You might show this program and then assign students to small groups to evaluate the belief in the effectiveness of facilitated communication.

Another popular therapeutic approach to evaluate is the controversial EMDR, or "eye-movement desensitization and reprocessing," in which counselors pass two fingers rapidly back and forth in front of the client's face. Touted by a Yale psychiatrist as "the most significant advance since the introduction of pharmacological drugs," and often used in the treatment of post-traumatic stress, this therapy, too, has little scientific support. ABC's 20/20 segment entitled "When All Else Fails" and broadcast July 29, 1994, (Call 800-913-3434 to order) covers EMDR and like "Prisoners of Silence" it will stimulate a lively classroom discussion. Newsweek's "Waving Away the Pain" published June 20, 1994, provides a good overview of the therapy and the controversy surrounding it.

Both of these case studies will reinforce the text's conclusion that psychologists must test their preconceptions before presenting them as truth. Propositions that imply observable results are best evaluated by systematic observation and experiment, which is the whole point of social psychology.

2. Recovered Memories

The text discusses how some skeptics argue that therapists' search for hunch-confirming information explains many "recovered memories" of childhood abuse. In some cases, the confirmation-seeking tactics may lead clients to create memories for events that have never happened. You can introduce this topic with the ABC 20/20 clip, "From the Mouths of Babes." In 16 minutes it provides one of the best news-feature treatments of the accuracy of children's reports of sexual abuse. The clip moves from coverage of the famous Kelly Michaels case to the laboratories of Steven Ceci and colleagues who have studied the misinformation effect in young children. In perhaps the most dramatic study, simply repeating a leading question directs children to construct false memories. The clip is available for purchase from ABC News for about $40. Call 800-913-3434 and ask for the 20/20 segment entitled "From the Mouths of Babes" that was broadcast October 22, 1993.

Elsewhere Myers (1998) provides a synopsis of the public statements of the major psychological and medical associations on this critical issue. First, incest occurs more frequently than we once supposed and leaves its victims predisposed to problems ranging from sexual dysfunction to depression. Second, forgetting of isolated past events, both positive and negative, is an ordinary part of life. Moreover, some people are abused at a very early age and may not have understood the meaning of their experience—circumstances under which forgetting is "utterly common." Third, recovered memories are commonplace. What is debated is whether the unconscious mind represses painful experiences and whether they can be retrieved by certain therapist-aided techniques. Fourth, memories recovered under hypnosis or the influence of drugs are especially unreliable. Fifth, memories of experiences before age three are also unreliable. Finally, memories, whether real or false, can be emotionally upsetting. If a false memory of abuse becomes a part of one's history, the client as well as the family may suffer.

3. Illusory Thinking and Fringe Medicine

The text considers how illusory thinking may contaminate clinical judgments, recommendations, and predictions. You might extend this discussion to a consideration of why so many people believe in the effectiveness of what Karl Sabbagh (1985) called "fringe medicine." Practitioners of the fringe therapies (among them homeopathy and acupuncture) make extravagant claims, which are simply not supported by careful research. Yet people continue to believe. Why? Most obviously people believe because they want to believe. But there are additional reasons.

Sabbagh reviewed Emil J. Freireich's tongue-in-cheek "Experimental Plan," which enables anyone to set himself up as a therapist and is "guaranteed to produce beneficial results." The plan has two essential requirements. The first is a treatment of some sort—it doesn't matter what. It can be a form of psychotherapy or some physical procedure, a type of rubbing or handwaving or the administration of a drug, plant, or chemical. The second requirement is that the treatment be absolutely harmless.

Freireich proceeds to show how almost any fringe technique can lead to an outcome confirming its success. The crucial factor is the natural variability of all disease. Every disease has important periods of remission in which the patient feels better. This is true even if there is an inexorable trend downward. From this principle, Freireich recommends that treatment be applied only after a period in which the patient has been getting progressively worse. If it is applied during one of the "ups" and the patient continues to improve, he can always say he would have improved anyway. If the treatment is applied when the patient is getting worse, four possible things could happen. The patient could improve, given the natural variability of the illness. Such an outcome immediately "proves" the treatment is effective. Second, the disease may remain stable, which proves the treatment has arrested the problem. A third possibility is that the patient may continue to get worse, which merely means the dosage was inadequate and must be increased. Finally, the patient may die. In this case the treatment was obviously delayed too long and applied too late.

When a patient improves one must reduce the treatment. Two possible outcomes will again "prove" the effectiveness of the therapy. If the patient continues to improve, the treatment was obviously effective. If he or she gets worse, reducing the treatment has obviously made the disease active again.

4. Depression on Campus

Depression is the leading psychological disorder on college campuses. Roughly 25 percent of the student population suffers some symptoms at any given time. Suicides are 50 percent more frequent among college students than among nonstudents of the same age. Beck and Young (1978) suggest that college students may be especially prone to psychological problems because they simultaneously experience all the transitions that are major stresses in adulthood. Entering college, they lose family, friends, and familiar surroundings and are provided no ready-made substitutes. Furthermore, while in high school they were the able students. In college they must compare their own abilities with equally able students.

Moreover, students' frequent misperceptions of these stresses may be as important a cause of depression as the stresses themselves. While they do not hallucinate their problems of academic or social adjustment, they often inflate the importance of temporary setbacks and misjudge the severity of rejections. They may overestimate academic difficulties on the basis of one mediocre grade. They may grieve over their social isolation, even though they often have caring and supportive friends. Their pessimism and dissatisfaction may lead to clinical depression that in turn interferes with actual performance. A vicious cycle is created in which misperceptions of academic and social difficulties result in still poorer grades and greater social isolation.

5. Renewed Commitment to the Commons

Seligman (1990) suggests that the present epidemic of depression stems from a rise in individualism and a decline in commitment to the common good. Thus, while he agrees that depression follows from a pessimistic way of thinking about failure, and that learning to think more optimistically when we fail gives us a skill in warding off depression, he does not believe learned optimism alone will stop the tide of depression on a society-wide basis. It has to be coupled with a renewed commitment to the commons. He writes, "Optimism is a tool to help the individual achieve the goals he has set for himself. It is in the choice of the goals themselves that meaning—or emptiness—resides. When learned optimism is coupled with a renewed commitment to the commons, our epidemic of depression and meaninglessness may end."

Seligman argues that renewed commitment to the commons will not come easily in a society as individualistic as our own. He suggests that we begin by thinking of it as moral jogging in which a little daily self-denial is exchanged for long-term self-enhancement. In our own self-interest, we must begin to reduce our investment in ourselves and heighten our investment in the commons. Some of his specific suggestions follow:

- Give 5 percent of last year's income away. Do it personally, not through a charity. Advertise among potential recipients in a charitable field of interest that you are giving, say, $2,000 away. Interview applicants, give out the money, and follow its use to a successful conclusion.

- Give up eating out once a week, shopping for new shoes, watching a rented movie on Tuesday night, and spend the time promoting the well-being of others. Help in a soup kitchen, visit AIDS patients, clean the public park, raise funds for your alma mater.

- Visit areas where you will encounter the homeless. Talk to beggars and judge as well as you can whether they will use the money for nondestructive purposes. Spend three hours a week doing this.

- When you read of particularly virtuous or evil acts write letters. Compose fan letters to people who could use your praise, "mend-your-ways" letters to people and organizations you detest. Follow up with letters to elected officials who can act directly. Again spend three hours weekly in this activity.

- Teach your children to give things away. Suggest they set aside one-fourth of their allowance to give to a needy person or project. Further suggest that they do this personally.

6. The Role of Childhood Experiences and Self-Esteem in Depression?

In a provocative address at the 1994 American Psychological Convention, Martin Seligman denounced two "sacred cows" of psychotherapy (Azar, 1994). In describing how to combat depression, he argued that psychologists cannot change problems of adulthood by looking to childhood experiences for the answer. He noted that blaming one's early experiences appeals to many people because in so doing one becomes a victim and being a victim brings consolation. After examining the data, however, Seligman reports finding almost no specific nongenetic influences on depression. In contrast, genetic influence is very clear. Blaming genes, however, does not give people the assortment of consoling explanations that blaming parents, race, age, or sex does.

And it is the latter explanations, argues Seligman, that make us feel better by shifting the blame to others, thereby raising self-esteem.

Increasing self-esteem is a popular goal of many therapies and undeniably, admits Seligman, depressed people have low self-esteem. But "bolstering self-esteem without changing hopelessness, without changing passivity, accomplishes nothing." In fact, building self-esteem may increase hopelessness and passivity. What needs improving is not self-esteem but skill in dealing with the world. Seligman maintains that "psychological immunization" is the key to stopping the depression epidemic. Depressed people are strongly pessimistic—they believe that bad events are permanent, pervasive, and will undermine everything. Moreover, nondepressed people who have such pessimistic explanatory styles are four to eight times more likely to develop depression than those with optimistic explanatory styles. Cognitive therapy aims to prevent depression by changing explanatory styles.

Seligman summarized the results of a prevention program, which taught coping skills to college freshman and 10- and 11-year-olds at risk for depression. Small to moderate reductions in rates of depression were found among college students, and a much larger positive effect was found with the children. "Two years after treatment, there is between 50 and 100 percent less depression in the preventive than in the control kids," reported Seligman.

7. Optimism

Michael Scheier and Charles Carver (1993) provide an excellent review of research on optimism that can be used to extend the text's brief discussion on optimism and health. They report that several studies now indicate that optimists maintain higher levels of subjective well-being during times of stress. For example, a study of undergraduate students' adjustment to their first semester of college indicated that optimism was associated with lower distress three months after starting school. Similarly, a study of women having their first child indicated that initial optimism was inversely associated with depression three weeks postpartum, even when the initial level of depression was controlled statistically.

Optimism also confers benefits on physical well-being. In men undergoing heart bypass surgery, optimism is negatively associated with physiological changes that make one susceptible to suffer a heart attack during surgery. Optimism also predicted rate of recovery including the attainment of behavioral milestones such as sitting up in bed and walking. In a six-month follow-up, optimistic patients were more likely to have resumed vigorous physical exercise and to have returned to work full-time.

Optimists are more likely to take direct action to solve their problems, are better at making plans to deal with adversity, and are more focused in their coping efforts. Optimists tend to accept the reality of the stressful situations they encounter, and they seem intent on growing personally from negative experiences. They try to make the best of bad situations.

Differences in optimism-pessimism may be partly inherited. In a study of more than 500 same-sex pairs of middle-aged Swedish twins, the heritability of optimism and pessimism was estimated to be about 25 percent. Prior experiences with success and failure are also important. To the degree people have been successful in the past, they should expect success in the future. Children may acquire a sense of optimism from their parents through modeling. Parents may also shape children's tendencies by instructing them in problem solving. Parents who teach adaptive coping skills will produce children who are better problem solvers and thus ultimately more optimistic.

8. Loneliness

Sociologist Robert Weiss estimates that between 50 and 60 million Americans or as much as a quarter of the population feel extremely lonely at some time during any given month (Meer, 1985). Survey research has suggested that the highest rate of loneliness is found in 18-to-25-year-olds. However, it is not uncommon for children between the ages of 7 and 11 to report they feel "lonely and wish they had more friends." While we hold a stereotype of the elderly as especially lonely, the frequency of loneliness actually drops steadily with age and reaches a minimum in those over 70. Psychologist Ann Gerson suggests that "Older people become more self-sufficient and their lives are simpler. They have a better idea than younger people of what to expect from relationships" (Meer, 1985).

The number of social contacts someone has is only one factor in loneliness. Psychologist Cecilia Solano points out that loneliness is partly a matter of expectation—how many contacts people expect or think are normal—as well as how many they actually have. The contacts that make one person feel lonely may make another feel overburdened with attention. Similarly, Letitia Ann Peplau believes that loneliness develops when desires or needs for intimacy don't match the quality or quantity of social contacts one has or thinks one has. Peplau states, "Experience is filtered through our individual evaluation process. The amount of time spent with another person, the degree to which two lives are intertwined, and the desirability of the arrangement are all in the eye of the beholder."

Jeffrey Young notes that while some lonely people are afraid of any social contact, most do not avoid contact but find themselves unable to perform up to their own expectations in intimate situations. Eventually they may avoid depending upon any of their relationships. Warren Jones found that lonely students did not get to know new people as well during a 15-minute conversation as did students who were not lonely. The lonely students also believed that their new acquaintances didn't like them. Interestingly the new acquaintances didn't report dislike but stated the lonely students did not seem to like themselves.

Karen Rook suggests that cognitive behavior therapy may help some chronically lonely people. The therapy aims to isolate the sources of distorted self-images and to help lonely people monitor their behavior. Rook states, "We can get people to stop seeing themselves as 'incurable', and start them toward challenging and eradicating these thoughts." Social-skills groups teach lonely people how to open conversation and to handle conflict or disappointment when they develop. Rook explains, "In social-skills training groups, we often find it useful to teach people how to match the level of disclosure of their partner. If lonely people disclose too much of themselves, they may make their partner uncomfortable, but if they disclose too little they may never reach the level of intimacy they are looking for" (Meer, 1985).

9. Stress: Hassles and Uplifts

What is more stressful? Major life events or everyday hassles? Richard Lazarus (1981) suggests that the petty annoyances and unpleasant surprises we experience every day may add up to more grief than life's major stressful events. Such hassles may range from getting stuck in a traffic jam or losing a wallet to arguing with a relative or employer. Lazarus argues that the impact of hassles on our physical and mental health depends on their frequency, duration, and intensity. Furthermore, a person's response to a given hassle depends on a variety of factors including personality, coping style, and how the rest of the day has gone. Lazarus writes, "Psychological stress resides neither in the situation nor the person; it depends on the transaction between the two. It arises from how the person appraises an event and adapts to it."

The counterpart to daily hassles is daily uplifts: pleasant and satisfying experiences like hearing good news, getting a good night's sleep, solving a difficult problem. Lazarus reasons that just as hassles may cause physical and psychological changes that may result in illness, uplifts may serve as emotional buffers against those disorders.

You might ask your students for their own list of hassles and uplifts. One sample of college students reported the following:

Hassles	Uplifts
1. Troubling thoughts about the future	1. Completing a task
2. Not getting enough sleep	2. Relating well with friends
3. Wasting time	3. Giving a present
4. Inconsiderate smokers	4. Having fun
5. Physical appearance	5. Getting love
6. Too many things to do	6. Giving love
7. Misplacing or losing things	7. Being visited, phoned
8. Not enough time to do necessary things	8. Laughing
9. Concerns about meeting high standards	9. Entertainment
10. Being lonely	10. Music

To measure the effects of hassles and uplifts, Lazarus had subjects complete physical and mental health questionnaires at the beginning and end of the year. As predicted, hassles turned out to be much better predictors of psychological and physical health than major life events. The more frequent and intense the hassles people reported, the poorer their overall health. Major events did have some long-term effects, but in the short term, hassles seemed more strongly correlated with health. Lazarus suggests that major life events may affect us indirectly through the daily hassles they provoke. Divorce, for example, might force an inexperienced man to make his own meals and it might compel a woman to repair a leaky faucet.

10. Overcoming Dating Anxiety

We experience social anxiety when we are motivated to impress others but are doubting our ability to do so. As Benjamin Lahey (1986) suggests, dating is a prime example. Anxiety over approaching, asking out, and interacting with new acquaintances is overwhelming for some and is one of the major reasons why college students seek help from their campus counseling centers. Christiansen and Arkowitz (1974) describe a program that is both effective and easy to implement.

College men and women troubled by dating anxiety were paired for "practice dates." Each student went on six dates with six different students who were matched with him or her on such characteristics as age, height, race, etc. At the conclusion of each practice date, the students provided each other written feedback through the therapist. They provided four positive aspects of their date's behavior and one that could be improved. The therapist's only task was to arrange the dates and serve as a consultant when needed. Students in the project reported significant decreases in anxiety and marked increased in the frequency of later dating.

11. Following Doctors' Orders

Adler and Stone (1984) report that as many as half of all patients fail to follow their physician's recommendations. Other research indicates that of people with dangerously high blood pressure who seek treatment, only about half adhere to the prescribed treatment regimen. And even among women who have had breast cancer, fewer than half follow their doctor's recommendation of breast self-examination. Why do so many fail to follow their doctor's orders? As Myers (1992) elsewhere points out, a surprising number do not understand the instructions. If told to "take the pill as needed for water retention," some may think this means to "take the pill when you need to retain water." And does the instruction "Take one every six hours" apply only to waking hours? Sometimes patients understand the orders but find the delayed rewards of a more healthful lifestyle outweighed by the immediate pleasure of smoking or eating high-calorie, junk foods.

Baddeley (1990) reports research which suggests how doctors' instructions might be made more memorable. First, findings suggest a primacy effect; that is, retention of advice was enhanced when more important and salient features were presented first. Second, patients remembered more when doctors explicitly divided their statements into clear categories. For example, the doctor might say, "I am going to tell you what is wrong with you: I think you have bronchitis. Second, what tests will be needed: You will have to have an x-ray and a blood test to make sure. Third, what the treatment will be: I'll give you an antibiotic to take. Take it on an empty stomach at least one hour before a meal." Finally, recall of advice can be improved by using specific rather than general instructions. Statements such as "You must weigh yourself regularly," or "You must lose weight," were less likely to be recalled than more specific statements, such as "Weigh yourself every Monday before breakfast," or "You must lose 15 pounds."

12. The "Up" Side and "Down" Side of Holistic Medicine

Whereas traditional medicine seeks to find the organic cause of a disease or illness and to alleviate it with some physical intervention, holistic medicine emphasizes the "whole person" and is more likely to consider psychological factors as either the cause or the remedy for a given condition. Holists are more likely to emphasize personal responsibility in maintaining or regaining health.

Gilovich (1991) cites both the potential benefits and dangers in this approach. On the "up" side, it is very much in our own interest to be well informed about the nature of an illness, and to take an active role in determining the course of treatment. Holistic medicine's emphasis on our personal role in prevention is also positive, given the fact that half the mortality from the 10 leading causes of death in the United States have been traced to people's behavior. Finally, holistic medicine's outlook may help people cope with their illness, disability, and pain. The practices of meditation, deep muscle relaxation, and positive mental imagery can assist people in managing their symptoms. Research suggests a sense of personal control can be beneficial even if it turns out to be illusory.

The down side, however, is that if appropriate thoughts and feelings promote health, it readily follows that sickness reflects a failure to adopt the right attitude. The sick and disabled are subject to blame by themselves and others for their misfortune. Gilovich notes how various comments by the representatives of holistic medicine reflect victim blaming. For example, New Age faith healer Elizabeth Stratton states that "Disease is merely a symptom of a deep psychological problem that the person probably isn't even aware of. . . . What I look for is why they created the illness and why they're hanging on to it." Similarly, Eileen Gardner, who served for a brief period in the Reagan administration as an aide to Education Secretary William Bennett, once wrote that handicapped individuals ". . . falsely assume that the lottery of life has penalized them at random. This is not so. Nothing comes to an individual that has not been, at some point in his development, summoned." Finally, there is the oft-quoted holistic slogan that "It is much more important to know what sort of patient has the disease than what sort of disease the patient has."

We run the danger, writes Gilovich, of compounding the tragedy of a disease with the torment of believing that it stems from a person's own mental and spiritual shortcomings. What could be more cruel than adding self-blame to a victim's misfortune? Note the anguish reflected in this letter to the editors of New Age magazine:

> I am physically disabled by a chronic inflammatory disease. I have not healed myself. I have visualized until I can hardly stand to do it anymore; I have been on countless diets and fasts. I have worked courageously and consistently in every possible area that might be an avenue. Last winter I finally understood that I was hurting rather than helping myself with my fanatic, stress-filled desire to heal. Everyone was telling me that what was preventing me from healing was that I was doing

something wrong. I believed them. It has been very hurtful to me to have everyone around me blame me for my illness.

Gilovich concludes by noting that the relationship between mental states and illness remains uncertain. While the uncertainty exists, perhaps we should err on the side of caution and assume that those who are ill did nothing to contribute psychologically or spiritually to their disease. The burden of illness is heavy enough.

13. Social Ties and Colds

You can extend the text's discussion of the relationship between social support and well-being with the interesting finding that those with a broad array of social ties are significantly less likely to catch colds than those with few social networks.

Sheldon Cohen and his colleagues (1997) at Carnegie Mellon asked a total of 276 healthy adults from 18 to 55 years to identify the types of relationships in their social circle from a list of 12 categories. These included spouse, children, other relatives, neighbors, friends, colleagues at work, members of social organizations, and members of religious groups. A category was included if a participant spoke either directly or by phone with a member of it at least once every two weeks.

After being given nose drops containing one of two cold viruses, the volunteers were quarantined in a hotel for five days. They were tested daily for signs of the cold virus in their nasal secretions and observed for typical cold symptoms. Results indicated that those with the most categories of social relationships had the lowest susceptibility to colds. Diversity of social ties was a better predictor than smoking, drinking, vitamin C intake, or level of stress hormones. Interestingly, the total number of people in a person's social world showed no relationship to developing a cold. "It's not the number of people in your network," concludes Sheldon, "it's the diversity of relationships you have."

14. The Benefits of Solitude

Although close, supportive relationships foster well-being, solitude also has benefits (McIntosh, 1996). For those who face many social demands and experience much social stimulation, solitude can restore coping resources and rejuvenate.

From his research on privacy, Darhl Pedersen of Brigham Young University suggests four other benefits. Contemplation may be the most important. "It gives people the chance to contemplate who they are, what their relationships are to other people, and what their goals will be," he claims. Solitude can also foster creativity by providing opportunity to consider new ideas without censorship or evaluation.

Two additional needs that solitude can meet are autonomy—"the chance to do your own thing, to act freely, and be who you are"—as well as "confiding," argues Pedersen. The latter was an unexpected result from research participants who used the term to describe a prayerful relationship with a deity.

15. Illusion and Well-Being: A Social Psychological Perspective on Mental Health

One question that will most assuredly interest students considers material from both this chapter and Chapter 2 (The Self). "Is it mentally healthy for people to have illusions of control over situations, unrealistic optimism regarding the future, and favorable self-other comparisons as described in Chapter 2?" You may present the case more clearly by providing an example something like the following: most people believe they are a better-than-average driver (as noted in the text)—is it good for them personally to feel this way? Is it good for society that most people feel this way? You can support the negative by noting that for virtually all of psychology's history it has been presumed that the psychologically healthy person is the one who maintains close contact with reality (e.g., Jahoda, 1958) (After all, don't you want drivers who are on the roads to be very aware of what they are capable and incapable of doing?). You can, however, support the affirmative by noting some of the points raised by Taylor and Brown (1988; 1994). They argue that illusion (mild not severe) is a hallmark of mentally healthy people. Positive illusions regarding the self, they note, correlate with happiness, ability to care for others and the capacity for creative, productive work. Some of the material presented in Mod A concerning the "sadder but wiser" effect may also be fodder for discussion.

16. Popular Sources for Additional Classroom Material

Dawes, R. (1994). House of cards: Psychology and psychotherapy built on myth. New York: Free Press. Dawes examines popular clinical assumptions and methods. For example, he challenges the belief that high self-esteem is essential to productive living, that one's childhood determines one's fate as an adult, and that "you have to love yourself before you can love another."

Myers, D. G. (1992). The pursuit of happiness: What makes a person happy—and why. New York: William Morrow. A survey of research on well-being. An excellent extension of the chapter's personal postscript.

Pennebaker, J. W. (1997). Opening up: The healing power of expressing emotions. New York: Guilford. Explains how personal self-disclosure contributes to emotional health and boosts our immune system functioning. Describes benefits of both talking and writing about trauma.

Peterson, C., & Bossio, L. (1991). Health and optimism. New York: Free Press. A leading researcher shows how social cognition—especially, an optimistic versus pessimistic explanatory style—influences physical well-being.

Seligman, M. E. P. (1998). Learned optimism: How to change your mind and your life. New York: Pocket Books. Reviews the benefits of optimism. Suggests strategies for choosing optimism as a route to greater freedom and well-being.

Snyder, C. R. (1994). The psychology of hope. New York: The Free Press. Drawing on both case studies and research with his hope scale, Snyder shows that hopeful people have the ability to envision a broader range of goals, greater energy and will power in pursing those goals, and the skills to generate a greater variety of routes to reach those objectives.

Snyder, C. R., & Forsyth, D. F. (Eds.). (1991). Handbook of social and clinical psychology: The health perspective. New York: Pergamon Press. Experts offer state-of-the-art summaries of social psychology's contributions to the diagnosis, understanding, and treatment of mental and physical disorder.

Taylor, S. E. (1995). Health psychology (3rd ed.). New York: McGraw-Hill. Excellent resource to complement this chapter. Surveys psychological influences on how people remain healthy, why they become ill, and how they respond when they do become ill.

Wedding, D., & Boyd, M. A. (1999). Movies and mental health: Using films to understand psychopathology. Boston: McGraw-Hill. Although more directly relevant to an abnormal or therapeutic class, most of the scenes referenced in the manual have strong social components.

DEMONSTRATION AND PROJECT IDEAS

1. Social Psychology in the Clinic Quiz

Demonstration MA-1 may be used to stimulate student interest and to show the value of social psychological research in the clinic. The correct answers to most of these questions are not obvious, apart from research. As the chapter will reveal, statements 3, and 5 are false; the rest are true. Naturally, this demonstration will be most effective BEFORE students have read the chapter.

2. Problem Behaviors on the Web

Students may pursue the problem behaviors discussed in the text more fully on the World Wide Web. For example, New York University's site at http://www.med.nyu.edu/Psych/public.html makes the text material on depression and anxiety personally relevant with on-line screening tests for each disorder. In addition there is comprehensive information on diagnosis, treatment, self-help programs, and advocacy groups, with links to the National Institute of Mental Health. The Cheek and Buss Revised Shyness Scale is presented below but can also be found at Johnathan Cheek's homepage www.wellesley.edu/Psychology/Cheek/jcheek.html along with helpful information on shyness research and treatment including links to other shyness sites. Mind Tools' How to Master Stress at www.psychwww.com/mtsite/smpage.html is a comprehensive site that emphasizes the applications of the theory and research on stress and includes separate sections on understanding, recognizing, and managing stress. Students will also find directions for keeping a stress diary.

3. Attributional Style

The text notes that depressed people are more likely than nondepressed people to exhibit a negative "attributional style." That is, they are more likely to attribute failure and setbacks to causes that are stable, global, and internal. The result of this pessimistic, overgeneralized, self-blaming thinking is a depressing sense of hopelessness.

You can illustrate attributional style as well as attempts to assess it with an example provided by Peterson and Seligman (1984). Ask your students to imagine that their bank has just notified them that their checking account is overdrawn. After thinking a bit about the possible reasons for this notification, have them write down what they believe to be the single most important cause. Then have them answer the following questions:

A. Does the cause you wrote about reflect more about you or something more about other people or circumstances? (Is it an internal or external cause?)

B. Is the cause something that is permanent or temporary; that is, is the cause likely to be present in the future (stable or unstable)?

C. Is the cause something that influences other areas of your life or only your checking account balance (global or specific)?

Ask volunteers to share some of their answers and reiterate that attributions that are internal, stable, and global are more likely to be associated with depression. Peterson and Seligman give the following attributions that you can use as examples in class:

"I'm incapable of doing anything right" (internal, stable, global).

"I always have trouble figuring my balance" (internal, stable, specific).

"I've been sick for a week, and I've let everything go" (internal, unstable, global).

"The one time I didn't enter a check is the one time my account gets overdrawn" (internal, unstable, specific).

"All institutions chronically make mistakes" (external, stable, global).

"This bank has always used antiquated techniques" (external, stable, specific).

"Holiday shopping demands that one throw oneself into it" (external, unstable, global).

"I'm surprised—my bank has never made an error before" (external, unstable, specific).

4. Perfectionism Scale

Demonstration MA-2 is the Perfectionism Scale designed by David Burns. Total score is the sum of all responses and higher scores reflect greater perfectionism. (Be sure to remind students that plus and minus numbers cancel each other out.) You can extend the text's treatment of psychological disorders by presenting Burns' (1980) ideas on how perfectionism contributes to anxiety or depression.

According to Burns, perfectionism is not to be confused with the healthy pursuit of excellence. For perfectionists, the drive to excel is self-defeating for they measure their own worth entirely in terms of productivity and achievement. Thus any failure or feeling of inadequacy leads to a precipitous loss of self-esteem.

A common cognitive distortion of perfectionists is all-or-none thinking. For example, a straight-A student who receives a B may conclude: "Now I am a total failure." Perfectionists also tend to overgeneralize. For example, when they make mistakes, they tell themselves, "I'm always goofing up. I'll never get this right." Finally, perfectionists seem to plague themselves with "should" statements. When they fail to reach a goal they are not likely to ask, "What can I learn from this?" Rather they harangue themselves saying, "I shouldn't have messed up! I ought to do better. I must not do that again!" Such statements lead to frustration and to guilt that may cause them to repeat the error.

There is little evidence that perfectionism helps people achieve success. In a study of insurance agents, those who linked self-worth with achievement earned an average of $15,000 less than nonperfectionists did. Among first-year law students, a perfectionistic thinking pattern was associated with a desire to leave school and feelings of either anxiety or depression. Burns observes that when these students, who had been successful in the past, realized that their performance might place them in the middle of the pack, they began to see themselves as losers. They reacted with frustration, anger, and panic.

Perfectionists are also plagued by loneliness and disturbances in interpersonal relationships. Because they anticipate rejection when they are judged as imperfect, they tend to react defensively to criticism. This response usually alienates others and may bring about the very disapproval feared. This, in turn, reinforces the irrational belief that, to be accepted, one must never fail.

5. Shyness Scale

Demonstration MA-3 is the 13-item Revised Cheek and Buss Shyness Scale, developed by Jonathan Cheek of Wellesley College and Arnold Buss of the University of Texas (Austin). It can be used to introduce and extend the text's discussion of social anxiety. As presented, the scale has been simplified for self-scoring by rewording reverse-scored items to eliminate need for recoding. Simply have each student add up his or her score. If it is over 50, the respondent is very shy; if it is between 36 and 50, he or she is somewhat shy; if it is below 36, he or she is probably not shy. A scale mean of 33 has been obtained for college students.

Several points are worth making regarding shyness. Surveys indicate that about 40 percent of Americans consider themselves to be shy, and that over 80 percent of these people do not like being shy (Pilkonis, 1977; Zimbardo, 1977). Only 7 percent of Americans say they have never experienced feelings of shyness. Cheek and Melchior (1990) note that interactions with strangers, particularly those of the opposite sex, and situations requiring assertive behavior provoke the strongest feelings of social anxiety. Among the typical reactions of shy people are tension, inhibition, awkwardness, acute self-consciousness, physical distress, worry about receiving negative evaluations from others, and reticence. Shyness is defined as the tendency to feel tense, worried, or awkward during social interactions, especially with unfamiliar people.

One model of shyness suggests three components: First, the emotional or physiological involving upset stomach, pounding heart, sweating, and blushing. Second, the cognitive including acute public self-consciousness, self-deprecating thoughts, and worries about being negatively evaluated. Third, the behavioral involving social incompetence, reticence, and inhibition. Although all three frequently occur together, shy individuals may differ in the extent to which they suffer from problems of each component.

Cheek and Melchior indicate that shy people have one obvious thing in common: they think of themselves as being shy. From this perspective they argue that it is essential to understand the self-concept of the shy person. Their emphasis on the social cognitions associated with shyness extends the text's treatment of social anxiety. Shy people typically experience low self-esteem, attribute more personal responsibility to themselves when they are unsuccessful than when they are successful, demonstrate a selective memory for negative information about themselves, have a low expectancy for social success, adopt a protective self-presentation style, show anxious self-preoccupation and worry about receiving negative evaluations from others. <u>Shyness: Perspectives on Research and Treatment</u> by W. H. Jones, J. M. Cheek, and S. R. Briggs (New York: Plenum, 1986) provides an excellent resource for additional information.

6. The UCLA Loneliness Scale

Demonstration MA-4, provided by Daniel Russell, is a 10-item version of the UCLA Loneliness Scale. These items actually came from the original version of the scale published in 1978. For each question students should give themselves one point for a "never" response, two points for "rarely," three points for "sometimes," and four points for "often." Total score is computed by adding responses on the 10 items together. Mean scores for college students, nurses, public school teachers, and elderly persons have been 20, 20, 19, and 16, respectively. A score above 30 indicates the person is experiencing severe levels of loneliness.

7. Perceived Stress

How much stress do your students feel in their lives? You might introduce this topic with the questions researchers Sheldon Cohen and Gail Williamson (1988) asked a representative sample of Americans. After writing the response scale on the chalkboard (0 = never, 1 = almost never, 2 = sometimes, 3 = fairly often, 4 = very often) ask students, "In the last month, how often have you felt... A. unable to control the important things in your life? B. confident about your ability to handle personal problems? C. that things were going your way? D. that difficulties were piling up so high that you could not overcome them?

For questions B and C students should first reverse their response numbers, i.e., 0 = 4, 1 = 3, 2 = 2, 3 = 1, 4 = 0, and then add up the numbers they gave in response to all four questions. In Cohen and Williamson's national study, men and women averaged 4.2 and 4.7 points, respectively.

8. Illusory Correlation

People have difficulty discerning the presence and absence of correlations. Demonstration MA-5 presents data in which a correlation of +.57 exists. Do students correctly judge the presence of a correlation? (Most will not.)

Demonstration MA-6 presents data, which have zero correlation. (The interview is three times as likely to yield a positive diagnosis as not, <u>regardless</u> of the Rorschach diagnosis. A chi square analysis therefore yields a result of 0.0.) However, most students perceive that there <u>is</u> a relationship. Why the illusory correlation? Are people overly impressed by confirming instances?

You can use these demonstrations to illustrate how difficult it is to discern with our unaided intuition the presence or absence of relationships—and why, just as a biologist needs a microscope to see what the eye cannot see, so too a psychologist needs statistics.

9. Testing Social Beliefs with Confirmatory Strategies

There is an almost irresistible tendency to search for positive instances of one's beliefs or hypothesis. You can demonstrate this as Mark Snyder and Steve Gangestad (1981) did in their research. Ask students each to take a few moments to design an experiment that tests the following social stereotype: "Women are particularly susceptible to flattery and thus tend to comply with requests when smiled at and when given compliments."

The appropriate experimental design would observe compliance rates following requests made under at least four conditions:

	Flattery	No Flattery
Women		
Men		

Now ask for a show of hands. How many included a condition in which women are flattered? (Snyder and Gangestad report that virtually all their participants did.) How many included all three of the other necessary conditions? (Snyder and Gangestad report that only one-third did so.) This demonstrates that people seem to find information that is hypothesis confirming more relevant than information that is disconfirming. This bias contributes to the illusory correlation phenomenon reported in the chapter.

10. Self-Confirming Diagnoses

You can replicate the first stage of Mark Snyder and William Swann's research, described in the text. Distribute each form of Demonstration MA-7 to half the class. (If they have already read the module, have them each be experimenters and give the forms to two others.) When all have finished, have them count the number of introverted questions checked. Were those who were testing for introversion more likely than those who were testing for extraversion to prefer questions that would elicit examples of introverted behavior? (Snyder and Swann report that those testing for introversion chose 5.8 introverted and 4.6 extraverted questions; those testing for extraversion chose 2.7 introverted and 7.4 extraverted questions.) Point out that people who are actually asked these introverted questions are later observed to behave less sociably than those who have been asked extraverted questions. This illustrates how easy it can be for clinicians to confirm their diagnoses, indeed, how easy it is for all of us to confirm our beliefs about others.

Here is the scoring key (E = extraverted questions, I = introverted questions, N = neutral questions).

1. I	7. I	13. N	19. E	25. E
2. E	8. I	14. I	20. N	26. E
3. E	9. E	15. E	21. I	
4. I	10. E	16. I	22. E	
5. N	11. I	17. I	23. E	
6. I	12. E	18. N	24. I	

As the text indicates, some research suggests that when subjects make up their <u>own</u> questions, rather than choosing from Snyder's list, the confirmatory bias is absent. Surely, however, the last word on this important issue has not been spoken.

11. After-the-Fact Psychologizing

To demonstrate how easy it is to "explain" people's personalities with hindsight analysis, present each form of Demonstration MA-8, which is adapted from Kahneman and Tversky (1973), to half the class. Regardless of which outcome they are given, most students will have little difficulty discerning the psychological signs pointing to that outcome. You might even form the class into small groups, give each version to half the groups, and then invite each group to read to the class a short written report of its findings.

12. The Life Orientation Test

Demonstration MA-9 is Michael Scheier and Charles Carver's Life Orientation Test, which measures a respondent's optimism, or expectations regarding the favorability of future outcomes. In scoring the scale, students should reverse their responses to items 3, 8, 9 and 12 (0 = 4, 1 = 3, 2 = 2, 3 = 1, 4 = 0), and then add up their responses to items 1, 3, 4, 5, 8, 9, 11, and 12 to obtain a final score (items 2, 6, 7, and 10 are filler items). Scores can range from 0 to 32, with higher scores reflecting greater optimism. The mean score is approximately 21.

13. The Social Connection Video Series

One of the entries in the video instructional supplement (The Social Connection Video Series), entitled "Social Ostracism," discusses how we tend to be happier and healthier when we fell supported by close intimate relationships. See the Faculty Guide accompanying the video series for a program summary, pause points, and a classroom activity.

Demonstration MA-1

True or False

1. Some studies have suggested that mental health workers often fall prey to judgmental errors like succumbing to the hindsight bias and forming illusory correlations. T F
2. Unfortunately, some research suggests clinical diagnosis can be influenced by mental health workers' preconceived ideas concerning attributes of the client and what their problem(s) might be. T F
3. Thankfully, there is little evidence suggesting trained clinicians engage in the same kind of "confirming information only" searches in which so many other people naively engage. T F
4. A clinical diagnosis generated by a statistical model is much more likely to be accurate than a diagnosis made by an actual clinician T F
5. Not surprisingly, research suggests nondepressed people are more evenhanded in recalling their successes and failures than are depressed people. T F
6. Both Joe and Zack failed their last Social Psychology exam. Joe, however, a depressed classmate, is much more likely than Zack, a nondepressed classmate, to attribute that failure to his own general inability to understand college-level material. T F
7. Many studies suggest the emotional fluctuation many women experience prior to menstruation is best understood as a social construction as opposed to a biologically-based syndrome. T F
8. Experiencing uncontrollable stress does seem to negatively impact the bodies immune functioning. T F
9. Research with overweight patients wishing to diet suggests merely giving the patient the power to choose which technique to use improves their chances of success. T F
10. Thankfully, numerous therapeutic techniques are available to help patients successfully break the vicious cycle of depression, loneliness, and social anxiety. T F

Demonstration MA-2

(with permission of D. Burns)

Indicate how much you agree with each statement according to the following code: +2 = I agree very much; +1 = I agree somewhat; 0 = I feel neutral about this; -1 = I disagree slightly; -2 = I disagree strongly. Fill in the blank preceding each statement with the number that best describes how you think most of the time. Be sure to choose only one answer for each attitude. There are no "right" or "wrong" answers, so try to respond according to the way you usually feel or behave.

___ 1. If I don't set the highest standards for myself, I am likely to end up a second-rate person.

___ 2. People will probably think less of me if I make a mistake.

___ 3. If I cannot do something really well, there is little point in doing it at all.

___ 4. I should be upset if I make a mistake.

___ 5. If I try hard enough, I should be able to excel at anything I attempt.

___ 6. It is shameful for me to display weaknesses or foolish behavior.

___ 7. I shouldn't have to repeat the same mistake many times.

___ 8. An average performance is bound to be unsatisfying to me.

___ 9. Failing at something important means I'm less of a person.

___ 10. If I scold myself for failing to live up to my expectations, it will help me to do better in the future.

(This scale was designed by David D. Burns, M.D., author of Feeling Good: The New Mood Therapy, Morrow, 1980, and is used by permission.)

Demonstration MA-3

(with permission of J. Cheek)

Revised Cheek and Buss Shyness Scale

<u>How Shy are You?</u>

Read each item carefully and decide to what extent it is characteristic of your feelings and behavior. Answer each question by choosing a number from the scale below.

    1 = very uncharacteristic or untrue, strongly disagree
    2 = uncharacteristic
    3 = neutral
    4 = characteristic
    5 = very characteristic or true, strongly agree

___ 1. I feel tense when I'm with people I don't know well.
___ 2. I am socially somewhat awkward.
___ 3. I find it difficult to ask other people for information.
___ 4. I am often uncomfortable at parties and other social functions.
___ 5. When in a group of people, I have trouble thinking of the right thing to say.
___ 6. It takes me a long time to overcome my shyness in new situations.
___ 7. It is hard for me to act natural when I am meeting new people.
___ 8. I feel nervous when speaking to someone in authority.
___ 9. I have doubts about my social competence.
___ 10. I have trouble looking someone right in the eye.
___ 11. I feel inhibited in social situations.
___ 12. I find it hard to talk to strangers.
___ 13. I am more shy with members of the opposite sex.

Add up your score. If it is over 50, you are very shy; if it is between 36 and 50, you are somewhat shy; if it is below 36, you are probably not shy.

Demonstration MA-4

(with permission of D. Russell)

UCLA Loneliness Scale

Indicate how often each of the statements below is descriptive of you.

<u>Circle</u> one letter for each statement:

    O indicates "I <u>often</u> feel this way"

    S indicates "I <u>sometimes</u> feel this way"

    R indicates "I <u>rarely</u> feel this way"

    N indicates "I <u>never</u> feel this way"

1.	How often do you feel unhappy doing so many things alone?	O S R N
2.	How often do you feel you have nobody to talk to?	O S R N
3.	How often do you feel you cannot tolerate being so alone?	O S R N
4.	How often do you feel as if nobody really understands you?	O S R N
5.	How often do you find yourself waiting for people to call or write?	O S R N
6.	How often do you feel completely alone?	O S R N
7.	How often do you feel you are unable to reach out and communicate with those around you?	O S R N
8.	How often do you feel starved for company?	O S R N
9.	How often do you feel it is difficult for you to make friends?	O S R N
10.	How often do you feel shut out and excluded by others?	O S R N

Demonstration MA-5

Bolt & Myers

©McGraw-Hill, 1999

Elaine is examining the relationship between height and hair thickness among adult men. She has someone measure the height of twenty men, and has someone else measure their hair thickness (from 0, no hair, to 100, maximum thickness).

Subject #	Height in inches	Hair Thickness
1	80	75
2	63	66
3	61	60
4	79	90
5	74	60
6	69	42
7	62	42
8	75	60
9	77	81
10	60	39
11	64	48
12	76	69
13	71	72
14	66	57
15	73	63
16	70	75
17	63	30
18	71	30
19	68	84
20	70	39

What did Elaine observe?

___Height is very positively correlated with hair thickness.

___Height is moderately positively correlated with hair thickness.

___Height is slightly positively correlated with hair thickness.

___Height is not at all correlated with hair thickness.

___Height is slightly negatively correlated with hair thickness.

___Height is moderately negatively correlated with hair thickness.

___Height is very negatively correlated with hair thickness.

Demonstration MA-6

©McGraw-Hill, 1999

Roger wonders whether people's responses to Rorschach inkblots reveal unresolved childhood tensions with their parents. He assigns a different person to each of twenty clinicians who administer the Rorschach and judge the presence or absence of unresolved tension in the person. Each of the persons also visits a second clinician, who conducts an in-depth interview to assess the presence or absence of unresolved tension. Here are the results:

Is Unresolved Tension Present?

Person #	Rorschach result	Interview result
1	yes	yes
2	yes	yes
3	no	yes
4	yes	yes
5	yes	yes
6	yes	yes
7	no	yes
8	no	no
9	yes	yes
10	yes	no
11	yes	yes
12	yes	yes
13	no	yes
14	yes	no
15	yes	yes
16	yes	no
17	yes	yes
18	yes	yes
19	yes	no
20	yes	yes

What did Roger find? The Rorschach result is:

__ very positively correlated with interview result

__ moderately positively correlated with interview result

__ slightly positively correlated with interview result

__ not at all correlated with interview result

__ slightly negatively correlated with interview result

__ moderately negatively correlated with interview result

__ very negatively correlated with interview result

Demonstration MA-7

(with permission of M. Snyder)

Pretend that you are a psychologist who is about to talk with someone in order to assess how introverted this person is. Introverts are typically shy, timid, reserved, quiet, distant, and retiring. In your conversation, you can ask 12 questions that will help you get to know the person by finding out concrete information and specific facts about what that person actually thinks, feels, and does. To assess how introverted this person is, which 12 of the following questions would you most like to ask? Circle the number of each question that you'd like to ask.

1. Think about times when you felt lonely. What events brought on these feelings?
2. What events make you feel popular with people?
3. What activities do you really excel in?
4. In what situations do you wish you could be more outgoing?
5. What do you do to keep yourself in good spirits?
6. Tell me about some time when you felt left out from some social group. How did you handle these feelings?
7. What kinds of events make you feel like being along?
8. What factors make it hard for you to really open up to people?
9. What social activities (e.g., clubs, groups, fraternities or sororities) have you been active in over the years?
10. What do you like about living situations in which there are always lots of people around?
11. What do you usually think about when you're in a serious mood?
12. What kinds of situations do you seek out if you want to meet new people?
13. What kinds of charities do you like to contribute to?
14. Describe to me a type of social situation that invariably makes you feel ill at ease and awkward. What is it about such situations that makes you uncomfortable?
15. In what social situations are you likely to be outgoing and friendly?
16. Think about times when your shyness in social situations has made you come across as being aloof. Give me an example.
17. What things do you dislike about loud parties?
18. What do you think the good and bad points of acting friendly and open are?
19. In what social situations are you most likely to feel self-assured and confident of yourself?
20. What are some of your favorite books? Can you recall a time that you got into a book so much that you could hardly put it down?
21. What are your career goals?
22. Think about times you have engaged in a lively and spirited debate with someone. What are some typical things you like to debate?
23. In what situations are you most talkative? What is it about these situations that makes you like to talk?
24. Think about a time when you really wanted to talk to someone, but just couldn't bring yourself to initiate conversation. What types of situations are most likely to make you feel this way?
25. What do you like to do when you are feeling really energetic?
26. What would you do if you wanted to liven things up at a party?

Demonstration MA-7

(with permission of M. Snyder)

Pretend that you are a psychologist who is about to talk with someone in order to assess how extraverted this person is. Extraverts are typically outgoing, sociable, energetic, confident, talkative, and enthusiastic. In your conversation, you can ask 12 questions that will help you get to know the person by finding out concrete information and specific facts about what that person actually thinks, feels, and does. To assess how extraverted this person is, which 12 of the following questions would you most like to ask? Circle the number of each question that you'd like to ask.

1. Think about times when you felt lonely. What events brought on these feelings?
2. What events make you feel popular with people?
3. What activities do you really excel in?
4. In what situations do you wish you could be more outgoing?
5. What do you do to keep yourself in good spirits?
6. Tell me about some time when you felt left out from some social group. How did you handle these feelings?
7. What kinds of events make you feel like being along?
8. What factors make it hard for you to really open up to people?
9. What social activities (e.g., clubs, groups, fraternities or sororities) have you been active in over the years?
10. What do you like about living situations in which there are always lots of people around?
11. What do you usually think about when you're in a serious mood?
12. What kinds of situations do you seek out if you want to meet new people?
13. What kinds of charities do you like to contribute to?
14. Describe to me a type of social situation that invariably makes you feel ill at ease and awkward. What is it about such situations that makes you uncomfortable?
15. In what social situations are you likely to be outgoing and friendly?
16. Think about times when your shyness in social situations has made you come across as being aloof. Give me an example.
17. What things do you dislike about loud parties?
18. What do you think the good and bad points of acting friendly and open are?
19. In what social situations are you most likely to feel self-assured and confident of yourself?
20. What are some of your favorite books? Can you recall a time that you got into a book so much that you could hardly put it down?
21. What are your career goals?
22. Think about times you have engaged in a lively and spirited debate with someone. What are some typical things you like to debate?
23. In what situations are you most talkative? What is it about these situations that makes you like to talk?
24. Think about a time when you really wanted to talk to someone, but just couldn't bring yourself to initiate conversation. What types of situations are most likely to make you feel this way?
25. What do you like to do when you are feeling really energetic?
26. What would you do if you wanted to liven things up at a party?

Demonstration MA-8

Pretend the following description of Tom W. was written by a clinical psychologist five years ago, when Tom was a senior in high school. Please read it carefully before responding to the question below.

> Tom W. is of high intelligence, although lacking in true creativity. He has a need for order and clarity, and for neat and tidy systems in which every detail finds its appropriate place. His writing is rather dull and mechanical, occasionally enlivened by somewhat corny puns and flashes of imagination of the sci-fi type. He has a strong drive for competence. He seems to have little feeling and little sympathy for other people and does not enjoy interacting with others. Self-centered, he nonetheless has a deep moral sense.

Today, Tom is a mental patient in a state hospital. Might that outcome have been predicted when Tom was a senior in high school? On what basis?

Demonstration MA-8

Pretend the following description of Tom W. was written by a clinical psychologist five years ago, when Tom was a senior in high school. Please read it carefully before responding to the question below.

> Tom W. is of high intelligence, although lacking in true creativity. He has a need for order and clarity, and for neat and tidy systems in which every detail finds its appropriate place. His writing is rather dull and mechanical, occasionally enlivened by somewhat corny puns and flashes of imagination of the sci-fi type. He has a strong drive for competence. He seems to have little feeling and little sympathy for other people and does not enjoy interacting with others. Self-centered, he nonetheless has a deep moral sense.

Today, Tom is a graduate student in the School of Education in a state university and hopes to work eventually with training handicapped children. Might that outcome have been predicted when Tom was a senior in high school? On what basis?

Demonstration MA-9

(with permission of M. Scheier)

Scheier & Carver's Life Orientation Test

Indicate the degree to which you agree with the statements using the following response scale:

    0 = strongly disagree
    1 = disagree
    2 = neutral
    3 = agree
    4 = strongly agree

__ 1. In uncertain times, I usually expect the best.
__ 2. It's easy for me to relax.
__ 3. If something can go wrong for me, it will.
__ 4. I always look on the bright side of things.
__ 5. I'm always optimistic about my future.
__ 6. I enjoy my friends a lot.
__ 7. It's important for me to keep busy.
__ 8. I hardly ever expect things to go my way.
__ 9. Things never work out the way I want them.
__ 10. I don't get upset too easily.
__ 11. I'm a believer in the idea that "every cloud has a silver lining."
__ 12. I rarely count on good things happening to me.

Scheier, M., & Carver, C. (1985). Optimism, coping, and health: Assessment and implications of generalized outcome expectancies. Health Psychology, 4, p. 219–247. Copyright © 1985 by Lawrence Erlbaum Associates, Inc. Reprinted with permission.

FILMS/VIDEOS

Depression: A Study in Abnormal Behavior (CRM, 26 min., 1973). Follows the case of Helen, a 29-year-old school teacher, who suffers from chronic depression. Highlights causes, symptoms, and treatment.

Depression: Beating the Blues (FIL, 28 min., 1984). An overview of the physical, psychological, and social aspects of depression. Various therapeutic interventions are also reviewed including electroconvulsive therapy.

Depression: The Dark Side of the Blues (BAR, 25 min., 1986). Film takes viewers into the lives of five fictitious depressives. Discusses both chronic and manic depression as well as possible treatments.

Health, Stress, and Coping (INS, 30 min., 1990). Uses case studies to illuminate the intimate link between biology and psychology in understanding stress and learning how to cope. Norman Cousins discusses Selye's General Adaptation Syndrome.

Managing Stress—Revised Edition (CRM, 33 min., 1989). Provides everyday examples of stress, examines our physiological responses, and considers various ways of coping with stress.

The Pain of Shyness (FIL, 17 min., 1987). Produced by ABC's 20/20, this film first demonstrates the inhibiting effects of shyness and then illustrates some successful therapeutic interventions.

The Stress Mess (BAR, 25 min., 1981). Humorous, yet highly instructional, this film teaches stress management techniques. A 16-page instructional guide accompanies it and provides discussion questions, role-playing exercises.

Understanding Depression: Through the Darkness (FHS, 24 min., 1996). Features three patients who suffer from depression. Covers the effects the disorder has had on them, the roles of their families and friends during their illness, and how they have fared in their treatment programs.

MODULE B
SOCIAL PSYCHOLOGY IN COURT

Eyewitness Testimony
    How Persuasive is Eyewitness Testimony?
    How Accurate are Eyewitnesses?
    The Misinformation Effect
    Retelling
    Feedback to Witnesses
    Reducing Error
    Train Police Interviewers
    Minimize False Lineup Identifications
    Educate Jurors
Other Influences on Judgments
    The Defendant's Characteristics
    Physical Attractiveness
    Similarity to the Jurors
    The Judge's Instructions
    Other Issues
The Jurors as Individuals
    Juror Comprehension
    Jury Selection
    "Death-Qualified" Jurors
The Jury as a Group
    Minority Influence
    Group Polarization
    Leniency
    Are 12 Heads Better than 1?
    Are 6 Heads as Good as 12?
From Lab to Life: Simulated and Real Juries
Personal Postscript: Thinking Smart with Psychological Science

LECTURE AND DISCUSSION IDEAS

1. "Enter the Jury Room"

CBS Reports' "Enter the Jury Room" broadcast on April 16, 1997, provides an outstanding introduction to the issues discussed in Module B. Narrated by Ed Bradley and Richard Schlesinger, and produced in cooperation with the American Bar Association, this program reviews three cases tried in the Arizona judicial system. Students see the case presented in court and then the actual deliberations of the jury as each seeks to reach a verdict. Questions of jury selection, the reliability of eyewitness testimony, the impact of the judge's instructions, and minority influence all come alive with these real life examples. Interviews with jurors, attorneys, and judges address the question of what influences jury decisions and ultimately whether they serve justice. Although the total program is two hours, the cases can be easily separated so that you can show just one in class. Order "Enter the Jury Room" for $24.98 + $4.95 S&H by calling 1-800-934-NEWS.

2. The Rodney King Case

Like the O. J. Simpson trial described in the opening to Module B, the first trial of the four police officers in the Rodney King beating raises important questions about the courtroom that social psychology seeks to address.

First, the videotape of King's beating made every viewer an eyewitness to apparent police brutality, convincing most with overpowering evidence of excessive force. Seeing is believing. Still the jury saw differently, surely partly as the result of the defense's expert witnesses (most of whom were police officers) reassuring the jury that the force used against King was appropriate. For example, Sgt. Charles Duke, a Los Angeles SWAT team member, testified, "Once an officer is attacked, to allow a suspect to rise to his feet, you allow the possibility of escalating to the use of deadly force." Some speculated that the absence of Rodney King's personal testimony was the critical factor. One unnamed juror later admitted, "Had King been able to talk with us, the video might have been looked at differently." In addition to introducing the text's discussion of eyewitness testimony, you can use the King case to review the nature of perception, particularly its inherent subjectivity as described in Chapter 3.

The Rodney King case highlights the question of how the defendant's characteristics such as attractiveness, status, and similarity to the jurors influence verdicts. The defendants were four white police officers for whom the all-white jury likely had respect and sympathy from the start. Note one juror's comment after the trial: "They're policemen, not angels. They're out there to do a low-down dirty job. Would you want your husband doing it, or your son or your father?" Less sympathy was probably felt for King, a black man with a criminal record.

The trial raises questions about the effects of pretrial publicity and the judge's instructions. At the request of the defense, which argued that publicity in Los Angeles made a fair trial there unlikely, the trial was moved to Simi Valley. Some saw this shift as critical. And several jurors suggested that the judge's final instructions before they began deliberations constituted the key reason for the not guilty verdict. To find the officers guilty of assault, Judge Stanley Weisberg said, jurors had to agree that they had a "general criminal intent" and that the beating was not done "in lawful defense of another" officer. On the charge of assault "under color of authority," the judge said, "If you have a reasonable doubt that the use of force was unlawful and without lawful necessity, you must find the defendant not guilty." "I had to go by what evidence was given me," said one juror. "and there was a reasonable doubt."

Much was made of the jury's composition in explaining its verdict. The panel was drawn from an initial pool of 400, less than 10 of whom were black. It constituted six men, six women, one Asian, one Hispanic. There was an even division among Democrats and Republicans; the age range was 38 to 65. They were selected from what most considered to be a politically conservative community, Simi Valley and surrounding Ventura County. The prosecution did not object to the trial site, although some civil rights leaders forecast the results. NAACP leader John Hatcher III stated, "They would be better going to Mississippi. King will lose and the officers will win."

Finally, the case raised questions about how, after deliberations begin, jurors influence one another. For example, does a minority ever sway the majority? The jury in the Rodney King case deliberated for a week, although they had apparently agreed on all counts but one by the end of the first day. They eventually deadlocked by a vote of 8 to 4 on one charge of excessive force against the officer who had delivered the most blows. Perhaps most revealing were juror Virginia Loya's (the lone Hispanic on the panel) comments a few days after the trial. She claimed that her fellow members on the panel had made up their minds before deliberations began. Moreover, they mocked and pressured her when she fought for at least one conviction. "The people's eyes weren't open and I said to God, 'If you give me one more person on my side I would know.'"

3. Case Study of a Jury: Twelve Angry Men

The feature film Twelve Angry Men (see Chapter 3) is also very useful in introducing the research of this chapter (both the 1957 original or the 1997 remake). The entire film deals with the deliberations of a jury deciding the fate of a young man accused of murder. Questions relating to eyewitness testimony, defendant characteristics, juror characteristics, and the jury as a group are all raised. The film is particularly applicable to a discussion of minority influence. In the course of the jury's deliberations, an 11 to 1 vote for a guilty verdict becomes a unanimous vote for acquittal.

The film highlights a host of social psychological processes and thus may also provide a good summary and ending to the course. For their final, possibly "take-home" exam, students could be asked to apply their knowledge of social psychological theory and research to an understanding of the events of the film.

Dana Anderson (1992) suggests specific ways of using feature films to stimulate discussion of psycholegal issues. One strategy is to have students identify research findings relevant to the films and critique the accuracy of the films' representation of this material. A second assignment requires students to analyze the psycholegal issues the films evoke, critique the films' presentation of the issues, and evaluate their impact on the students' own positions. Among the films Anderson recommends are Nuts, which portrays the relationship between a woman charged with manslaughter and her attorney who suspects she may be too mentally ill to stand trial; The Onion Field, which concerns the aftermath of a police officer's killing for his partner and accused killers; and Taxi Driver, which shows the mental deterioration of a would-be political assassin who turns vigilante.

4. Eyewitness Testimony

In addition to the findings reported in the text on eyewitness testimony, you may wish to add the following, as reported by Elizabeth Loftus (1984):

- In spite of the fact that most people believe police officers make better witnesses, research indicates that neither training nor experience increases their accuracy.
- Witnesses do not remember the details of a violent crime better than those of a nonviolent one. In fact research suggests the opposite: the stress that violence creates clouds perceptions.

- Witnesses almost invariably think a crime took longer than it did. Moreover, the more violent and stressful the crime, the more witnesses overestimate its duration.
- The unreliability of confidence as a guide to accuracy has been demonstrated outside as well as inside the courtroom. For example, of several people who provided accounts of an aircraft accident killing nine people, one observer was certain that the plane "was heading right toward the ground, straight down." Photographs made it clear the airplane hit flat and at a low enough angle to skid almost 1,000 feet.

5. Challenging Memories of Sex Abuse

Many recent court cases have involved testimonies from individuals asserting they have recovered memories of sexual abuse during childhood. One of the topics in this module concerns the degree of confidence we can attach to personal memories and the accuracy of eyewitness testimony. An interesting debate concerning the legitimacy of these memories can be found in the Taking Sides series (Clashing Views on Controversial Psychological Issues, 9th Ed) edited by Brent Slife (1996). Issue 8 asks the question "Are memories of sex abuse always real?" Ellen Bass and Laura Davis respond in the affirmative while Lee Coleman responds in the negative. The two theses are followed by a series of challenge questions, which can be used to generate discussion in small groups.

6. Eliciting False Confessions

The text discusses police interrogations of eyewitnesses. You can readily extend this topic in the classroom to the research on police interviews of criminal suspects. Kassin's (1997) review of the psychology of confession evidence is an excellent source. Perhaps most startling is his research indicating that false incriminating evidence can lead people to accept guilt for a crime they did not commit.

Kassin and Kiechel (1996) had two college students (one of whom was a confederate) participate in a reaction time experiment. The confederate read a list of letters, which the participant was to type as quickly as possible on a computer keyboard. Participants were forewarned not to press the "ALT" because the computer would malfunction and the data would be lost. Sixty seconds into the task the computer crashes and the experimenter accuses the participant of hitting the key. All are in fact innocent and initially deny the charge. Independent variables include the speed of the task (letters are presented at a slow or fast pace) and the presentation of false incriminating evidence (the confederate did not see what happened or accuses the participant of hitting the forbidden key).

To assess social influence, the experimenter handwrote a standardized confession and prodded the participants to sign it. In addition, as they left the experiment they met another waiting participant (a second confederate) who asked about the commotion. The participant's reply was coded as to whether he or she accepted blame. Finally, the experimenter brought the participants back to ask if they could reconstruct what had happened. This procedure was used to test for evidence of confabulation. Overall an amazing 69 percent signed the confession, 28 percent internalized guilt, and 9 percent confabulated details to support their false beliefs. Of 17 participants in the fast pace-witness group, all signed the confession, 65 percent came to believe they were guilty, and 35 percent confabulated details to fit the newly created belief.

7. Defendant Versus Plaintiff Attractiveness

The text's discussion of the defendant's physical attractiveness can be readily extended by introducing Wilbur Castellow and his colleagues' (1990) intriguing research on the effects of the attractiveness of both the plaintiff and defendant in sexual harassment judgments.

Male and female college students read a three-page summary of a sexual harassment trial. Attached to the upper right hand corner of the first page were photographs of an attractive or unattractive female plaintiff and an attractive or unattractive male defendant. Results indicated that the appearance of both individuals had a significant impact on students' judgments. A total of 83 percent of the subjects found the defendant guilty when he was unattractive and the plaintiff was attractive, 71 percent voted guilty when both the defendant and plaintiff were attractive, 69 percent voted guilty when both were unattractive, and only 41 percent found the defendant guilty when he was attractive and the plaintiff was unattractive.

8. Inadmissible Testimony and the Judge's Instructions

The text indicates that jurors often have difficulty following a judge's instructions to ignore pretrial publicity and inadmissible evidence. Recent research clarifies conditions under which jurors do ignore such information.

Kassin and Sommers (1997) presented research participants with a murder trial summary in which a wiretap was ruled inadmissible either because it was unreliable (the tape was barely audible and thus it was difficult to be sure what was said) or because it was illegally obtained. A no-wiretap control condition and a fourth group where the wiretap was admissible evidence completed the experimental design. A low 24 percent conviction rate in the control group contrasted with a high 79 percent for the admissible wiretap group. The conviction rates for the inadmissible/due-process and inadmissible/unreliable groups were 55 percent and 24 percent, respectively. Kassin and Sommers concluded that jurors are influenced not by the judge's instructions per se but by the causal basis for the ruling. Jurors discount inadmissible evidence for reasons that are substantive rather than procedural.

Fein, McCloskey, and Tomlinson (1997) presented mock jurors with incriminating information about a defendant in the context of pretrial publicity or testimony during the trial that was ruled inadmissible. In spite of the judge's instructions to disregard the information, jurors' judgments were significantly influenced unless they were made suspicious about the motives underlying the introduction of this information. That is, some jurors were led to believe that the media manipulated information to sell papers (pretrial publicity) or the prosecuting attorney was intentionally trying to manipulate jurors' judgements (inadmissible testimony). When jurors were given reason to be suspicious about why the incriminating information was introduced, their verdicts did not differ from those jurors not exposed to the incriminating information.

9. The Insanity Plea

Consideration of the insanity plea can be presented in the context of the text's treatment of defendant characteristics. It is certain to stimulate lively classroom discussion and debate.

"Sanity" is actually a legal rather than a psychological term and is reflected in the fact that "insanity" is not a diagnostic category of the DSM-IV. The insanity defense can be traced back to the 1843 British case of Daniel M'Naghten who tried to kill the prime minister but shot the prime minister's secretary by mistake. M'Naghten, who was under the delusion that the prime minister was persecuting him, was acquitted as insane and hospitalized. After the verdict was upheld, the insanity rule emerged. Defendants were judged insane if they did not know what they were doing or did not know that it was wrong.

When John W. Hinckley, Jr., was brought to trial in 1982 for shooting President Reagan and his press secretary, the insanity defense had been broadened. The burden of proof was on the prosecution to prove that Hinckley had "a substantial capacity" not merely to "know" his act was wrong but to "appreciate" its wrongfulness and to act accordingly. When the prosecution was unable to prove Hinckley's sanity to the jury's satisfaction, he was sent to a mental hospital.

Partly in response to public outcry at the Hinckley verdict, some states, including Montana, Idaho, and Utah, have abolished the insanity defense. Furthermore, in Canada and in three-fourths of the U.S. states where the insanity defense remains, defendants must now show that they did not understand the wrongfulness of their acts. Some states have also instituted a "guilty but mentally ill" plea. This verdict acknowledges the need for treatment but holds people responsible and sends them to prison if they are judged sane before their sentence is over.

The general public vastly overestimates both the frequency with which defendants plead insanity as well as their success. The public estimates that it is raised in 37 percent of all felony cases when in fact it is used in less than 1 percent. And while the public estimates that 44 percent who plead insanity are acquitted, the actual rate is 26 percent.

10. Police Lineups as Experiments

Wells and Luus (1990), as the text briefly notes, draw a useful analogy between a methodologically sound social psychology experiment and a properly conducted police lineup. You can review and extend that analogy in class. In addition to introducing the specific research findings on lineups, it provides a good review of experimental design and its potential relevance for helping solve social problems.

Wells and Luus show how, in the image of a social psychology experiment, the police officer conducting the lineup is an <u>experimenter</u>, the <u>experimenter's hypothesis</u> is that the suspect is the perpetrator, and the <u>null hypothesis</u> is that the suspect is not the perpetrator. The <u>subjects</u> are the eyewitnesses, the <u>stimulus</u> is the suspect, and the <u>confederates</u> are the foils in the lineup. The <u>design</u> has the suspect embedded among the distractors or foils, and the <u>procedure</u> consists of the instructions to the eyewitnesses. <u>Possible manipulations</u> include the number of foils, the appearance of the foils, and the presence or absence of the suspect. <u>Dependent measures</u> include the recognition as well as the certainty of recognition. The <u>outcome</u> is the eyewitnesses identifying the suspect, identifying a foil, or identifying no one. Wells and Luus suggest that the analogy between an experiment and a lineup fits so well that experimental social psychologists are well-suited to the task of defining the best ways to conduct lineups.

The authors show how this analysis and simple extensions of it have led to improvements in the procedures used in police lineups. For example, in a typical lineup, a suspect is placed among nonsuspects and paraded before the eyewitnesses. A problem with this procedure, that follows from the lineup-as-experiment analogy, is lack of a control group. One solution has been to have subjects, who were not eyewitnesses, attempt to identify the suspect from the lineup (this is called the mock-witness control, a between-subjects type of control). Another approach is to show the eyewitnesses a lineup that does not contain a suspect before showing a lineup that does (this is called a blank-lineup control, a within-subjects kind of control). Mock witnesses not only help to define and control chance (e.g., could merely having read a general description of the culprit enable one to pick out the suspect?), they are also helpful in determining whether the witness was able to discern the police investigator's hypothesis. The blank line-up can be a powerful way to detect any response bias in the eyewitness, for example, simply to choose anyone or to choose someone who most looks like the culprit relative to the other lineup members.

Finally, Wells and Luus give examples of specific recommendations for the conduct of lineups or photo spreads that have experimental analogues. Witnesses should be separated as soon as possible (if subjects interact before responding to the dependent measure, then their data cannot be analyzed as though they were independent); at no time should a witness be led to believe that the actual perpetrator is in the set of mugshots (experimenter protocols should be worded in a way that does not create demands on the subject to respond in a particular way); if there is more than one witness, the position of the suspect in the photo spread should be changed for each witness (stimulus presentation order should be randomized or counterbalanced across subjects).

11. Jury Selection

Paul Olczak and his colleagues (1991) report a series of studies, which explored the jury selection strategies of trial attorneys and naive subjects. In the first experiment they examined the kinds of information attorneys use in juror selection and whether their selections are helpful to their case. The specific characteristics they said they sought or avoided (in order of importance) were intelligence, age, appearance, occupation, open-mindedness, gender, attentiveness, impressibility, and race. (Intelligence was mentioned most often as a desirable trait for the defense. The voir dire questions they most often reported using were general attitude toward the police, exposure to prejudicial pretrial publicity, whether the juror was ever victimized, attitude toward people who are arrested, racial bias, any acquaintance ever arrested or convicted, any relationship to the parties in the case. Olczak and his colleagues report that none of the juror characteristics have significant predictive validity.

In a second experiment, the researchers compared attorneys' and introductory psychology students' selection strategies. Both groups were given the same information about the characteristics of hypothetical jurors in a rape case and were asked to rate the acceptability of each from a defense perspective. The attorneys and naive subjects showed simple and identical patterns of using juror characteristics in judging desirability. The researchers concluded that attorneys, despite their trial experience, use a narrow range of characteristics in judging jurors, which suggests the influence of lay psychology or everyday stereotypes.

In a third experiment, trial attorneys and law students were presented with the characteristics of jurors who had served in a prior mock trial and judged their desirability from a defense standpoint. Both attorneys and students were more in error than accurate. Both groups judged jurors who had convicted as more desirable than those who had acquitted.

12. Primacy and Recency Effects: Interpreting Ambiguous Evidence

Kassin and his colleagues (1990) demonstrate how the same piece of evidence takes on a very different meaning depending on which side introduces it in a trial. They also show how the personal characteristics of the jurors make a difference.

Subjects read a summary of an actual murder case and then watched a 45-minute police interrogation of the female defendant. (Police will often videotape their interrogations, and confessions are replayed in court.) She maintained her innocence throughout but made some very implausible assertions. Her ambiguous statement could be interpreted as evidence of guilt or innocence. The researchers created two conditions. In the first, the defense attorney introduced the tape and noted his client's consistent disclaimers in the face of heavy pressure to confess. The tape was played and the prosecutor cited serious flaws in the defendant's account. In the second condition the prosecutor introduced the tape as evidence of guilt, played it, and the defense counterargued.

Results indicated that judgments of guilt or innocence were clearly influenced by which attorney introduced the tape. However, the direction of influence was different for subjects who were either high or low in need for cognition. High need-for-cognition subjects showed a primacy effect, sharing the perspective of whoever introduced the tape. Low need-for-cognition subjects demonstrated a recency effect. Their judgment agreed with whoever had the final word about the tape.

13. Social Psychology in Court

The text reveals that attempts to introduce research on simulated juries into court proceedings has had a mixed response. Recently Loftus (1991) described the expanding role that psychology is playing in the legal world. She cites two examples in which <u>social framework data</u> (use of general conclusions from social science research in determining factual issues in a specific case) has been used in court.

One case involved the employment of Ann Hopkins at Price Waterhouse (a leading accounting firm). Although competent, committed, and hard-working, Hopkins was denied partnership and she promptly filed a complaint in federal court. Social psychologist Susan Fiske testified on her behalf, citing research findings on stereotyping, including its causes, symptoms, and consequences. The judge ruled in Hopkins' favor. Price Waterhouse appealed and eventually the case was heard by the U.S. Supreme Court. Although research on sex stereotyping had been introduced in other legal proceedings, it was the first Supreme Court case to examine psychological research on sex stereotyping. The American Psychological Association entered with an amicus curiae brief, expanding psychology's involvement. The result, perhaps due in part to psychology's role, was in favor of Hopkins.

In another case tried in South Africa, defendants were convicted of murdering a number of workers who had refused to join a strike. Several had not actually committed the killings but were found guilty by virtue of "common purpose." In the postconviction phase of the trial, Andrew Coleman described to the court such basic psychological phenomena as conformity, obedience to authority, deindividuation, bystander apathy, and the fundamental attribution error. Research findings were at the heart of his expert testimony. The outcome, possibly attributable in part to this testimony, was that several defendants were ultimately spared the death penalty.

Loftus discusses how judges and attorneys reacted to the testimony, considers whether the psychologist's expert testimony should have been admitted in court, and explains possible benefits to psychology of involvement in legal cases.

14. "Death-Qualified" Jurors and the "Witherspoon" Standards

The text indicates that when a court dismisses potential jurors opposed to the death penalty it also creates a more conviction-prone jury. In 1968, William C. Witherspoon appealed his conviction and death sentence to the U.S. Supreme Court on the grounds that the "death-qualified" jury that deliberated the case was not representative. Before his murder trial, 47 of the 100 prospective jurors had been dismissed with the judge's statement, "Let's get these conscientious objectors out of the way without wasting any time on them" (Ellsworth, 1985). Although the court did reverse the death sentence, it allowed the verdict to stand, stating that the results of research were "too tentative and fragmentary" to conclude that a "death-qualified" jury was more likely to return a guilty verdict. It did state, however, that the criteria used to exclude jurors should be more stringent, applying only to those who say that their opposition to the death penalty would prevent them from fairly determining the defendant's guilt or innocence. Interestingly the court also invited further research to determine whether death-qualified juries are conviction-prone. Since 1968, the "Witherspoon" standards have been used in most capital trials in the United States.

Phoebe Ellsworth (1985) provides an overview of the research since the Witherspoon case including her investigations with Robert Fitzgerald which involved attitudinal comparisons between those excluded and death-qualified using the Witherspoon criteria. Interviews with 717 jurors revealed that the "death-qualified" were significantly more punitive and more likely to reject basic due-process guarantees such as the protection against self-incrimination and the insanity defense. Excluded jurors were equally skeptical of defense and prosecution attorneys but death-qualified jurors trusted the prosecutor much more than the defense. The survey also found that, on the basis of their death penalty attitudes, blacks were more likely to be excluded than members of other groups, and women were more likely to be excluded than men. Further research indicated that the death-qualified jurors were much more likely to find a defendant guilty. After watching a 2 1/2 hour videotape of a homicide trial, 78 percent of the death-qualified jurors found the defendant guilty, compared to 53 percent of those excluded. Other studies have replicated this finding and have shown differences in the willingness to believe prosecution and defense witnesses, in the willingness to convict defendants who plead insanity, and in thresholds of reasonable doubt. In addition, Craig Haney reports that the standard practice of questioning potential jurors about their attitudes toward capital punishment suggests to them that the defendant is probably guilty. In essence they think: "If the judges and lawyers didn't think the defendant was guilty, why would they spend so much time asking about the appropriate punishment?"

In early 1986, the U.S. Supreme Court heard the case of Lockhart vs. McCree. Ardia McCree was convicted of capital murder in Arkansas in 1978. Because the state originally sought the death penalty (later it asked for and obtained the life sentence) eight prospective jurors were excluded from his jury because they would not impose the death penalty under any circumstances. While McCree's appeal that he was denied a fair trial was rejected by the state supreme court, the federal district court as well as the federal district court of appeals agreed that the death-qualified jury violated McCree's constitutional rights. Arkansas appealed the decision to the Supreme Court. On May 5, 1986, in a 6-3 ruling, the justices stated that death penalty opponents may be excluded from juries deciding the guilt or innocence of defendants who face possible death sentences. Justice William H. Rehnquist, writing for the majority, expressed "serious doubts about the value" of studies supporting the conviction-prone theory. Arkansas Attorney General Steve Clark called the ruling a "home run" that could clear the way for the first execution in that state since 1964. In a dissenting opinion, Justice Thurgood Marshall accused the court of "a glib nonchalance ill-suited to the gravity of the issue present." He further stated, "Such a blatant disregard for the rights of a capital defendant offends logic, fairness, and the Constitution."

15. Language in the Courtroom

Lori Andrews (1984) states, "Far from being a straightforward fact-finding mission, a trial is a labyrinth of language, with the words of the judge, lawyers and witnesses creating numerous obstacles that prevent juries from making accurate decisions." She indicates that a review of research done in the last 10 years clearly demonstrates that the language of the courtroom is far more influential than anyone had previously imagined. Included among the findings are the following:

- Winning prosecutors asked more questions referring to the witness, spoke longer, and made more assertive statements than did the losing prosecutors.

- Successful defense attorneys used more abstract language, more legal jargon, and more ambiguous words than losers did.

- Jurors who heard emotionally laden questions like "How much of the fight did you see?" were more likely to convict a defendant than those who heard neutral versions of the same question, "How much of the incident did you see?"

- When a lawyer used an aggravating, aggressive, active manner to ask about an incident, a witness was more likely to describe it as noisier and more violent than when the lawyer used a neutral form of questioning.

- Juries form unwarranted poor impressions of defendants whose native tongue is not English.
- When a lawyer permitted a witness to testify in a narrative style rather than one interrupted by many questions, listeners believed that the lawyer thought his witness was more intelligent and competent and in turn tended to judge the witness the same way.
- When 14 widely used jury instructions were read to jurors and they were asked to paraphrase each instruction after they heard it, only 32 percent of the instructions were given back correctly.
- In John Hinckley's trial for the attempted assassination of President Reagan, a defense attorney pointed to Hinckley's "bizarre poetry" as evidence of insanity, while a prosecution psychiatrist said Hinckley was a sane man whose poetry was "eccentric fiction." The jurors wondered, "Was all poetry fiction?" If so, the prosecution witness might be correct and Hinckley was sane. Their request to the judge for a dictionary was denied and the jurors were forced to decide the case on some other basis.

16. Nonunanimous Juries

In 1972, the Supreme Court, in a 5-4 (nonunanimous!) ruling, declared that states could establish nonunanimous juries to speed up trials and to reduce costs. A study by Robert Foss (1981) of West Virginia University raises serious questions about whether the verdicts reached by such juries are comparable to those of unanimous juries. A total of 28 simulated juries heard the case of a businessman who had been shot by a colleague. Their task was to determine whether the shooting was intentional or not. Half of the juries were instructed to reach a unanimous verdict while the other half were told to reach a decision in which only 10 people had to agree. In a second manipulation, Foss presented more, or less, ambiguous versions of the evidence.

Juries were polled before deliberating and then after each 15-minute interval. A jury was considered hung if no change occurred in its voting after being polled three times, or if it made three consecutive requests to declare itself hung.

Results indicated that, while all 14 juries operating under the 10-vote rule reached a verdict, only eight of those requiring unanimity reached a decision. Of the six hung juries, all but one had heard the ambiguous case.

An even more interesting finding was that of the hung juries, four had not even reached enough agreement for a verdict under the majority rule of 10. In other words, the failure of unanimous juries to reach a decision was not the result of one or two holdouts. More disagreement clearly existed in the juries required to reach unanimity. Foss reports that while the extent of disagreement was initially the same in the two types of juries, by the end of the first 15 minutes disagreement in majority-rule juries was about half the level of that in unanimous juries.

In attempting to explain these findings Foss reasoned that members of a majority-rule jury know that one or two people cannot prevent a verdict. Thus there is a greater tendency to reach agreement. Jurors who might otherwise be more argumentative do not insist on their own view because they know they cannot prevent a contrary verdict anyway.

As the text suggests, majority-rule juries do appear to deliberate differently, and their decisions are not necessarily comparable to those requiring unanimity.

Discussion Questions:

1. In what ways may simulated juries be different from actual juries?

2. Should all juries be required to reach a unanimous verdict? Why or why not? Is the severity of the crime likely to influence how juries deliberate?

17. Plea Bargaining

Most felony convictions are reached through the plea bargaining process. Plea bargaining refers to the process by which defendants agree to plead guilty in exchange for the promise of a reduction either in what they are charged with or in the actual sentence they receive.

The major reason for plea bargaining on the part of the prosecution is the tremendous pressure courts are under from the large backload of cases. The obvious incentive for defendants is the prospect of a significantly lighter sentence than that which might be received if they were convicted in jury trials. For example, in 1978, in a plea bargain approved by the Supreme Court, a defendant was offered a five-year prison term if he would plead guilty. He was told he might receive a mandatory life sentence if found guilty by trial. Such a disparity might even lead an innocent person to plea bargain, and helps explain why the process has come under attack. Plea bargaining assumes the defendant is guilty, short-circuits the trial process, and thus may result in an abridgment of the individual's rights. Similarly, the guilty may receive an unduly light sentence.

Two experiments on plea bargaining were conducted by Gregory, Mowen, and Linder (1978). In the first experiment, male college students were asked to imagine that they were innocent or guilty of having committed an armed robbery. After hearing a summary of the evidence that would be presented for and against them at their trial (the same for both "innocent" and "guilty" subjects), the number of charges against them (four versus one), as well as the sentence if convicted (10 to 15 years versus 1 to 2 years), a plea bargain was offered them. Since a jury's verdict is to rest solely on the evidence presented, a defendant's private knowledge of guilt should not affect his or her estimate of the probability of conviction. Nevertheless 18 percent of the subjects playing the role of innocent defendants accepted the plea bargain, while 83 percent of the guilty defendants accepted. Moreover, the number of charges and severity of punishment influenced willingness to accept the plea bargain by guilty defendants only.

The second experiment was conducted to provide validation for the major finding of the first study. Introductory psychology students were given a difficult exam after being given prior information by a confederate that most of the answers were "B" (guilty condition). Students were led to believe that they had scored extremely high on the test, arousing the experimenter's suspicion that the student had obtained prior information about the test. Students were informed that they would have to appear before an ethics committee that would evaluate the situation and make a decision that might involve costly punishment. Students were then given the opportunity to plea bargain, that is, to confess and receive a lesser penalty. As in the first study, innocent defendants overwhelmingly refused the plea bargain, whereas guilty defendants accepted it. (The investigators, sensitive to the ethical issues raised by the experiment, informed the subjects that the procedures would involve stress, thoroughly debriefed them after the experiment, and telephoned each subject three to seven days following the study to assess the students' feelings and to answer further questions.)

Discussion Questions:

1. Should plea bargaining be permitted?
2. What ethical issues are raised by these studies? Did the researchers address them satisfactorily?
3. What other variables might influence the defendant's willingness to accept a plea bargain?

18. Popular Sources for Additional Classroom Material

Costanzo, M. (1997). <u>Just revenge: Costs and consequences of the death penalty</u>. New York: St. Martin's Press. Provides a comprehensive, research-based analysis of capital punishment. Examines the costs, benefits, and implications of the death penalty.

Hans, V., & Vidmar, N. (1986). <u>Judging the jury</u>. New York: Plenum. Reviews the history of the jury, of two decades of jury research, and of highly publicized trials. Examines issues involved in insanity, rape, and death penalty cases.

Kassin, S., & Wrightsman, L. (1988). <u>The American jury on trial: Psychological perspectives</u>. New York: Hemisphere. An easy-to-read and authoritative review of the entire process of trial by jury, from jury selection to verdict.

Loftus, E., & Ketcham, K. (1991). <u>Witness for the defense</u>. New York: St. Martin's Press. Good source of material for classroom discussion of eyewitness testimony. The authors show how memory construction can produce persuasive but flawed eyewitness reports, by adults and children.

Pecoraro, T. (1981, October). Jurors go easy on handsome rapists with homely victims. <u>Psychology Today</u>, pp. 15, 27. Briefly describes the results of a study showing that the attractiveness of both the victim and the defendant are potentially important in understanding the judgments of jurors.

Wrightsman, L. S. (1989, August). Psychology and the law: Recurring dilemmas. G. Stanley Hall Lecture presented at the meetings of the American Psychological Association, New Orleans. Presents a number of classroom discussion topics for each of five dilemmas, which include definitions of justice and the law versus social science as a means of making decisions.

DEMONSTRATION AND PROJECT IDEAS

1. Courtroom Quiz

Demonstration MB-1 may be used to introduce the research findings discussed in Module B. Many of the correct answers are likely to surprise your students. As the chapter will reveal, answers to the first three questions are false, the rest are true.

2. Eyewitness Accuracy

The persuasiveness and accuracy of eyewitness testimony is an important topic of this chapter. William Dragon (1992) utilizes a very useful class project/demonstration in which students stage and videotape an instructor's assassination. You can receive a free copy of the segment he created with his students by sending a blank video cassette or CD-R to Prof. William Dragon, Dept. of Psychology, Cornell College, 600 First St. West, Mt. Vernon, IA 52314-1098. Include a postage-paid envelope for return of the tape to you. The tape depicts the first few minutes of a lecture on short-term memory. About three minutes into the lecture a student stands and fires a starter's pistol at the instructor who falls to the floor. The assailant flees, several students rush to assist the instructor, and the segment ends.

Dragon shows the brief tape to other classes and simply instructs the students to write down what they saw. Then small groups of students construct a description with the requirement that all members must agree on the description. The assignment forces students to deal with their own assumptions of how accurately they perceive the world as well as their assumptions about how others see the world. Once each group has reached agreement the groups read their descriptions to the full class. At the end of the session, the tape is shown again. Ask students how comfortable they feel about being an eyewitness in court or having their own court case depend on eyewitness testimony. Most students readily acknowledge significant differences between their memory of an event and the actual event.

Dragon suggests some different ways in which the videotape can be used. For example, you can construct true-false questions about the scene to test viewer accuracy. You might even create two lists with one list utilizing some leading questions, e.g. "Did you see the gun?" or "Did you see a gun?" You might also vary the length of time between viewing the scene and its recall. That is, you might delay recall until the next class period or the following week with clear instructions that the class is not to discuss the tape. The small group assignment may also be used to demonstrate the dynamics of social influence, for example, how individuals maintain or fail to maintain their own opinions in group situations.

3. Knowledge of Eyewitness Behavior Questionnaire

Demonstration MB-2 is the Knowledge of Eyewitness Behavior Questionnaire (Deffenbacher & Loftus, 1982) which provides a good introduction to the test's discussion of eyewitness testimony. The correct answers follow:

1.	b	6.	a	11.	b
2.	d	7.	b	12.	d
3.	a	8.	d	13.	c
4.	c	9.	c	14.	a
5.	c	10.	a		

A majority of American subjects gave wrong answers to questions 3, 4, 7, 8, 9, 10, 12, and 14 (Deffenbacher and Loftus, 1982). Noon and Hollin's (1987) replication using a British sample found a majority giving incorrect answers to questions 3, 7, 8, 9, 12, and 14. As the text states, lay people are insensitive to most of the factors known to influence eyewitness testimony.

4. Group Polarization in Simulated Juries

You can illustrate group polarization of juror judgments with the materials of Demonstration MB-3 (from Kaplan & Kemmerick, 1974). Distribute the cases to students for their individual responses, and then have them turn these in and pick up fresh items on their way to their simulated juries (groups of four or five). Instruct the groups to discuss each case as a jury would (to consensus) or, at least to a point where they are hung. In either case, after the discussion they should each mark their judgments.

Before the next class, you can compute the average response to each item before and after discussion. The gross negligence case generally triggers lenient judgments that become even more lenient after discussion. The wrongful death case generally triggers harsher judgments, which become more so after discussion.

5. The Social Connection Video Series

One of the entries in the video instructional supplement (The Social Connection Video Series), entitled "Eyewitness Memory," discusses Gary Wells' important work on the limits of eyewitness testimony. See the Faculty Guide accompanying the video series for a program summary, pause points, and a classroom activity.

Demonstration MB-1

True or False?

    T   F

1. ___ ___ An eyewitness who testifies against a defendant in court and then is discredited is more damaging to the prosecutor's case than having no eyewitness at all.
2. ___ ___ Eyewitnesses who can correctly remember trivial details of a crime are also more likely to correctly identify the guilty person.
3. ___ ___ Eyewitnesses who are more certain of what they saw also tend to be more accurate.
4. ___ ___ Attractive defendants are less likely to be found guilty.
5. ___ ___ Jurors are more sympathetic to defendants who share their own religious beliefs.
6. ___ ___ A judge's order to ignore inadmissible evidence can actually add to the testimony's impact.
7. ___ ___ A more severe potential punishment makes jurors less likely to convict.
8. ___ ___ People who do not oppose the death penalty are also more likely to find a defendant guilty.
9. ___ ___ A minority that favors acquittal stands a better chance of convincing the majority than a minority that favors conviction.
10. ___ ___ When a judge disagrees with the jury's decision it is usually because the jury acquits someone the judge would have convicted.

Demonstration MB-2

(with permission of E. Loftus)

KNOWLEDGE OF EYEWITNESS BEHAVIOR QUESTIONNAIRE

Choose the best answer for each of the following:

1. Two women are walking to school one morning, one of them an Asian and the other white. Suddenly two men, one black and one white, jump into their path and attempt to grab their purses. Later the women are shown photographs of known purse snatchers in the area. Which statement describes your view of the women's ability to identify the purse snatchers?

   (a) Both the Asian and the white woman will find the white man harder to identify than the black man.

   (b) The white woman will find the black man more difficult to identify than the white man.

   (c) The Asian woman will have an easier time than the white woman making an accurate identification of both men.

   (d) The white woman will find the black man easier to identify than the white man.

2. When a person experiences extreme stress as the victim of a crime, there will be:

   (a) generally a greater than normal ability to perceive and recall the details of the crime.

   (b) generally the same ability to perceive and recall the details of the crime as under normal conditions.

   (c) a majority of people will become better at perceiving and recalling crime details whereas others will become worse at it.

   (d) generally a reduced ability to perceive and recall the details.

3. Suppose that a man and a woman both witness two crimes. One crime involves violence while the other is nonviolent. Which statement do you believe is true?

   (a) Both the man and the woman will remember the details of the nonviolent crime better than the details of the violent crime.

   (b) Both the man and the woman will remember the details of the violent crime better than the details of the nonviolent crime.

   (c) The man will remember the details of the violent crime better than the details of the nonviolent crime and the reverse will be true for the woman.

   (d) The woman will remember the details of the violent crime better, and the man will remember the details of the nonviolent crime better.

4. Consider a situation in which a person is being robbed. The robber is standing a few feet from the victim and is pointing a gun at him/her. The victim later reports to a police officer, 'I was so frightened, I'll never forget that face.' Which of the following do you feel best describes what the victim experienced at the time of the robbery?

   (a) The victim was so concerned about being able to identify the robber that he/she didn't even notice the gun.

   (b) The victim focused on the robber's face and only slightly noticed the gun.

   (c) The victim focused on the gun, which would interfere with his/her ability to remember the robber's face.

   (d) The victim got a good look at both the gun and the face.

5. Suppose a person is mugged in a darkened hotel hallway. He/She is later asked questions about the incident. (1) 'Did you see a scar on the left side of the assailant's neck?' or (2) 'Did you see the scar on the left side of the assailant's neck?'

   (a) There is no important difference between these two questions in information provided to the witness.
   (b) The slight difference in question wording would make no difference in witness accuracy since the witness would know whether or not he/she had seen a scar.
   (c) Even a slight difference in question wording such as that here might affect the witness's accuracy in responding.
   (d) When asked to remember a stressful event, a witness would certainly not be affected by a difference in wording as small as the distinction between 'a' and 'the.'

6. A robbery is committed. Later, the clerk who was robbed at gunpoint identifies someone from a set of photographs as the person who perpetrated the crime. Still later, the clerk is asked whether the robber is present in a line-up of several somewhat similar individuals. Which of the following statements is true?

   (a) Guilty or not, if the person identified in the photo is present, he/she is likely to be identified from the line-up as well.
   (b) Having seen the photos, the witness (victim) is not likely to choose someone from the line-up if the robber is not present.
   (c) If the robber is present in the line-up, having seen his/her photo previously does not add significantly to his/her chances of being identified from the line-up.
   (d) The effect of viewing the photos on accuracy of identification later at the line-up is not affected by how good a look the witness got of the robber.

7. Under less than optimal viewing conditions, such as those of a violent crime, which of the following statements would be true?

   (a) The relationship between a witness's stated confidence and his/her accuracy of identification is moderately strong.
   (b) The relationship between confidence and accuracy is zero.
   (c) The relationship between confidence and accuracy is very strong.
   (d) The relationship between confidence and accuracy is very strong only for those of above-average intelligence.

8. Which of the following statements do you feel best represents the truth about an eyewitness's memory for faces seen only once?

   (a) Even after several months, memory is still 90–95 percent accurate.
   (b) Amazingly enough, physically attractive and unattractive faces are remembered no better over the long term than are faces of average attractiveness.
   (c) Memory accuracy drops after only 2 weeks to a level where a face seen once before becomes indistinguishable from those never before seen.
   (d) It is 6–12 months before memory accuracy drops to a level where a face seen once becomes indistinguishable from ones never before seen.

9. Concerning the effects of the amount of training or experience a person has had in making eyewitness identifications, which of the following statements seems most reasonable to you?

   (a) Police officers in general are better than civilians at recalling details of another person encountered for only a few seconds.

   (b) When asked to watch a busy street for incidents of an illegal nature, civilians report more 'possible' thefts than do police.

   (c) It appears to be quite difficult to train people to become better at recognizing faces seen previously.

   (d) Only police officers with 20 years or more experience possess greater ability than civilians to recognize faces seen previously.

10. Sometimes during a criminal trial the age of the eyewitness is assumed to be a factor in the accuracy of identification. Which statement do you think describes the actual relationship between age and identification accuracy?

    (a) Ability to recognize previously seen faces increases steadily to early adulthood and then declines after age 60.

    (b) Ability to recognize faces increases up until the early school years and then remains constant through old age.

    (c) Face recognition ability remains relatively constant in accuracy after 3-4 years of age.

    (d) Because of their much greater experience, people over age 60 have greater ability to recognize faces seen under brief and/or stressful viewing conditions than do young adults.

11. Suppose an armed robbery took place in a grocery store. The entire incident lasted 4 minutes. If 100 people saw the robbery and were asked how long it had taken:

    (a) some would say less than 4 minutes, some would say more than 4 minutes, but the average would be about 4 minutes;

    (b) a few would say less than 4 minutes, most would say more than 4 minutes, and the average would be more than 4 minutes;

    (c) most would say less than 4 minutes, a few would say more than 4 minutes, and the average would be less than 4 minutes;

    (d) in general, people are fairly good at estimating time durations and most estimates would be very close to 4 minutes.

12. Witnesses to crimes are sometimes asked by police to tell what happened in their own words; in other words to report freely. Sometimes the police ask them specific questions. Compared to a free report, a witness's answers to specific questions are:

    (a) more accurate and complete;

    (b) less accurate and complete;

    (c) more accurate, but less complete;

    (d) less accurate, but more complete.

13. Suppose a house were burglarized and the resident got a glimpse of the burglar through the window. At a later line-up the resident attempts to make an identification. Assume there is a 10 percent chance that the resident will be mistaken. Now in addition to the above facts, assume that the resident was first shown photographs by the police, but recognized none of the people in the photos. Assume further that the person the resident later picked in the line-up was shown in

one of the photos that had earlier been viewed. The chance of an incorrect identification in this latter situation would then:

(a) remain about 10 percent;

(b) decrease below 10 percent;

(c) increase above 10 percent;

(d) decrease below 10 percent for women and increase above 10 percent for men.

14. Appropriate to the situation where people of one racial group view those of another, you may have heard the expression: 'They all look alike.' Which of the following statements best reflects your personal view of this expression?

(a) It is true.

(b) It is a myth.

(c) It is more applicable to white viewing non-whites than the reverse.

(d) It is more applicable to non-whites viewing whites than the reverse.

Demonstration MB-3

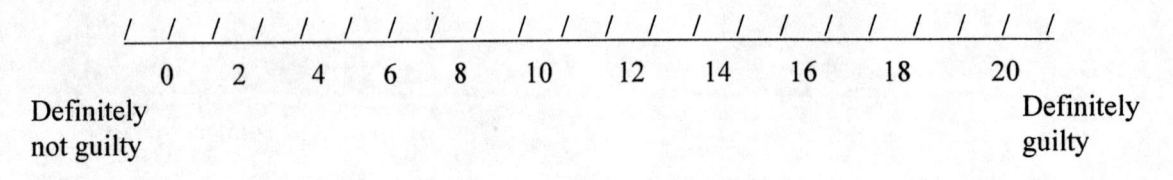

(with permission of M. Kaplan)

Gross Negligence

The defendant had bought his automobile from an acquaintance about three weeks prior to the accident. The vehicle was six years old, and the seller testified, without dispute from the defendant, that he warned the defendant that the brakes were in poor condition and probably needed replacement. Two days later, the defendant had new brake linings and brake shoes installed. The mechanic testified that he did not inspect the emergency brake system, which is a completely separate system from the brakes.

About two weeks after purchasing the car, the defendant and a friend drove to San Diego. While visiting some other friends, the defendant parked his car on_____ Street, at the top of a moderately steep hill.

The defendant was unable to turn his wheel to the curb, as prescribed by law, as this particular block had no curb at the time. He did set the emergency handbrake and he placed the gearshift into "park," and this was verified by his friend and by investigating police officers. Shortly after the defendant and his companion left the vehicle, the car rolled downhill.

The street right-angles into _____ Street at the bottom of the incline. The rolling vehicle crashed through the window of Jeff's Grocery, hitting a 14-year-old boy standing at the counter and the grocer. The boy was not seriously injured, but the grocer received serious injuries, requiring ten months' hospitalization.

Police investigating the accident testified that the emergency brake cable was badly rusted and had broken.

Degree of guilt

```
/ / / / / / / / / / / / / / / / / / / / /
0   2   4   6   8   10  12  14  16  18  20
```
Definitely   Definitely
not guilty   guilty

Demonstration MB-3

(with permission of M. Kaplan)

Wrongful Death

The collision between the ambulance and state-owned dump truck occurred about 1:30 p.m. on S.R. 117-A between Monterey and Salinas on a straight stretch of two-lane highway just east of a gradual curve known as the Toro curve. The dump truck was hauling dirt from the south side of the highway to the north side, where it was used to widen the shoulder on the north side. At the time, a subforeman was controlling traffic. He was standing approximately 1,350 feet east of a "Men and Equipment Working" sign erected at the west end of the project. The sign was clearly visible. The loading operation was some 250 feet east of the subforeman. No vehicles were in sight of the driver or nearby workers at the time the truck driver commenced his U-turn on the highway.

The ambulance driven by the defendant, was carrying Mrs. P., an invalid, on a nonemergency run from her home to the county hospital. Mr. S., driving a sedan behind the ambulance, estimated his speed at about 50 miles an hour. Mr. S. testified that the subforeman was holding up the warning paddle with the "Slow" side facing traffic. The testimony was corroborated by the subforeman. Mr. S. also testified that the ambulance did not slow down when passing the subforeman, and that 5 pieces of equipment were visible on the shoulder to the right. Shortly after overtaking the parked equipment, the ambulance put on its siren.

Just as the ambulance passed the parked equipment, the dump truck collided with it, swinging it around onto the shoulder where it was thrown into a roll. The truck was stopped at the point of impact, and the ambulance, after rolling over 1-1/2 times, rested on its top 96 feet from the point of impact. There were no skid marks. Mrs. P., thrown from the ambulance, subsequently died from injuries.

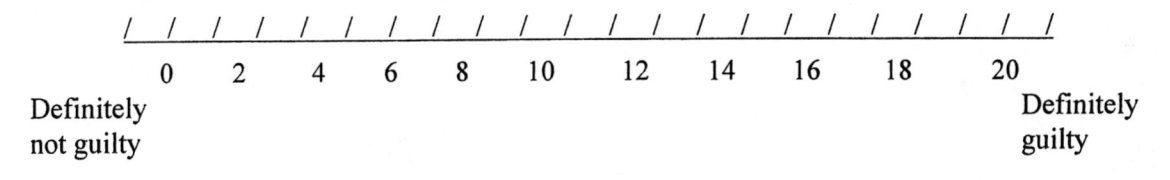

Degree of guilt

```
/ / / / / / / / / / / / / / / / / / / / /
0   2   4   6   8   10  12  14  16  18  20
```
Definitely   Definitely
not guilty   guilty

FILMS/VIDEOS

And Justice For All? (PBS, 60 min., 1992). Examines the crisis in the American court system. Narrated by Bill Moyers, the program shows how public defenders and legal aid attorneys are in short supply, leaving the poor without adequate and timely representation.

Criminal Justice (INS, 58 min., 1986). Looks at the criminal justice system by focusing on three cases—a robbery, a homicide, and a rape. The program traces the activities and statements of prosecutors, defense attorneys, police officers, defendants, and plaintiffs.

The Death Penalty (FHS, 26 min., 1991). Examines the death penalty in light of evidence that it is imposed arbitrarily and is not a deterrent. Examines the cases of two men who committed virtually identical murders and were tried in the same courtroom two weeks apart.

Enter the Jury Room (CBS, 120 min., 1997). Viewers hear three separate cases and then view the deliberations of the juries. Many of the issues raised in Module B are illustrated by these trials conducted in Arizona. Order by calling 1-800-934-NEWS.

From the Mouths of Babes (ABC, 16 min., 1993). An ABC 20/20 segment that features Stephen Ceci and Maggie Bruck's research demonstrating young children's suggestibility, as discussed in Module B. Highly recommended! (Available for purchase by calling 1-800-913-3434.)

Inside the Jury Room (MINN, 58 min., 1986). From the Frontline series, this program examines the efforts of 12 men and women as they weigh the evidence in the case of Leroy Reed. Asks whether jurors should be told that they have power to disregard the law. In Georgia, Maryland, and Indiana, judges are required to inform juries that they may follow their own consciences.

The Rodney King Case: What the Jury Saw in California vs. Powell (INS, 120 min., 1992). Presents the prosecution and defense arguments in the first Rodney King trial. Includes the videotape of Rodney King's beating, played frame by frame as seen by the jury, as well as eyewitness accounts of what occurred after he got out of his car.

The Study of Memory (FHS, 74 min., 1986). This program on memory includes a videoclip of a robbery to test recall for eyewitness testimony.

MODULE C
SOCIAL PSYCHOLOGY AND THE SUSTAINABLE FUTURE

The Global Crisis
      Overshooting the Earth's Carrying Capacity
      World Population Will Double
      Economic Growth Is Increasing Consumption
      Enabling Sustainable Lifestyles
      Increasing Efficiency and Productivity
      Reducing Consumption
The Social Psychology of Materialism and Simplicity
      Increased Materialism
      Wealth and Well-Being
      Are Rich People Happier?
      Does Economic Growth Improve Human Morale?
      Why Materialism Fails to Satisfy
      The Adaptation-Level Phenomenon
      Social Comparison
Toward Sustainable Consumption
Personal Postscript: A Final Word

LECTURE AND DISCUSSION IDEAS

1. Simple Living Resources on the Web

Mod C suggests one of the mandatory adjustments needed for reaching long-term sustainability given the current population boom is to start living more simply. Learning how to live and function with less material wealth and learning how to decrease consumption of nonrenewable energies seems to be more important now than ever before. Lectures about simple living and addressing the problem of "Affluenza" can be informed from resources on the Internet. The following cites are just a few of the available resources.

Natural Life Magazine has a "Voluntary Simplicity Index" (www.life.ca/subject/simplicity.html), which helps you find 1) alternatives to consumerism, 2) ways to reduce your dependence on mainstream economics, 3) and happiness with fewer purchases. It lists resources about sustainable living, voluntary simplicity, frugality and other ways to live earth-friendly.

Seeds of Simplicity (www.seedsofsimplicity.org/default.asp) is national, nonprofit membership organization working to help mainstream and symbolize voluntary simplicity as an authentic social and environmental issue. It is a Los Angeles-based program of the Center for Religion, Ethics & Social Policy at Cornell University.

The Simple Living Network (www.simpleliving.net/default.asp) contains tools (newsletter, web addresses, discussion boards, etc.) and examples for those who are serious about learning to live more simply.

PBS has a one-hour TV special that explores the high social and environmental costs of materialism and over-consumption entitled "Affluenza." The home page is found at www.pbs.org/kcts/affluenza. The page includes links for more information about the show, diagnosis, treatment, and escape.

2. Who Is Happy?

Mod C discusses some of the counterintuitive research on subjective well-being (happiness); what correlates and what does not. Recently, David Myers and Ed Diener (1995) put together an easy-to-read review of several contemporary studies. Topics covered include the myths of happiness, happiness and gender/race/culture/, money and happiness, the traits of happy people, faith and happy people, and elements of a theory of happiness. Instructors might precede the reading of this article with a survey of students' perceptions regarding the relationship between many of these variables and happiness. An interesting concluding exercise (after having students read and discuss the article) involves having students look at the ideas they registered before reading the article, reflect on what the research shows, and generate for themselves some of the "myths of happiness" and explore reasons for why these myths persist.

3. Popular Sources for Additional Classroom Material

Dittmar, H. (1992). The social psychology of material possessions. New York: St. Martin's Press. This book reviews a massive amount of research on the relationship between ownership of material possessions and social identity. Some topics include biological accounts of possessions and property, material possessions as extensions of the self, and material possessions as reflections of identity.

Myers, D. G. (2000). The American paradox: Spiritual hunger in an age of plenty. Yale University Press. This book looks at the question of why we have less happiness and more depression while our incomes are doubling and then some.

Myers, D. G. (1993). <u>The pursuit of happiness: Discovering the pathway to fulfillment, well-being, and enduring personal joy.</u> Avon books. This book is a scientific study of well-being, which identifies common factors happy people share.

DEMONSTRATION AND PROJECT IDEAS

1. Sustainability, Materialism, and Happiness Quiz

Demonstration MC-1 may be used to stimulate student interest and to show the value of using social psychology research to address contemporary issues of sustainability, materialism, and happiness. The correct answers to most of these questions are not obvious, apart from research. As the chapter will reveal, statements 2, 7, and 9 are true; the rest are false. Naturally, this demonstration will be most effective BEFORE students have read the chapter.

2. Simplicity Exercise

Modular C, in part, examines the curative role that simple living might play in a world overpopulated and full of excessive consumption. Of course, living simply and "going without" have been disciplines practiced and extolled throughout history. Many of these ideas are grounded in religious thought, but other secular writers have addressed them as well (e.g., Thoreau).

Having students personally experience the process of adjustment that necessarily comes when people willingly choose to go without has been argued by some to be a necessary exercise for anyone who wishes to call themselves "educated." Instructors can facilitate just such an experience by presenting their students with a simplicity exercise. First, provide students with a list of items from which they may choose to abstain for a certain period of time (e.g., one week). Second, have them keep a journal noting 1) all of the various adjustments they had to make to continue meeting the demands placed upon them; 2) their feelings toward the project (at the beginning of the exercise and at the end); 3) a measure of their perceived inconvenience by not using the item (at the beginning of the exercise and at the end); and 4) the unimagined benefits they experienced from going without the item. Third, have students reflect on their experience in a paper and/or class discussion. Many students will note (with surprise) how quickly they adjusted to life without something they would have never imagined they could have lived without prior to the exercise. Some ideas of items for your list include one's cell phone (or some form of electronic communication), personal make-up, electronic media, car, bike, computer, TV, radio, CD player, bed, sugared foods, meat, household appliances (e.g., dishwasher, air conditioner, electric vacuum) and alcohol.

Of course, some students may already abstain from some of these items. In order to create a meaningful experience, students must choose something that would be seen as sacrificial. Also, make sure students are not allowed to choose something that could be harmful (e.g., food, water, sleep). Going without these basic necessities is not implied in the idea of living simply.

Note: Some of the items mentioned in this list are not as harmful to the environment as others. An instructor may choose to just list items which, when used frequently by many people, harm the environment so as to have students experience simplicity for environmental protection reasons. Other instructors may want their students to experience simplicity in a broader sense and, as a result, include items that are not necessarily tied to environmental harm (e.g., bike, bed, and alcohol).

3. Materialism Scale

Materialism and it's inability to satisfy is discussed in Module C. Richins and Dawson (1992) developed and validated a scale of materialistic attitudes and values which is found in Demonstration MC-2.

Richins and Dawson make four proposals regarding materialism: 1) Materialistic people value acquisition and the means to acquire possessions more highly than those low in materialism; 2) Materialistic people are self-centered; 3) Materialists will pursue a life of material complexity rather than material simplicity; and 4) Materialists tend to be less satisfied than others with their lot in life. The 18-item scale provides a measure of overall materialistic attitudes and values as well as a measure of three sub-components labeled "success" (the use of possessions as an indicator of success in life—items 3, 6, 9, 12, 15, & 17), "centrality" (the importance of acquisition and possession generally—items 2, 5, 8, 11, 14, 16, & 18) and "happiness" (the perception that possessions are needed for happiness—items 1, 4, 7, 10, & 13). To tally, reverse score items 1, 2, 5, 7, 8, 9, 17, & 18 (1 goes to 5, 2 goes to 4, 3 stays 3, 4 goes to 2, and 5 goes to 1) and then sum the numbers.

The sample mean for consumers who filled out one version of the survey was 47.9 with a standard deviation of 10.2. Respondents scored as low as 20 and as high as 84. The sub-scale findings for this version of the survey are as follows: centrality (mean = 19.8; s.d. = 4.2); happiness (mean = 13.3; s.d. = 4.2); and success (mean = 14.7; s.d. = 3.9).

Richins and Dawson also looked for relationships between materialism and some demographic variables. All correlations were quite low, with the exception of age. It appears that as age increases, materialism declines (median correlation with age was -.19)

4. Happiness Scale

Module C looks at some of the recent research on happiness (subjective well-being) and, in particular, the relationship between wealth and happiness. Demonstration MC-3 contains a brief, but well researched, "satisfaction with life" scale. The scale, and other information about research on happiness and life satisfaction can be found at Ed Diener's web page (www.psych.uiuc.edu/~ediener/index.html). To score the scale, simply sum the responses. The following markers may be helpful:

> 35–31 Extremely satisfied
> 26–30 Satisfied
> 21–25 Slightly satisfied
> 20 Neutral
> 15–19 Slightly dissatisfied
> 10–14 Dissatisfied
> 5–9 Extremely dissatisfied

The text notes the rather weak relationship that exists between material wealth and subjective well-being (at least for those not excessively poor). An exploration of the relationship between personal wealth, materialistic attitudes/values, and personal happiness can be accomplished in the classroom by having students complete both Demonstrations MC-2 and MC-3 and, in addition, noting their personal wealth (e.g., personal annual income or parents annual income). Of course an instructor wishing to examine these variables in a classroom format should take every precaution needed to ensure anonymity.

5. Adaptation Level

Royce Singleton (1978) suggests question #1 of Demonstration MC-4, which should work if your students come from various geographic regions. When Singleton divided students into those who were and weren't from Southern California, he found the former had a much narrower range of temperature tolerance.

Question #2 attempts a related demonstration with family income. Do students from poorer families require less income to define someone as "well off"?

Demonstration MC-1

True or False

1. The moral and social decline of our culture is well evidenced by the increase of heavy drinking rates, hard liquor consumption and drunken driving fatalities. T F
2. Modern technology has allowed food production to increase faster than the world population is growing. T F
3. The average American needs just about 10 acres of biologically productive space to support their consumption and absorb their waste. T F
4. Since 1950, the world's poorest fifth have nearly doubled their per person meat and timber consumption. T F
5. Although there exists a perception of a massive social-cultural shift between 1960 and the 1990s, there is actually very little evidence of this in markers such as divorce rates, teen suicide rates, juvenile violence rates and the number of babies born out of wedlock. T F
6. Research on happiness suggests money does buy happiness—especially for the very wealthy. T F
7. Contrary to collegians up to 30 years ago, today's collegians value being well off financially more than developing a meaningful philosophy of life. T F
8. Research on the interplay of economic growth and human morale shows a strikingly positive relationship, especially in affluent countries. T F
9. Our feelings of success versus failure and satisfaction versus dissatisfaction are generated more from comparisons we make with our previous accomplishments than with objective norms. T F
10. Research suggests adapting to an enhanced lifestyle as a result of a pay increase takes very little time, but recovering from a pay cut may not happen at all. T F

Demonstration MC-2

(with permission of U of Chicago Press and Richins)

Read each of the following statements as if it referred to you. Then, please indicate your agreement or disagreement with the statement by registering a number in the blank next to the question. The numbers correspond to the following responses (1 = strongly disagree; 2 = disagree; 3 = don't agree or disagree; 4 = agree; and 5 = strongly agree):

1. _____ I have all the things I really need to enjoy life.
2. _____ I usually buy only the things I need.
3. _____ I admire people who own expensive homes, cars, and clothes.
4. _____ My life would be better if I owned certain things I don't have.
5. _____ I try to keep my life simply, as fare as possessions are concerned.
6. _____ Some of the most important achievements in life include acquiring material possessions.
7. _____ I wouldn't be any happier if I owned nicer things.
8. _____ The things I own aren't all that important to me.
9. _____ I don't place much emphasis on the amount of material objects people own as a sign of success.
10. _____ I'd be happier if I could afford to buy more things.
11. _____ I enjoy spending money on things that aren't practical.
12. _____ The things I own say a lot about how well I am doing in life.
13. _____ It sometimes bothers me quite a bit that I can't afford to buy all the things that I'd like.
14. _____ Buying things gives me a lot of pleasure.
15. _____ I like to own things that impress people.
16. _____ I like a lot of luxury in my life.
17. _____ I don't pay much attention to the material objects other people own.
18. _____ I put less emphasis on material things then most people I know.

Reprinted from Richins and Dawson, <u>Journal of Consumer Research</u>, vol. 19, p. 303–316. Copyright by the University of Chicago Press. Used with permission.

Demonstration MC-3

Below are five statements that you may agree or disagree with. Using the 1–7 scale below indicate your agreement with each item by placing the appropriate number on the line preceding that item. Please be open and honest in your responding.

       7   Strongly agree
       6   Agree
       5   Slightly agree
       4   Neither agree nor disagree
       3   Slightly disagree
       2   Disagree
       1   Strongly disagree

_____ In most ways my life is close to my ideal.
_____ The conditions of my life are excellent.
_____ I am satisfied with my life.
_____ So far I have gotten the important things I want in life.
_____ If I could live my life over, I would change almost nothing.

Demonstration MC-4

(with permission of R. Singleton)

Temperature:

a. <u>Above</u> what temperature would you consider the weather uncomfortably hot?
_____

b. <u>Below</u> what temperature would you consider the weather uncomfortably cold?
_____

c. Where (city area and state) have you lived most of your life?
_____

Income:

a. <u>Above</u> what annual income level would you consider a family well off?
_____

b. <u>Below</u> what annual income level would you consider a family to be poor?
_____

c. Roughly estimate your family's income for the past year.
_____

FILMS/VIDEOS

The 1900 House (PBS, 240 min., 2000). Viewers of this four-part "docu-soap" observe the Bowler family as they are transplanted from modern London life to an upper middle-class lifestyle at the turn of the last century. The series clearly shows the dramatic changes in domestic life brought about by the scientific and technological innovations of the last 100 years.

FILM PRODUCER/DISTRIBUTOR LIST

ABC
American Broadcasting Company
P.O. Box 807
New Hudson, MI

AIM
Aims Instructional Media Services
9710 De Soto Avenue
Chatworth, CA 91311

ANN
The Annenberg/CPB Collection
Dept. HB01
901 E Street
Washington, DC 20004

AVA
Avanti Films
8271 Melrose Avenue
Los Angeles, CA 90046

BAR
Barr Films
100 Wilshire Blvd.
Santa Monica, CA

BOS
Steve Bosustow Productions
20548 Pacific Coast Highway
Malibu, CA 90265

CAR
Carousel Films, Inc.
1501 Broadway
New York, NY 10036

CATT
The Catticus Corporation
2600 Tenth Street
Berkeley, CA 94710

CBC
C.B. Communications
P.O. Box 7541 Oakland Station
Pittsburgh, PA 19113

CBS
Columbia Broadcasting Service
1830 Avenue of the Americas
New York, NY 10019

CDF
Cambridge Educational
90 MacCorkle Avenue, SW
South Charleston, WY 25311

CHU
Churchill Media
P.O. Box 3121
Paso Robles, CA 93447

CRM
CRM/McGraw-Hill Films
2215 Faraday Avenue
Carlsbad, CA 92008

DOC
Document Associates, Inc.
211 East 43rd Street
New York, NY 10017

EBE
Encyclopedia Britannica
Education Corporation
310 South Michigan Avenue
Chicago, IL 60604

FHS
Films for the Humanities and
Sciences
PO Box 2053
Princeton, NJ 08543

FIL
Filmakers Library
124 East 40th Street, Suite 901
New York, NY 10016

HAR
Harper & Row Publishers, Inc.
108 Wilmot Road
Deerfield, IL 60015

HBJ
Harcourt, Brace, and Jovanovich
176 E. Adams Street
Chicago, IL 60603

IFF
International Film Foundations, Inc.
475 Fifth Avenue
Room 916
New York, NY 10017

INS
Insight Media
2162 Broadway
New York, NY 10024

KIN
King Screen Productions
Division of King Broadcasting Co.
320 Aurora Avenue N
Seattle, WA 98109

LCA
Learning Corporation of America
P.O. Box 2649
Columbus Ohio 43216-2649

MINN
University of Minnesota
University Film and Video
1313 Fifth Street, Suite 108
Minneapolis, MN 55414

MTI
MTI Teleprograms Inc.
P.O. Box 2649
Columbus, Ohio 43216

NBC
National Broadcasting Co.
30 Rockefeller Plaza
New York, NY 10020

NEW
New Day Films
22D Hollywood Avenue
Ho-Ho-Kus, NJ 07423

OAS
Oasis
15 Willoughby Street
Boston, MA 02135

PBS
Public Broadcasting System
1320 Braddock Place
Alexandria, VA 22314

PYR
Pyramid Film and Video
2801 Colorado Avenue
Santa Monica, CA 90404

PSU
Audio-Visual Services
Pennsylvania State University
Special Services Building
1127 Fox Hill Road
University Park, PA 16803

REY
Stuart Reynold Productions
9465 Wilshire Boulevard
Beverly Hills, CA 90212

STE
Sterling Educational Films, Inc.
241 East 3rd Street
New York, NY 10016

TEX
Texture Films
PO Box 1337
Skokie, IL 60076

UCE
University of California
Extension Media Center
2000 Center Street, Fourth Floor
Berkeley, CA 94720

UFC
University Films of Canada
115 Melrose Avenue
Toronto, Ontario
Canada M5M 148

UNA
United Artists
727 Seventh Avenue
New York, NY 10019

WIL
John Wiley and Sons, Inc.
605 Third Avenue
New York, NY 10016

REFERENCES

Adler, R., & Stone, G. (1984). Psychology and the health system. In J. Ruffini (Ed.), <u>Advances in medical social science</u>. New York: Gordon & Breach (p. 527).

Adorno, T., Frenkel-Brunswik, E., Levinson, D., & Sanford, N. (1950). <u>The authoritarian personality</u>. New York: Harper.

Ahmad, S. (1998, January 5). Time for a Twinkie tax? <u>U.S. News & World Report</u>, pp. 62-63.

Ajzen, I. (1985). From intentions to actions: A theory of planned behavior. In J. Kuhland & J. Beckman (Eds.), <u>Action-control: From cognitions to behavior</u> (pp. 11-39). Heidelberg: Springer.

Albert, S., & Dobbs, J.M., Jr. (1970). Physical distance and persuasion. <u>Journal of Personality and Social Psychology, 15,</u> 265-270.

Allman, W.F. (1984, October). Nice guys finish first. <u>Science/84</u>, pp. 25-32.

Allport, G., & Postman, L. (1947). <u>The psychology of rumor</u>. New York: Henry Holt.

Altman, I. (1975). <u>The environment and social behavior</u>. Monterey, CA: Brooks/Cole.

Anderson, D.D. (1992). Using feature films as tools for analysis in a psychology and law course. <u>Teaching of Psychology, 19,</u> 155-158.

Andrews, L. (1984, February). Exhibit A: Language. <u>Psychology Today</u>, pp. 28-33.

Archer, D., Iritani, B., Kines, D., & Barrios, M. (1983). Face-ism: Five studies of sex difference in facial prominence. <u>Journal of Personality and Social Psychology, 45,</u> 725-735.

Aron, A., Aron, E. N., & Smollan, D. (1992). Inclusion of Other in the Self Scale and the structure of interpersonal closeness. <u>Journal of Personality and Social Psychology, 63,</u> 596-612.

Aron, A., Melinat, E., Aron, E. N., Vallone, R. D., & Bator, R. J. (1997). The experimental generation of interpersonal closeness: A procedure and some preliminary findings. <u>Personality and Social Psychology Bulletin, 23,</u> 363-377.

Aronson, E. (1997, May). <u>Adventures in applied social psychology: How to convince sexually active teenagers to use condoms.</u> Paper presented at the annual meeting of the American Psychological Society, Washington, DC.

Aronson, E. (Ed.). (1999). <u>Readings about the social animal</u>. New York: Worth/W. H. Freeman.

Aronson, E. (2000). <u>Nobody left to hate: Compassion after Columbine</u>. W. H. Freeman & Co.

Aronson, E., & Cope, V. (1968). My enemy's enemy is my friend. <u>Journal of Personality and Social Psychology, 8,</u> 3-12.

Aronson, E., & Mills, J. (1959). The effect of severity of initiation on linking for a group. <u>Journal of Abnormal and Social Psychology, 59,</u> 177-181.

Averill, J. (1983). Studies on anger and aggression: Implications for theories of emotion. <u>American Psychologist, 38,</u> 1145-1160.

Axelrod, R. (1980a). Effective choice in the Prisoner's Dilemma. <u>Journal of Conflict Resolution, 24,</u> 3-25.

Axelrod, R. (1980b). More effective choice in the Prisoner's Dilemma. <u>Journal of Conflict Resolution, 24,</u> 379-403.

Ayeroff, F., & Abelson, R.P. (1976). ESP and ESB: Belief in personal success at mental telepathy. <u>Journal of Personality and Social Psychology, 34,</u> 240-247.

Azar, B. (1994). Seligman recommends a depression 'vaccine.' <u>The APA Monitor, 27,</u> 4.

Babineck, M. (1997, October 14). 11-year-old puts 'Baby Jessica' in past. <u>USA Today</u>, p. 3A.

Baddeley, A. (1990). <u>Human memory: Theory and practice</u>. Boston: Allyn and Bacon.

Baechler, J. (1979). <u>Suicides</u>. New York: Basic Books.

Balch, W.R. (1980). Testing the validity of astrology in class. <u>Teaching of Psychology, 7,</u> 247-250.

Ball-Rokeach, S.J., Rokeach, M., & Grube, J. (1984, November). The great American values test. Psychology Today, pp. 34-41.

Baron, R. (1997). The sweet smell of helping...Helping: Effects of pleasant ambient fragrance on prosocial behavior in shopping malls.
Personality and Social Psychology Bulletin, 23, 498-503.

Barringer, F. (1991, October 14). Psychologists try to explain reason for opposing views. New York Times, p. All.

Barr-Hillel, M. (1980). The base-rate fallacy in probability judgments. Acta Psychologica, 44, 211-233.

Baumeister, R.F. (1982). A self-presentational view of social phenomena. Psychological Bulletin, 91, 3-26.

Baumeister, R. F. (1999). Low self-esteem does not cause aggression. APA Monitor, January.

Baumeister, R.F., Smart, L., Boden, J.M. (1996). Relation of threatened egotism to violence and aggression: The dark side of high self-esteem. Psychological Review, 103, 5-33.

Baumrind, D., & Baron, R.A. (1981, August). Deceiving human subjects: An exchange. SASP Newsletter, 7(4), 1-11.

Bazerman, M. (1986, June). Why negotiations go wrong. Psychology Today, pp. 54-58.

Beck, A., & Young, J. (1978, September). College blues. Psychology Today, pp. 80-92.

Beggan, J. K. (1992). On the social nature of nonsocial perception: The mere ownership effect. Journal of Personality and Social Psychology, 62, 229-237.

Beloff, J. (1978, December). Why parapsychology is still on trial. Human Nature, pp. 68-74.

Bem, D.J. (1970). Beliefs, attitudes, and human affairs. Belmont, CA: Brooks/Cole.

Bem, S.L. (1974). The measurement of psychological androgyny. Journal of Consulting and Clinical Psychology, 42, 155-162.

Bem, S.L. (1981). Bem sex-role inventory: Professional manual. 577 College Ave., Palo Alto, CA 94306: Consulting Psychologists Press.

Benac, N. (1997, September 14). 'Good Samaritan' laws. Grand Rapids Press, p. A3

Benjamin, L.T., Jr. (1985). Defining aggression: An exercise for classroom discussion. Teaching of Psychology, 12, 40-42.

Ben-Zur, H., & Breznitz, S. (1991). What makes people angry: Dimensions of anger-evoking events. Journal of Research in Personality, 25, 1-22.

Bernhardt, P. (1997). Influences of serotonin and testosterone in aggression and dominance: Convergence with social psychology. Current Directions in Psychological Science, 6, 44-48.

Beroldi, G. (1994). Critique of the Seville Statement on Violence. American Psychologist, 49, 847-848.

Berzins, J., Welling, M.A., & Wetter, R.E. (1978). A new measure of psychological androgyny based on the Personality Research Form. Journal of Consulting and Clinical Psychology, 46, 126-138.

Blau, K. (1974). Instructor's manual for Secord and Backman's Social Psychology (2nd ed.). New York: McGraw-Hill.

Bohner, G., Bless, H., Schwarz, N., & Strack, F. (1988). What triggers causal attributions? The impact of valence and subjective probability. European Journal of Social Psychology, 18, 335-345.

Borgida, E., & Nisbett, R.E. (1977). The differential impact of abstract vs. concrete information on decisions. Journal of Applied Social Psychology, 7, 258-271.

Breckler, S. (1984). Empirical validation of affect, behavior, and cognition as distinct components of attitude. Journal of Personality and Social Psychology, 47, 1191-1205.

Brehm, S. (1985). Intimate relationships. New York: Random House.

Brewer, M.B. (1991). The social self: On being the same and different at the same time. Personality and Social Psychology Bulletin, 17, 475-482.

Brewer, M.B., & Weber, J.G. (1994). Self-evaluation effects of interpersonal versus intergroup social comparison. Journal of Personality and Social Psychology, 66, 268-275

Brickman, P., Rabinowitz, V., Karuza, J., Coates, D., Cohn, E., & Kidder, L. (1982). Models of helping and coping. American Psychologist, 37, 368-384.

Brigham, J. (1986). Social psychology. Boston: Little, Brown.

Brislin, R. (1988). Increasing awareness of class, ethnicity, culture, and race by expanding on students' own experiences. In I.S. Cohen (Ed.), The G. Stanley Hall lecture series, Vol. 8 (pp. 137-180). Washington, DC: American Psychological Association.

Brodansky, D. (1980). Electricity generation choices for the near term. Science, 207, 721-728.

Broverman, I.K., Broverman, D.M., Clarkson, F.E., Rosenkrantz, P.S., & Vogel, S.R. (1970). Sex-role stereotypes and clinical judgments of mental health. Journal of Consulting and Clinical Psychology, 34, 1-7.

Brown, R. (1965). Social psychology. New York: Free Press.

Brown, R. (1985). Social psychology (2nd ed). New York: Free Press.

Burger, J. (1990). Personality (2nd ed.). Belmont, CA: Wadsworth.

Burns, D. (1980, November). The perfectionist's script for self-defeat. Psychology Today, pp. 34-52.

Burstin, K., Doughtie, E.B., & Raphaeli, A. (1980). Contrastive vignette technique: An indirect methodology designed to address reactive social attitude measurement. Journal of Applied Social Psychology, 10, 147-165.

Burt, M. (1980). Cultural myths and supports for rape. Journal of Personality and Social Psychology, 38, 217-230.

Burtoff, B. (1980, January 27). Is prejudice a fairy tale? Grand Rapids Press, pp. 1b-2b.

Buss, A.H., & Perry, M. (1992). The aggression questionnaire. Journal of Personality and Social Psychology, 63, 452-459.

Buss, D.M. (1989). Sex differences in human mate preferences: Evolutionary hypotheses in 37 cultures. Behavioral and Brain Sciences, 12, 1-49.

Buss, D.M. et al. (1990). International preferences in selecting mates: A study of 37 cultures. Journal of Cross-Cultural Psychology, 21, 5-47.

Buunk, B.P., Angleitner, A., Oubaid, V., & Buss, D.M. (1996). Sex differences in jealousy in evolutionary and cultural perspective: Tests from the Netherlands, Germany, and the United States. Psychological Science, 7, 359-363.

Buys, C. (1978). Humans would do better without groups. Personality and Social Psychology Bulletin, 4, 123-125.

Cacioppo, J., & Petty, R. (1981). Electromyograms as measures of extent and affectivity of information processing. American Psychologist, 36, 441-456.

Cacioppo, J., & Petty, R. (1982). The need for cognition. Journal of Personality and Social Psychology, 42, 116-131.

Calhoun, J.B. (1962). Population density and social pathology. Scientific American, 206, 139-148.

Calhoun, L.G., Selby, J.W., & Faulstich, M.E. (1980). Reaction to the parents of childhood suicide: A study of social impressions. Journal of Consulting and Clinical Psychology, 98, 535-536.

Carkenord, D.M., & Bullington, J. (1993). Bringing cognitive dissonance to the classroom. Teaching of Psychology, 20, 41-43.

Casscells, W., Schoenberger, A., & Graboys, T. (1978). Interpretation by physicians of clinical laboratory results. New England Journal of Medicine, 299, 999-1001.

Castellow, W.A., Wuensch, K.L., & Moore, C.H. (1990). Effects of physical attractiveness of the plaintiff and defendant in sexual harassment judgments. Journal of Social Behavior and Personality, 5, 547-562.

Ceci, S., & Peters, D. (1984). Letters of reference: A naturalistic study of the effects of confidentiality. American Psychologist, 39, 29-31.

Chapman, L. J. (1967). Illusory correlation in observational report. Journal of Verbal Learning and Verbal Behavior, 6, 151-155.

Cheek, J.M., & Mechior, L.A. (1990). Shyness, self-esteem, and self-consciousness. In H. Lietenberg (Ed.), Handbook of social and evaluation anxiety. New York: Plenum.

Cheek, J. M., Tropp, L. R., Chen, L., & Underwood, M. K. (1994). Identity orientations: Personal, social and collective. Paper presented at the 102nd Annual Convention of the American Psychological Association, Los Angeles.

Christensen, A., & Arkowitz, H. (1974). Preliminary report on practice dating and feedback on treatment for college dating problems. Journal of Counseling Psychology, 21, 92-95.

Christie, R. (1970, November). The Machiavellis among us. Psychology Today, pp. 82-86.

Christie, R. (1992). Authoritarianism and related constructs. In J. Robinson, P. Shaver, & L. Wrightsman (Eds.), Measures of personality and social psychological attitudes. San Diego, CA: Academic Press (pp. 501-572).

Christie, R., & Geis, F. (1970). The ten dollar game. In R. Christie & F.L. Geis (Eds.), Studies in Machiavellianism. New York: Academic Press.

Cialdini, R.B. (2001). Influence: Science and Practice (4rd ed.). New York: HarperCollins.

Cialdini, R.B., Petty, R.E. & Cacioppo, J.T. (1981). Attitude and attitude change. Annual Review of Psychology, 32, 357-404.

Clary, E.G. et al. (1994). Matching messages to motives in persuasion: A functional approach to promoting volunteerism. Journal of Applied Social Psychology, 24, 1129-1149.

Cohen, D., & Nisbett, R.E. (1997). Field experiments examining the culture of honor: The role of institutions in perpetuating norms about violence. Personality and Social Psychology Bulletin, 23, 1188-1199.

Cohen, S., et al. (1997). Social ties and susceptibility to the common cold. The Journal of the American Medical Association, 277, 1940-1944.

Cohen, S., & Williamson, G.M. (1988). Perceived stress in a probability sample of the United States. In S. Spacapan & S. Oskamp (Eds.), The social psychology of health. Newbury Park, CA: Sage.

Conroy, J., III, & Sundstrom, E. (1977). Territorial dominance in a dyadic conversation as a function of similarity of opinion. Journal of Personality and Social Psychology, 35, 570-576.

Cook, T.D., Appleton, H., Conner, R.F., Shaffer, A., Tomkin, G., & Weber, S.J. (1975). Sesame Street revisited. New York: Russell Sage.

Crawford, M. (1994). Rethinking the romance: Teaching the content and function of gender stereotypes in the psychology of women course. Teaching of Psychology, 21, 151-153.

Crosby, F. (1976). A model of egoistic relative deprivation. Psychological Review, 83, 85-113.

Cutler, G. (1998, January). Using personal want ads to teach interpersonal attraction. Poster session presented at the Twentieth Annual National Institute on the Teaching of Psychology, St. Petersburg Beach, FL

Davis, K.E. (1985, February). Near and dear: Friendship and love compared. Psychology Today, pp. 22-30.

Davis, M.H. (1980). A multidimensional approach to individual differences in empathy. Catalog of Selected Documents in Psychology, 10(4), 85.

Deci, E.L. (1985, March). The well-tempered classroom. Psychology Today, pp. 52-53.

Deffenbacher, K.A., & Loftus, E.F. (1982). Do jurors share a common understanding concerning eyewitness behavior? Law and Human Behavior, 6, 15-30.

Dember, W.M., & Penwell, L. (1980). Happiness, depression, and the Pollyanna Principle. Bulletin of Psychonomic Society, 15, 321-323.

Deutsch, M., & Krauss, R.M. (1960). The effect of threat upon interpersonal bargaining. Journal of Abnormal and Social Psychology, 61, 181-189.

Deutsch, R. (1982). Unpublished study, York University.

Dodd, D. (1985). Robbers in the classroom: A deindividuation exercise. Teaching of Psychology, 12, 89-91.

Doise, W. (1986). Levels of explanation in social psychology. Cambridge: Cambridge University Press.

Dollinger, S.J. (1986, August). Simulations for an undergraduate seminar in personality. Paper presented at the American Psychological Association convention, Washington, D.C.

Dowd, E.T. (in press). Toward a briefer therapy: Overcoming resistance and reactance in the therapeutic process. In W.J. Matthews & J.H. Edgette (Eds.), Current thinking and research in brief therapy, Vol. III. Bristol, PA: Brunner/Mazel Publishers.

Dowd, E.T., Milne, C.R., & Wise, S.L. (1991). The therapeutic reactance scale: A measure of psychological reactance. Journal of Counseling & Development, 69, 541-545.

Dragon, W. (1992). To be or not to be: Uses for a videotaped shooting in the classroom. Paper presented at the meeting of the Midwestern Psychological Assocation, Chicago, IL.

Driscoll, R., Davis, K.E., & Lipitz, M.E. (1972). Parental interference and romantic love: The Romeo and Juliet effect. Journal of Personality and Social Psychology, 24, 1-10.

Dunn, D. (1989). Demonstrating a self-serving bias. Teaching of Psychology, 16, 21-22.

Dunn, D. (1992). Perspectives on human aggression: Writing to Einstein and Freud on "Why War?" Teaching of Psychology, 19, 112-113.

Eagly, A., & Steffen, V. (1984). Gender stereotypes stem from the distribution of men and women into social roles. Journal of Personality and Social Psychology, 46, 735-754.

Eagly, A., & Steffen, V. (1986). Gender and aggressive behavior: A meta-analytic review of the social psychological literature. Psychological Bulletin, 100, 309-330.

Eagly, A., & Steffen, V. (1988). A note on assessing stereotypes. Personality and Social Psychology Bulletin, 14, 676-680.

Eisenberger, R., & Cameron, J. (1996). Detrimental effects of reward: Reality or myth? American Psychologist, 51, 1153-1166.

Ellsworth, P. (1985, July). Juries on trial. Psychology Today, pp. 44-46.

Elms, A. (1995). Obedience in retrospect. Journal of Social Issues, 51, 21-31.

Eysenck, H. (1981). The causes and effects of smoking. London: Sage.

Fein, S., McCloskey, A. L., & Tomlinson, T. M. (1997). Can the jury disregard that information? The use of suspicion to reduce the prejudicial effects of pretrial publicity and inadmissible testimony. Personality and Social Psychology Bulletin, 23, 1215-1226.

Feingold, A. (1983). Happiness, unselfishness and popularity. Journal of Psychology, 115, 3-5.

Feldman-Summers, S., & Kiesler, S.B. (1974). Those who are number two try harder: The effect of six on attributions of causality. Journal of Personality and Social Psychology, 30, 846-855.

Ferraro, F. (1990). Field experiments in personal space invasion for introductory psychology. Teaching of Psychology, 17, 124-125.

Fischhoff, B. (1975, April). The silly certainty of hindsight. Psychology Today, pp. 70-76.

Fischhoff, B. (1977). Perceived informativeness of facts. Journal of Experimental Psychology: Human Perception and Performance, 3, 349-358.

Fischhoff, B., & Beyth, R. (1975). "I knew it would happen"--Remembered probabilities of once-future things. Organizational Behavior and Human Performance, 13, 1-16.

Fischhoff, B., Slovic, P., & Lichtenstein, S. (1977). Knowing with certainty: The appropriateness of extreme confidence. Journal of Experimental Psychology: Human Perception and Performance, 3, 552-564.

Fishbein, M., & Ajzen, I. (1985). Belief, attitude, intention, and behavior: An introduction to theory and research. Reading, MA: Addison-Wesley.

Fisher, J. (1979). Body magic. New York: Stein and Day.

Fisher, J.D., & Nadler, A. (1974). The effect of similarity between donor and recipient on recipient's reactions to aid. Journal of Applied Social Psychology, 4, 230-243.

Fisher, J.D., Nadler, A., & Whitcher-Alagna, S. (1982). Recipient reactions to aid. Psychological Bulletin, 91, 27-54.

Fiske, S., & Taylor, S. (1991). Social cognition. New York: McGraw-Hill.

Fletcher, G., Danilovics, P., Fernandez, G., Peterson, D., & Reeder, G. (1986). Attributional complexity: An individual differences measure. Journal of Personality and Social Psychology, 51, 875-884.

Fordyce, M.W. (1988). A review of research on the happiness measures: A sixty second index of happiness and mental health. Social Indicators Research, 20, 355-381.

Forer, B.R. (1949). The fallacy of personal validation: A classroom demonstration of gullibility. Journal of Abnormal and Social Psychology, 44, 118-123.

Forsyth, D.R. (1983). An introduction to group dynamics. Monterey, CA: Brooks/Cole.

Forsyth, D. (1990). Group dynamics (2nd ed.). Pacific Grove, CA: Brooks/Cole.

Foss, R. (1981). Structural effects in simulated jury decision-making. Journal of Personality and Social Psychology, 40, 1055-1062.

Fox, R. (1988). On the Seville Statement on Violence. Human Ethology Newsletter, 5, 4.

Fox, J. A., 7 Tracy, P. E. (1980). The randomized response approach: Applicability to criminal justice research and evaluation. Evaluation Review, 4, 601-622.

Friedrich, J. (1996). On seeing oneself as less self-serving than others: The ultimate self-serving bias. Teaching of Psychology, 23, 107-109.

Gaertner, S., & Bickman, L. (1972). A nonreactive indicator of racial discrimination: The wrong number technique. In L. Bickman & T. Henchy (Eds.), Beyond the laboratory: Field research in social psychology. New York: McGraw-Hill.

Garfinkle, H. (1967). Studies in ethnomethodology. Englewood Cliffs, NJ: Prentice-Hall.

Gergen, K.J., Gergen, M.M., & Barton, W.N. (1973, October). Deviance in the dark. Psychology Today, pp. 129-130.

Gergen, K.J., Ellsworth, P., Maslach, C., & Seipel, M. (1975). Obligation, donor resources, and reactions to aid in three cultures. Journal of Personality and Social Psychology, 31, 390-400.

Gilmour, R. (1988). Desirable and negative qualities. In P. Marsh (Ed.), Eye to eye. Topsfield, MA: Salem House Publishers (p. 197).

Gilovich, T. (1991). How we know what isn't so. New York: Free Press.

Glick, P., Diebold, J., Bailey-Werner, B., & Zhu, L. (1997). The two faces of Adam: Ambivalent sexism and polarized attitudes toward women. Personality and Social Psychology Bulletin, 23, 1323-1334.

Glick, P., & Fiske, S.T. (1995). The ambivalent sexism inventory: Differentiating hostile and benevolent sexism. Journal of Personality and Social Psychology, 70, 491-512.

Glick, P., Gottesman, D., & Jolton, J. (1989). The fault is not in the stars: Susceptibility of skeptics and believers in astrology to the Barnum effect. Personality and Social Psychology Bulletin, 15, 572-583.

Gmelch, G. (1978, August). Baseball magic. Human Nature, pp. 32-39.

Goethals, G.R., & Demorest, A.P. (1979). The risky shift is a sure bet. Teaching of Psychology, 6, 177-179.

Goggin, W.C., & Range, L.M. (1985). The disadvantages of hindsight in the perception of suicide. Journal of Social and Clinical Psychology, 3, 232-237.

Goldstein, S.B. (1997). The power of stereotypes: A labeling exercise. Teaching of Psychology, 24, 256-258.

Gonzales, M.H., & Meyers, S.A. (1993). "Your mother would like me": Self-presentation in the personal ads of heterosexual and homosexual men and women. Personality and Social Psychology Bulletin, 19, 131-142.

Graves, R. (1997, July 3). Heroes' courage, kindness rewarded by Carnegie fund. Grand Rapids Press, D11.

Green, S.K., & Gross, A.E. (1979). Self-serving biases in implicit evaluations. Personality and Social Psychology Bulletin, 5, 214-217.

Gregory, W.L., Mowen, J.C., & Linder, D.E. (1978). Social psychology and plea bargaining: Applications, methodology, and theory. Journal of Personality and Social Psychology, 36, 1521-1530.

Hall, E.T. (1966). The hidden dimension. New York: Doubleday.

Haney, W.V. (1979). Communication and interpersonal relations (4th ed.). Homewood, IL: Richard D. Irwin, Inc.

Hansel, C.E.M. (1980). ESP and parapsychology: A critical evaluation. Buffalo, NY: Prometheus.

Hansen, R.D. (1980). Commonsense attribution. Journal of Personality and Social Psychology, 39, 996-1009.

Hass, R. (1984). Perspective taking and self-awareness. Journal of Personality and Social Psychology, 46, 788-798.

Hatfield, E., & Sprecher, S. (1985). Measuring passionate love in intimate relationships. Unpublished manuscript. University of Hawaii at Manoa, Honolulu, HI.

Hazan, C., & Shaver, P. (1987). Romantic love conceptualized as an attachment process. Journal of Personality and Social Psychology, 52, 511-524.

Helweg-Larsen, M., & Collins, B. E. (1997). A social psychological perspective on the role of knowledge about AIDS in AIDS prevention. Current Directions in Psychological Science, April, 23-26.

Hendrick, C., Hendrick, S. S., & Dicke, A. (1998). The love attitudes scale: Short form. Journal of Social and Personal Relationships, 15, 147-159.

Herek, G. (1987). Can functions be measured? A new perspective on the functional approach to attitudes. Social Psychology Quarterly, 50, 285-303.

Higgins, E.T. (1989). Self-discrepancy theory: What patterns of self-beliefs cause people to suffer? In L. Berkowitz (Ed.), Advances in experimental social psychology (Vol. 22, pp. 93-136). New York: Academic Press.

Hill, C.A. (1987). Affiliation motivation: People who need people...but in different ways. Journal of Personality and Social Psychology, 52, 1008-1018.

Hill, R. (1945). Campus values in mate selection. Journal of Home Economics, 37, 554-558.

Hinsz, V., & Tomhave, J. (1991). Smile and (half) the world smiles with you, frown and you frown alone. Personality and Social Psychology Bulletin, 17, 586-592.

Hofling, C.K., Brotzman, E., Dalrymple, S., Graves, N., & Pierce, C.M. (1966). An experimental study of nurse-physician relationships. Journal of Nervous and Mental Disease, 143, 171-180.

Hogan, R., Curphy, G.J., & Hogan, J. (1994). What we know about leadership: Effectiveness and personality. American Psychologist, 49, 493-504.

Hom, H. (1994). Can you predict the overjustification effect? Teaching of Psychology, 21, 36-37.

Horovitz, D. G. Greenberg, B. G., & Abernathy, J. R. (1976). Randomized response: A data gathering device for sensitive questions. International Statistical Review, 44, 181-196.

Hunt, M. (1982). The universe within: A new science explores the human mind. New York: Simon and Schuster.

Hyman, R., & Vogt, E.Z. (1967, May). Water witching: Magic ritual in contemporary U.S. Psychology Today, pp. 35-42.

Infante, D., & Rancer, A.S. (1982). A conceptualization and measure of argumentativeness. Journal of Personality Assessment, 46, 72-80.

Jahoda, M. (1958). Current concepts of positive mental health. New York: basic Books.

James, W. (1890). The principles of psychology. New York: Holt.

Janis, I. (1989). Crucial decisions: Leadership in policymaking and crisis management. New York: Free Press.

Janis, I., & Mann, L. (1977). Decision making: A psychological analysis of conflict, choice, and commitment. New York: Free Press.

Jones, E.E. (1990). Interpersonal perception. New York: W. H. Freeman.

Jones, E.E., & Davis, K.E. (1965). From acts to dispositions: The attribution process in person perception. In L. Berkowitz (Ed.), Advances in experimental social psychology (Vol. 2). New York: Academic Press.

Jones, E.E., & Rhodewalt, F. (1982). Self-handicapping scale. Available from the authors at the Department of Psychology, University of Utah.

Jones, M. (1994). Linking dispositions and social behavior: Self-monitoring and advertising preferences. Teaching of Psychology, 21, 160-161.

Jonides, J., & Rozin, P. (1981). Study guide for Gleitman's Psychology. New York: Norton.

Jourard, S.M. (1971). Self-disclosure: An experimental analysis of the transparent self. New York: Wiley.

Kahneman, D., & Tversky, A. (1972). Subjective probability: A judgment of representativeness. Cognitive Psychology, 3, 430-454.

Kahneman, D., & Tversky, A. (1973). On the psychology of prediction. Psychological Review, 80, 237-251.

Kaplan, D.A., Lewis, S.D., & Hammer, J. (1993, December 20). Is it torture or tradition? Newsweek, p. 124.

Kaplan, M.F., & Kemmerick, G.D. (1974). Juror judgment as information integration: Combining evidential and nonevidential information. Journal of Personality and Social Psychology, 30, 493-499.

Karylowski, J. (1985). Regression toward the mean effect; No statistical background required. Teaching of Psychology, 12, 229-230.

Kassin, S. (1997). The psychology of confession evidence. American Psychologist, 52, 221-233.

Kassin, S., & Kiechel, K. (1996). The social psychology of false confessions. Psychological Science, 7, 125-128.

Kassin, S., Reddy, M., & Tulloch, W. (1990). Juror interpretations of ambiguous evidence: The need for cognition, presentation order, and persuasion. Law and Human Behavior, 14, 43-55.

Kassin, S., & Sommers, S. (1997). Inadmissible testimony, instructions to disregard, and the jury: Substantive versus procedural considerations. Personality and Social Psychology Bulletin, 23, 1046-1054.

Katz, I. (1960). The functional approach to the study of attitudes. Public Opinion Quarterly, 24, 163-204.

Katz, I., & Hass, R. (1988). Racial ambivalence and American value conflict: Correlational and priming studies of dual cognitive structures. Journal of Personality and Social Psychology, 55, 893-905.

Kelley, H., & Grzelak, J. (1972). Conflict between individual and common interest in an N-person relationship. Journal of Personality and Social Psychology, 21, 190-197.

Kelman, H. C. (1997). Group processes in the resolution of international conflicts: Experiences from the Israeli-Palestinian case. American Psychologist, 52, 212-220.

Keltner, D., & Robinson, R.J. (1996). Extremism, power, and the imagined basis of social conflict. Current Directions in Psychological Science, 5, 101-105.

Kerber, K.W. (1980). Rewards, costs, and helping: A demonstration of the complementary nature of experimental and correlational research. Teaching of Psychology, 7, 50-52.

Kendzierski, D., & Whitaker, D.J. (1997). The role of self-schema in linking intentions with behavior. Personality and Social Psychology Bulletin, 23, 139-147.

Kinzel, A.S. (1970). Body-buffer zone in violent prisoners. American Journal of Psychiatry, 127, 59-64.

Kipnis, D. (1984, December). The view from the top. Psychology Today, pp. 30-36.

Kipnis, D., & Schmidt, S. (1985, April). The language of persuasion. Psychology Today, pp. 40-46.

Kite, M. (1991). Observer biases in the classroom. Teaching of Psychology, 18, 161-164.

Klar, Y., & Giladi, E. E. (1997). No one in my group can be below the group's average: A robust positivity bias in favor of anonymous peers. Journal of Personality and Social Psychology, 73, 885-901.

Kunda, Z. (1999). Social cogntion: Making sense of people. Cambridge, Mass: The MIT Press.

Lahey, B.J. (1986). Psychology, second edition. Dubuque, IA: William C. Brown.

Lambert, W., Moghaddam, F., Sorin, J., & Sorin, S. (1990). Assimilation vs. multiculturalism: Views from a community in France. Sociological Forum, 5, 387-411.

Lambert, W., & Taylor, D. (1988). Assimilation vs. multiculturalism: The views of urban Americans. Sociological Forum, 3, 72-88.

Lashley, R. (1987). Using students' perceptions of their instructor to illustrate principles of person perception. Teaching of Psychology, 14, 179-180.

Laughlin, P.R., & Adamopoulos, J. (1980). Social combination processes and individual learning for six-person cooperative groups on an intellective task. Journal of Personality and Social Psychology, 38, 941-947.

Lazarus, R. (1981, July). Little hassles can be hazardous to health. Psychology Today, pp. 58-62.

Lerner, M. (1980). The belief in a just world. New York: Plenum.

Levine, R., & Wolff, E. (1985, March). Social time: The heartbeat of culture. Psychology Today, pp. 28-35.

Levine, R. V., Martinez, T. S., Brase, G. & Sorenson, K. (1994). Helping in 36 U.S. cities. Journal of Personality and Social Psychology, 67, 69-82.

Locke, D., & Pennington, D. (1982). Reasons and other causes: Their role in attribution processes. Journal of Personality and Social Psychology, 42, 212-223.

Loftus, E. (1984, February). Eyewitnesses: Essential but unreliable. Psychology Today, pp. 22-26.

Loftus, E. (1991). Resolving legal questions with psychological data. American Psychologist, 46, 1046-1048.

Long, K. (1992, February 16). Researchers offer some answers to schools' gender bias dilemma. Grand Rapids Press, p. F3.

Lovaglia, M. J. (2000). Knowing people: The personal use of social psychology. New York: McGraw-Hill

Luchins, A.S. (1957). Primacy-recency in impression formation. In C.I. Hovland et al. (Eds.), The order of presentation in persuasion. New Haven: Yale University Press.

Lutsky, N. (1993). A scheme and variations for studies of social influence in an experimental social psychology laboratory. Teaching of Psychology, 20, 105-107.

MacLachlan, J. (1979, November). What people really think of fast talkers. Psychology Today, pp. 112-117.

Madden, T., Ellen, P., & Ajzen, I. (1992). A comparison of the theory of planned behavior and the theory of reasoned action. Personality and Social Psychology Bulletin, 18, 3-9.

Makosky, V.P. (1985). Identifying major techniques of persuasion. Teaching of Psychology, 12, 42-43.

Marks, D., & Kamman, R. (1980). The psychology of the psychic. Buffalo, NY: Prometheus.

Marsh, H.W., & Parker, J.W. (1984). Determinants of student self-concept: Is it better to be a relatively large fish in a small pond even if you don't learn to swim as well? Journal of Personality and Social Psychology, 47, 213-231.

Martin, J. (1980). Relative deprivation: A theory of distributive injustice for an era of shrinking resources. In Research in Organizational Behavior (Vol. 3). Greenwich, CN: JAI Press.

Martindale, D.A. (1971). Territorial dominance behavior in dyadic verbal interaction. Proceedings of the 79th Annual Convention of the American Psychological Association, 6, 305-306.

Matlin, M., & Stang, D. (1978). The Pollyanna principle: Selectivity in language, memory, and cognition. Cambridge, MA: Schenkman.

McCauley, C., & Stitt, C. (1978). An individual and quantitative measure of stereotypes. Journal of Personality and Social Psychology, 36, 929-940.

McConahay, J.B. (1986). Modern racism, ambivalence, and modern racism scale. In J.F. Dovidio & S.L. Gaertner (Eds.), Prejudice, discrimination, and racism (pp. 91-125). Orlando, FL: Academic Press.

McGuire, A.M. (1994). Helping behaviors in the natural environment: Dimensions and correlates of helping. Personality and Social Psychology Bulletin, 20, 45-56.

McIntosh, H. (1996, March). Solitude provides an emotional tune-up. APA Monitor, pp. 1, 10.

McKean, K. (1985, June). Decisions, decisions. Discover, pp. 22-31.

Meer, J. (1985, July). Loneliness. Psychology Today, pp. 28-33.

Milgram, S. (1972). The lost letter technique. In L. Bickman & T. Henchy (Eds.), Beyond the laboratory: Field research in social psychology. New York: McGraw-Hill.

Miller, A.G. (1986). The obedience experiments: A case study of controversy in social science. New York: Praeger.

Miller, R. L., Brinkman, P., & Bolen, D. (1975). Attribution versus persuasion as a means for modifying behavior. Journal of Personality and Social Psychology, 31, 430-441.

Milojkovic, J.D., & Ross, L. (1981). Telling truths from lies: Miscalibration of confidence and base-rate utilization. Paper presented at the American Psychological Association Convention.

Mintz, A. (1951). Non-adaptive group behavior. Journal of Abnormal and Social Psychology, 46, 150-159.

Montgomery, R.L. (1971). Status, conformity, and resistance to compliance in natural groups. Journal of Social Psychology, 84, 197-206.

Montgomery, R.L., & Enzie, R.F. (1971). Social influence and the estimation of time. Psychonomic Science, 22, 77-78.

Moorhead, G. Ference, R. & Neck, C.P. (1991). Group Decision Fiascoes Continue: Space Shuttle Challenger and a Revised Groupthink Framework. Human Relations, pp.539-550.

Motowidlo, S.J. (1982). Sex role orientation and behavior in a work setting. Journal of Personality and Social Psychology, 42, 935-945.

Murray, S.L., & Holmes, J.G. (1997). A leap of faith? Positive illusions in romantic relationships. Personality and Social Psychology Bulletin, 23, 586-604.

Myers, D. (1992). Psychology (3rd ed.). New York: Worth Publishers, Inc.

Myers, D. (1998). Psychology (5th ed.). New York: Worth Publishers, Inc.

Myers, D.G., & Bishop, G.D. (1971). The enhancement of dominant attitudes in group discussion. Journal of Personality and Social Psychology, 20, 386-391.

Myers, D. G., & Diener, E. (1995). Who is happy? Psychological Science, 6, 10-19.

Myers, D.G., & Kaplan, M.F. (1976). Group-induced polarization in simulated juries. Personality and Social Psychology Bulletin, 2, 135-140.

Nadler, A., Altman, A., & Fisher, J.D. (1979). Helping is not enough: Recipient's reaction to aid as a function of positive and negative information about the self. Journal of Personality, 47, 615-628.

Notarius, C., & Markman, H. (1993). We can work it out: Making sense of marital conflict. New York: Putnam.

Nelson, L. (1991, April). Teaching and assessing conflict resolution abilities in social psychology courses. Paper presented at the meeting of the Western Psychological Association, San Francisco, CA.

Nelson, L. (1991). Psychological factors in war and peacemaking. Contemporary Social Psychology, 15, 172-178.

Nesselroade, K. P., Jr., Beggan, J. K., & Allison, S. T. (1998). Possession enhancement in an interpersonal context: An extension of the mere ownership effect. Psychology and Marketing, 16, 1-14.

Newcomb, T.M. (1961). The acquaintance process. New York: Holt Rinehart, & Winston.

Nisbett, R.E. (1993). Violence and the U.S. regional culture. American Psychologist, 48, 441-449.

Nisbett, R.E., Caputo, C., Legant, P., & Marecek, J. (1973). Behavior as seen by the actor and as seen by the observer. Journal of Personality and Social Psychology, 27, 154-164.

Nisbett, R.E., & Wilson, R.D. (1977). Telling more than we can know. Verbal reports on mental processes. Psychological Review, 84, 231-259.

Noon, E., & Hollin, C.R. (1987). Lay knowledge of eyewitness behavior. A British survey. Applied Cognitive Psychology, 1, 143-153.

Nowicki, S., & Strickland, B.R. (1973). A locus of control scale for children. Journal of Consulting and Clinical Psychology, 40, 148-154.

O'Driscoll, P. (1997, December 9). In hot pursuit of road rage. USA Today, p. 3A.

Olczak, P.V., Kaplan, M.F., & Penrod, S. (1991). Attorney's lay psychology and its effectiveness in selecting jurors: Three empirical studies. Journal of Social Behavior and Personality, 6, 431-452.

Omoto, A.M., & Snyder, M. (1990). Basic research in action: Volunteerism and society's response to AIDS. Personality and Social Psychology Bulletin, 16, 152-166.

Orbell, S., Hodgkins, S., & Sheeren, P. (1997). Implementation intentions and the theory of planned behavior. Personality and Social Psychology Bulletin, 23, 945-954.

Osberg, T. (1993). Psychology is not just common sense: An introductory psychology demonstration. Teaching of Psychology, 20, 110-111.

Osherow, N. (1999). Making sense of the nonsensical: An analysis of Jonestown. In E. Aronson (Ed.), Readings about the social animal (8th ed.). New York: Worth/Freeman.

Oskamp, S. (1965). Attitudes toward U.S. and Russian actions: A double standard. Psychological Reports, 16, 43-46.

Parlee, M.B. (1979, October). The friendship bond. Psychology Today, pp. 13, 43-45.

Patterson, J., & Kimm, P. (1991). The day America told the truth. New York: Prentice-Hall.

Paul, A. M. (1998). Where bias begins: The truth about stereotypes. Psychology Today, May/June, 52-55.

Pearce, P.L., & Amato, P.R. (1980). A taxonomy of helping: A multidimensional scaling analysis. Social Psychology Quarterly, 43, 363-371.

Penrose, J. (1962). An investigation into some aspects of problem solving behavior. Unpublished doctoral dissertation, University of London.

Perloff, R.M. (1993). The dynamics of persuasion. Hillsdale, NJ: Lawrence Erlbaum.

Peterson, C., & Seligman, M. (1984). Causal explanations as a risk factor for depression: Theory and evidence. Psychological Review, 91, 347-374.

Pfeiffer, J.W., & Jones, J.E. (1972). Annual handbook for group facilitators, 1972. San Diego: University Associates.

Pfungst, O. (1965). Clever Hans, the horse of Mrs. Van Osten. New York: Holt, Rinehart, & Winston.

Phinney, J. (1990). Ethnic identity in adolescents and adults: Review of research. Psychological Bulletin, 108, 499-514.

Pilkonis, P.A. (1977). Shyness, public and private, and its relationship to other measures of social behavior. Journal of Personality, 45, 585-595.

Pines, A., & Maslach, C. (1979). Experiencing social psychology. New York: Knopf.

Pollis, N.P., & Montgomery, R.L. (1966). Conformity and resistance to compliance. Journal of Psychology, 63, 35-41.

Pollis, N.P., & Montgomery, R.L. (1968). Individual judgmental stability and the natural group. Journal of Social Psychology, 75, 75-81.

Poole, D.A., Lindsay, D.S., Memon, A., & Bull, R. (1995). Psychotherapy and the recovery of memories of childhood sexual abuse: U.S. and British practitioners' opinions, practices, and experiences. Journal of Consulting and Clinical Psychology, 63, 426-437.

Potera, C. (1988, November). Stress epidemics. Psychology Today, p. 16.

Pratkanis, A., & Aronson, E. (1992). Age of propaganda: The everyday use and abuse of persuasion. New York: W. H. Freeman.

Pratkanis, A., Farquhar, P., Silbert, S., & Hearst, J. (1989). Decoys produce contrast effects and alter choice probabilities. Unpublished manuscript. University of California, Santa Cruz.

Pruitt, D., & Rubin, J. (1986). Social conflict. New York: Random House.

Puente, M., & Castaneda, C.J. (1997, August 29). Rage starting to rule the nation's roads. USA Today, p. 3A.

Rank, S.G., & Jacobson, C.K. (1977). Hospital nurses' compliance with medication overdose orders: A failure to replicate. Journal of Health and Social Behavior, 18, 188-193.

Rempel, J.K., & Holmes, J.G. (1986, February). How do I trust thee? Psychology Today, pp. 28-34.

Rhodewalt, F., Saltzman, A.T., & Wittmer, J. (1984). Self-handicapping among competitive athletes: The role of practice in self-esteem protection. Basic and Applied Social Psychology, 5, 197-209.

Rider, E.A. (1992). Understanding and applying psychology through use of news clippings. Teaching of Psychology, 19, 161-163.

Rimland, B. (1982). The altruism paradox. The Southern Psychologist, 2(1), 8-9.

Rinzler, C.A. (1988, March/April). The annotated Adam and Eve. Hippocrates, pp. 78-79.

Rochat, F., & Modigliani, A. (1995). The ordinary quality of resistance: From Milgram's laboratory to the village of Le Chambon.
Journal of Social Issues, 51, 195-210.

Rocklin, T. (1985). Independent ratings are more valid than group consensus: A classroom demonstration. Teaching of Psychology, 12, 44-45.

Roediger, H. L. III., & McDermott, K. B. (1995). Creating false memories: Remembering words not presented in lists. Journal of Experimental Psychology: Learning, Memory, and Cognition, 21, 803-814.

Rokeach, M. (1973). The nature of human values. New York: Free Press.

Rokeach, M. (1974). Change and stability in American value systems. Public Opinion Quarterly, 38,(2), 222-238.

Rokeach, M., & Ball-Rokeach, S.J. (1989). Stability and change in American value priorities. American Psychologist, 44, 775-784.

Rosenthal, R. (1994). Interpersonal expectancy effects: A 30-year perspective. Current Directions in Psychological Science, 3, 176-179.

Ross, L., & Nisbett, R. (1991). The person and the situation. New York: McGraw-Hill.

Ross, M., & Sicoly, F. (1979). Egocentric biases in availability attribution. Journal of Personality and Social Psychology, 37, 322-336.

Rubin, D.C., & Schulkind, M.D. (1997). Distribution of important and word-cued autobiographical memories in 20-, 35-, and 70-year-old adults. Psychology and Aging, 12, 524-535.

Rubin, J.Z. (1981, March). Psychological traps. Psychology Today, pp. 52-63.

Rubin, J.Z., & Brockner, J. (1975). Factors affecting entrapment in waiting situations: The Rosencrantz and Guildenstern effect. Journal of Personality and Social Psychology, 31, 1054-1063.

Rubin, J.Z., Provenzano, F., & Luria, Z. (1974). The eye of the beholder: Parent's view on the sex of newborns. American Journal of Orthopsychiatry, 44, 512-519.

Rubin, Z. (1973). Liking and loving. New York: Holt, Rinehart, & Winston.

Rubin, Z., & Peplau, L.A. (1975). Who believes in a just world? Journal of Social Issues, 31, 65-89.

Rubinstein, E.A. (1978). Television and the young viewer. American Scientist, 66, 685-693.

Rule, B., Bisanz, G., & Kohn, M. (1985). Anatomy of a persuasion schema: Targets, goals, and strategies. Journal of Personality and Social Psychology, 48, 1127-1140.

Rusbult, C., & Zembrodt, I. (1983). Responses to dissatisfaction in romantic involvements: A multidimensional scaling analysis. Journal of Experimental Social Psychology, 19, 274-293.

Russell, D. (1982). The causal dimension scale: A measure of how individuals perceive causes. Journal of Personality and Social Psychology, 42, 1137-1145.

Russo, J., & Schoemaker, P. (1989). Decision traps. New York: Doubleday.

Sabbagh, K. (1985-1986). The psychopathology of fringe medicine. The Skeptical Inquirer, 10, 154-158.

Sadker, M., & Sadker, D. (1985, March). Sexism in the schoolroom of the 80's. Psychology Today, pp. 54-57.

Safer, M.A. (1980). Attributing evil to the subject, not the situation. Personality and Social Psychology Bulletin, 6, 205-209.

Saks, M.J. (1992). Obedience versus disobedience to legitimate versus illegitimate authorities issuing good versus bad directives. Psychological Science, 3, 221-223.

Sales, S.M. (1972, November). Authoritarianism: But as for me, give me liberty, or give me, maybe, a great, big, strong, powerful leader I can honor, admire, respect and obey. Psychology Today, pp. 94-98; 140-142.

Saltzman, A. (1994, November 7). Schooled in failure? U.S. News and World Report, pp. 88-93.

Salovey, P., & Rodin, J. (1985, September). The heart of jealousy. Psychology Today, pp. 22-29.

Salvador, D.S. et al. (1997, August). Quality of life and hormone levels in middle-aged men. Poster session presented at the annual meeting of the American Psychological Association, Chicago, IL.

Scheier, M., & Carver, C. (1985). Optimism, coping, and health: Assessment and implications of generalized outcome expectancies. Health Psychology, 4, 219-247.

Scheier, M., & Carver, C. (1993). On the power of positive thinking: The benefits of being optimistic. Current Directions in Psychological Science, 2, 26-30.

Schlenker, B.R., Forsyth, D.R., Leary, M.R., & Miller, R.S. (1980). Self-presentational analysis of the effects of incentives on attitude change following counterattitudinal behavior. Journal of Personality and Social Psychology, 39, 553-577.

Schutz, W. (1958). FIRO: A three dimensional theory of interpersonal behavior. New York: Rinehart.

Scoville, W. (1981). What would you do if. . .? Contemporary Social Psychology, 7(6), 20-21.

Sechrest, L., & Belew, J. (1983). Nonreactive measures of social attitudes. In L. Bickmann (Ed.), Applied Social Psychology Annual 4. Beverly Hills, CA: Sage Publishers.

Seepa, N. (1997, June). Children's TV remains steeped in violence. APA Monitor, p.36.

Segal, M.W. (1974). Alphabet and attraction: An unobtrusive measure of the effect of propinquity in a field setting. Journal of Personality and Social Psychology, 30, 654-657.

Seligman, M. (1990). Learned optimism. New York: Alfred A Knopf.

Seligman, M. (1998). The American way of blame. APA Monitor, July.

Shafir, E. (1993). Choosing versus rejecting: Why some options are both better and worse than others. Memory and Cognition, 21, 546-556.

Shaw, J. (1977). Some "real-life" accounts of influential relationships. Human Relations, 30, 363-372.

Shaw, M.E. (1981). Group dynamics: The psychology of small group behavior (3rd edition). New York: McGraw-Hill.

Sherer, M., Maddux, J.E., Mercandante, B., Prentice-Dunn, S., Jacobs, B., & Rogers, R.W. (1982). The self-efficacy scale: Construction and validation. Psychological Reports, 51, 663-671.

Sherman, S.J. (1980). On the self-erasing nature of errors of prediction. Journal of Personality and Social Psychology, 39, 211-221.

Shomer, R.W., David, A.H., & Kelley, H.H. (1966). Threats and the development of coordination: Further studies of the Deutsch and Krauss trucking game. Journal of Personality and Social Psychology, 4, 119-126.

Shotland, R.L. (1985, June). When bystanders just stand by. Psychology Today, pp. 50-55.

Shubik, M. (1971). The dollar auction game: A paradox in non-cooperating behavior and escalation. Journal of Conflict Resolution, 15, 109-111.

Simpson, J. (1988). Self-monitoring and commitment to dating relationships: A classroom demonstration. Teaching of Psychology, 15, 31-33.

Singelis, T.M. (1994). The measurement of independent and interdependent self-construals. Personality and Social Psychology Bulletin, 20, 580-591.

Singelis, T.M. (1995). Culture, self, and collectivist communication: Linking culture to individual behavior. Human Communication Research, 21, 354-389.

Singelis, T.M. (in press). Culture, self-construal, and embarrassability. Journal of Cross-Cultural Psychology.

Singer, B., & Benassi, V.A. (1980-81). Fooling some of the people all of the time. Skeptical Inquirer, 5(2), 17-24.

Singleton, R. (1978). Classroom demonstrations of social psychological principles. Teaching Sociology, 5, 187-200.

Singleton, R., & Kerber, K.W. (1980). Topics in social psychology. Teaching Sociology, 7, 439-452.

Sleek, S. (1996, September). Car wars: Taming drivers' aggression. APA Monitor, pp. 1, 13.

Slife, B., & Rubinstein, J. (Eds.) (1992). Taking sides: Clashing views on controversial psychological issues. Guilford, CT: Dushkin Publishing Group.

Snyder, C.R. (1997). Unique invulnerability: A classroom demonstration in estimating personal mortality. Teaching of Psychology, 24, 197-199.

Snyder, C.R., & Fromkin, H.L. (1977). Abnormality as a positive characteristic: The development and validation of a scale measuring need for uniqueness. Journal of Abnormal Psychology, 86, 518-527.

Snyder, C.R., & Fromkin, H.L. (1980). Uniqueness: The human pursuit of difference. New York: Plenum.
Snyder, M. (1974). Self-monitoring of expressive behavior. Journal of Personality and Social Psychology, 30, 526-537.
Snyder, M. (1987). Public appearance, private realities. New York: W. H. Freeman.
Snyder, M. (1992). Basic research and practical problems: The promise of a functional personality and social psychology. Paper presented at the annual meeting of the American Psychological Association, Washington, D.C.
Snyder, M., & Gangestad, S. (1981). Hypothesis-testing processes. In J.H. Harvey, W. Ickes, & R.F. Kidd (Eds.), New directions in attribution research. Hillsdale, NJ: Erlbaum.
Snyder, M., & Gangestad, S. (1986). On the nature of self-monitoring: Matters of assessment, matter of validity. Journal of Personality and Social Psychology, 51, 125-139.
Snyder, M., & Swann, W. B., Jr. (1976). When actions reflect attitudes: The politics of impression management. Journal of Personality and Social psychology, 34, 1034-1042.
Snyder, M., & Swann, W.B., Jr. (1978a). Behavioral confirmation in social interaction: From social perception to social reality. Journal of Experimental Social Psychology, 14, 148-162.
Snyder, M., & Swann, W.B., Jr. (1978b). Hypothesis-testing processes in social interaction. Journal of Personality and Social Psychology, 36, 1202-1212.
Sommer, R. (1969). Personal space. Englewood Cliffs, NJ: Prentice-Hall, Inc.
Sommer, R., & Olsen, H. (1980). The soft classroom. Environment and Behavior, 5, 3-16.
Sommer, R., & Ross, H. (1958). Social interaction on a geriatrics ward. International Journal of Social Psychiatry, 4, 128-133.
Stanovich, K. (1992). How to think straight about psychology (3rd ed.). New York: HarperCollins.
Stasson, M.F., & Bradshaw, S.D. (1995). Explanations of individual-group performance differences. Small Group Research, 26, 296-308.
Staub, E. (1999). Aggression and self-esteem. APA Monitor, January.
Steinzor, B. (1949). The development and evaluation of a measure of social interaction. Human Relations, 2, 103-121, 319-347.
Sternberg, R. J. (1988). Triangulating love. In R.J. Sternberg & M.L. Barnes (Eds.), The psychology of love. New Haven: Yale University Press.
Sternberg, R. J. (1998). Love is a story. New York: Oxford University Press.
Sternberg, R. J. (2000). What's your love story? Psychology Today, July/August, 52-59.
Stratton, L.O., Tekippe, D.J., & Flick, G.L. (1973). Personal space and self-concept. Sociometry, 36, 424-429.
Stroebe, W., Diehl, M., & Abakoumkin, G. (1992). The illusion of group effectivity. Personality and Social Psychology Bulletin, 18, 643-650.
Swim, J.K., & Hyers, L.L. (1997). Excuse me--What did you just say?! Women's public and private reactions to sexist remarks. Paper presented at the Joint European Association for Experimental Social Psychology and the Society for Experimental Social Psychology, and at the Empire State Social Psychology conference.
Taylor, S. E., & Brown, J. D. (1988). Illusion and well-being: A social psychological perspective on mental health. Psychological Bulletin, 103, 193-210.
Taylor, S. E., & Brown, J. D. (1994). Positive illusions and well-being revisited: Separating fact from fiction Psychological Bulletin, 116, 21-27.
Teger, A. I. (1980). Too much invested to quit. New York: Pergamon Press.
Thigpen, D. (1995, April 3). Confronting the killer. Time, p. 50.

Tierney, J. (1987, September/October). Good news! Better health linked to sin, sloth. Hippocrates, pp. 30-35.

Triandis, H., Brislin, R., & Hui, C. (1988). Cross-cultural training across the individualism-collectivism divide. International Journal of Intercultural Relations, 12, 269-289.

Trope, Y., & Bassok, M. (1982). Confirmatory and diagnosing strategies in social information gathering. Journal of Personality and Social Psychology, 43, 22-34.

Turkington, C. (1986, February). High court weighs value of research by social scientists. APA Monitor, pp. 1, 30.

Tversky, A., & Gati, I. (1978). Studies of similarity. In E. Rosch & B. Lloyd (Eds.), Cognition and categorization. Hillsdale, NJ: Erlbaum.

Tversky, A., & Kahneman, D. (1973). Availability: A heuristic for judging frequency and probability. Cognitive Psychology, 5, 207-232.

Tversky, A., & Kahneman, D. (1980). Causal schemas in judgments under uncertainty. In M. Fishbein (Ed.), Progress in social psychology (Vol. 1). Hillsdale, NJ: Erlbaum.

Tversky, A., & Kahneman, D. (1981). The framing of decisions and the psychology of choice. Science, 211, 453-458.

Tyler, T.R. (1990). Why people obey the law. New Haven: Yale Uniiversity Press.

Vallacher, R.R., & Wegner, D.M. (1985). A theory of action identification. Hillsdale, NJ: Erlbaum.

Vallacher, R.R., & Wegner, D.M. (1987). What do people think they're doing? Action identification and human behavior. Psychological Review, 94, 3-15.

Wann, D.L. (1993). Performing experiments in undergraduate social psychology classes. Teaching of Psychology, 4, 237-238.

Warner, S. L. (1965). Randomized response: A survey technique for eliminating evasive answer bias. Journal of the American Statistical Review, 60, 63-69.

Wason, P.C. (1960). On the failure to eliminate hypotheses in a conceptual task. Quarterly Journal of Experimental Psychology, 12, 129-140.

Wason, P.C. (1981). The importance of cognitive illusions. The Behavioral and Brain Sciences, 4, 356.

Wason, P.C., & Johnson-Laird, P.N. (Eds.). (1968). Thinking and reasoning. Baltimore: Penguin.

Webb, E.J., Campbell, D.T., Schwartz, R.D., Sechrest, L., & Grove, J.B. (1981). Nonreactive measures in the social sciences. Boston: Houghton Mifflin.

Weber, A. (1984). Teaching social psychology. Contemporary Social Psychology, 10(3), 9-10.

Wehr, P. (1979). Conflict regulation. Boulder, CO: Westview Press.

Weiner, B. (1985). "Spontaneous" causal thinking. Psychological Bulletin, 97, 74-84.

Weiner, B. (1992). Human motivation: Metaphors, theories, and research. Newbury Park, CA: Sage Publications.

Weinstein, N.D. (1982). Unrealistic optimism about susceptibility to health problems. Journal of Behavioral Medicine, 5, 441-460.

Wells, G., & Luus, E. (1990). Police lineups as experiments: Social methodology as a framework for properly conducted lineups. Personality and Social Psychology Bulletin, 16, 106-117.

Wells, W.D., Goi, F.J., & Seader, S. (1958). A change in a product image. Journal of Applied Psychology, 42, 120-121.

Wheeler, D.L., Jacobson, D.L., Paglieri, R.A., & Schwartz, A.A. (1993). An experimental assessment of facilitated communication. Mental Retardation, 31, 49-60.

Wood, G. (1984). Research methodology: A decision making perspective. In A. Rogers and C. Scheirer (Eds.), The G. Stanley Hall lecture series, Vol. 4. Washington, D.C.: American Psychological Association.

Zajonc, R. (1965). Social facilitation. Science, 149, 269-274.

Zajonc, R. (1970, February). Brainwash: Familiarity breeds comfort. <u>Psychology Today,</u> pp. 32-35, 60-64.

Zimbardo, P.G. (1977). <u>Shyness: What it is, what to do about it</u>. Reading, MA: Addison-Wesley.

Zimbardo, P.G. (1997, May). What messages are behind today's cults? <u>APA Monitor</u>, p. 14.